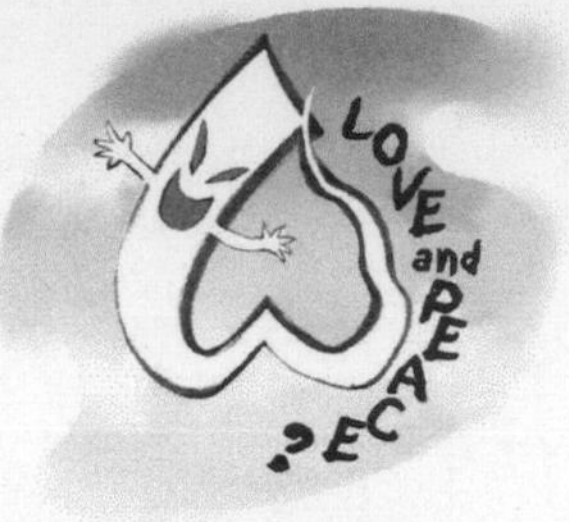
LOVE and PEACE?

池田晃久
AKIHISA IKEDA

Things seem kind of dangerous lately... A crime even occurred in my neighborhood. They say someone was stabbed—scary!! What's happening to this world? I like it when things are relatively peaceful and gentle. That's why the theme of this manga is "Let's all be friends"... That's right.

Akihisa Ikeda was born in 1977 in Miyazaki. He debuted as a mangaka with the four-volume magical warrior fantasy series *Kiruto* in 1999, which was serialized in *Monthly Shonen Jump*. *Rosario+Vampire* debuted in *Monthly Shonen Jump* in March of 2002, and is continuing in the new magazine *Jump Square* (Jump SQ). In Japan, *Rosario+Vampire* is also available as a drama CD. In 2008, the story was released as an anime.

Ikeda has been a huge fan of vampires and monsters since he was a little kid.

He says one of the perks of being a manga artist is being able to go for walks during the day when everybody else is stuck in the office.

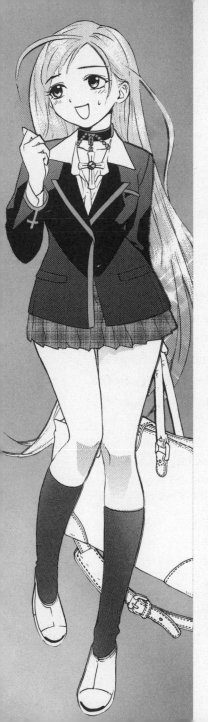

ROSARIO+VAMPIRE 4

SHONEN JUMP ADVANCED Manga Edition

STORY & ART BY AKIHISA IKEDA

Translation/Kaori Inoue
English Adaptation/Gerard Jones
Touch-up Art & Lettering/Stephen Dutro
Cover Design/Mark Griffin
Interior Design/ Julie Behn
Editor/Annette Roman

Printed in the U.S.A.

Published by VIZ Media, LLC
P.O. Box 77010
San Francisco, CA 94107

10 9
First printing, December 2008
Ninth printing, May 2015

VIZ media
www.viz.com

SHONEN JUMP ADVANCED
www.shonenjump.com

RATED T+ FOR OLDER TEEN

PARENTAL ADVISORY
ROSARIO+VAMPIRE is rated T+ for Older Teen and is recommended for ages 16 and up. It contains suggestive situations.

ratings.viz.com

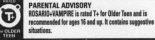

Rosario+Vampire

4

Carnivorous Plant

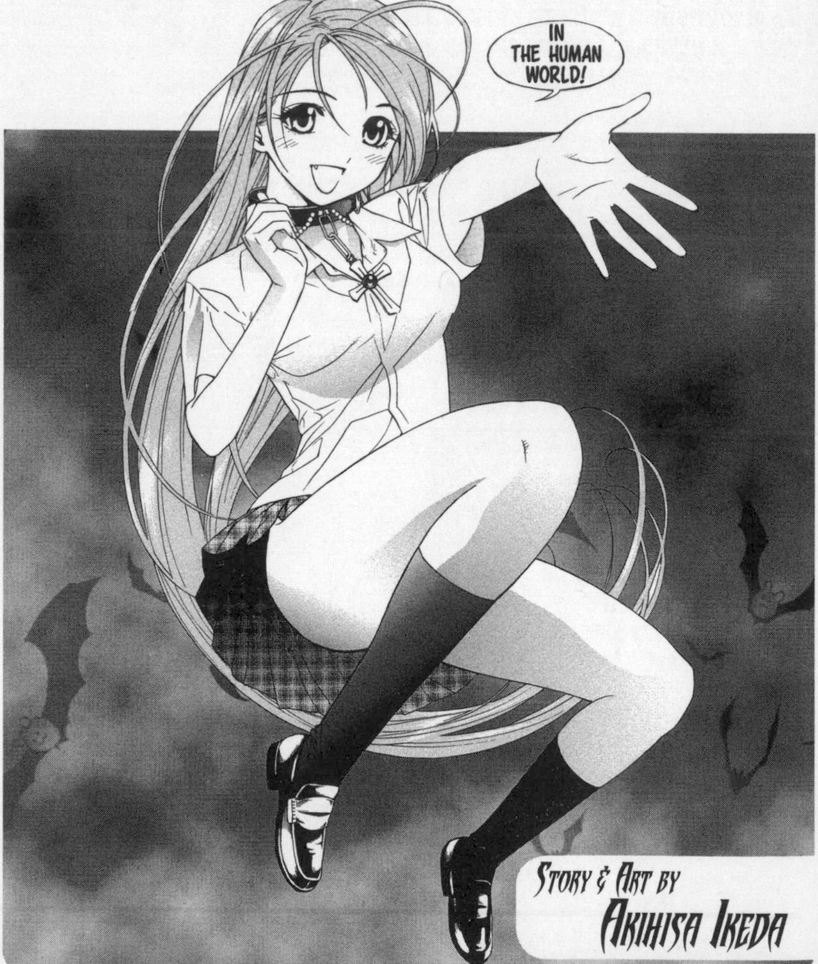
IN THE HUMAN WORLD!

Story & Art by

Akihisa Ikeda

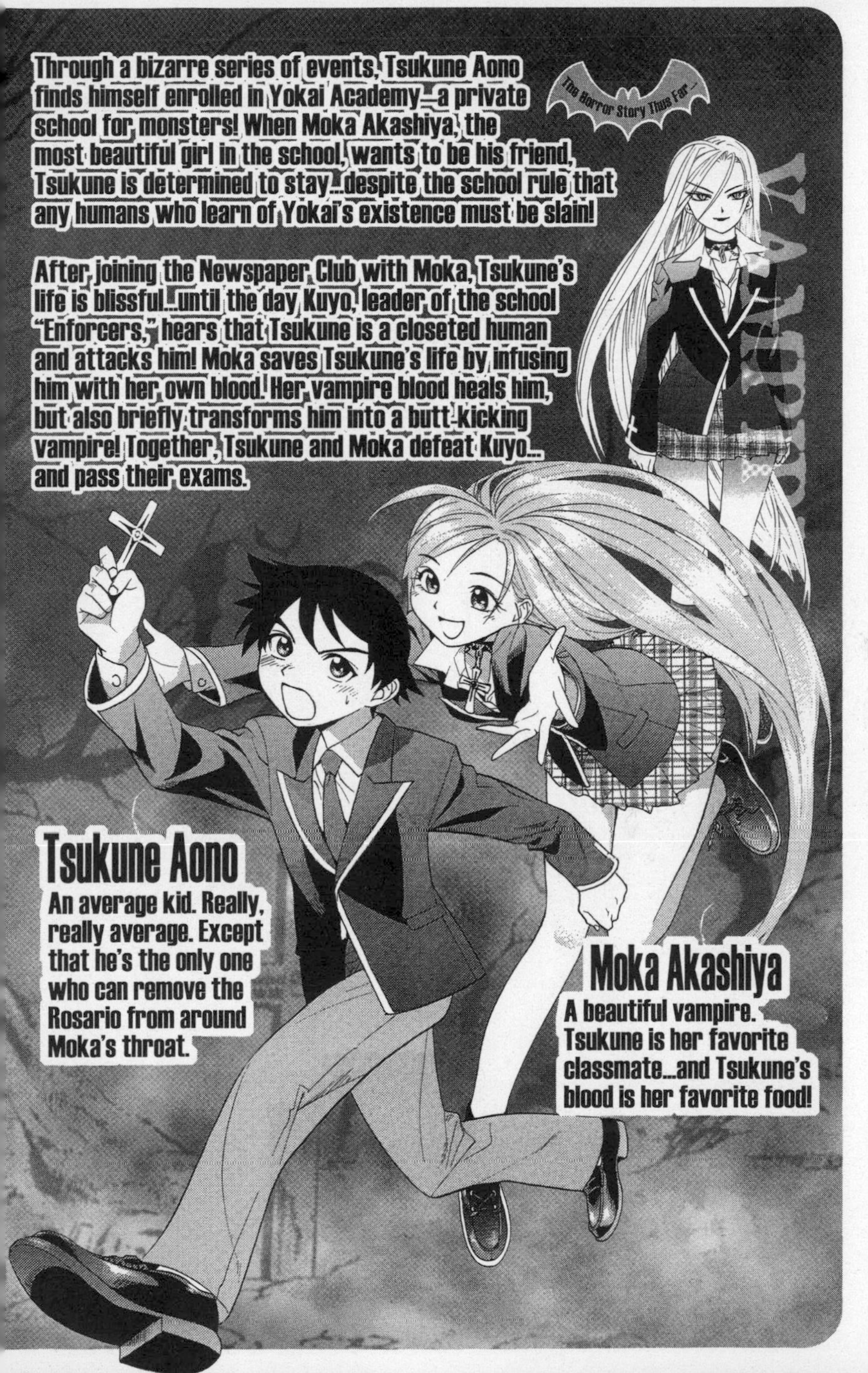
The Horror Story Thus Far...
Through a bizarre series of events, Tsukune Aono finds himself enrolled in Yokai Academy—a private school for monsters! When Moka Akashiya, the most beautiful girl in the school, wants to be his friend, Tsukune is determined to stay...despite the school rule that any humans who learn of Yokai's existence must be slain!
After joining the Newspaper Club with Moka, Tsukune's life is blissful...until the day Kuyo, leader of the school "Enforcers," hears that Tsukune is a closeted human and attacks him! Moka saves Tsukune's life by infusing him with her own blood. Her vampire blood heals him, but also briefly transforms him into a butt-kicking vampire! Together, Tsukune and Moka defeat Kuyo... and pass their exams.
Tsukune Aono
An average kid. Really, really average. Except that he's the only one who can remove the Rosario from around Moka's throat.
Moka Akashiya
A beautiful vampire. Tsukune is her favorite classmate...and Tsukune's blood is her favorite food!

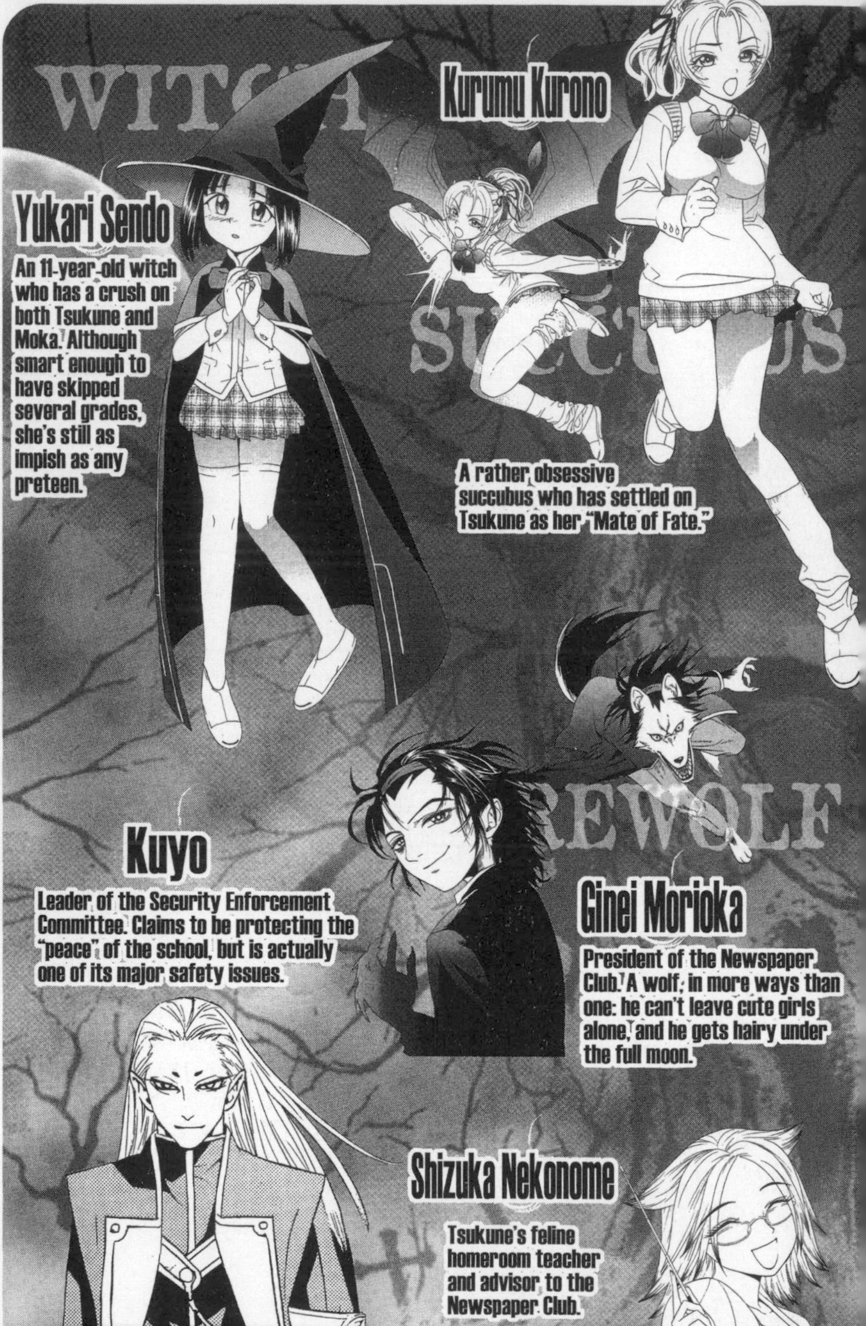

Kurumu Kurono
A rather obsessive succubus who has settled on Tsukune as her "Mate of Fate."
Yukari Sendo
An 11-year-old witch who has a crush on both Tsukune and Moka. Although smart enough to have skipped several grades, she's still as impish as any preteen.
Ginei Morioka
President of the Newspaper Club. A wolf, in more ways than one: he can't leave cute girls alone, and he gets hairy under the full moon.
Kuyo
Leader of the Security Enforcement Committee. Claims to be protecting the "peace" of the school, but is actually one of its major safety issues.
Shizuka Nekonome
Tsukune's feline homeroom teacher and advisor to the Newspaper Club.

CONTENTS

Volume 4: Carnivorous Plant

13: Summer the Color of Sunflowers

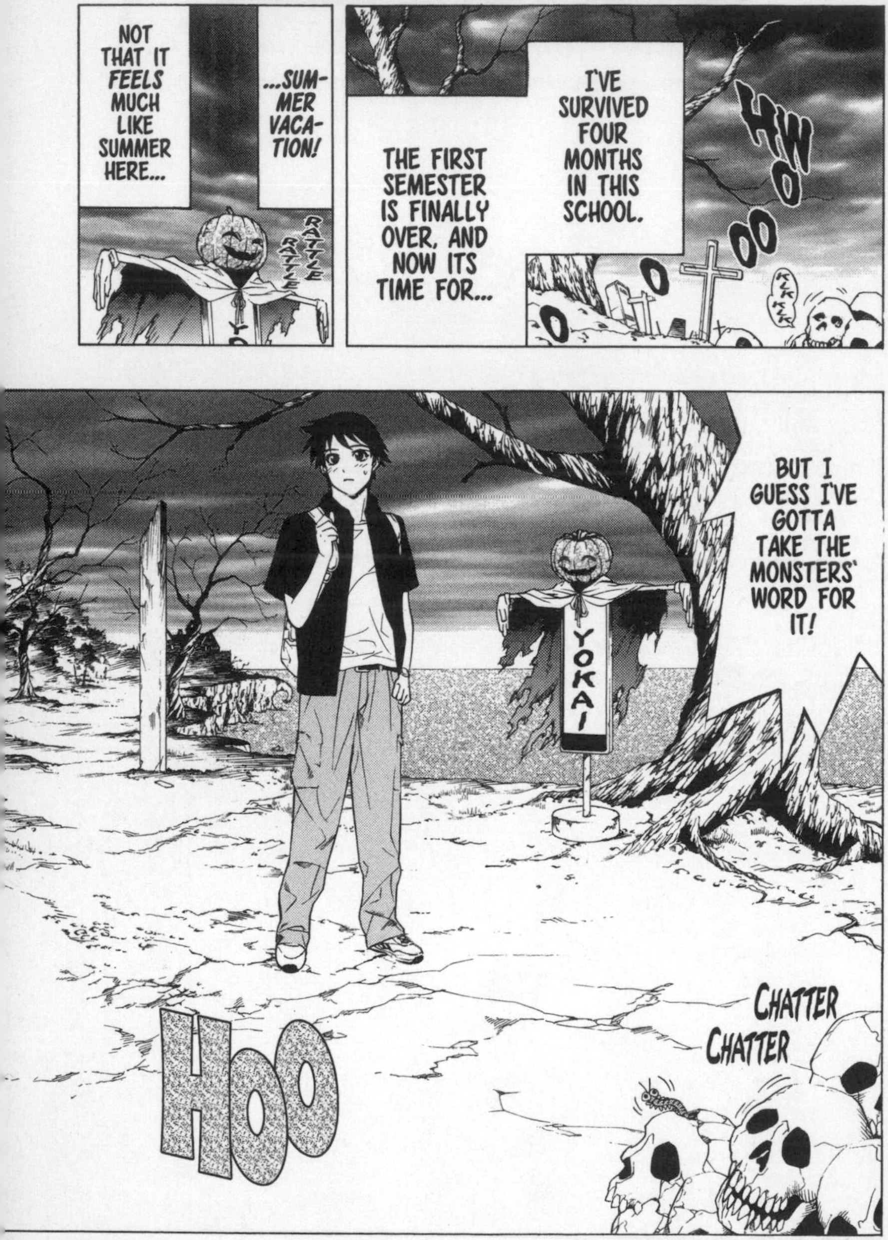
I'VE SURVIVED FOUR MONTHS IN THIS SCHOOL.
HWOOOOO
KLK KLK
THE FIRST SEMESTER IS FINALLY OVER, AND NOW ITS TIME FOR...
...SUMMER VACATION!
NOT THAT IT FEELS MUCH LIKE SUMMER HERE...
RATTLE RATTLE
BUT I GUESS I'VE GOTTA TAKE THE MONSTERS' WORD FOR IT!
YOKAI
CHATTER
CHATTER
HOO

13: Summer the Color of Sunflowers

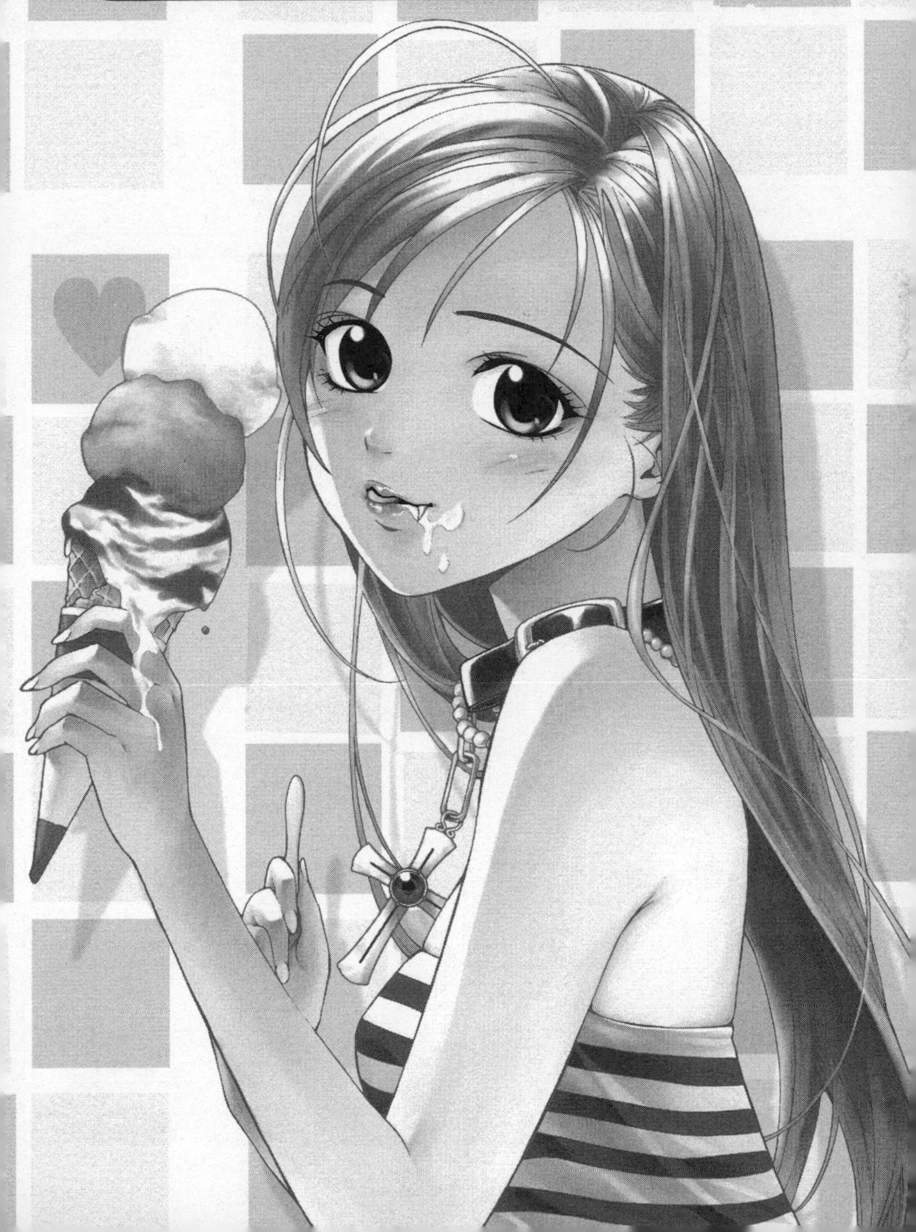

READ THIS WAY

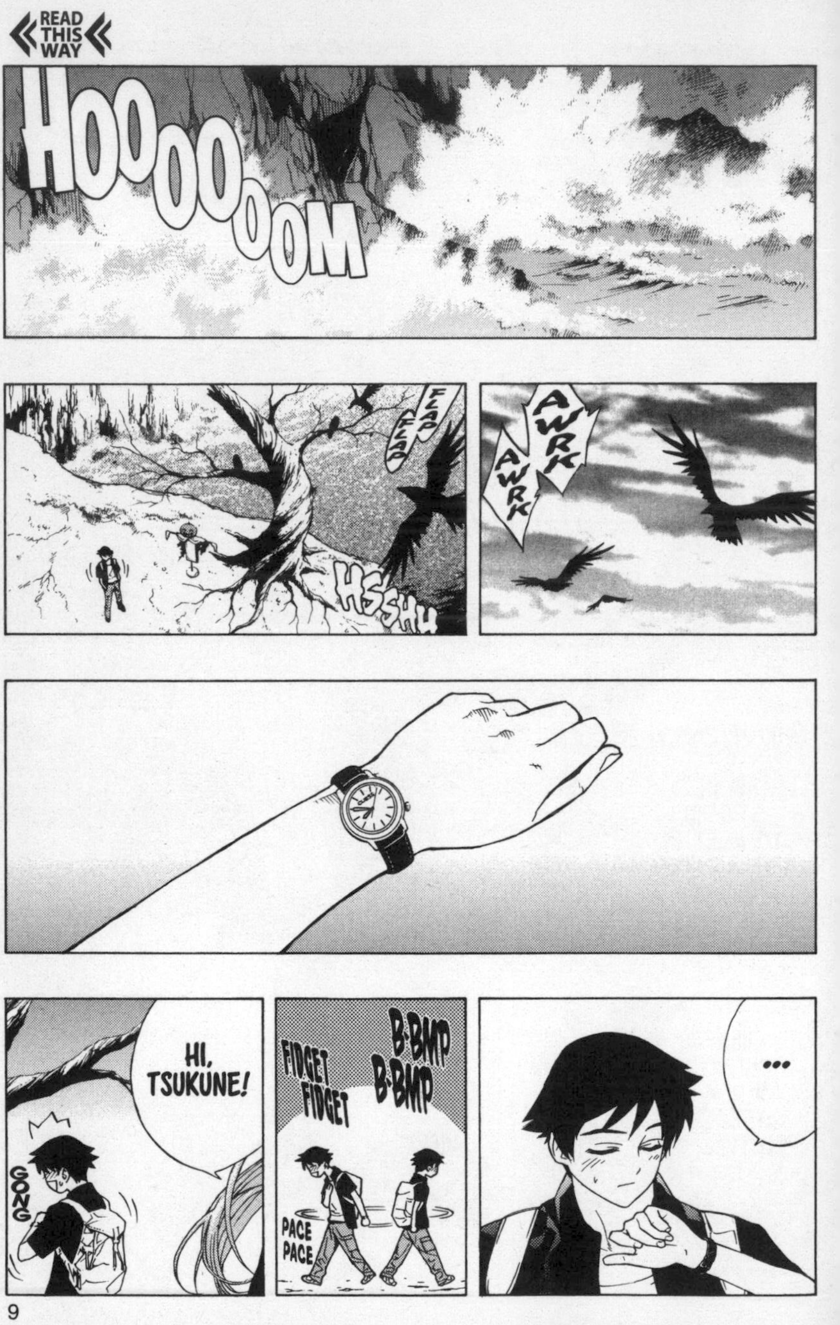
HOOOOOOOM
AWRK
AWRK
FLAP
FLAP
HSSHU
...
B-BMP
B-BMP
FIDGET
FIDGET
PACE
PACE
HI, TSUKUNE!
GONG

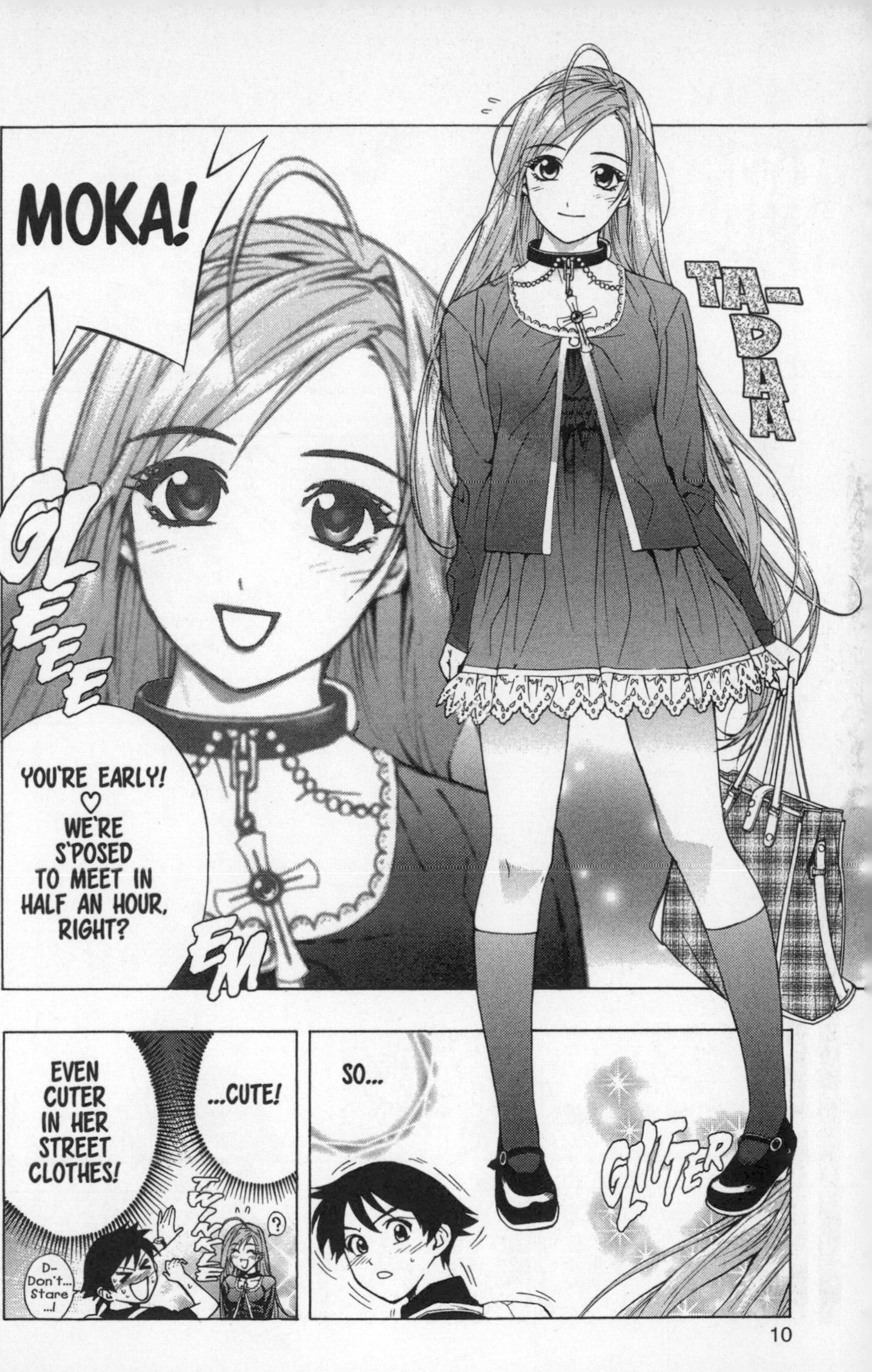
TA-DAA
MOKA!
GLEEEE
YOU'RE EARLY! ♡ WE'RE S'POSED TO MEET IN HALF AN HOUR, RIGHT?
EM
SO...
GLITTER
...CUTE!
EVEN CUTER IN HER STREET CLOTHES!
TWINKLE
?
D-Don't... Stare ...!

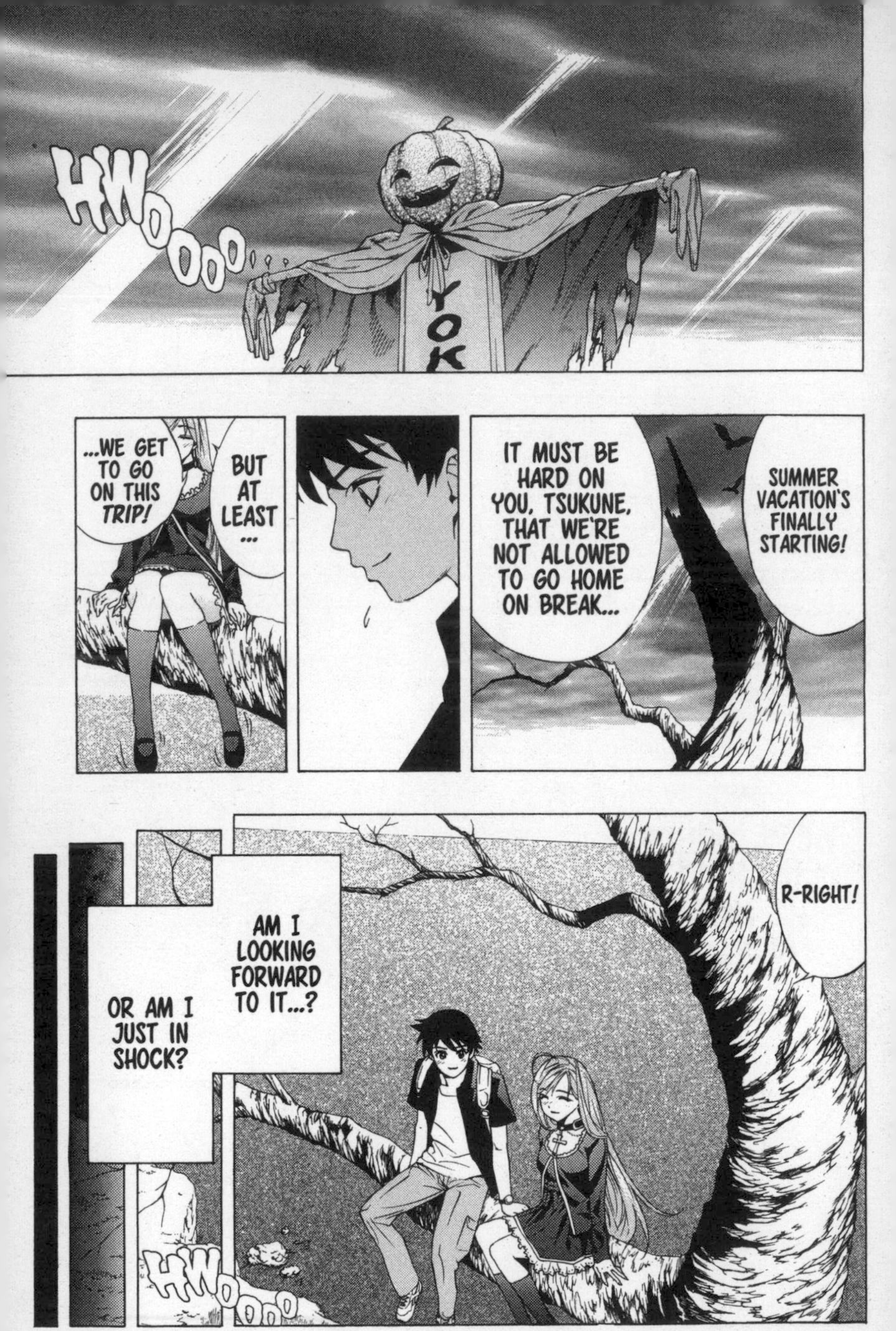
HWOOOO...
YOK
SUMMER VACATION'S FINALLY STARTING!
IT MUST BE HARD ON YOU, TSUKUNE, THAT WE'RE NOT ALLOWED TO GO HOME ON BREAK...
BUT AT LEAST...
...WE GET TO GO ON THIS TRIP!
R-RIGHT!
AM I LOOKING FORWARD TO IT...?
OR AM I JUST IN SHOCK?
HWOOOO

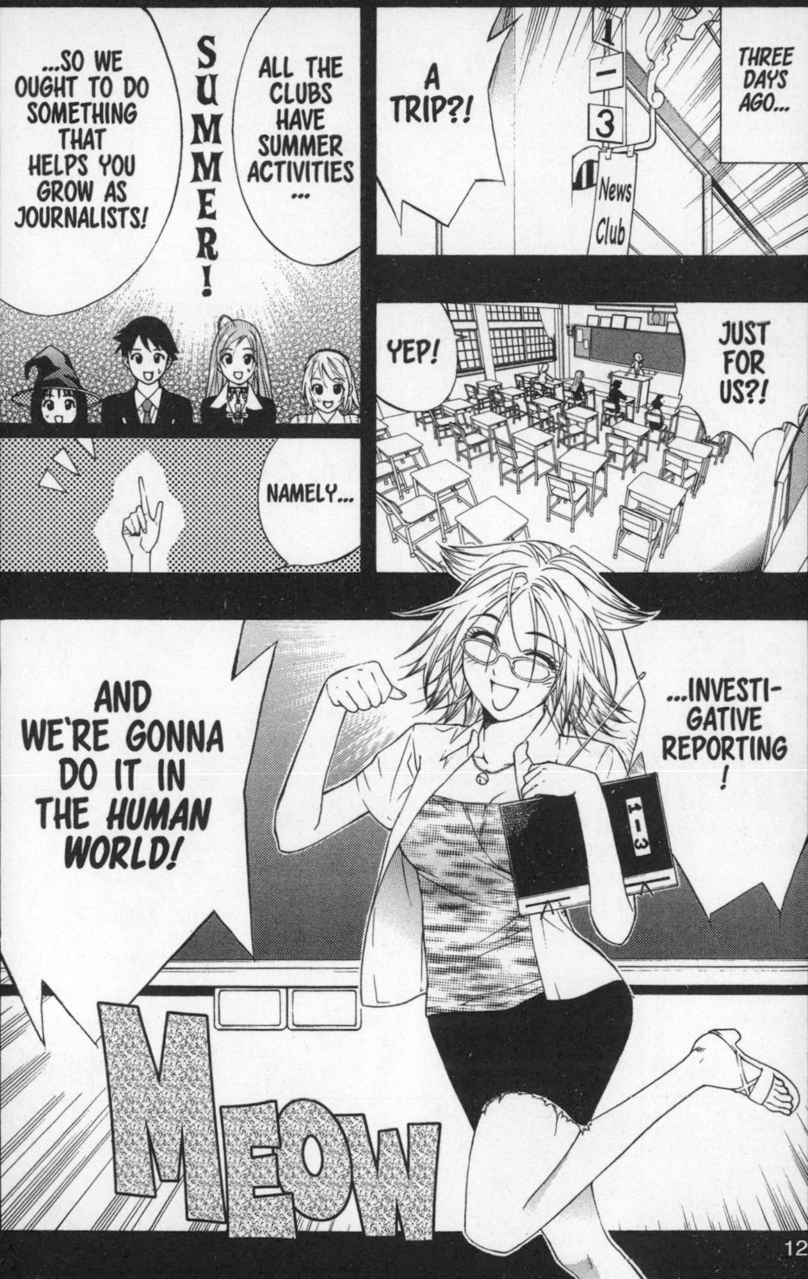
THREE DAYS AGO...
1-3
News Club
A TRIP?!
JUST FOR US?!
YEP!
ALL THE CLUBS HAVE SUMMER ACTIVITIES...
SUMMER!
...SO WE OUGHT TO DO SOMETHING THAT HELPS YOU GROW AS JOURNALISTS!
NAMELY...
...INVESTIGATIVE REPORTING!
AND WE'RE GONNA DO IT IN THE *HUMAN WORLD!*
1-3
MEOW

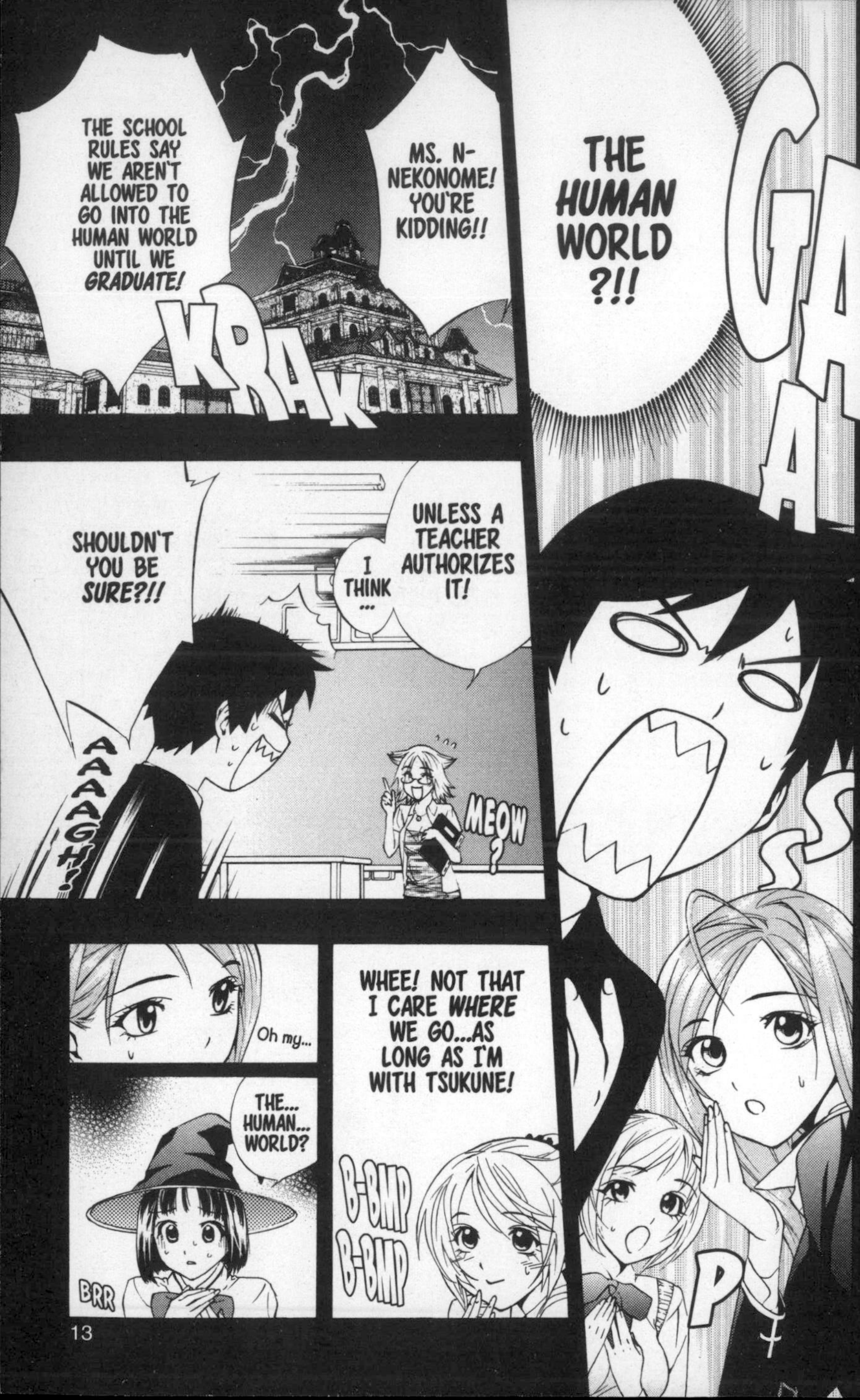
THE HUMAN WORLD ?!!
MS. N-NEKONOME! YOU'RE KIDDING!!
THE SCHOOL RULES SAY WE AREN'T ALLOWED TO GO INTO THE HUMAN WORLD UNTIL WE GRADUATE!
KRAK
UNLESS A TEACHER AUTHORIZES IT!
I THINK...
SHOULDN'T YOU BE SURE?!!
AAAAAGH!
MEOW?
WHEE! NOT THAT I CARE WHERE WE GO...AS LONG AS I'M WITH TSUKUNE!
B-BMP B-BMP
Oh my...
THE... HUMAN... WORLD?
BRR

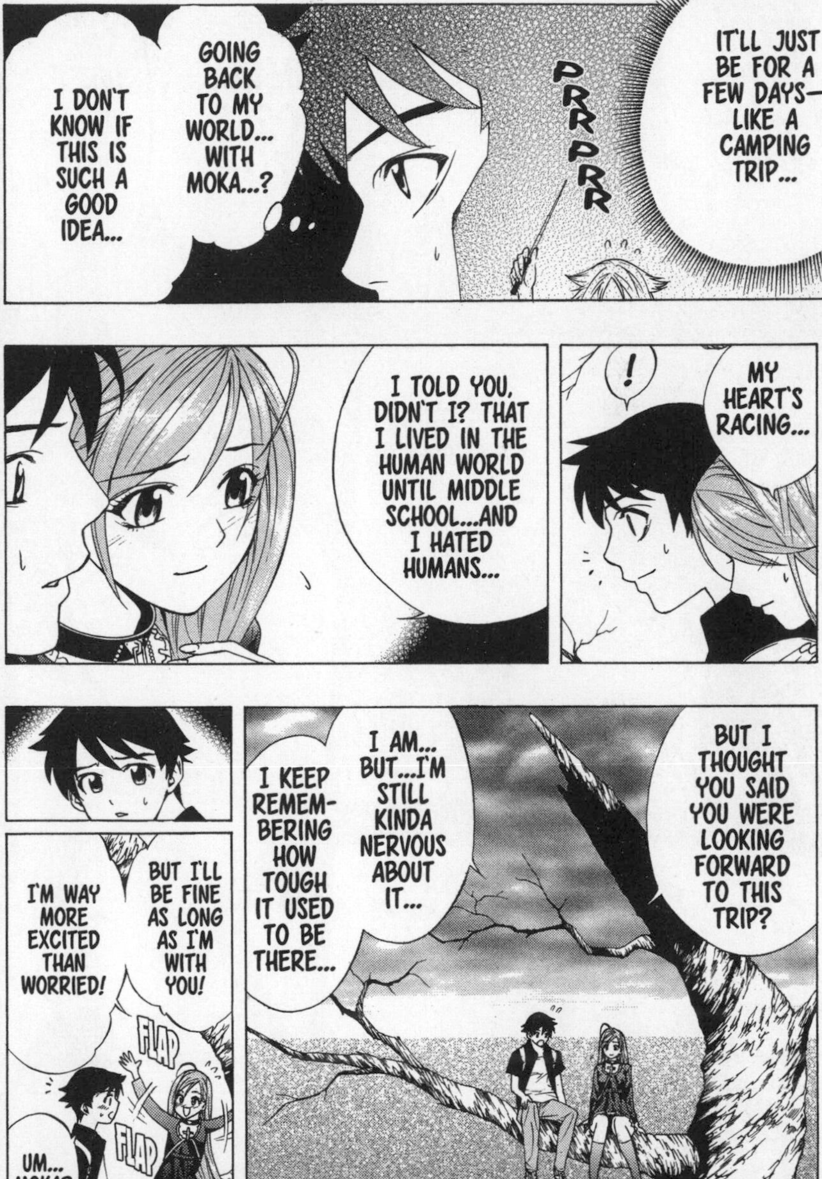
IT'LL JUST BE FOR A FEW DAYS—LIKE A CAMPING TRIP...
PRRRR
GOING BACK TO MY WORLD... WITH MOKA...?
I DON'T KNOW IF THIS IS SUCH A GOOD IDEA...
!
MY HEART'S RACING...
I TOLD YOU, DIDN'T I? THAT I LIVED IN THE HUMAN WORLD UNTIL MIDDLE SCHOOL...AND I HATED HUMANS...
BUT I THOUGHT YOU SAID YOU WERE LOOKING FORWARD TO THIS TRIP?
I AM... BUT...I'M STILL KINDA NERVOUS ABOUT IT...
I KEEP REMEMBERING HOW TOUGH IT USED TO BE THERE...
BUT I'LL BE FINE AS LONG AS I'M WITH YOU!
I'M WAY MORE EXCITED THAN WORRIED!
FLAP
FLAP
UM... MOKA?

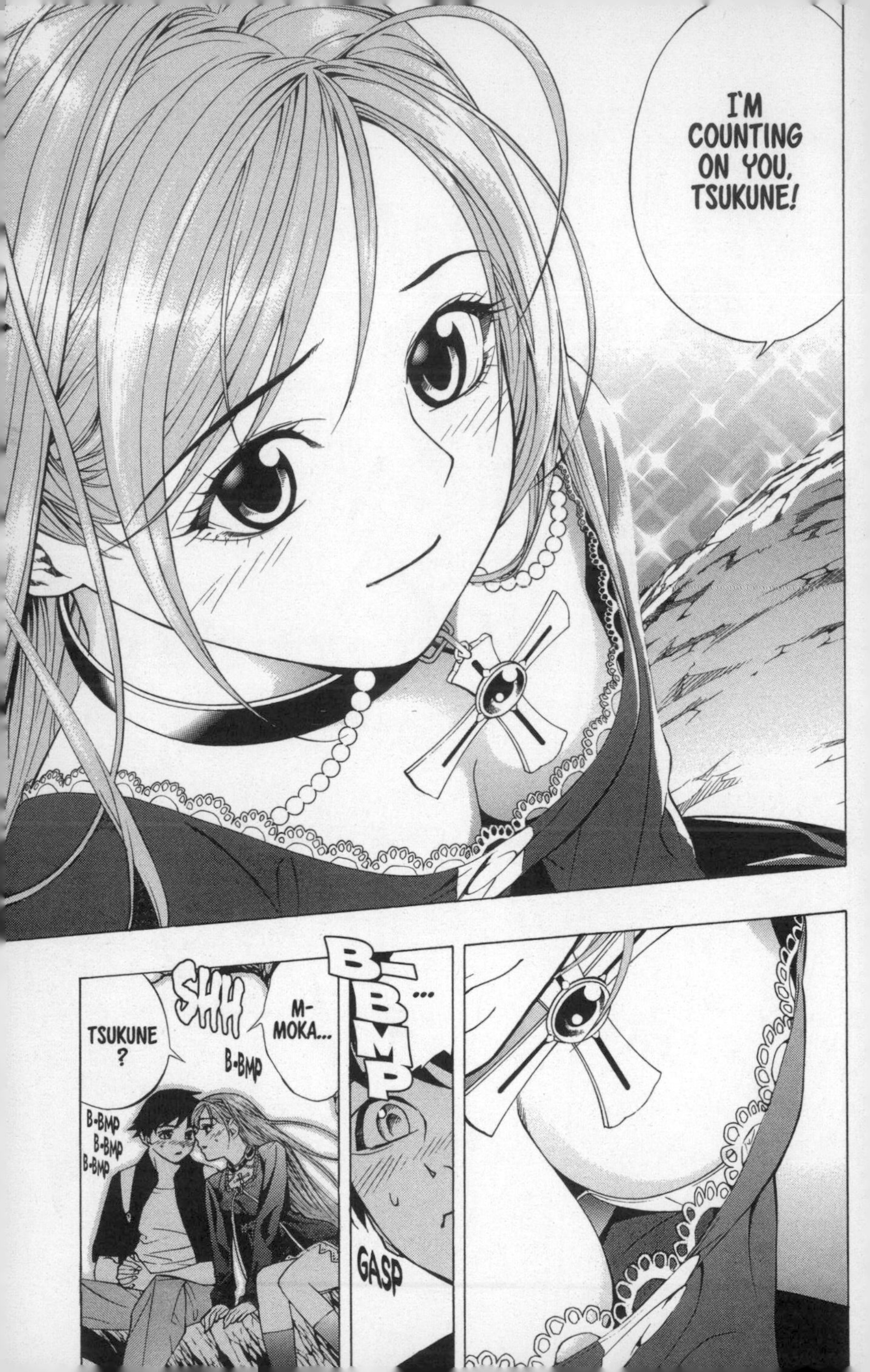
I'M COUNTING ON YOU, TSUKUNE!
B-BMP
...
GASP
M-MOKA...
SHH
TSUKUNE ?
B-BMP
B-BMP
B-BMP
B-BMP

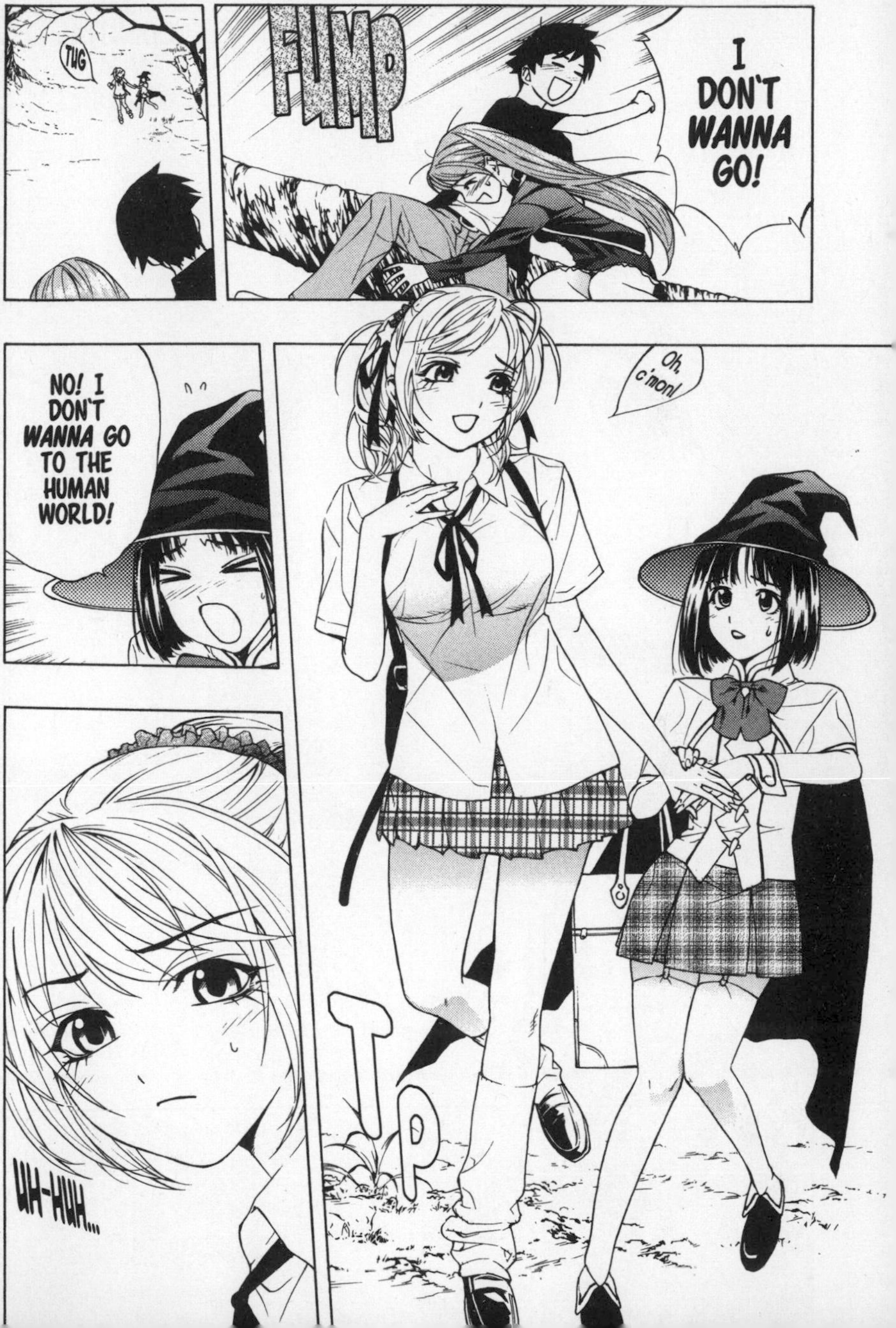
FUMP
I DON'T WANNA GO!
TUG
Oh, c'mon!
TP
NO! I DON'T WANNA GO TO THE HUMAN WORLD!
UH-HUH...

READ THIS WAY

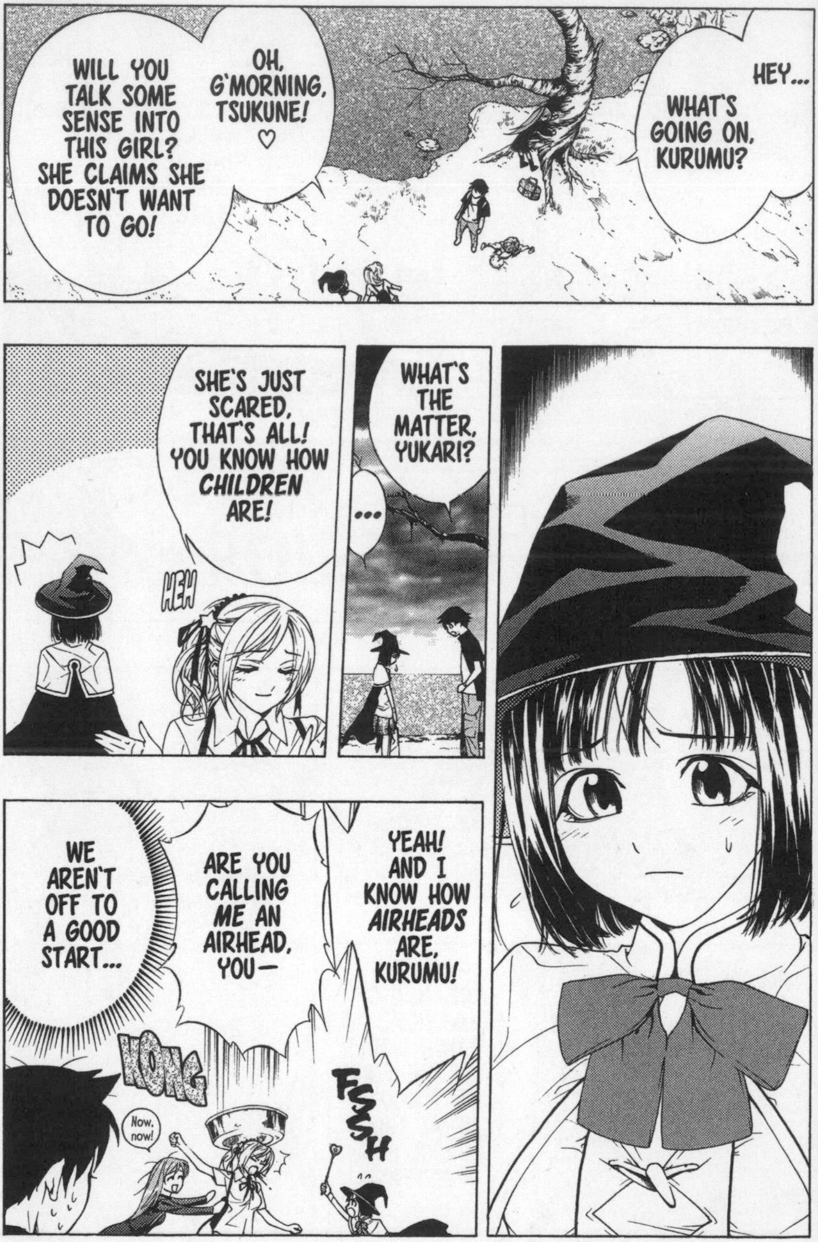
HEY... WHAT'S GOING ON, KURUMU?
OH, G'MORNING, TSUKUNE! ♡
WILL YOU TALK SOME SENSE INTO THIS GIRL? SHE CLAIMS SHE DOESN'T WANT TO GO!
WHAT'S THE MATTER, YUKARI?
...
SHE'S JUST SCARED, THAT'S ALL! YOU KNOW HOW CHILDREN ARE!
HEH
YEAH! AND I KNOW HOW AIRHEADS ARE, KURUMU!
ARE YOU CALLING ME AN AIRHEAD, YOU—
WE AREN'T OFF TO A GOOD START...
KONG
FSSH
Now, now!

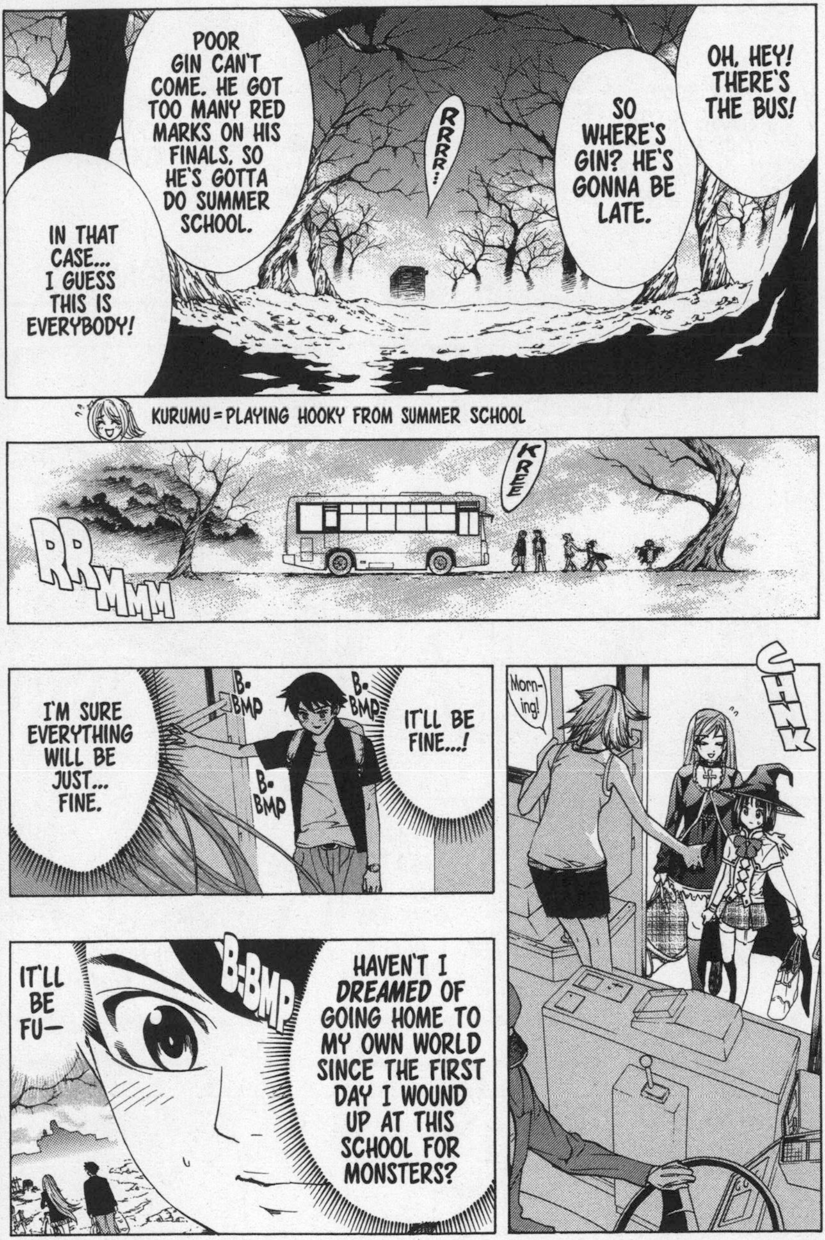
OH, HEY! THERE'S THE BUS!
SO WHERE'S GIN? HE'S GONNA BE LATE.
RRRR..
POOR GIN CAN'T COME. HE GOT TOO MANY RED MARKS ON HIS FINALS, SO HE'S GOTTA DO SUMMER SCHOOL.
IN THAT CASE... I GUESS THIS IS EVERYBODY!
KURUMU = PLAYING HOOKY FROM SUMMER SCHOOL
KREE
RRMMM
CHNK
Morn-ing!
IT'LL BE FINE...!
B-BMP
B-BMP
B-BMP
I'M SURE EVERYTHING WILL BE JUST... FINE.
HAVEN'T I *DREAMED* OF GOING HOME TO MY OWN WORLD SINCE THE FIRST DAY I WOUND UP AT THIS SCHOOL FOR MONSTERS?
B-BMP
IT'LL BE FU—

READ THIS WAY

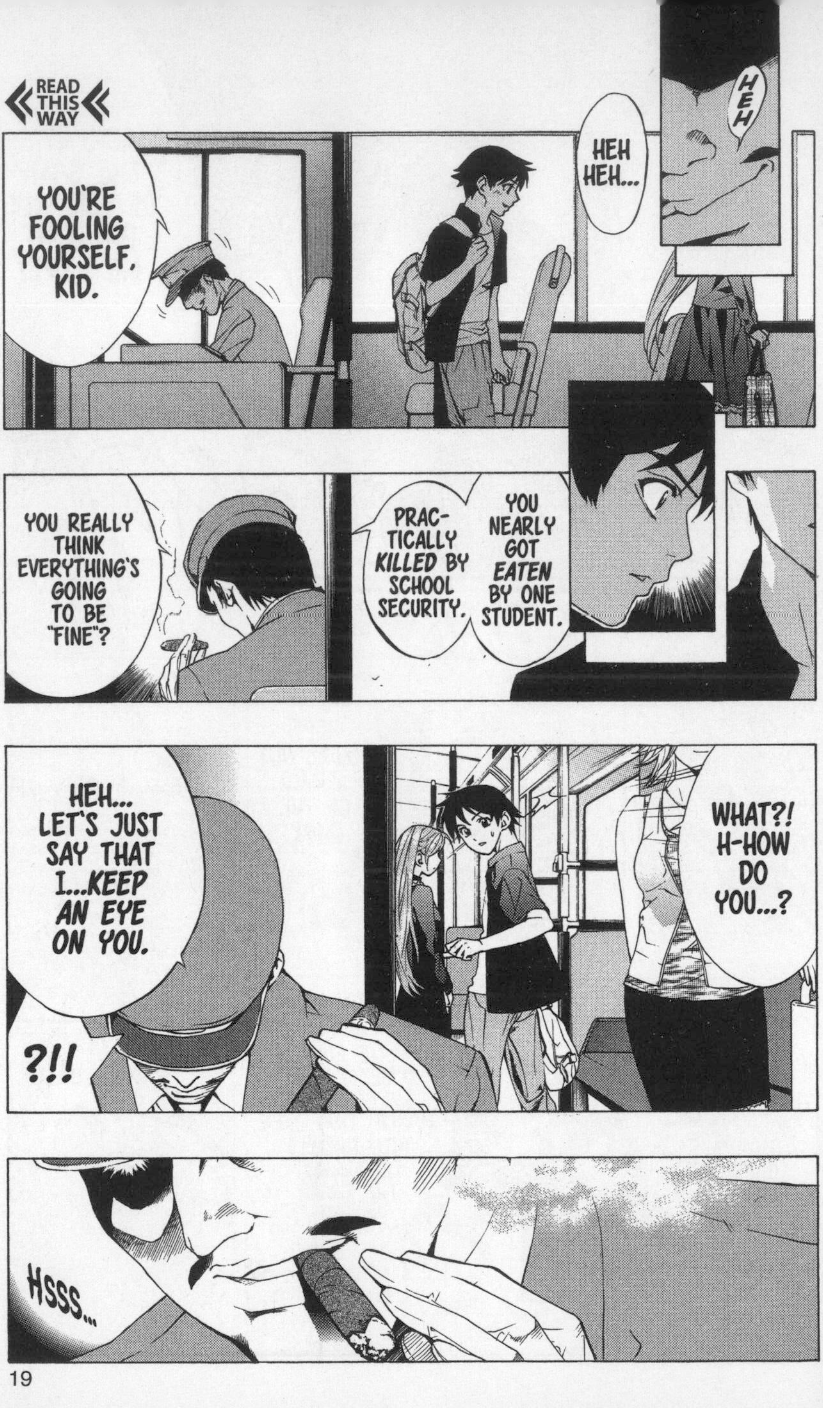
HEH
HEH HEH...
YOU'RE FOOLING YOURSELF, KID.
YOU NEARLY GOT *EATEN* BY ONE STUDENT.
PRAC-TICALLY *KILLED* BY SCHOOL SECURITY.
YOU REALLY THINK EVERYTHING'S GOING TO BE "FINE"?
WHAT?! H-HOW DO YOU...?
HEH... LET'S JUST SAY THAT I...*KEEP AN EYE* ON YOU.
?!!
HSSS...

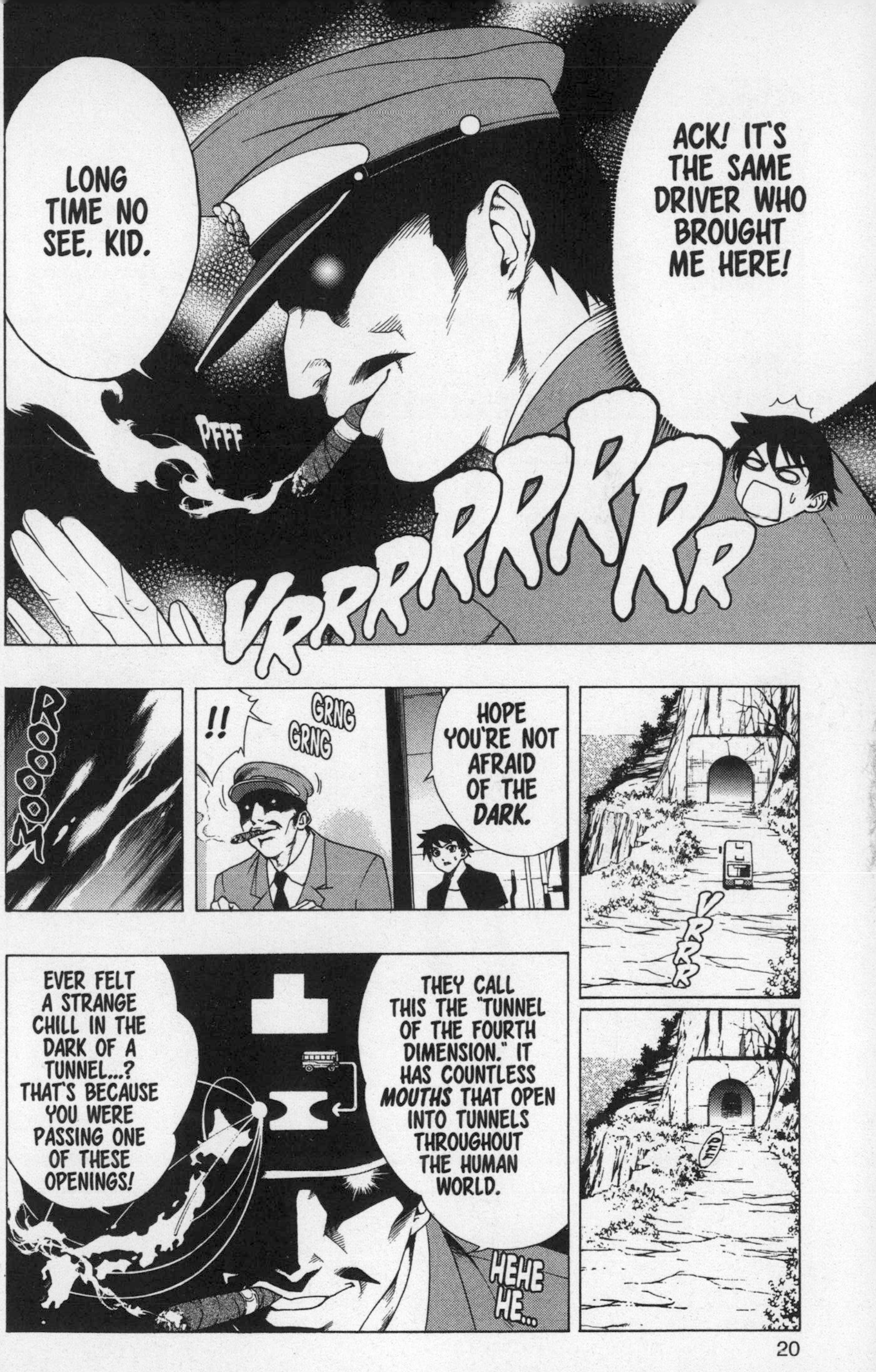
ACK! IT'S THE SAME DRIVER WHO BROUGHT ME HERE!
LONG TIME NO SEE, KID.
PFFF
VRRRRRRRRRR
VRRR
HOPE YOU'RE NOT AFRAID OF THE *DARK.*
GRNG GRNG
!!
ROOOOM
THEY CALL THIS THE "TUNNEL OF THE FOURTH DIMENSION." IT HAS COUNTLESS *MOUTHS* THAT OPEN INTO TUNNELS THROUGHOUT THE HUMAN WORLD.
EVER FELT A STRANGE CHILL IN THE DARK OF A TUNNEL...? THAT'S BECAUSE YOU WERE PASSING ONE OF THESE OPENINGS!
HEHE HE...

READ THIS WAY

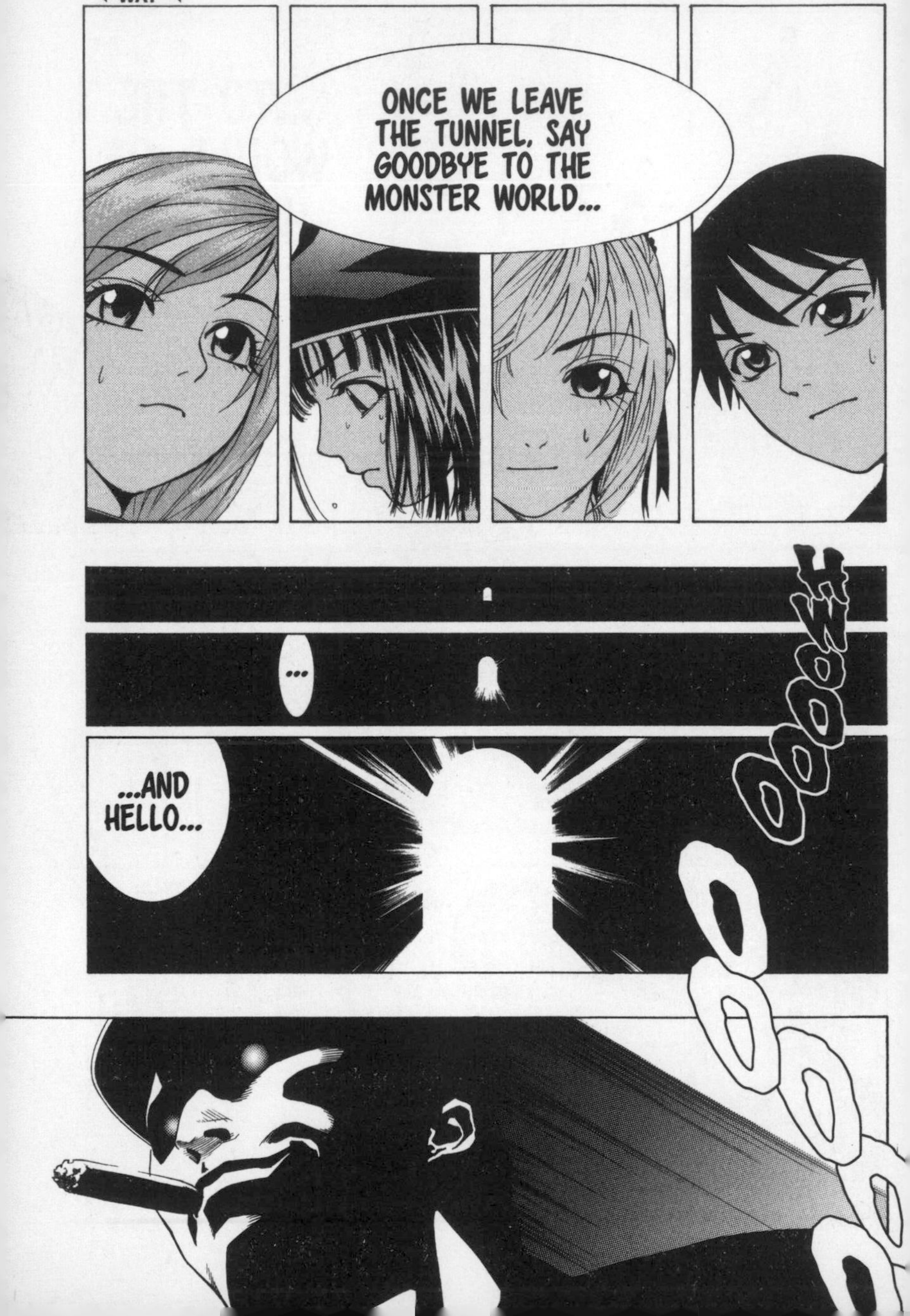
ONCE WE LEAVE THE TUNNEL, SAY GOODBYE TO THE MONSTER WORLD...
...
...AND HELLO...
HWOOOOOOOOOO

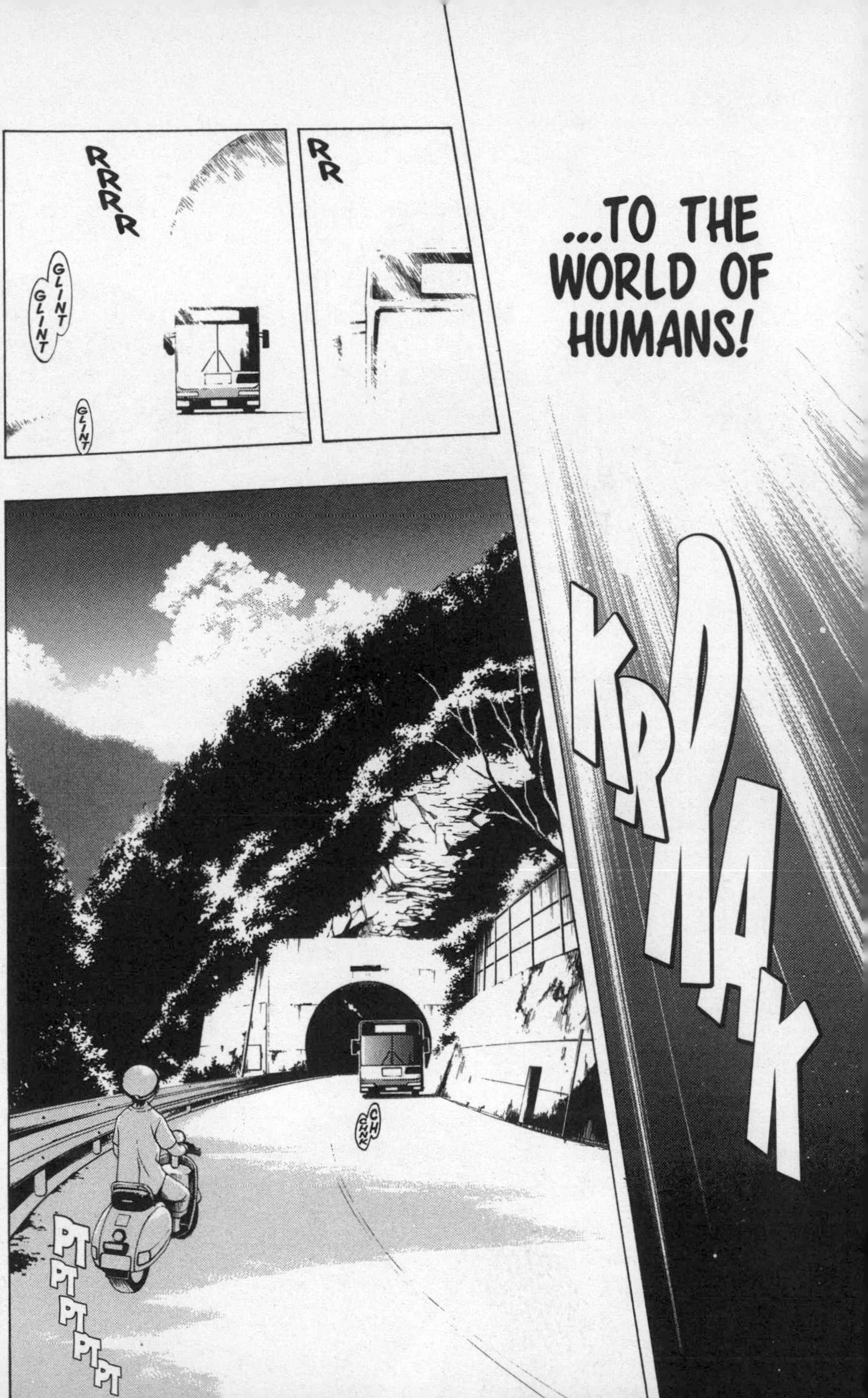
...TO THE WORLD OF HUMANS!
KRAAK
RR
RRRR
GLINT GLINT
GLINT
CH
CHNK
PT PT PT PT PT

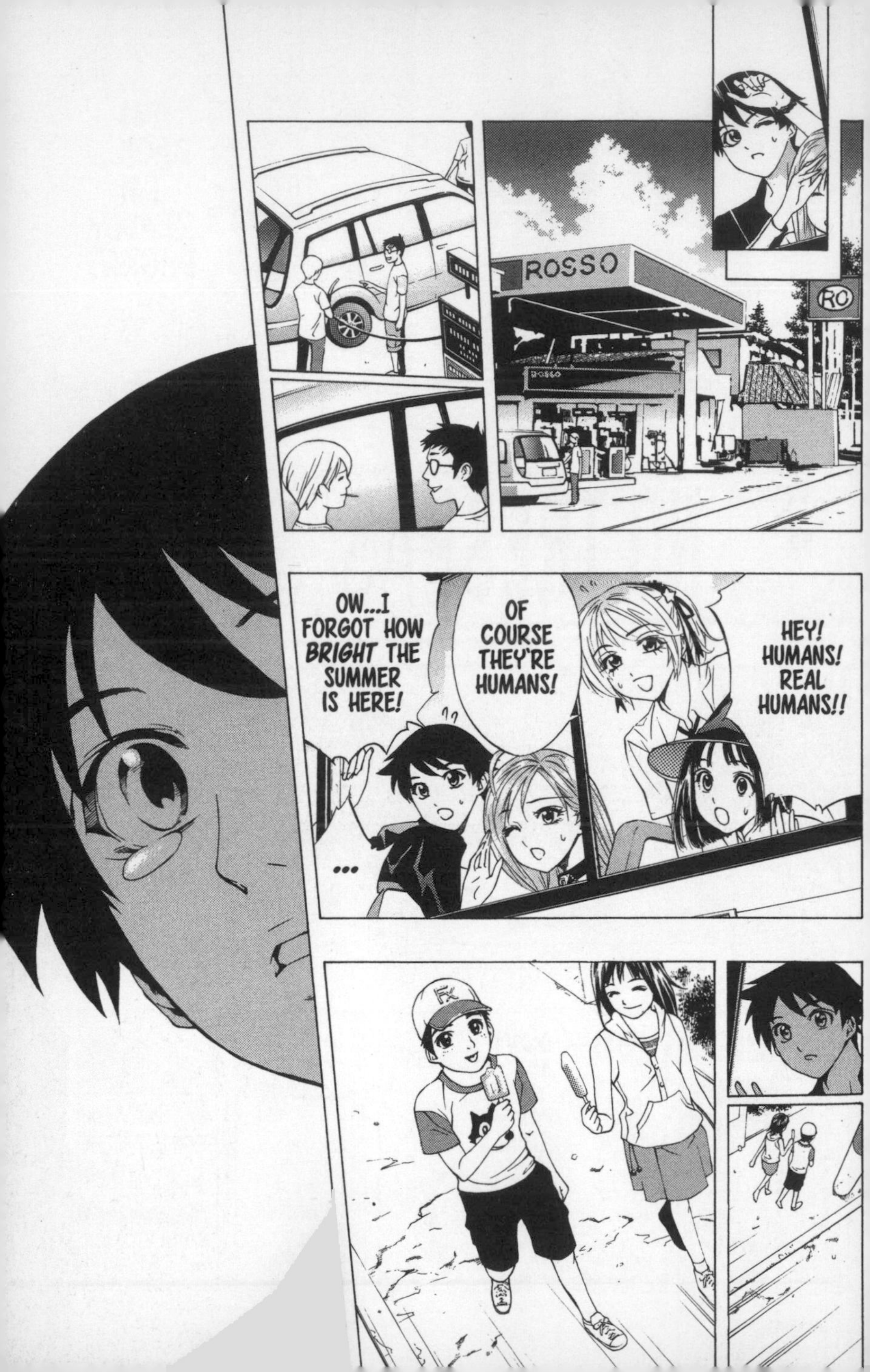
ROSSO
RC
HEY! HUMANS! REAL HUMANS!!
OF COURSE THEY'RE HUMANS!
OW...I FORGOT HOW *BRIGHT* THE SUMMER IS HERE!
...

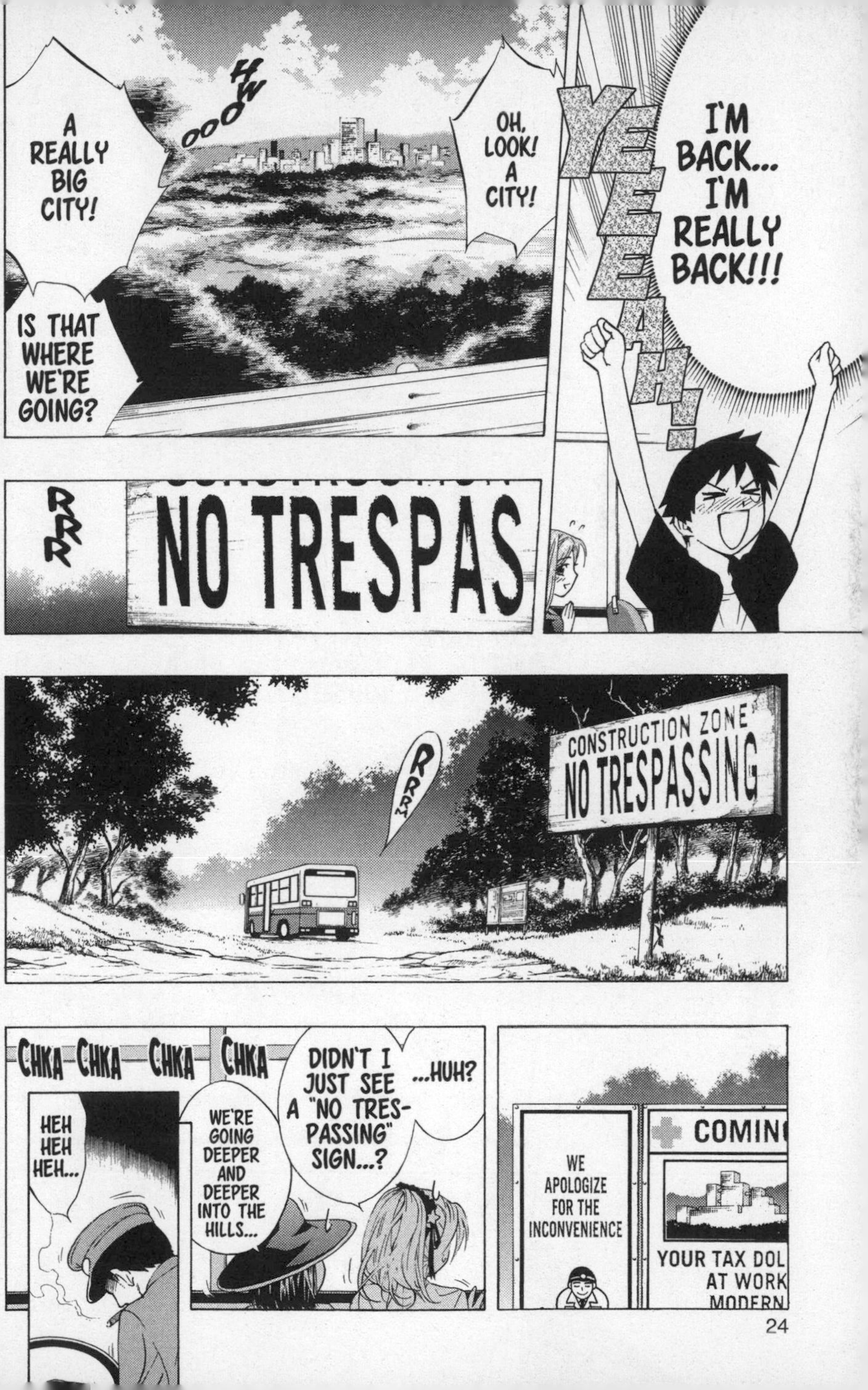
I'M BACK... I'M REALLY BACK!!!
YEEEEEAH!!
OH, LOOK! A CITY!
HWOOOO
A REALLY BIG CITY!
IS THAT WHERE WE'RE GOING?
NO TRESPAS
RRR
CONSTRUCTION ZONE
NO TRESPASSING
RRRR
COMIN
YOUR TAX DOL
AT WORK
MODERN
WE APOLOGIZE FOR THE INCONVENIENCE
...HUH?
DIDN'T I JUST SEE A "NO TRES-PASSING" SIGN...?
WE'RE GOING DEEPER AND DEEPER INTO THE HILLS...
CHKA CHKA CHKA CHKA
HEH HEH HEH...

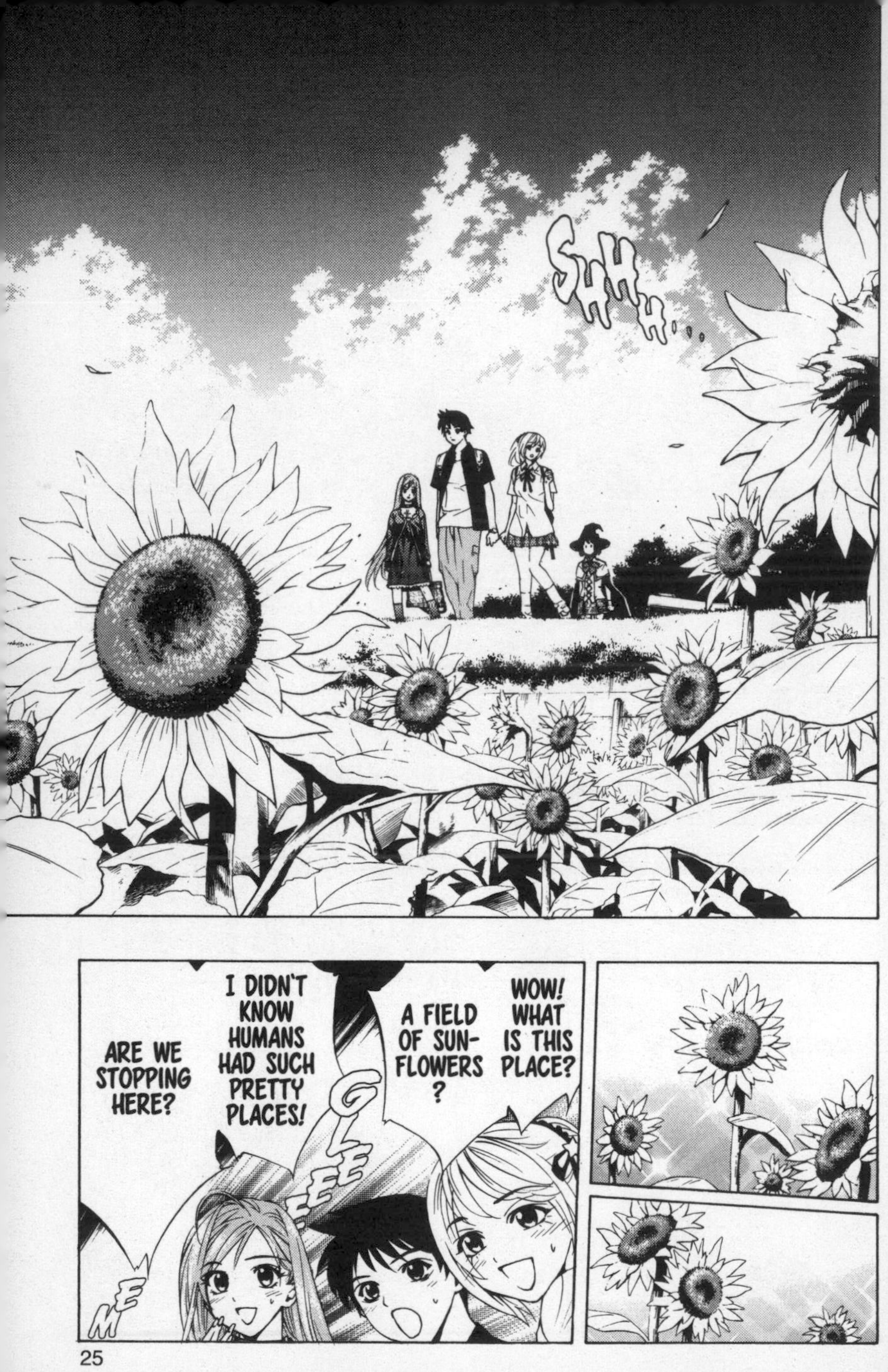
SHHH...
WOW! WHAT IS THIS PLACE?
A FIELD OF SUN-FLOWERS?
I DIDN'T KNOW HUMANS HAD SUCH PRETTY PLACES!
GLEEE
ARE WE STOPPING HERE?
ME

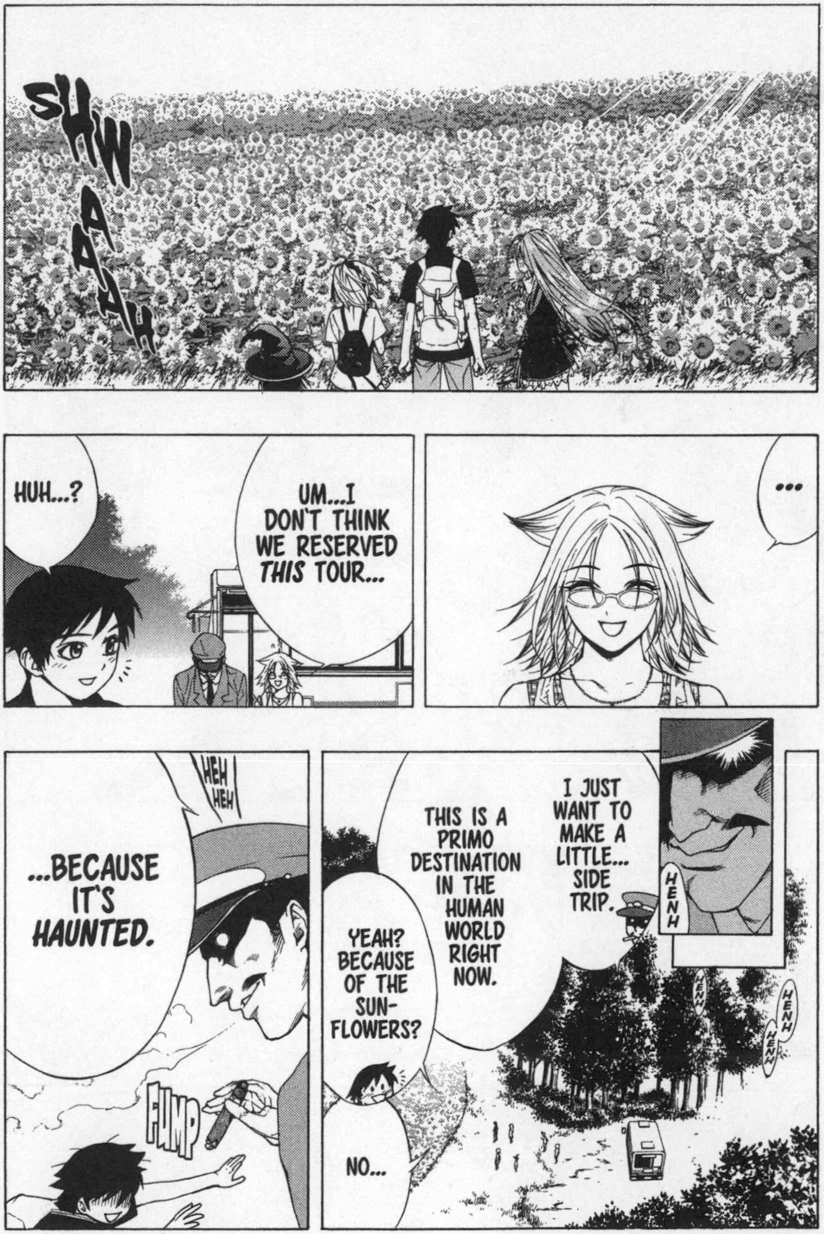
SHWAAAH
...
UM...I DON'T THINK WE RESERVED THIS TOUR...
HUH...?
I JUST WANT TO MAKE A LITTLE... SIDE TRIP.
HENH
THIS IS A PRIMO DESTINATION IN THE HUMAN WORLD RIGHT NOW.
HENH HENH HENH
YEAH? BECAUSE OF THE SUN-FLOWERS?
NO...
HEH HEH
...BECAUSE IT'S HAUNTED.
FUMP

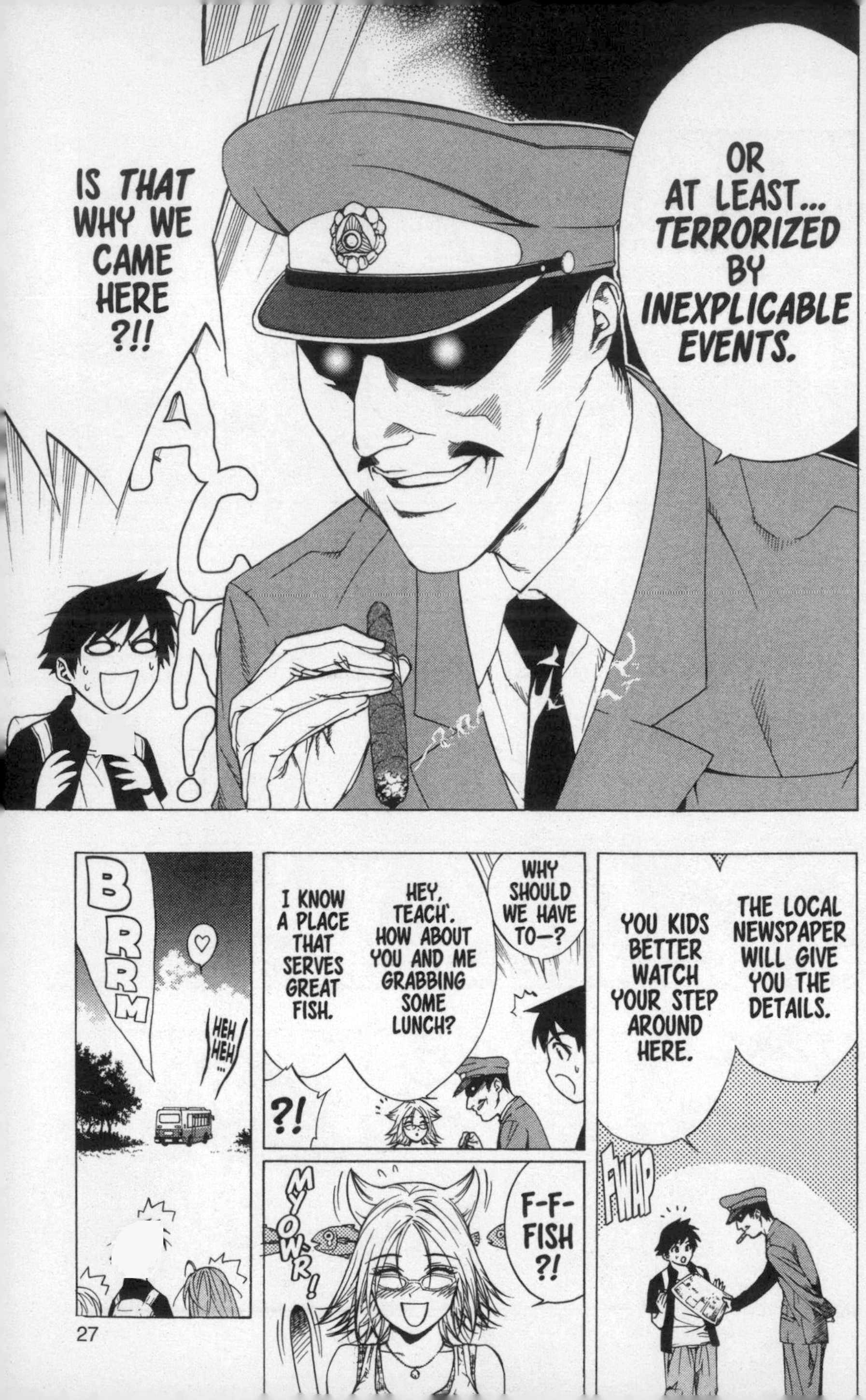
OR AT LEAST... TERRORIZED BY INEXPLICABLE EVENTS.
IS THAT WHY WE CAME HERE ?!!
ACK!
THE LOCAL NEWSPAPER WILL GIVE YOU THE DETAILS.
YOU KIDS BETTER WATCH YOUR STEP AROUND HERE.
FWAP
WHY SHOULD WE HAVE TO—?
HEY, TEACH'. HOW ABOUT YOU AND ME GRABBING SOME LUNCH?
I KNOW A PLACE THAT SERVES GREAT FISH.
?!
F-F-FISH ?!
MYOWR!
BRRRM
♡
HEH HEH...

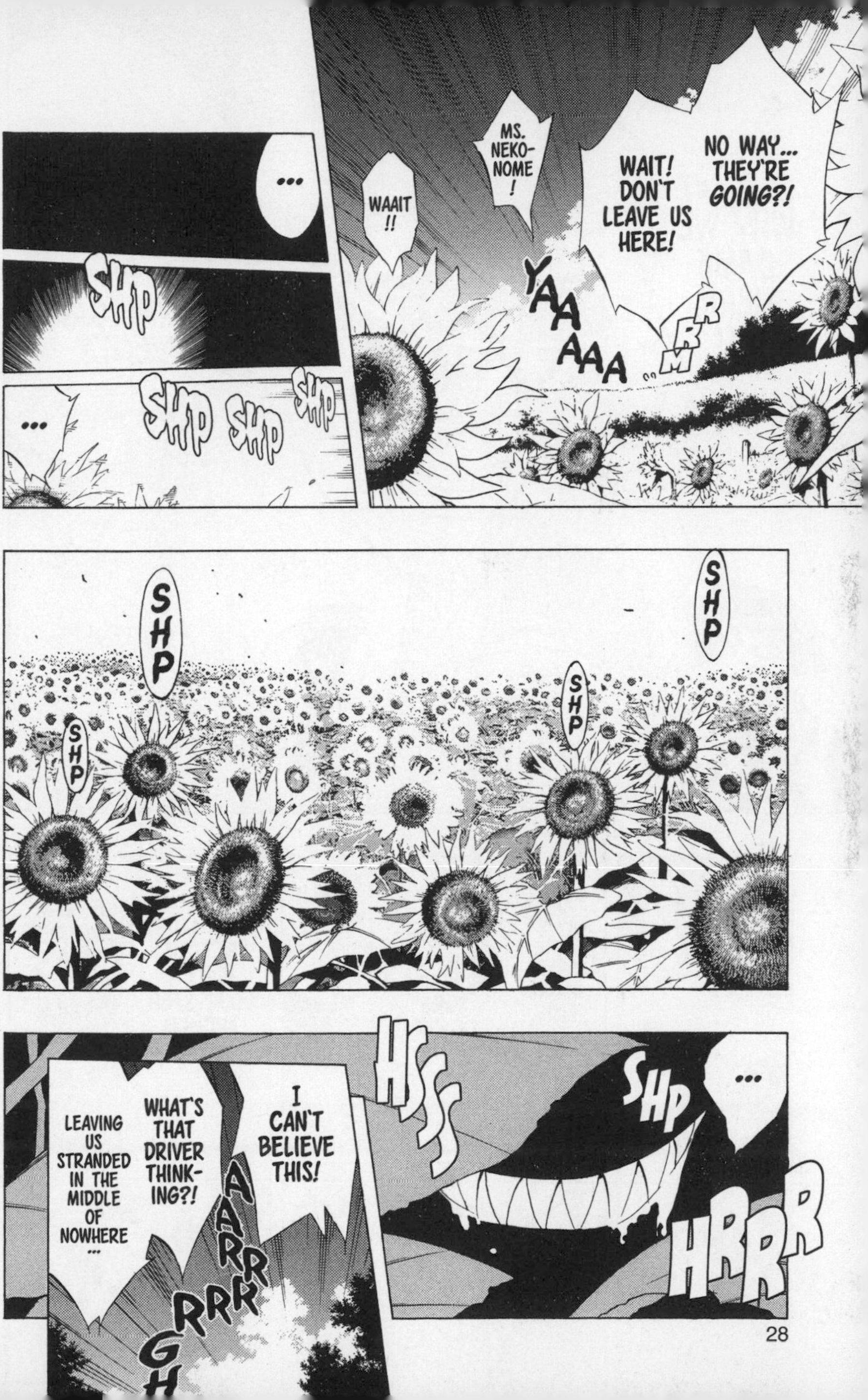
NO WAY... THEY'RE GOING?!
WAIT! DON'T LEAVE US HERE!
MS. NEKO-NOME!
WAAIT!!
YAAAAAA
RRM
...
SHP
...
SHP
SHP
SHP
SHP
SHP
SHP
SHP
...
SHP
HSSS
HRRR
I CAN'T BELIEVE THIS!
WHAT'S THAT DRIVER THINKING?!
LEAVING US STRANDED IN THE MIDDLE OF NOWHERE...
AARRRRRGH

READ THIS WAY

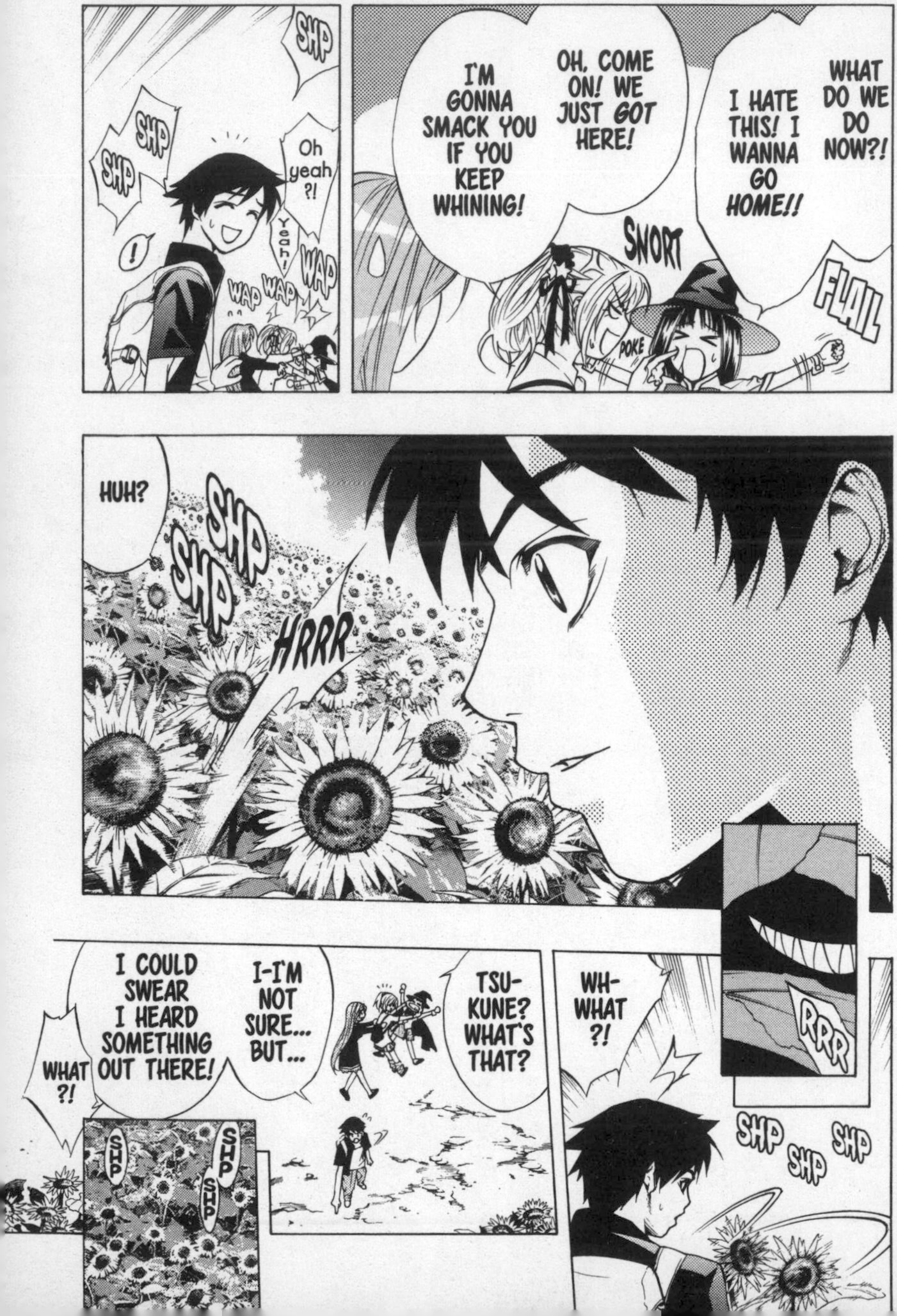
WHAT DO WE DO NOW?!
I HATE THIS! I WANNA GO HOME!!
FLAIL
OH, COME ON! WE JUST GOT HERE!
SNORT
I'M GONNA SMACK YOU IF YOU KEEP WHINING!
POKE
SHP
Oh yeah?!
Yeah!
WAP
SHP
SHP
!
WAP
WAP
HUH?
SHP
SHP
HRRR
RRR
WH-WHAT?!
SHP
SHP
SHP
TSU-KUNE? WHAT'S THAT?
I-I'M NOT SURE... BUT...
I COULD SWEAR I HEARD SOMETHING OUT THERE!
WHAT?!
SHP
SHP
SHP

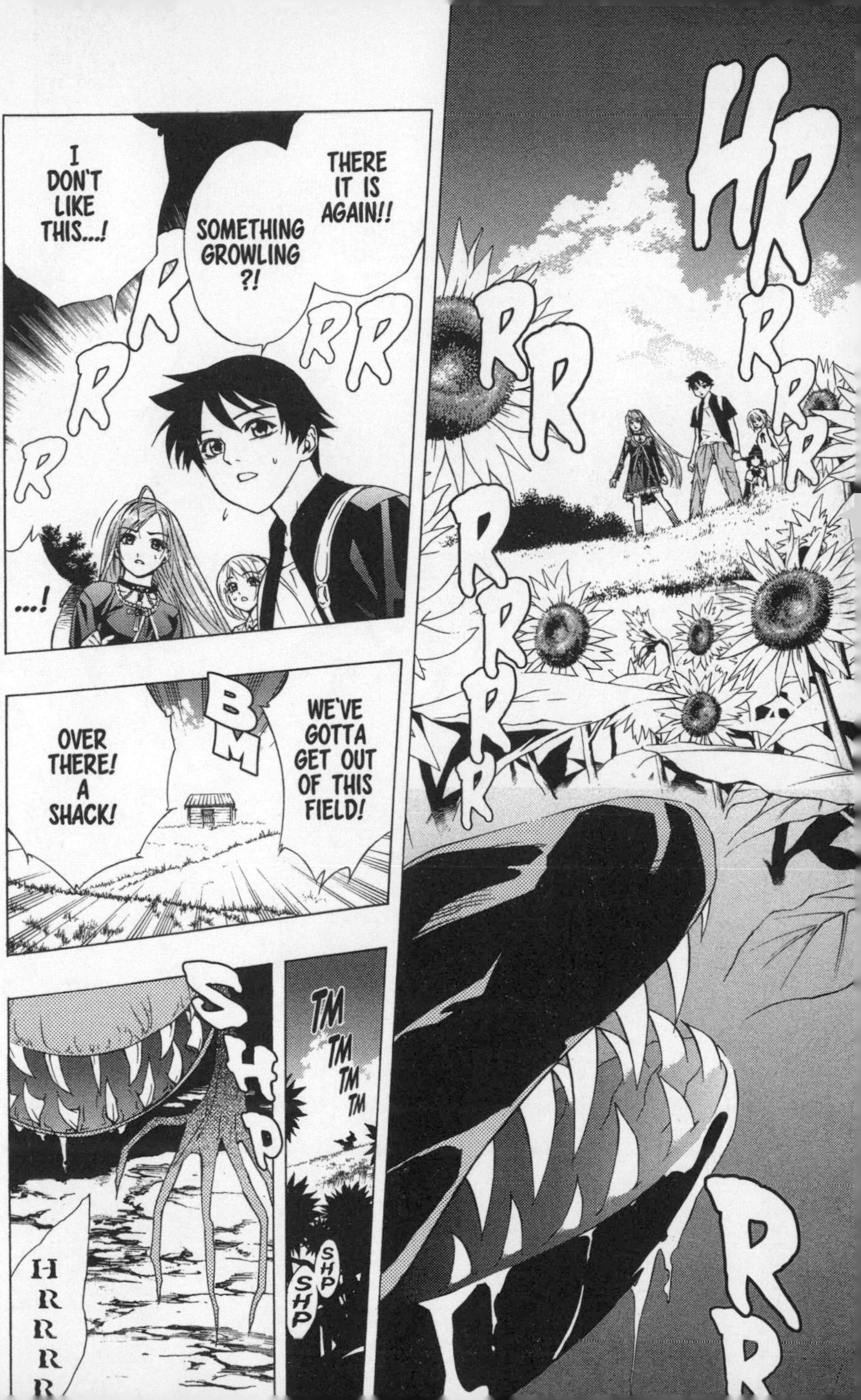
HRRRRR
RRR
RRRRRR
RR
THERE IT IS AGAIN!!
SOMETHING GROWLING?!
I DON'T LIKE THIS...!
RRRRRR
...!
BM
WE'VE GOTTA GET OUT OF THIS FIELD!
OVER THERE! A SHACK!
TM TM TM TM
SHP SHP SHP
SHP
HRRRR

READ THIS WAY

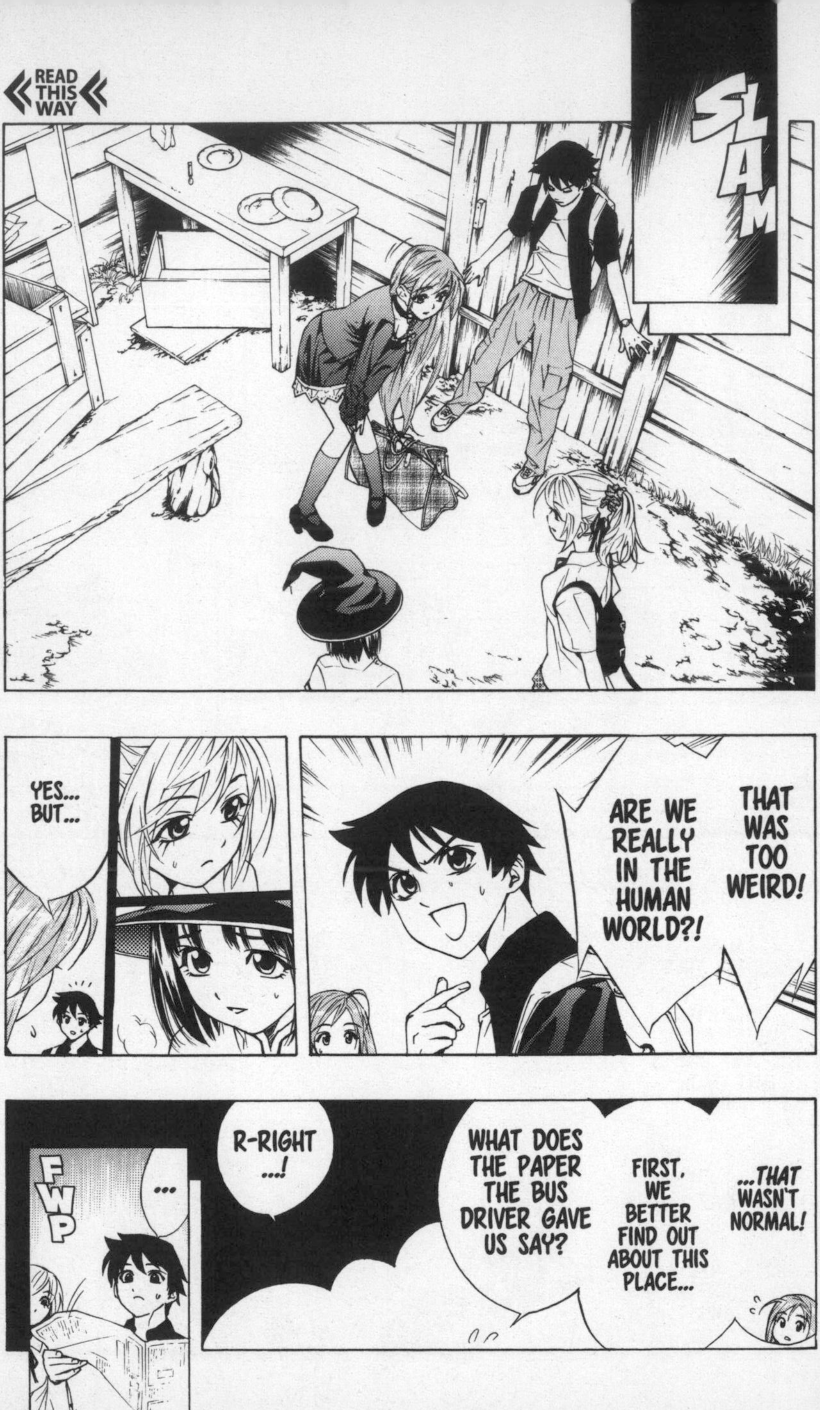

SLAM
THAT WAS TOO WEIRD!
ARE WE REALLY IN THE HUMAN WORLD?!
YES... BUT...
...THAT WASN'T NORMAL!
FIRST, WE BETTER FIND OUT ABOUT THIS PLACE...
WHAT DOES THE PAPER THE BUS DRIVER GAVE US SAY?
R-RIGHT ...!
...
FWP

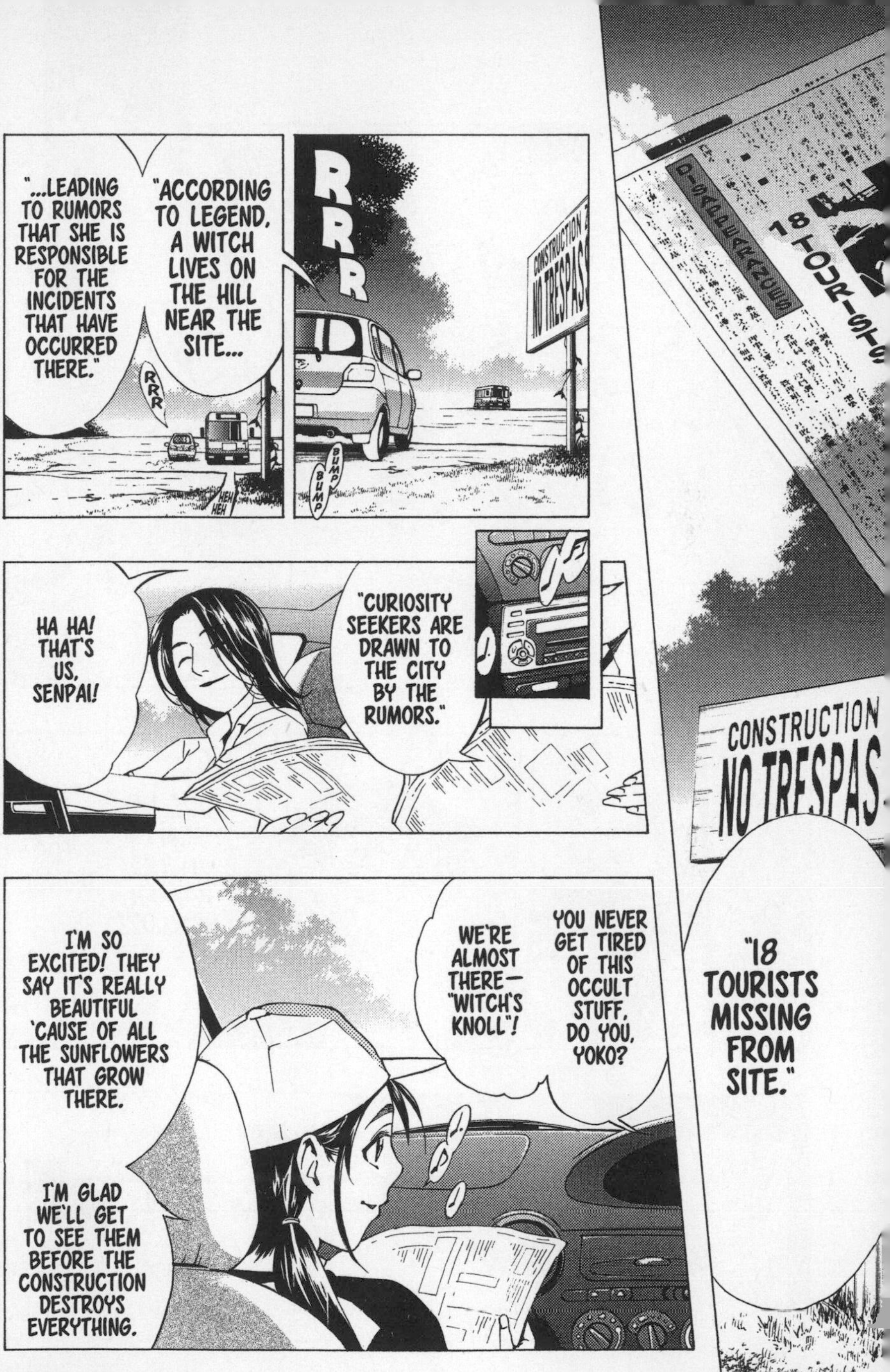
18 TOURISTS
CONSTRUCTION
NO TRESPAS
"18 TOURISTS MISSING FROM SITE."
RRR
CONSTRUCTION
NO TRESPAS
"ACCORDING TO LEGEND, A WITCH LIVES ON THE HILL NEAR THE SITE...
BUMP BUMP
"...LEADING TO RUMORS THAT SHE IS RESPONSIBLE FOR THE INCIDENTS THAT HAVE OCCURRED THERE."
RRR
HEH HEH
"CURIOSITY SEEKERS ARE DRAWN TO THE CITY BY THE RUMORS."
HA HA! THAT'S US, SENPAI!
YOU NEVER GET TIRED OF THIS OCCULT STUFF, DO YOU, YOKO?
WE'RE ALMOST THERE—"WITCH'S KNOLL"!
I'M SO EXCITED! THEY SAY IT'S REALLY BEAUTIFUL 'CAUSE OF ALL THE SUNFLOWERS THAT GROW THERE.
I'M GLAD WE'LL GET TO SEE THEM BEFORE THE CONSTRUCTION DESTROYS EVERYTHING.

READ THIS WAY

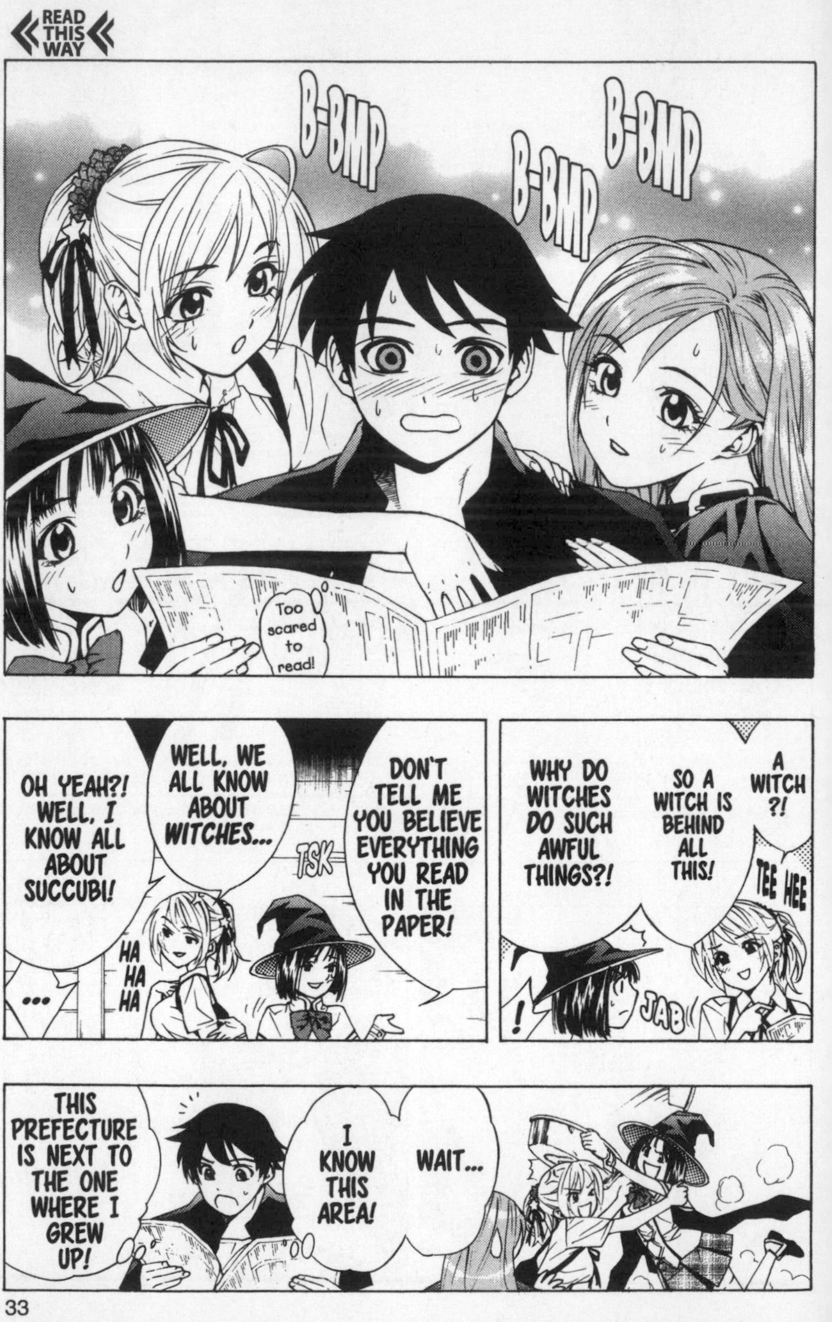
B-BMP
B-BMP
B-BMP
Too scared to read!
A WITCH?!
TEE HEE
SO A WITCH IS BEHIND ALL THIS!
WHY DO WITCHES DO SUCH AWFUL THINGS?!
JAB
!
DON'T TELL ME YOU BELIEVE EVERYTHING YOU READ IN THE PAPER!
TSK
WELL, WE ALL KNOW ABOUT WITCHES...
OH YEAH?! WELL, I KNOW ALL ABOUT SUCCUBI!
HA HA HA
...
WAIT...
I KNOW THIS AREA!
THIS PREFECTURE IS NEXT TO THE ONE WHERE I GREW UP!

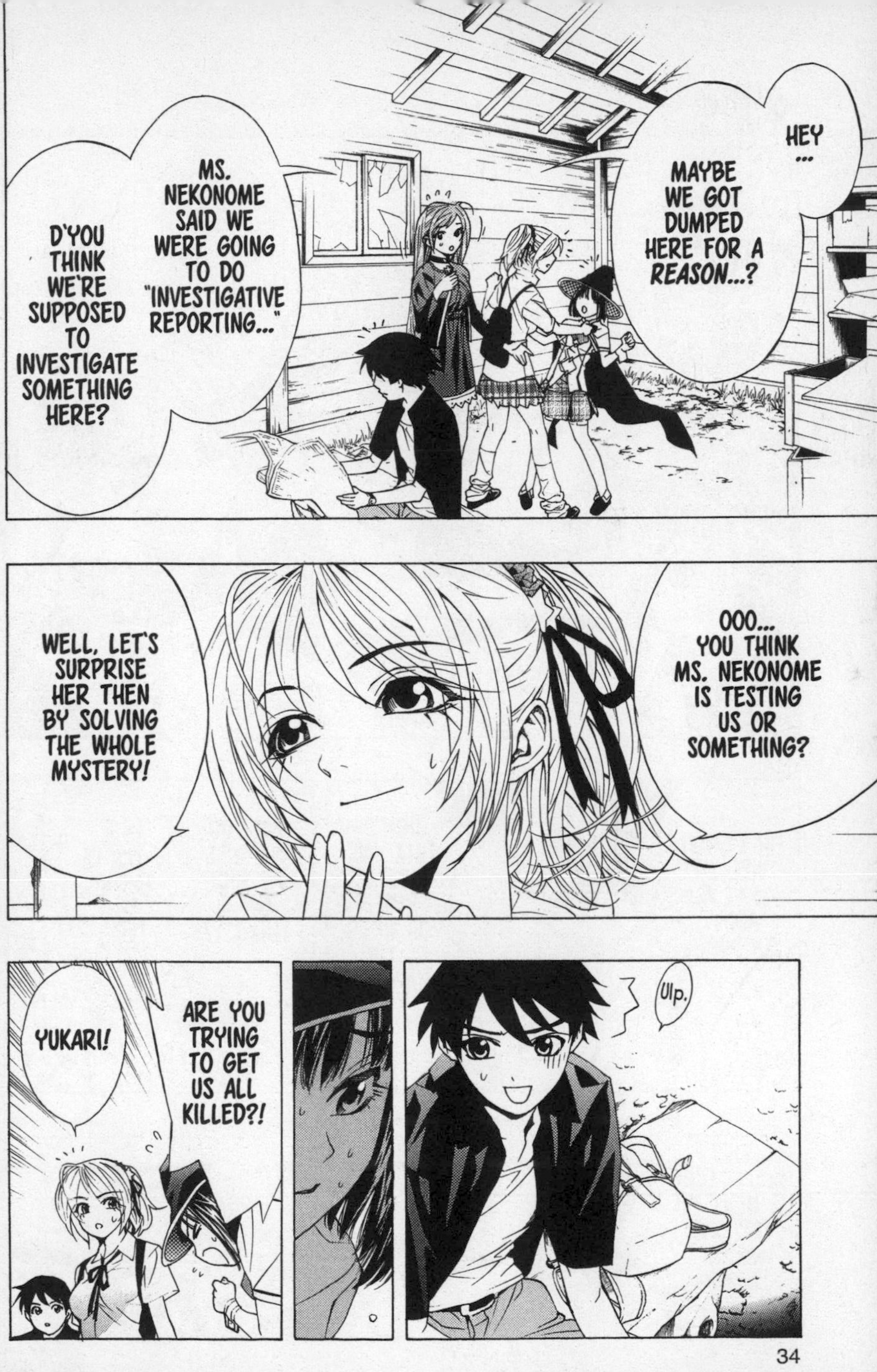
HEY ... MAYBE WE GOT DUMPED HERE FOR A REASON...?
MS. NEKONOME SAID WE WERE GOING TO DO "INVESTIGATIVE REPORTING..."
D'YOU THINK WE'RE SUPPOSED TO INVESTIGATE SOMETHING HERE?
OOO... YOU THINK MS. NEKONOME IS TESTING US OR SOMETHING?
WELL, LET'S SURPRISE HER THEN BY SOLVING THE WHOLE MYSTERY!
Ulp.
YUKARI!
ARE YOU TRYING TO GET US ALL KILLED?!

READ THIS WAY

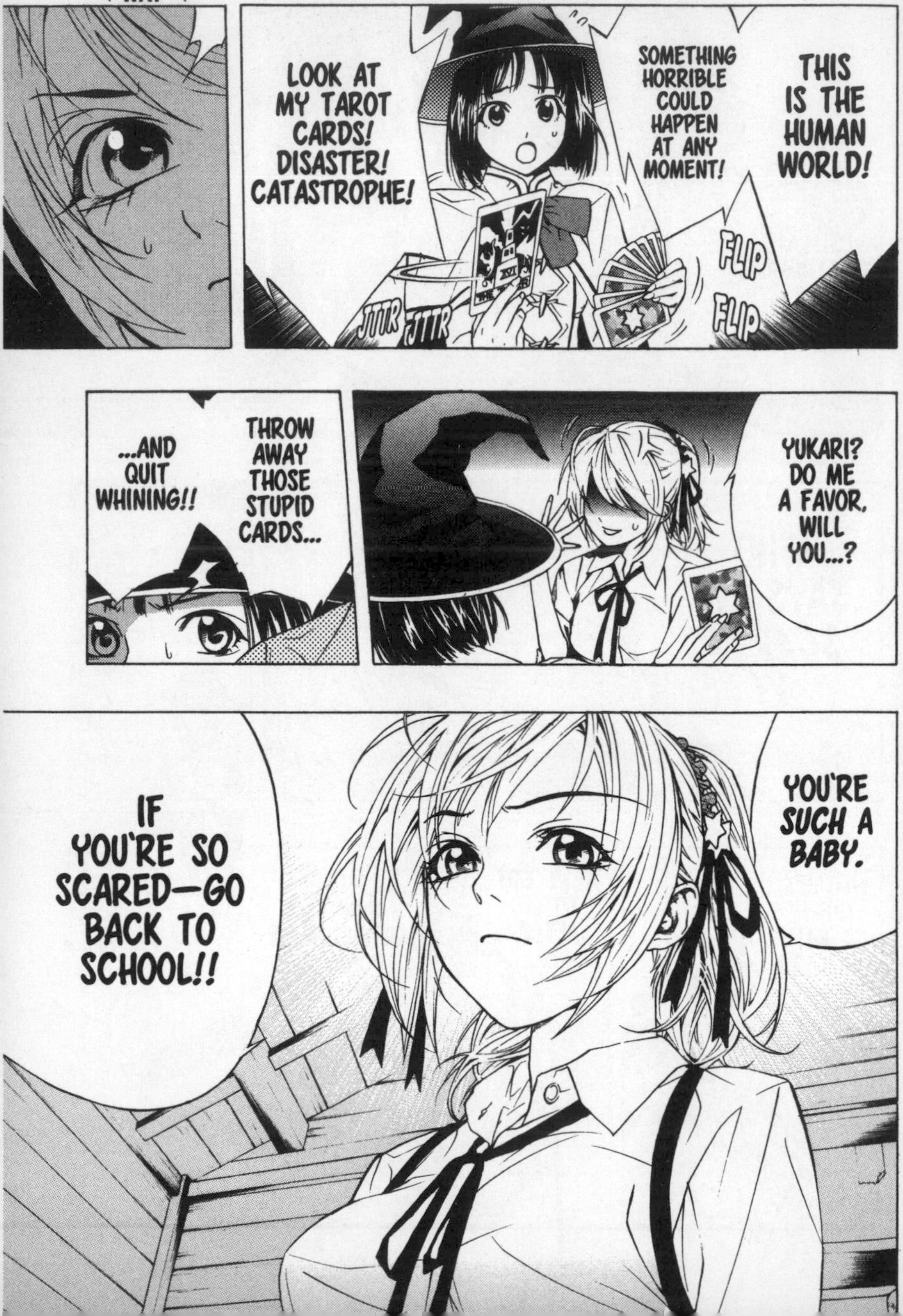
THIS IS THE HUMAN WORLD!
SOMETHING HORRIBLE COULD HAPPEN AT ANY MOMENT!
LOOK AT MY TAROT CARDS! DISASTER! CATASTROPHE!
FLIP
FLIP
JTTR
JTTR
YUKARI? DO ME A FAVOR, WILL YOU...?
THROW AWAY THOSE STUPID CARDS...
...AND QUIT WHINING!!
YOU'RE SUCH A BABY.
IF YOU'RE SO SCARED—GO BACK TO SCHOOL!!

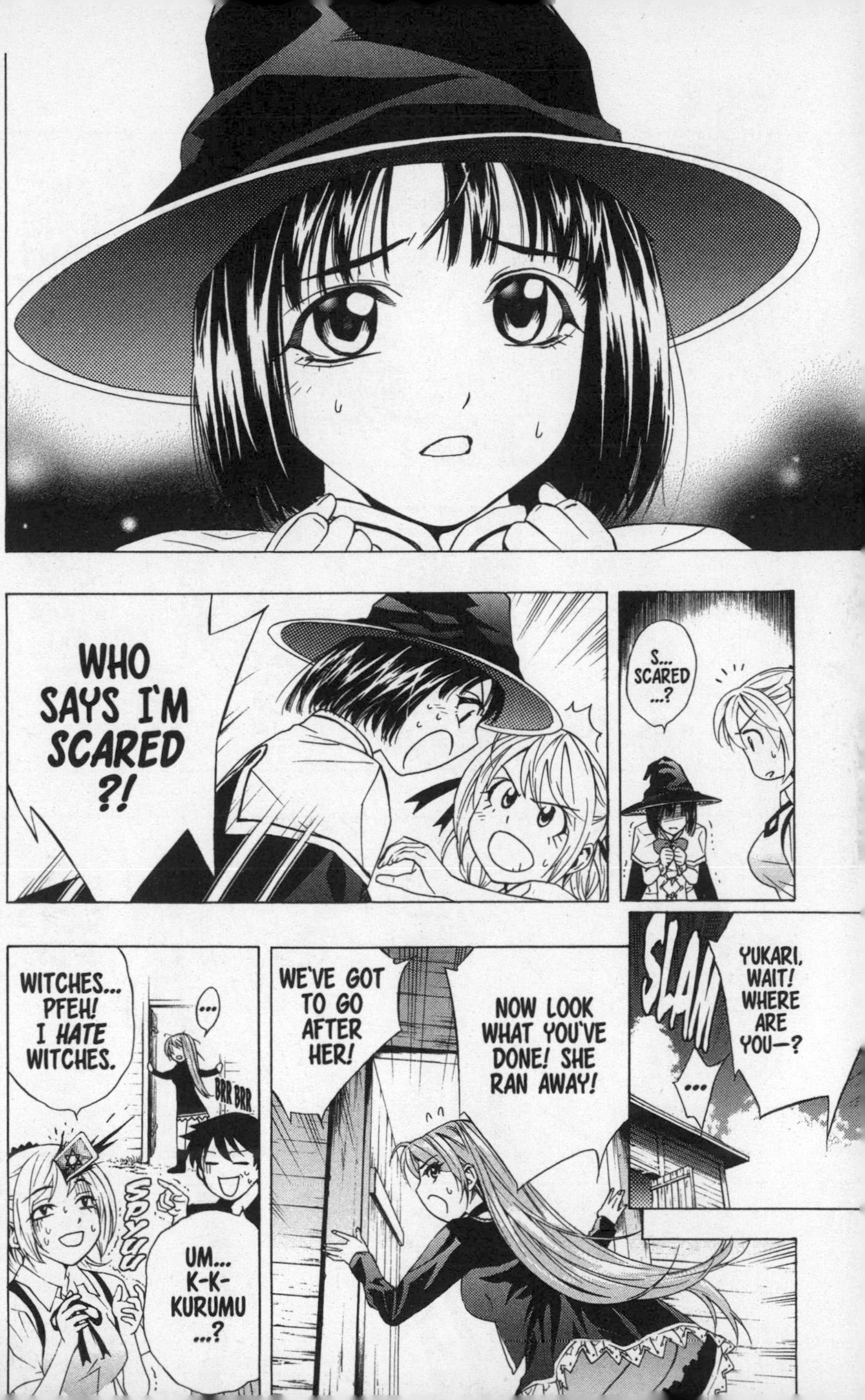
S... SCARED ...?
WHO SAYS I'M SCARED ?!
SLAM
YUKARI, WAIT! WHERE ARE YOU—?
...
NOW LOOK WHAT YOU'VE DONE! SHE RAN AWAY!
WE'VE GOT TO GO AFTER HER!
WITCHES... PFEH! I HATE WITCHES.
...
BRR BRR
UM... K-K-KURUMU ...?

READ THIS WAY

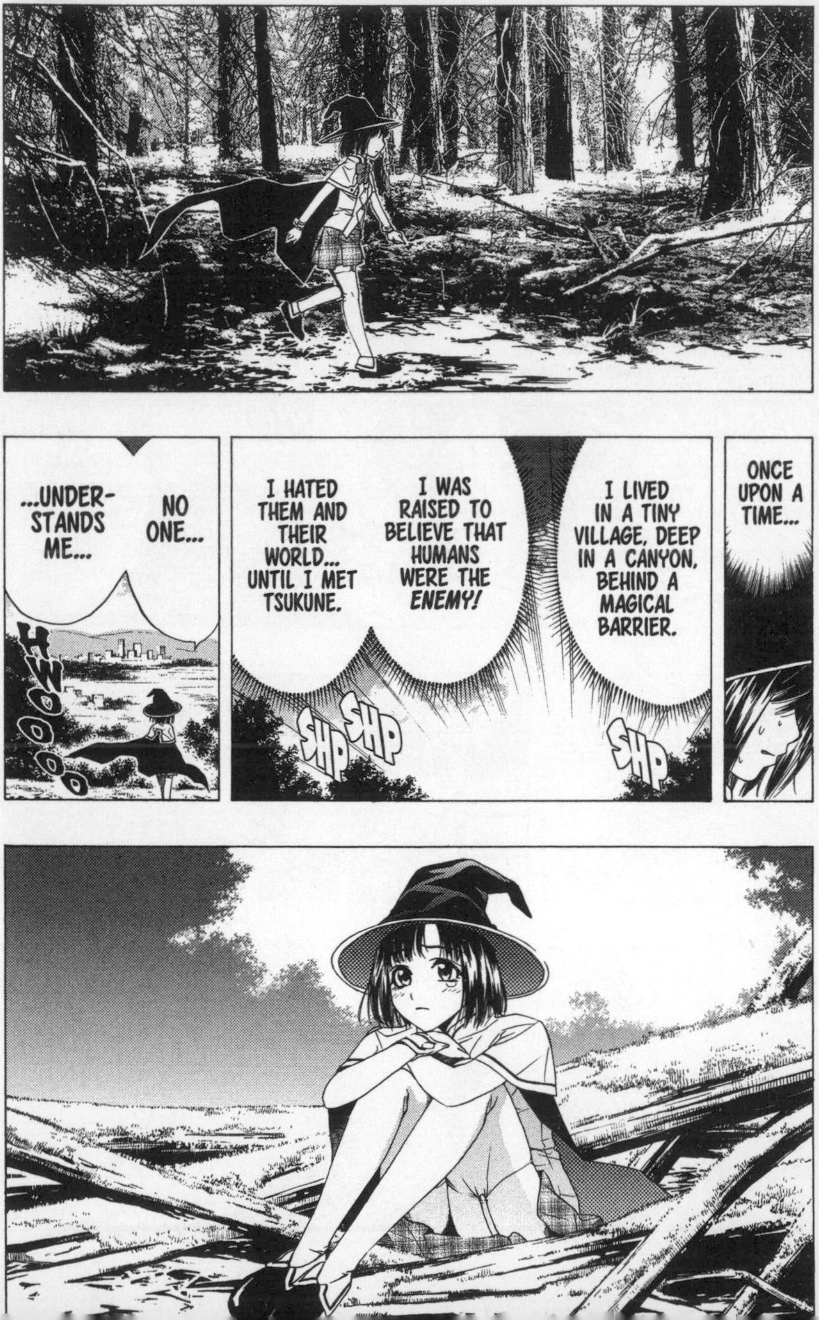
ONCE UPON A TIME...
I LIVED IN A TINY VILLAGE, DEEP IN A CANYON, BEHIND A MAGICAL BARRIER.
SHP
I WAS RAISED TO BELIEVE THAT HUMANS WERE THE *ENEMY!*
I HATED THEM AND THEIR WORLD... UNTIL I MET TSUKUNE.
SHP
SHP
NO ONE...
...UNDER-STANDS ME...
HWOOOOO

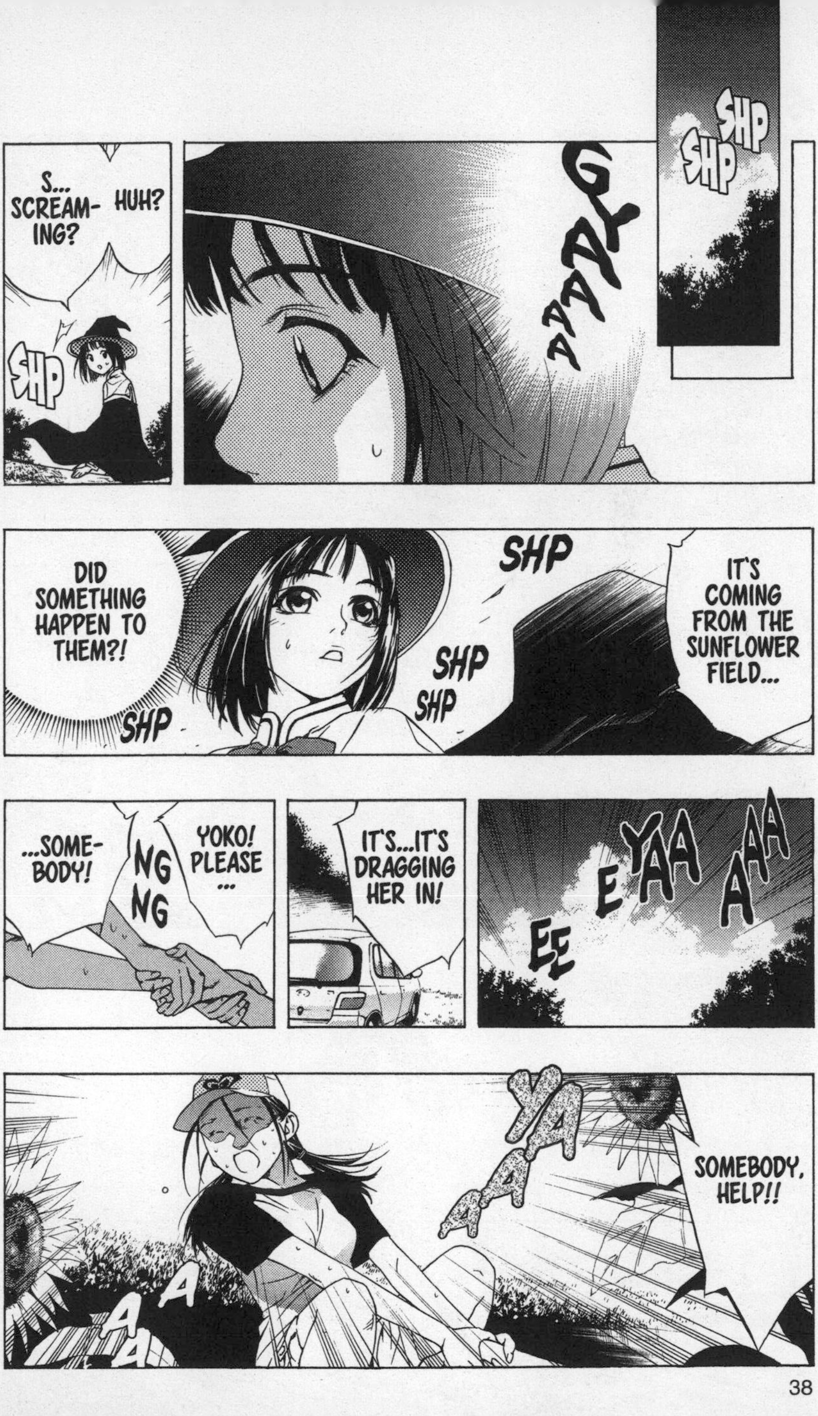
SHP SHP
GYAAAA
HUH?
S... SCREAMING?
SHP
IT'S COMING FROM THE SUNFLOWER FIELD...
SHP
SHP SHP
SHP
DID SOMETHING HAPPEN TO THEM?!
EEEYAAAAA
IT'S...IT'S DRAGGING HER IN!
YOKO! PLEASE ...
NG NG
...SOMEBODY!
SOMEBODY, HELP!!
YAAAA
AAAA

READ THIS WAY

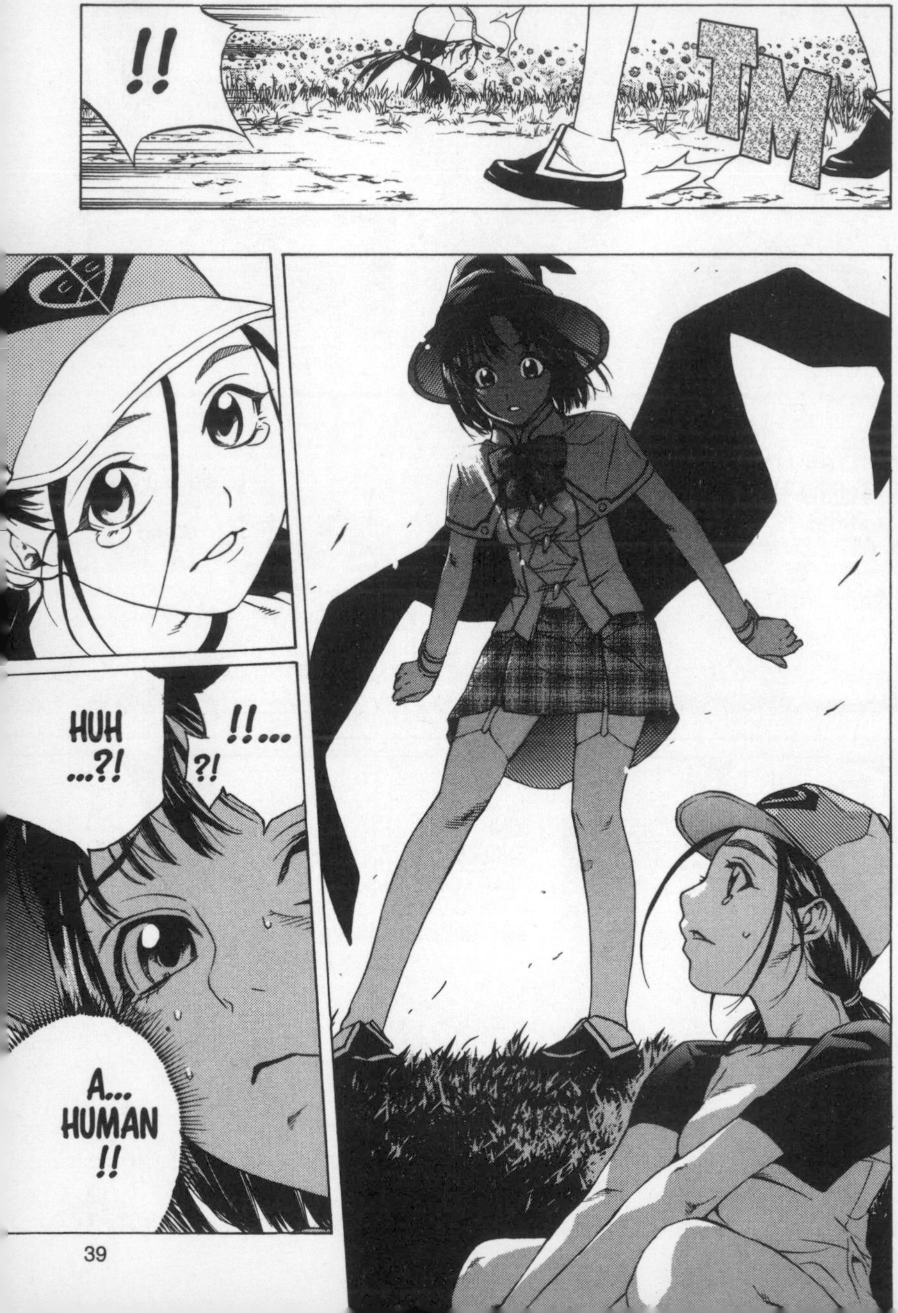
!!
TM
!!... ?!
HUH ...?!
A... HUMAN !!

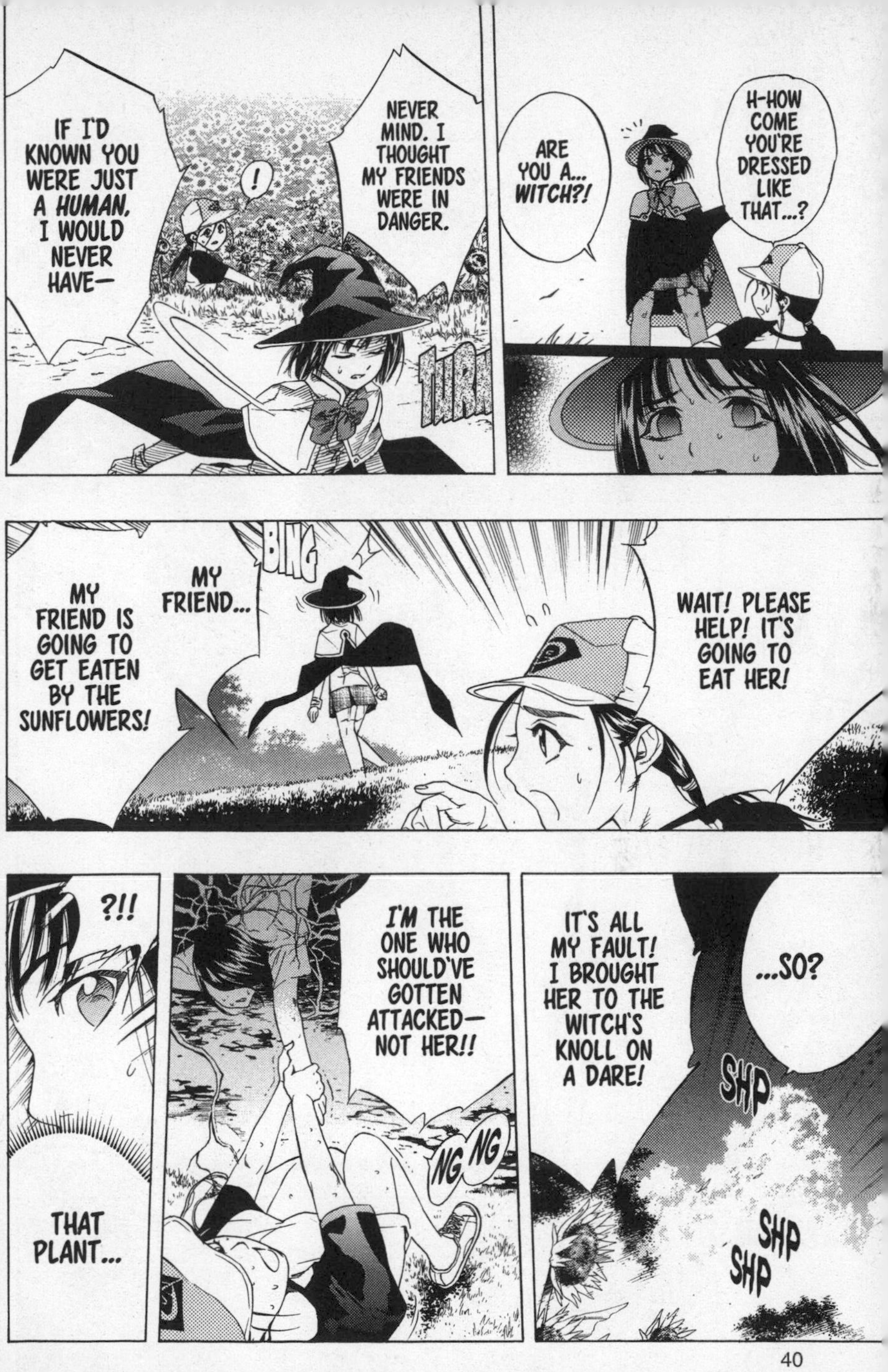
H-HOW COME YOU'RE DRESSED LIKE THAT...?
ARE YOU A... *WITCH?!*
NEVER MIND. I THOUGHT MY FRIENDS WERE IN DANGER.
!
IF I'D KNOWN YOU WERE JUST A *HUMAN*, I WOULD NEVER HAVE—
WAIT! PLEASE HELP! IT'S GOING TO EAT HER!
BING
MY FRIEND...
MY FRIEND IS GOING TO GET EATEN BY THE SUNFLOWERS!
...SO?
SHP
IT'S ALL MY FAULT! I BROUGHT HER TO THE WITCH'S KNOLL ON A DARE!
SHP
SHP
I'M THE ONE WHO SHOULD'VE GOTTEN ATTACKED—NOT HER!!
NG NG
?!!
THAT PLANT...

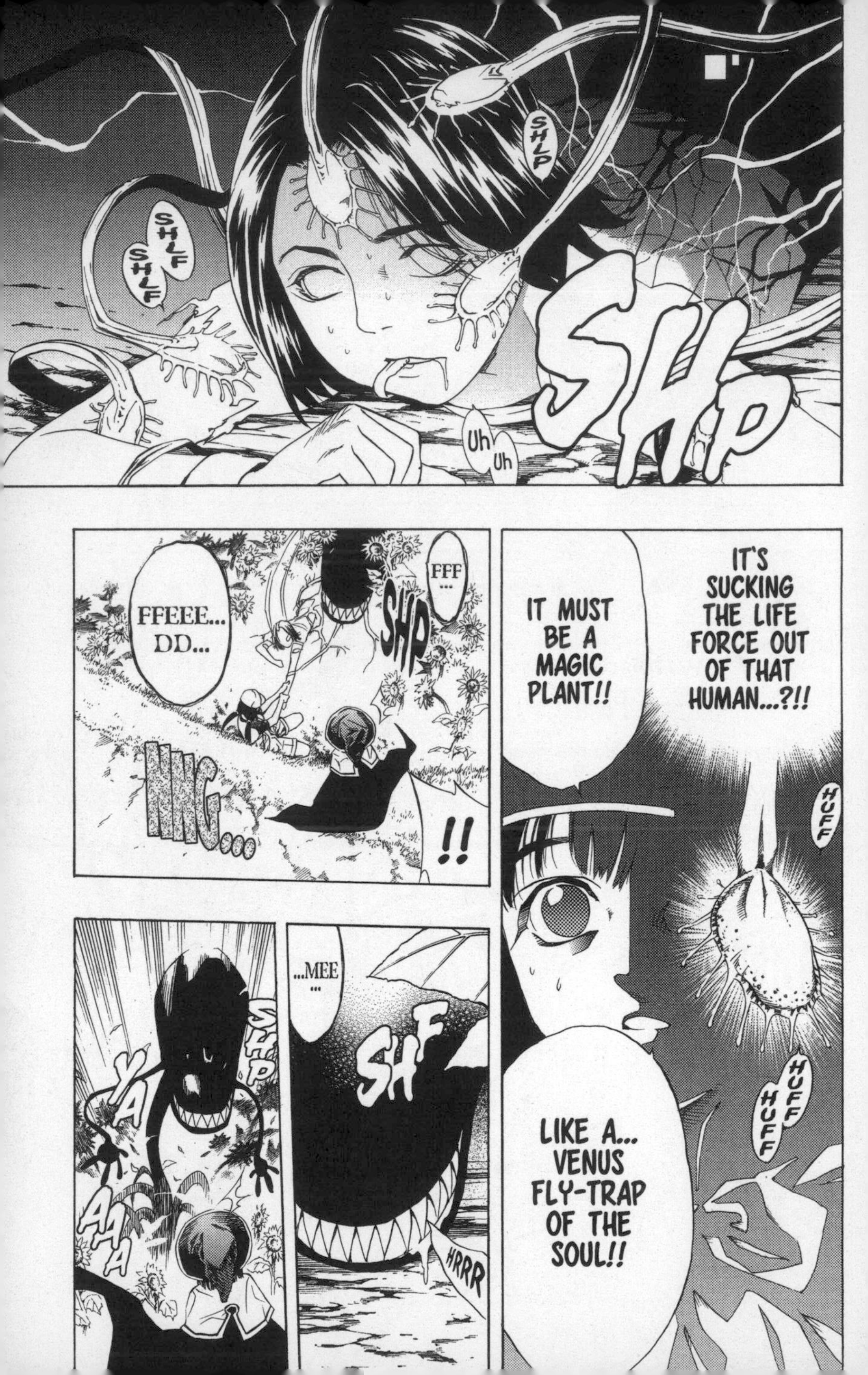
SHLP
SHP
SHLF
SHLF
Uh
Uh
IT'S SUCKING THE LIFE FORCE OUT OF THAT HUMAN...?!!
IT MUST BE A MAGIC PLANT!!
HUFF
HUFF
HUFF
LIKE A... VENUS FLY-TRAP OF THE SOUL!!
FFF...
SHP
FFEEE... DD...
!!
NNG...
...MEE...
SHF
HRRR
SHP
YA
AAA

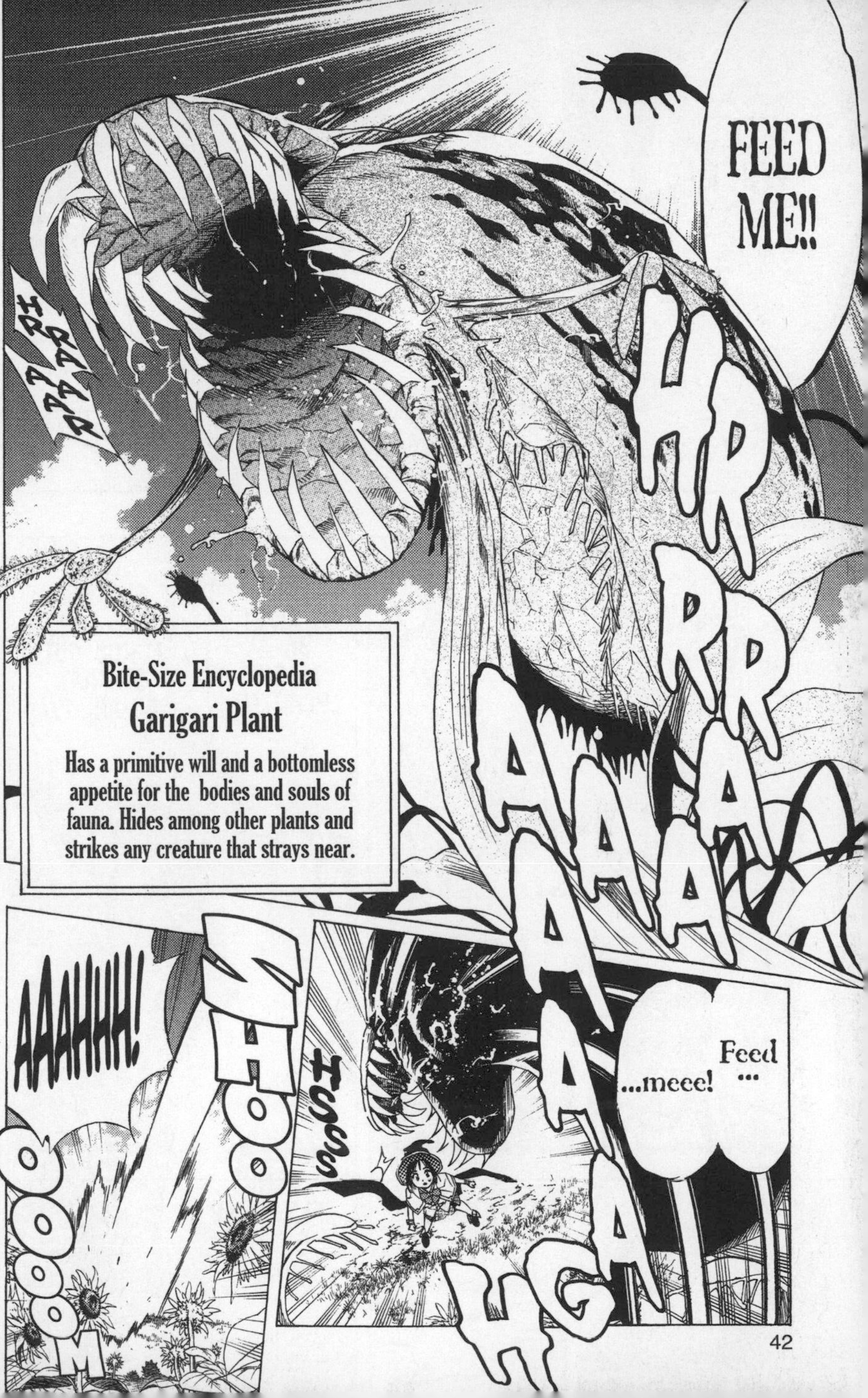
FEED ME!!
HRAAAAR
HRRRAAAAAAAGH
Bite-Size Encyclopedia
Garigari Plant
Has a primitive will and a bottomless appetite for the bodies and souls of fauna. Hides among other plants and strikes any creature that strays near.
Feed ...
...meee!
HSSSS
AAAHHH!
SHOOOOOOOM

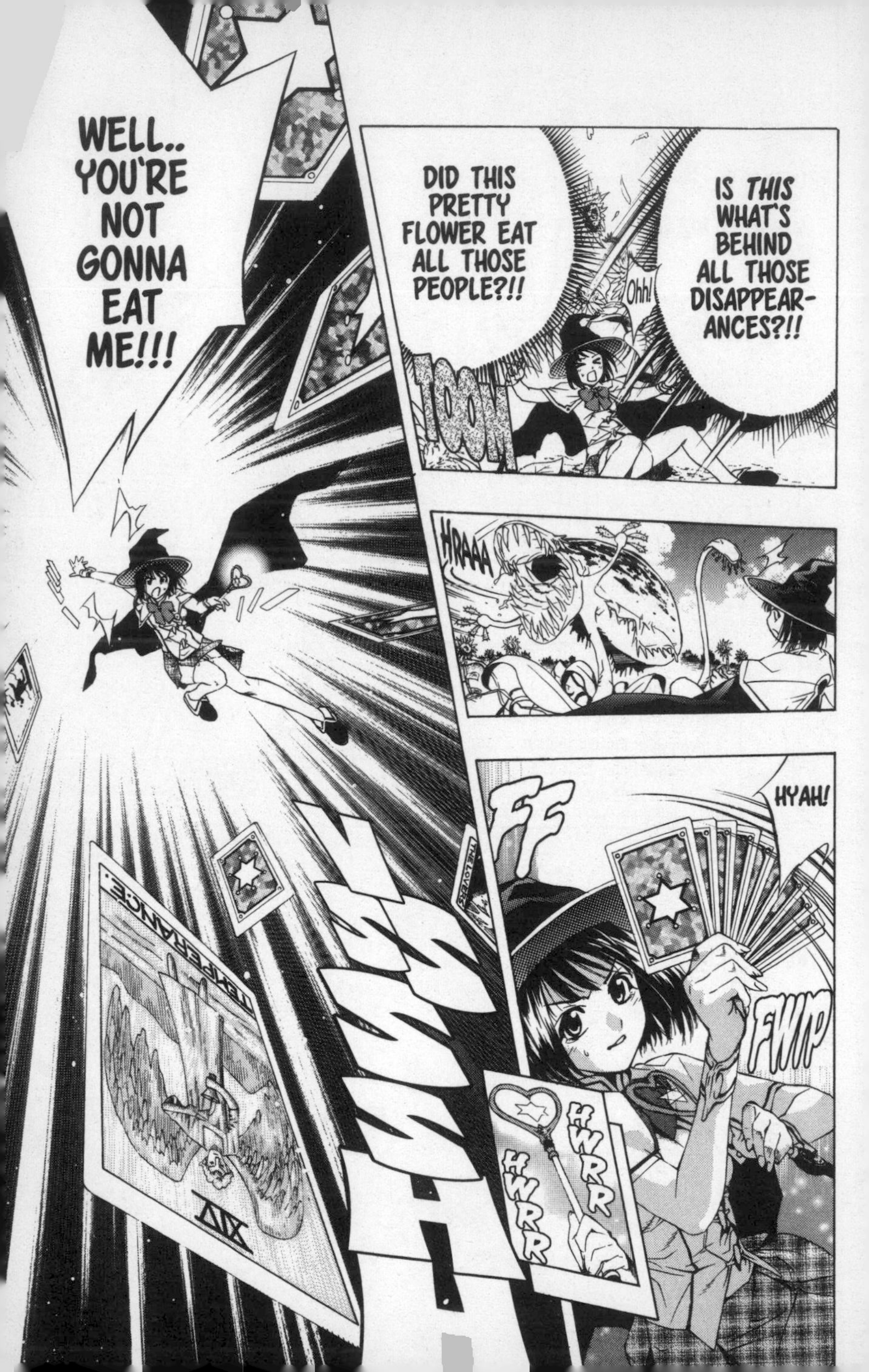
IS THIS WHAT'S BEHIND ALL THOSE DISAPPEARANCES?!!
DID THIS PRETTY FLOWER EAT ALL THOSE PEOPLE?!!
Ohh!
TOOM
HRAAA
HYAH!
FF
THE LOVERS
FWIP
HWRR
HWRR
WELL.. YOU'RE NOT GONNA EAT ME!!!
TEMPERANCE
XIV

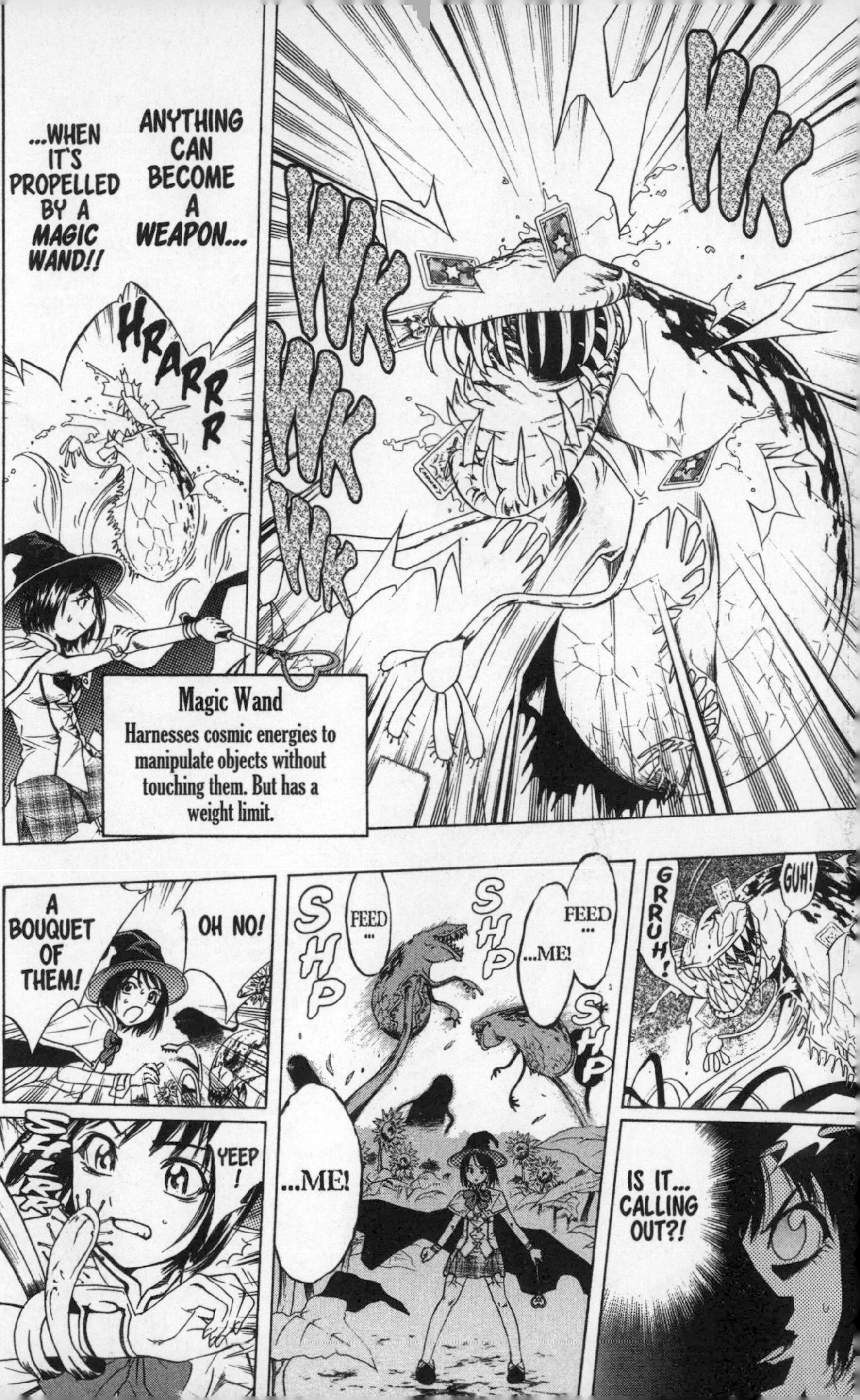
WK
WK
WK
WK
WK
ANYTHING CAN BECOME A WEAPON...
...WHEN IT'S PROPELLED BY A MAGIC WAND!!
HRARRR
Magic Wand
Harnesses cosmic energies to manipulate objects without touching them. But has a weight limit.
GRRUH!
GUH!
IS IT... CALLING OUT?!
FEED ...
...ME!
SHP
SHP
FEED ...
SHP
SHP
...ME!
OH NO!
A BOUQUET OF THEM!
YEEP!

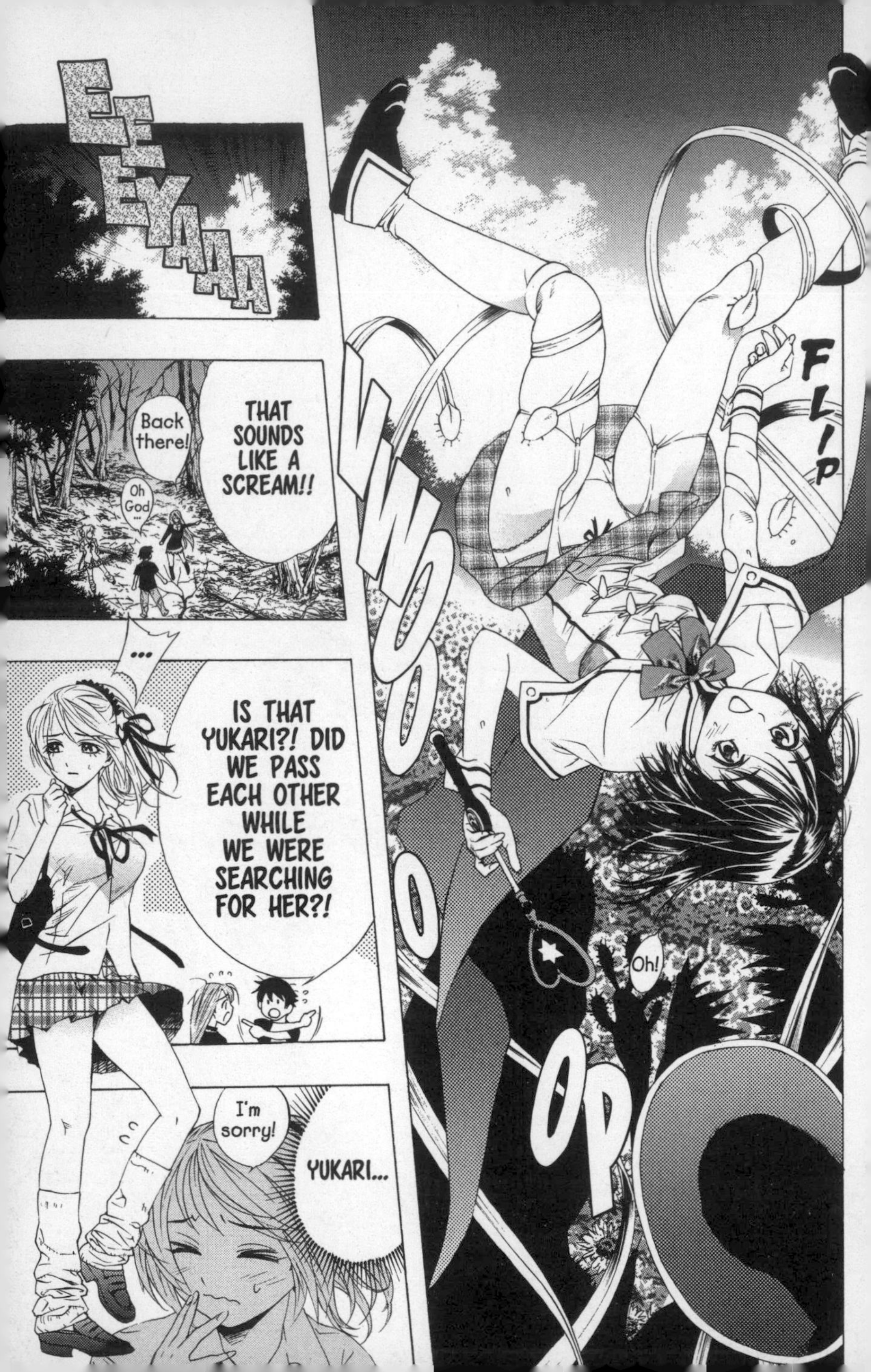
FLIP
VWOOOO
Oh!
OPS
EEEEYAAAA
THAT SOUNDS LIKE A SCREAM!!
Back there!
Oh God...
...
IS THAT YUKARI?! DID WE PASS EACH OTHER WHILE WE WERE SEARCHING FOR HER?!
I'm sorry!
YUKARI...

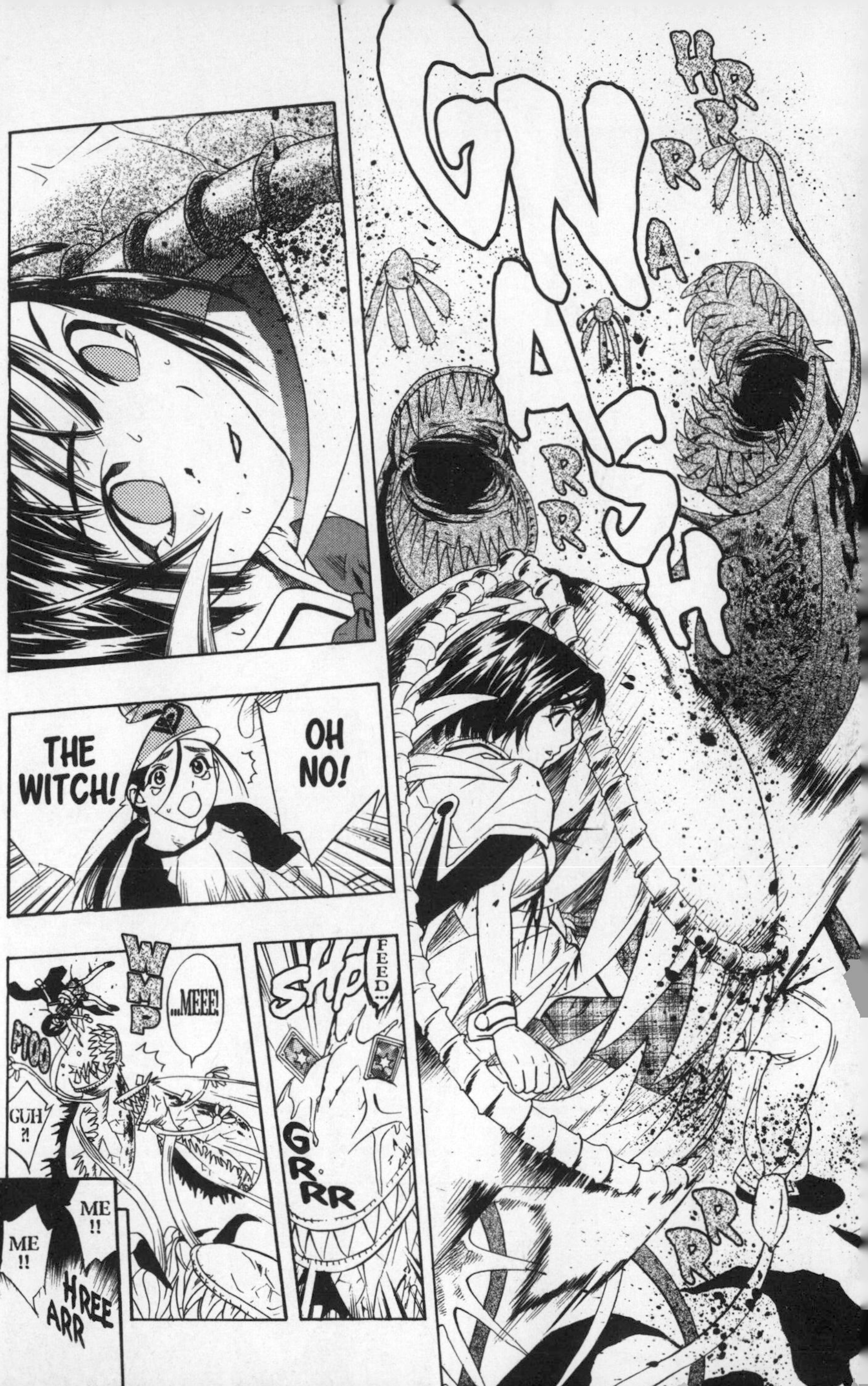
GNASH
HRRRARR
RRR
OH NO!
THE WITCH!
FEED...
SHP
GRRR
...MEEE!
WMP
GUH?!
ME!!
ME!!
HREE ARR

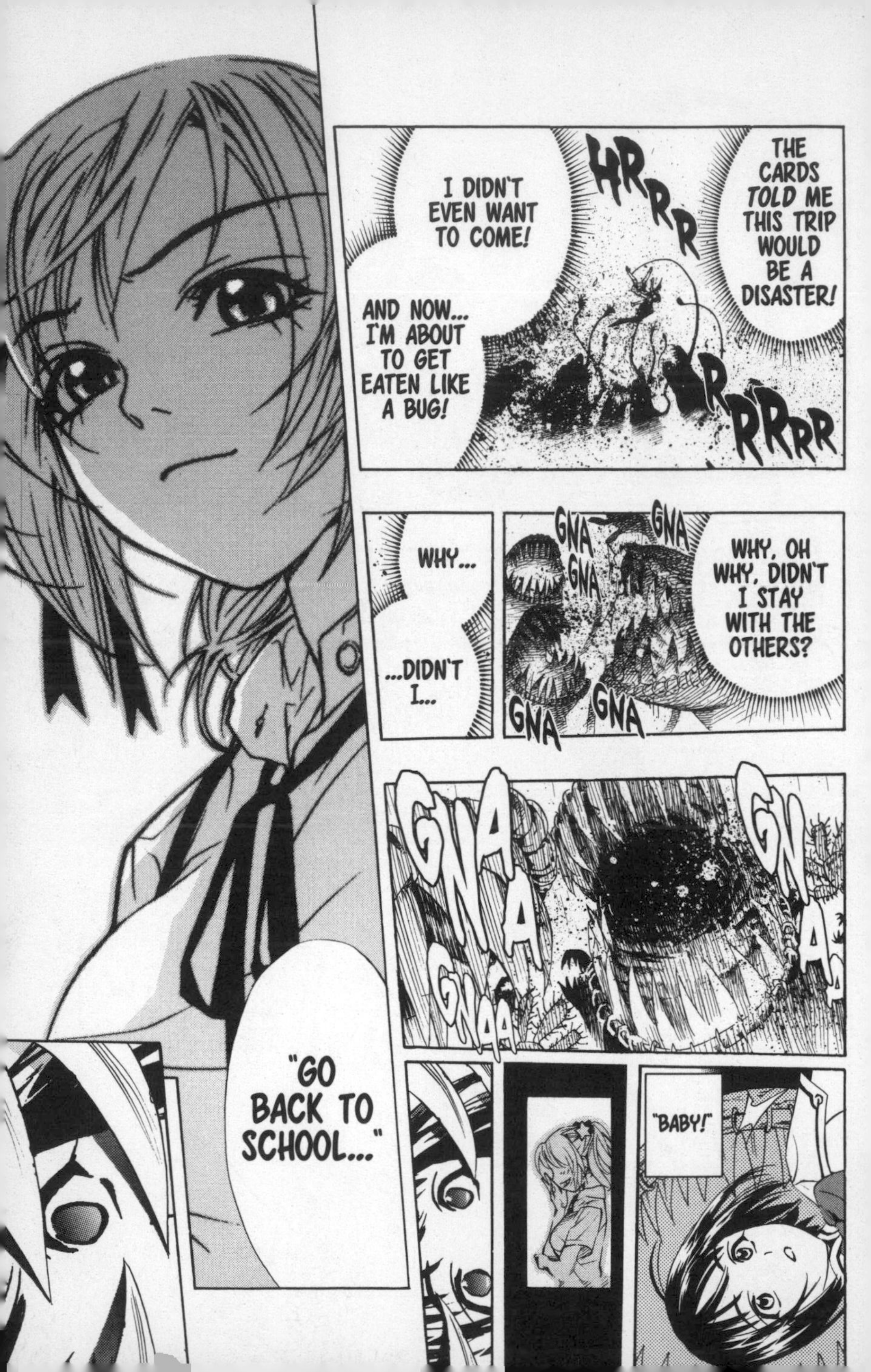
THE CARDS TOLD ME THIS TRIP WOULD BE A DISASTER!
HRRRR
I DIDN'T EVEN WANT TO COME!
AND NOW... I'M ABOUT TO GET EATEN LIKE A BUG!
RRRRR
GNA
GNA
GNA
WHY, OH WHY, DIDN'T I STAY WITH THE OTHERS?
GNA
GNA
WHY...
...DIDN'T I...
GNAA
GNAA
GNAA
"BABY!"
"GO BACK TO SCHOOL..."

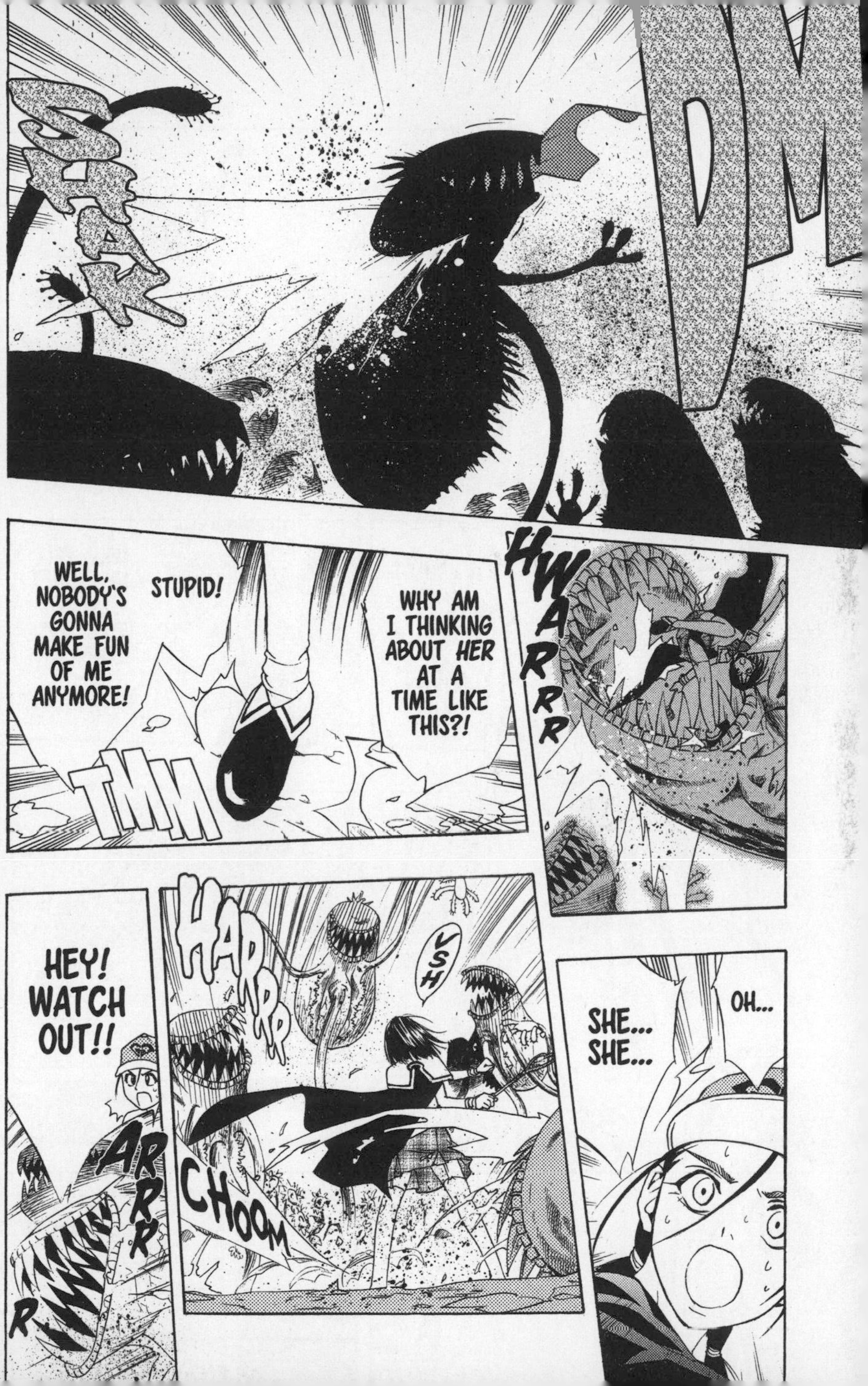
SHAK
HWARRRR
WHY AM I THINKING ABOUT HER AT A TIME LIKE THIS?!
STUPID!
WELL, NOBODY'S GONNA MAKE FUN OF ME ANYMORE!
TMM
OH...
SHE... SHE...
VSH
HARRR
CHOOM
HEY! WATCH OUT!!
ARRRR

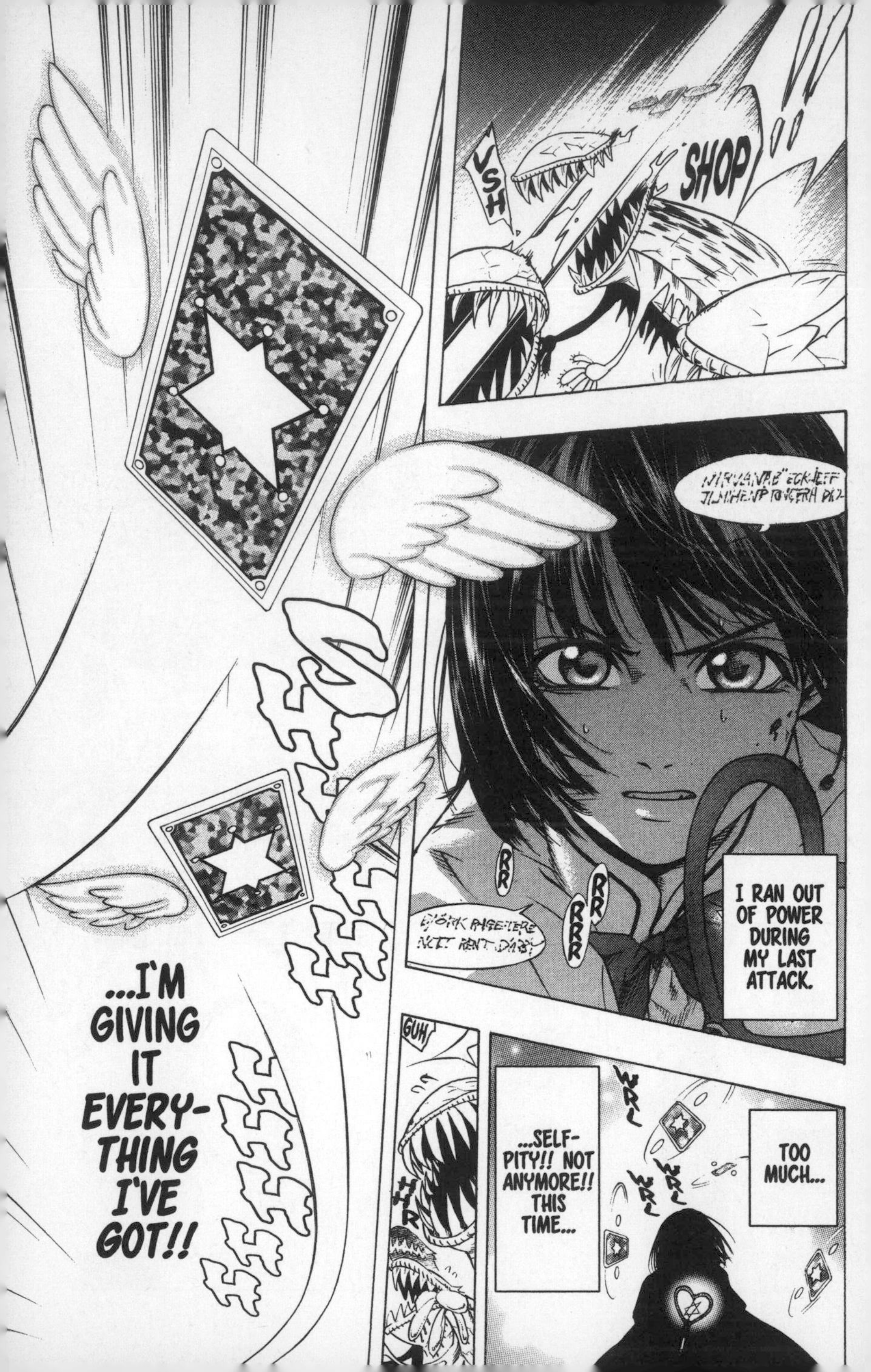
SHOP
VSH
RR
RR
RRR
I RAN OUT OF POWER DURING MY LAST ATTACK.
TOO MUCH...
WRL
WRL
WRL
...SELF-PITY!! NOT ANYMORE!! THIS TIME...
GUH
HHR
...I'M GIVING IT EVERYTHING I'VE GOT!!

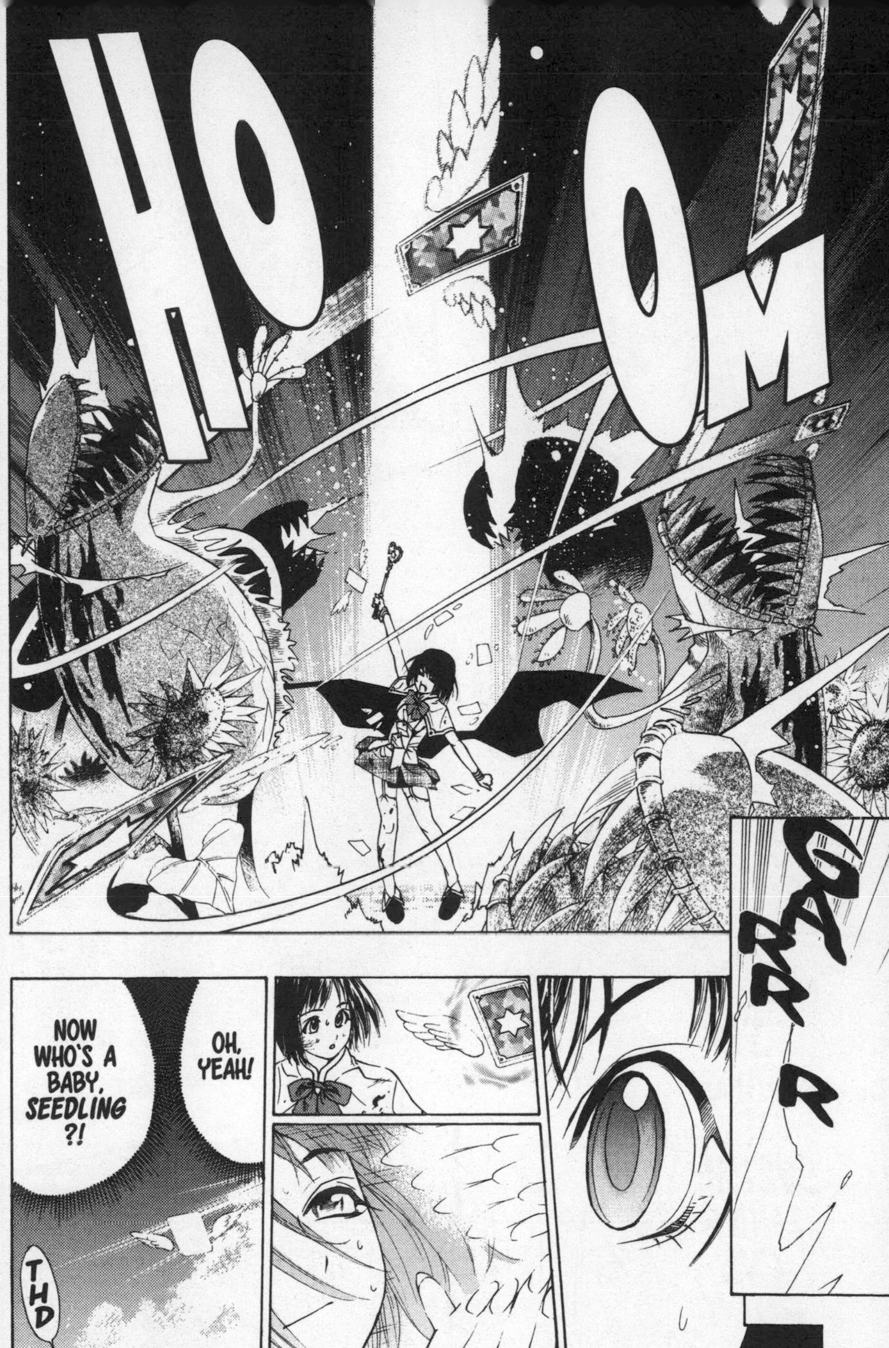
HOOM
GRRRR
OH, YEAH!
NOW WHO'S A BABY, SEEDLING?!
THD

READ THIS WAY

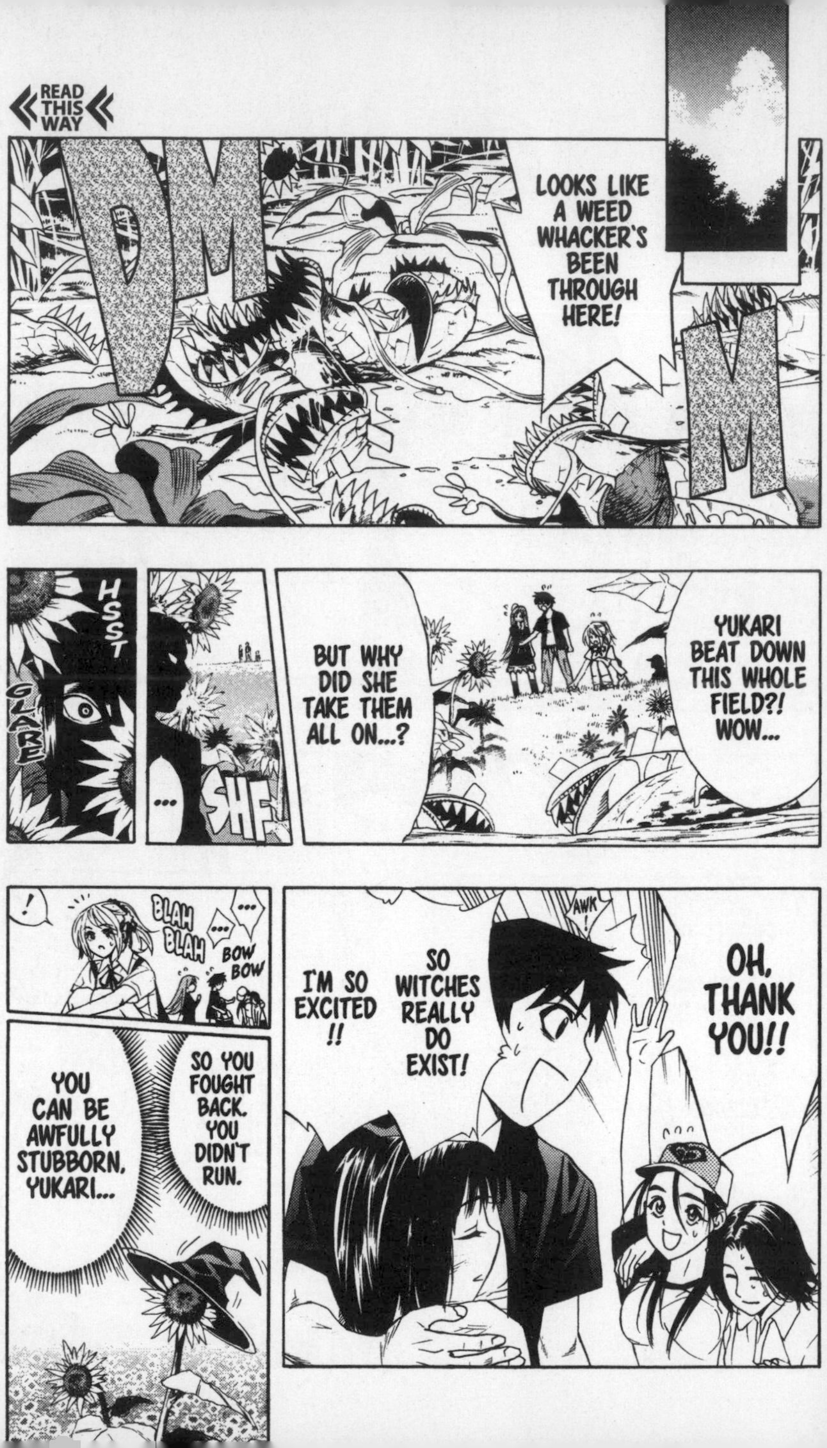
LOOKS LIKE A WEED WHACKER'S BEEN THROUGH HERE!
DM
M
YUKARI BEAT DOWN THIS WHOLE FIELD?! WOW...
BUT WHY DID SHE TAKE THEM ALL ON...?
...
SHF
HSST
GLARE
OH, THANK YOU!!
AWK
SO WITCHES REALLY DO EXIST!
I'M SO EXCITED !!
!
BLAH BLAH
...
...
BOW BOW
SO YOU FOUGHT BACK. YOU DIDN'T RUN.
YOU CAN BE AWFULLY STUBBORN, YUKARI...

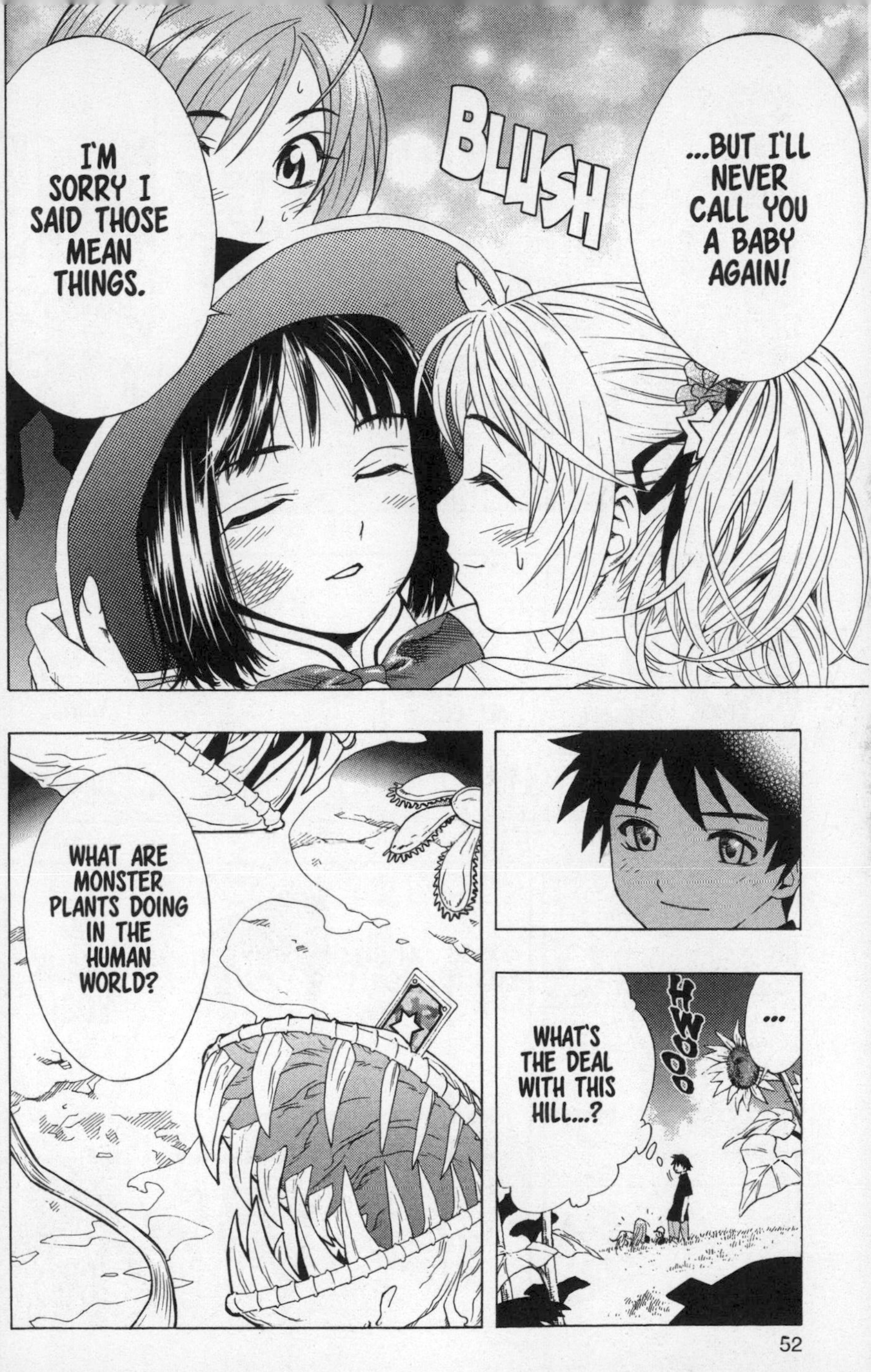
I'M SORRY I SAID THOSE MEAN THINGS.
BLUSH
...BUT I'LL NEVER CALL YOU A BABY AGAIN!
...
HWOOO
WHAT'S THE DEAL WITH THIS HILL...?
WHAT ARE MONSTER PLANTS DOING IN THE HUMAN WORLD?

READ THIS WAY

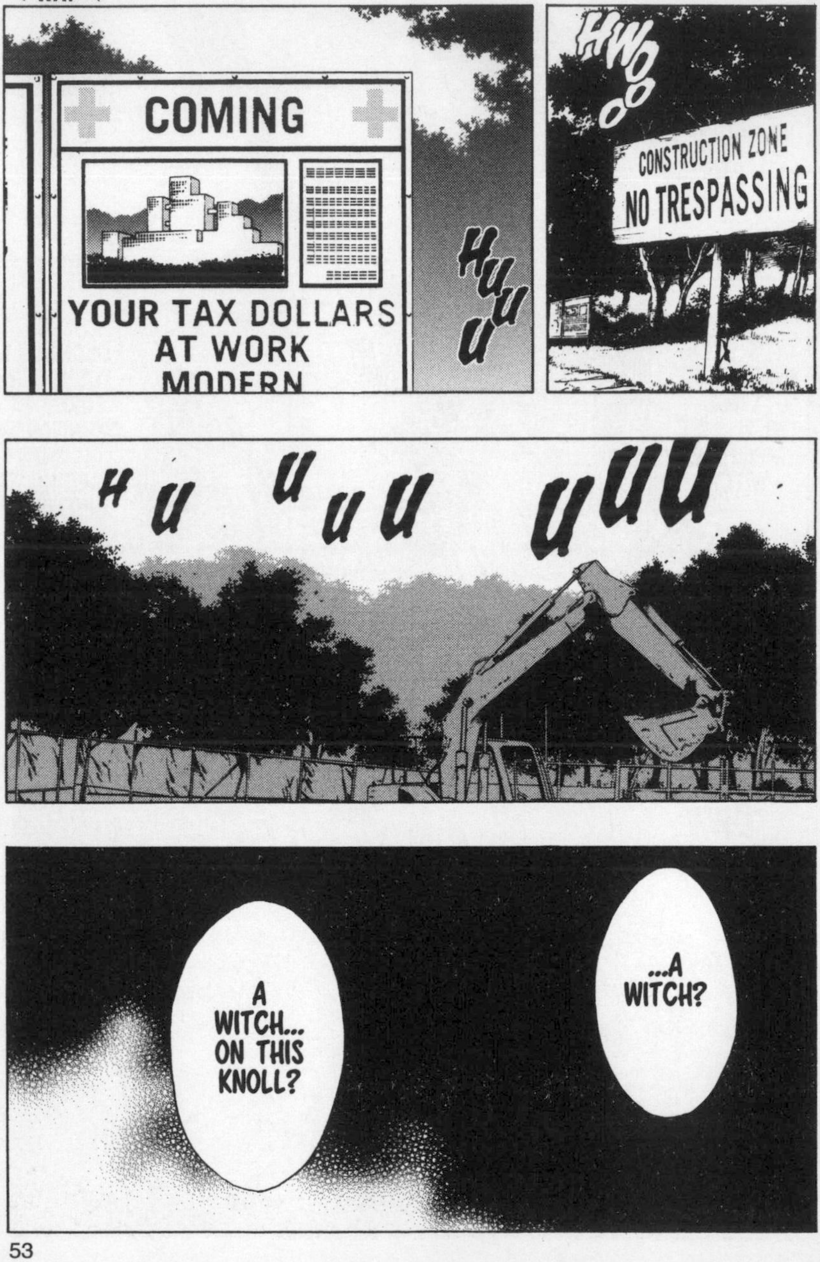
HWOOO
CONSTRUCTION ZONE
NO TRESPASSING
COMING
YOUR TAX DOLLARS AT WORK
MODERN
HUUU
HU UUU UUU
...A WITCH?
A WITCH... ON THIS KNOLL?

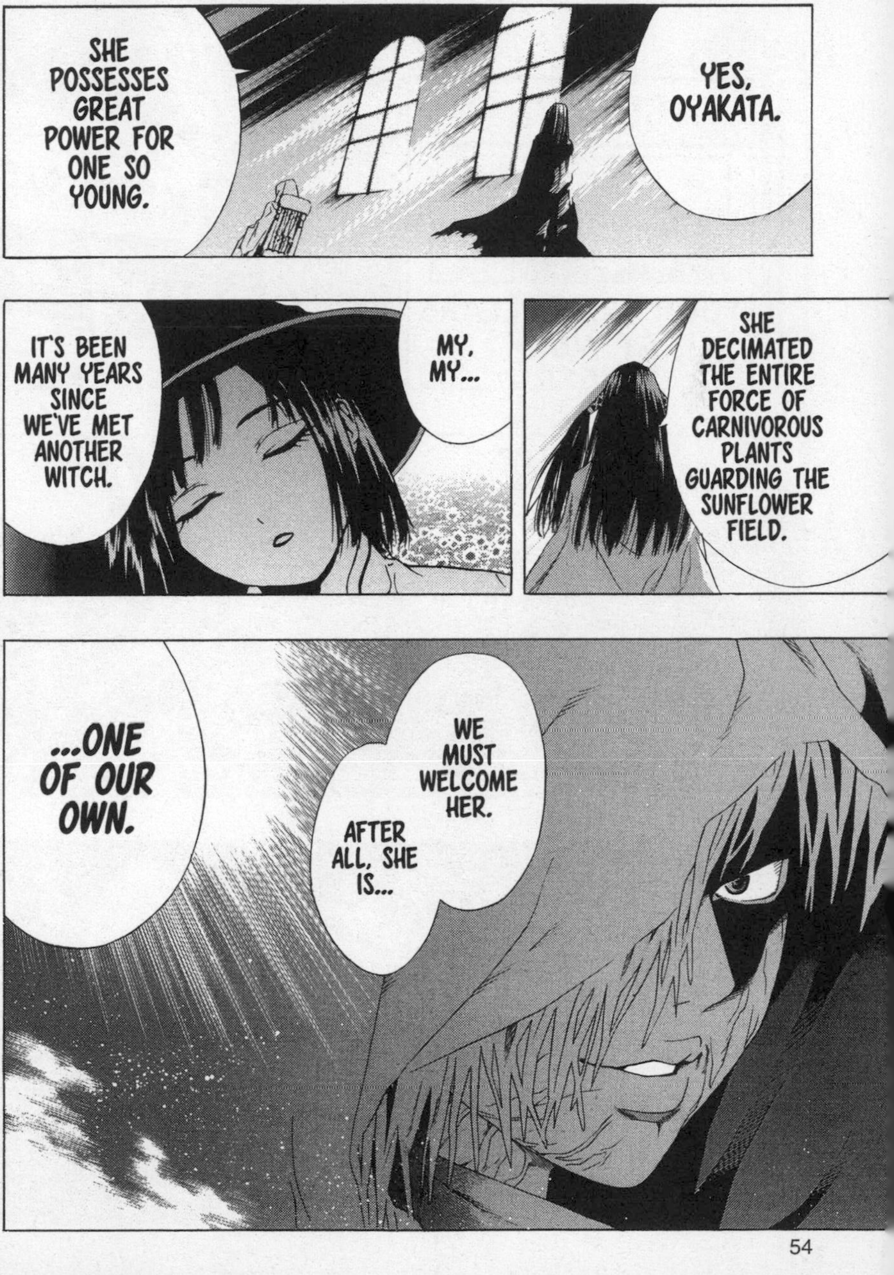
YES, OYAKATA.
SHE POSSESSES GREAT POWER FOR ONE SO YOUNG.
SHE DECIMATED THE ENTIRE FORCE OF CARNIVOROUS PLANTS GUARDING THE SUNFLOWER FIELD.
MY, MY...
IT'S BEEN MANY YEARS SINCE WE'VE MET ANOTHER WITCH.
WE MUST WELCOME HER.
AFTER ALL, SHE IS...
...ONE OF OUR OWN.

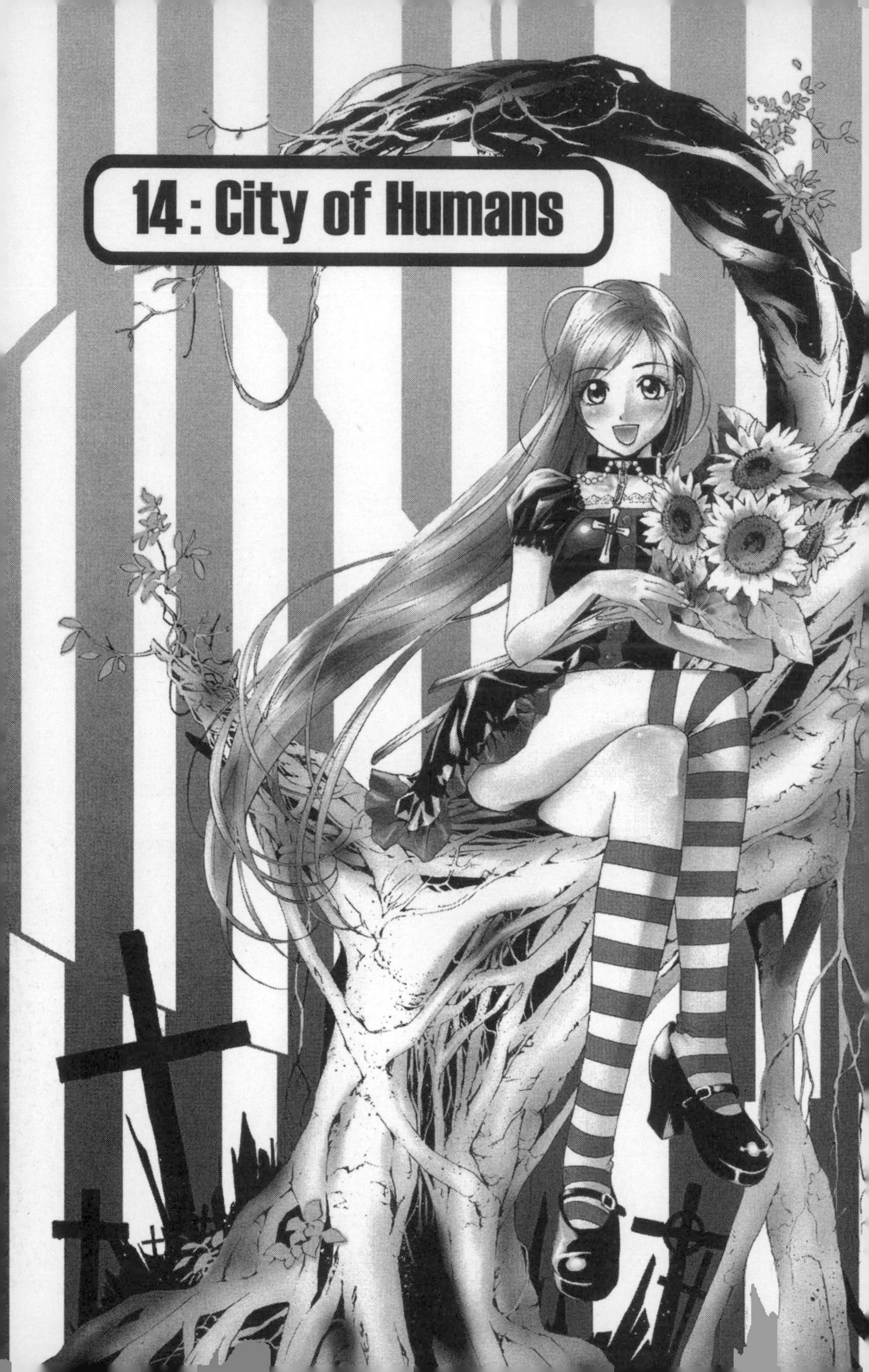
14 : City of Humans

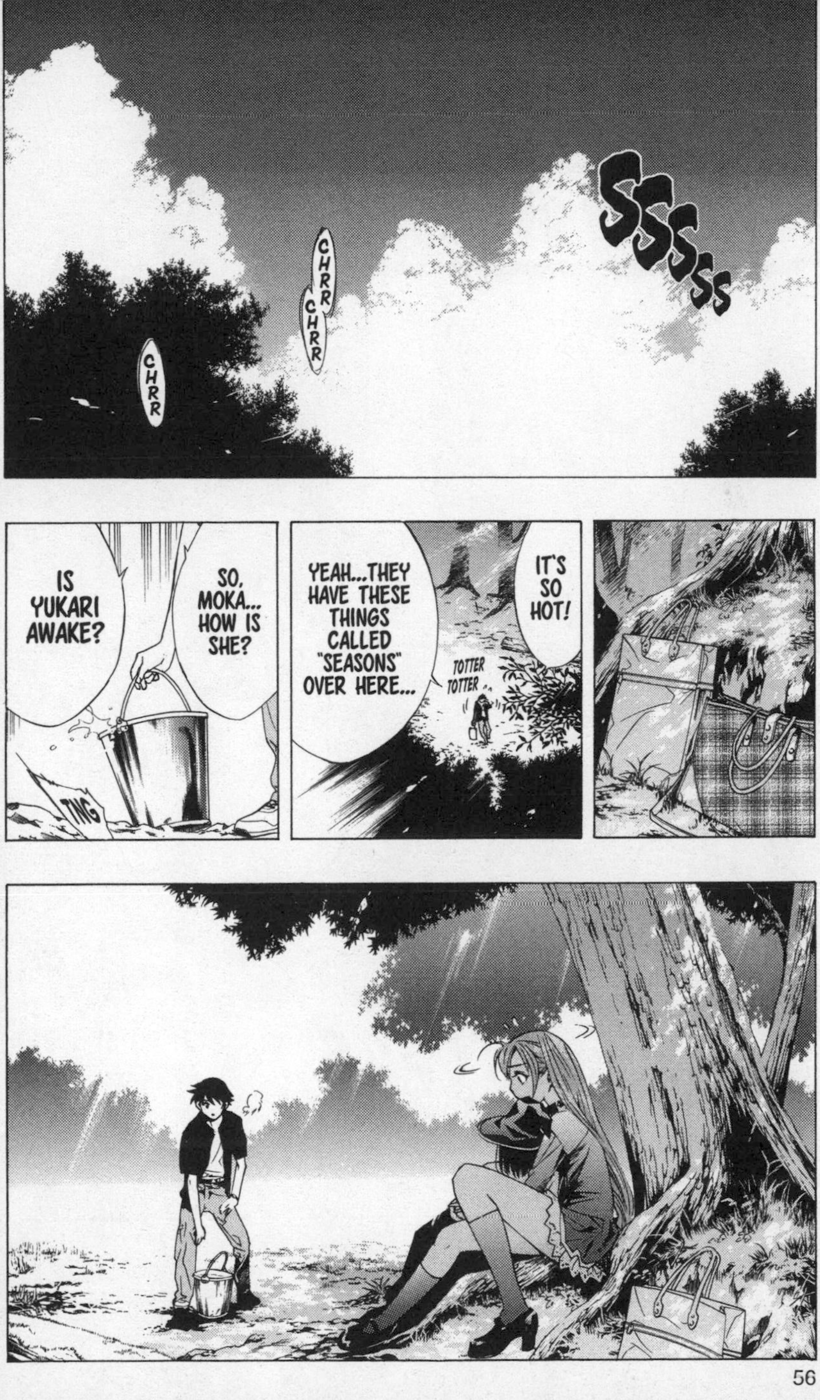
SSSSS
CHRR CHRR
CHRR
IT'S SO HOT!
YEAH...THEY HAVE THESE THINGS CALLED "SEASONS" OVER HERE...
TOTTER TOTTER
SO, MOKA... HOW IS SHE?
IS YUKARI AWAKE?
TNG

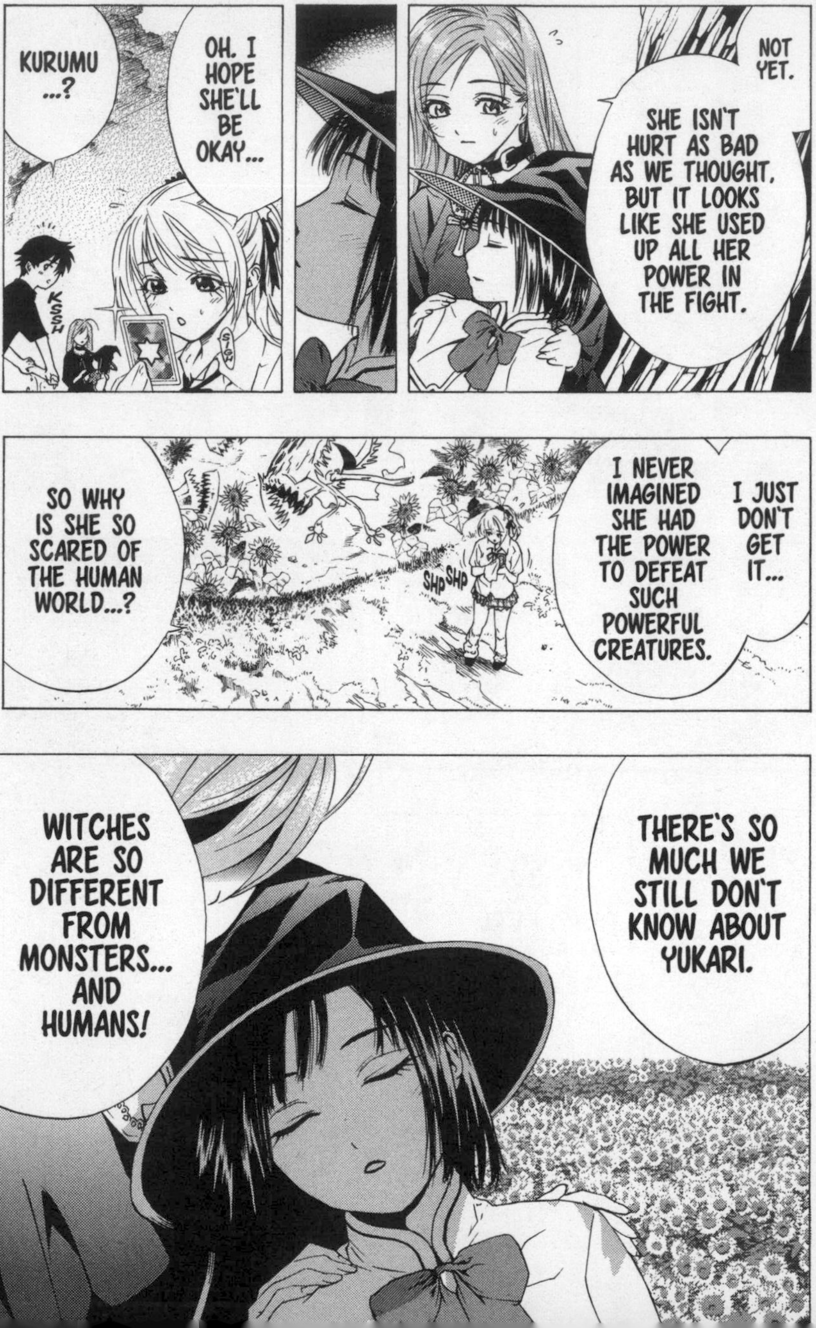
NOT YET.
SHE ISN'T HURT AS BAD AS WE THOUGHT, BUT IT LOOKS LIKE SHE USED UP ALL HER POWER IN THE FIGHT.
OH. I HOPE SHE'LL BE OKAY...
KURUMU ...?
SIGH
KSSH
I JUST DON'T GET IT...
I NEVER IMAGINED SHE HAD THE POWER TO DEFEAT SUCH POWERFUL CREATURES.
SHP SHP
SO WHY IS SHE SO SCARED OF THE HUMAN WORLD...?
THERE'S SO MUCH WE STILL DON'T KNOW ABOUT YUKARI.
WITCHES ARE SO DIFFERENT FROM MONSTERS... AND HUMANS!

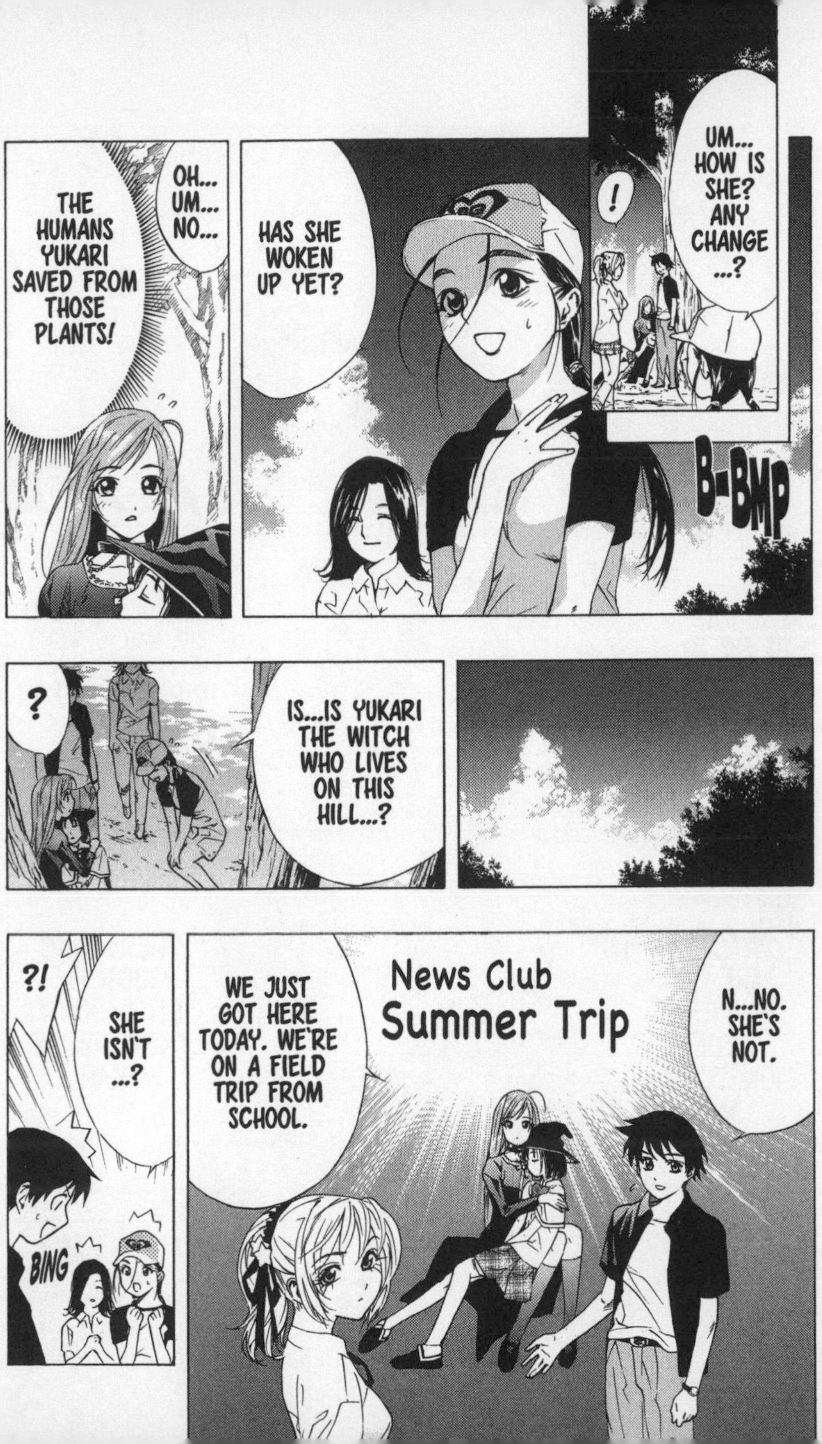
UM... HOW IS SHE? ANY CHANGE ...?
!
B-BMP
HAS SHE WOKEN UP YET?
OH... UM... NO...
THE HUMANS YUKARI SAVED FROM THOSE PLANTS!
IS...IS YUKARI THE WITCH WHO LIVES ON THIS HILL...?
?
N...NO. SHE'S NOT.
News Club Summer Trip
WE JUST GOT HERE TODAY. WE'RE ON A FIELD TRIP FROM SCHOOL.
SHE ISN'T ...?
?!
BING

READ THIS WAY

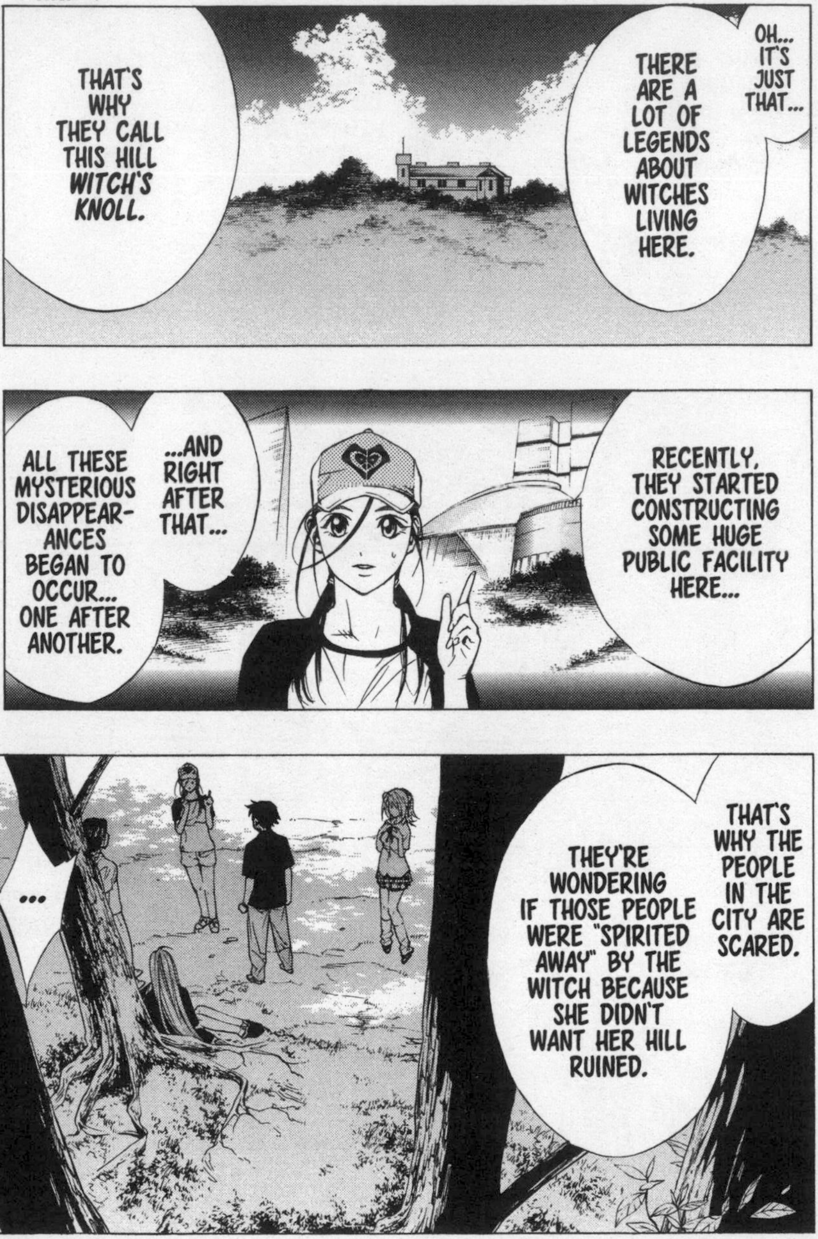
OH... IT'S JUST THAT...
THERE ARE A LOT OF LEGENDS ABOUT WITCHES LIVING HERE.
THAT'S WHY THEY CALL THIS HILL *WITCH'S KNOLL.*
RECENTLY, THEY STARTED CONSTRUCTING SOME HUGE PUBLIC FACILITY HERE...
...AND RIGHT AFTER THAT...
ALL THESE MYSTERIOUS DISAPPEAR-ANCES BEGAN TO OCCUR... ONE AFTER ANOTHER.
THAT'S WHY THE PEOPLE IN THE CITY ARE SCARED.
THEY'RE WONDERING IF THOSE PEOPLE WERE "SPIRITED AWAY" BY THE WITCH BECAUSE SHE DIDN'T WANT HER HILL RUINED.
...

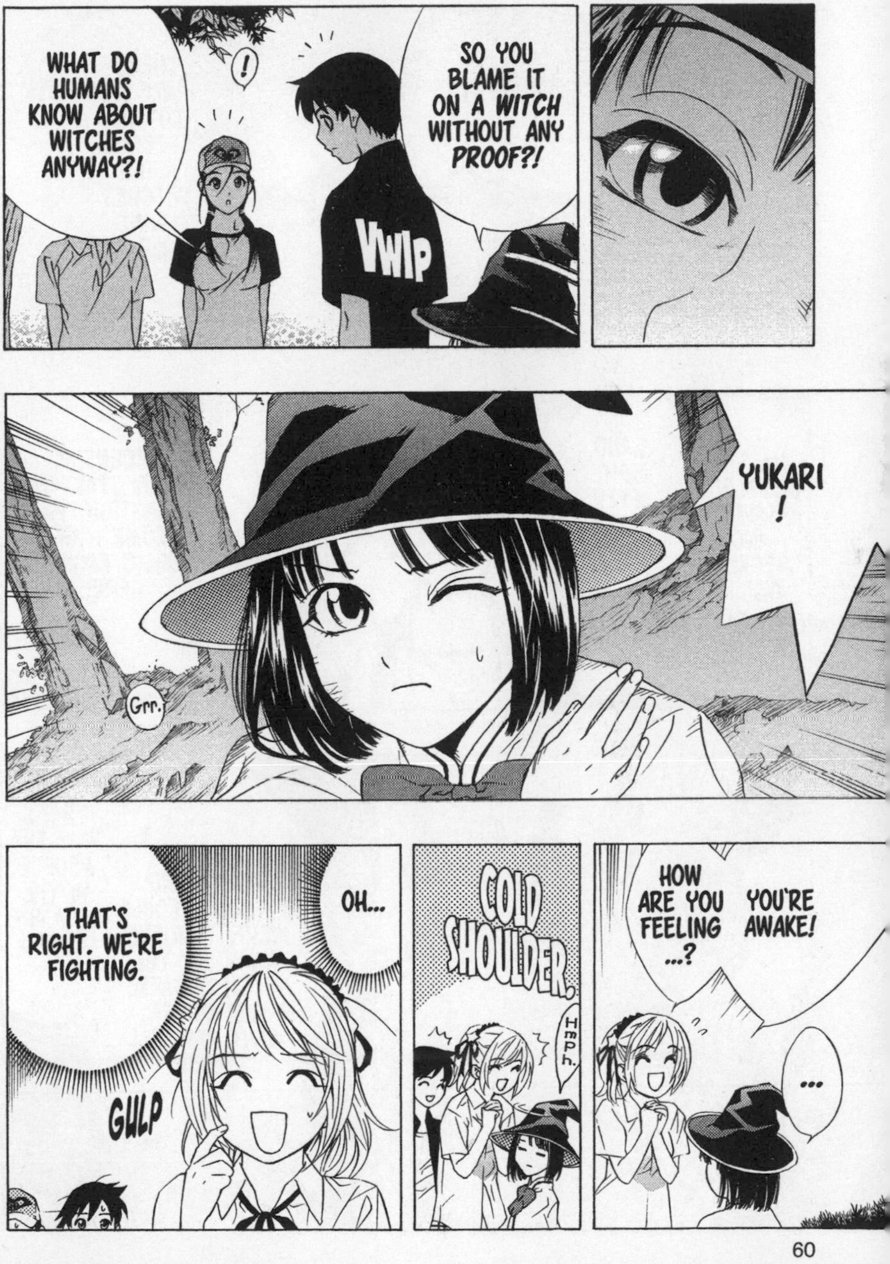
SO YOU BLAME IT ON A WITCH WITHOUT ANY PROOF?!
!
WHAT DO HUMANS KNOW ABOUT WITCHES ANYWAY?!
YUKARI!
Grr.
YOU'RE AWAKE!
HOW ARE YOU FEELING ...?
...
COLD SHOULDER.
Hmph.
OH...
THAT'S RIGHT. WE'RE FIGHTING.
GULP

READ THIS WAY

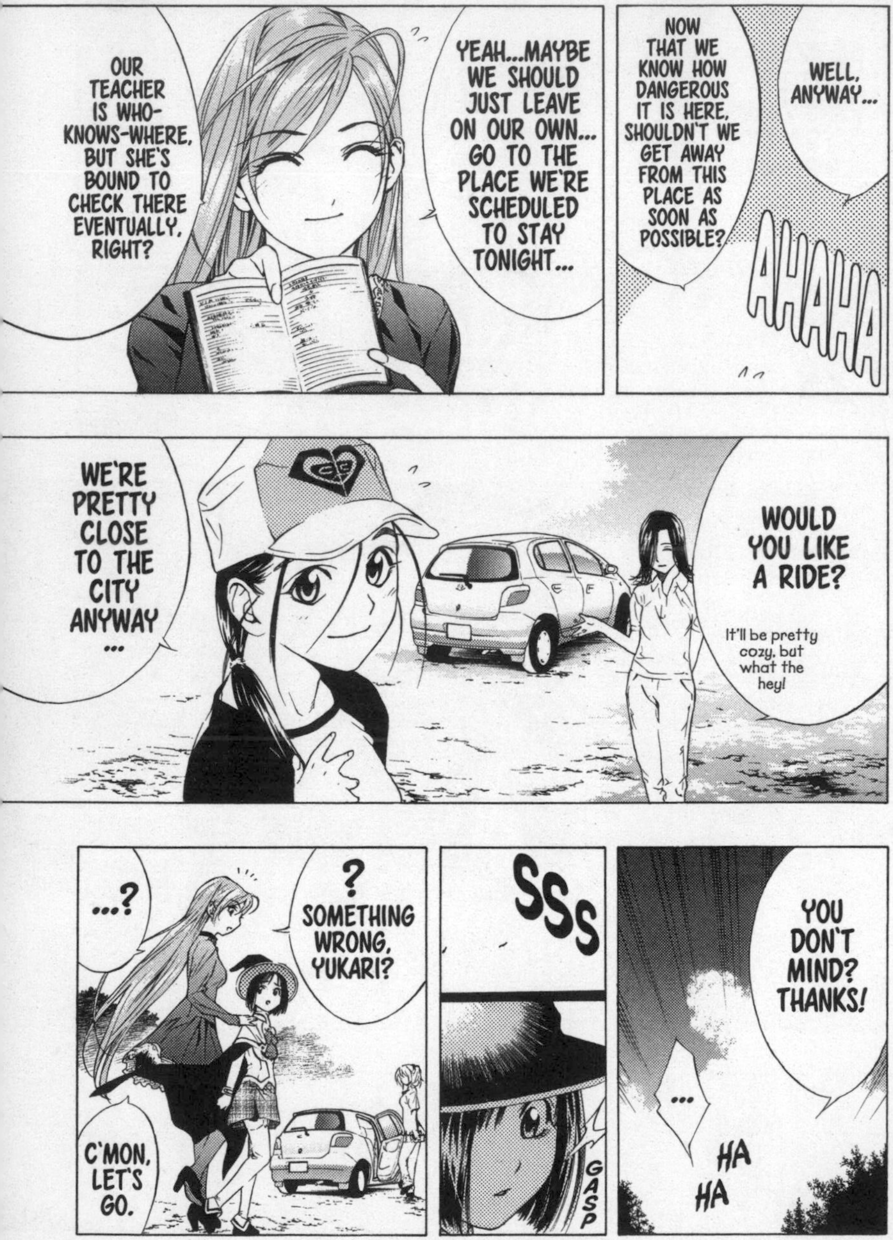
WELL, ANYWAY...
NOW THAT WE KNOW HOW DANGEROUS IT IS HERE, SHOULDN'T WE GET AWAY FROM THIS PLACE AS SOON AS POSSIBLE?
AHAHA
YEAH...MAYBE WE SHOULD JUST LEAVE ON OUR OWN... GO TO THE PLACE WE'RE SCHEDULED TO STAY TONIGHT...
OUR TEACHER IS WHO-KNOWS-WHERE, BUT SHE'S BOUND TO CHECK THERE EVENTUALLY, RIGHT?
WOULD YOU LIKE A RIDE?
It'll be pretty cozy, but what the hey!
WE'RE PRETTY CLOSE TO THE CITY ANYWAY...
YOU DON'T MIND? THANKS!
...
HA
HA
SSS
GASP
? SOMETHING WRONG, YUKARI?
...?
C'MON, LET'S GO.

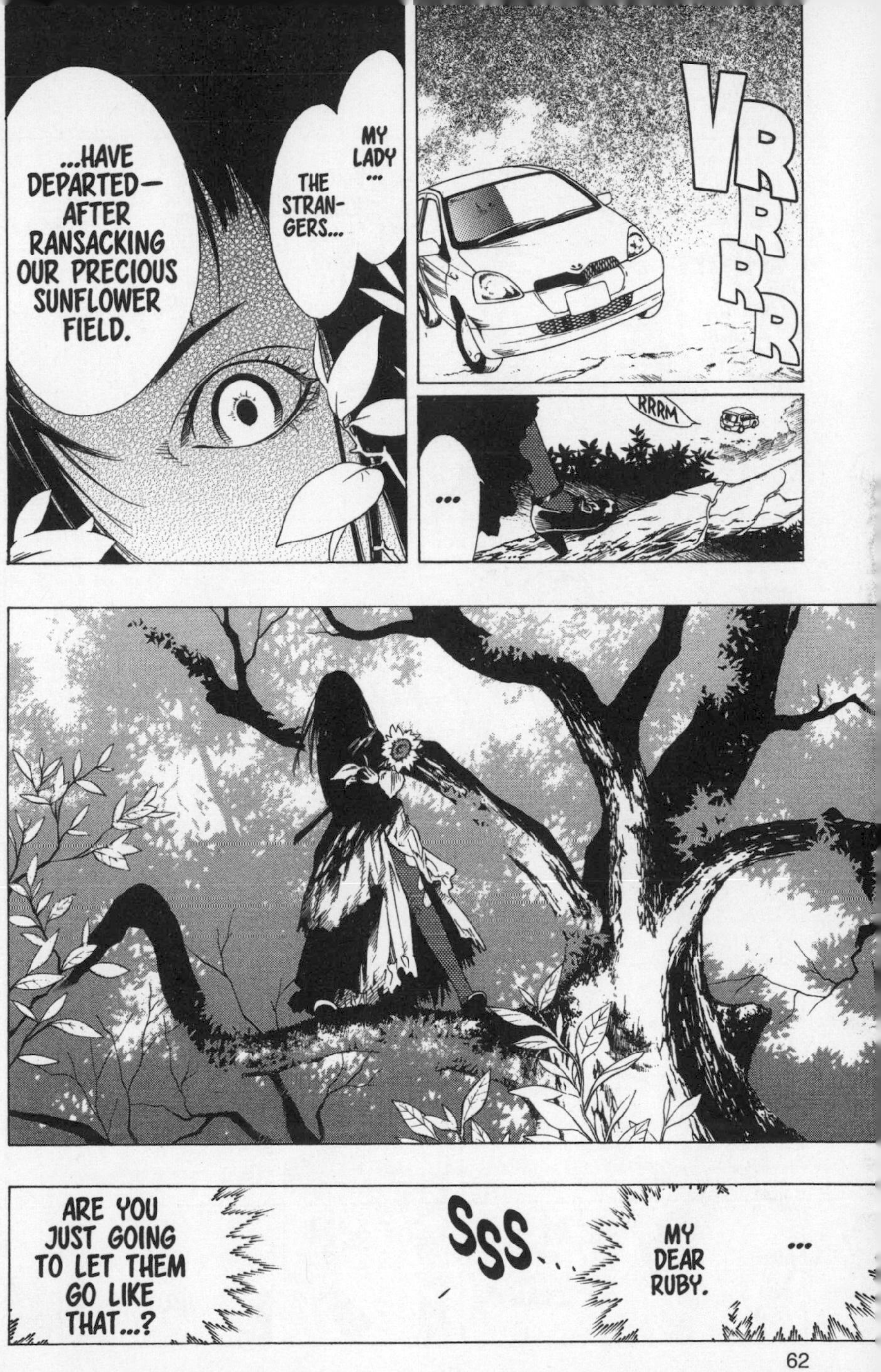
VRRRR
RRRM
...
MY LADY...
THE STRANGERS...
...HAVE DEPARTED— AFTER RANSACKING OUR PRECIOUS SUNFLOWER FIELD.
...
MY DEAR RUBY.
SSS...
ARE YOU JUST GOING TO LET THEM GO LIKE THAT...?

READ THIS WAY

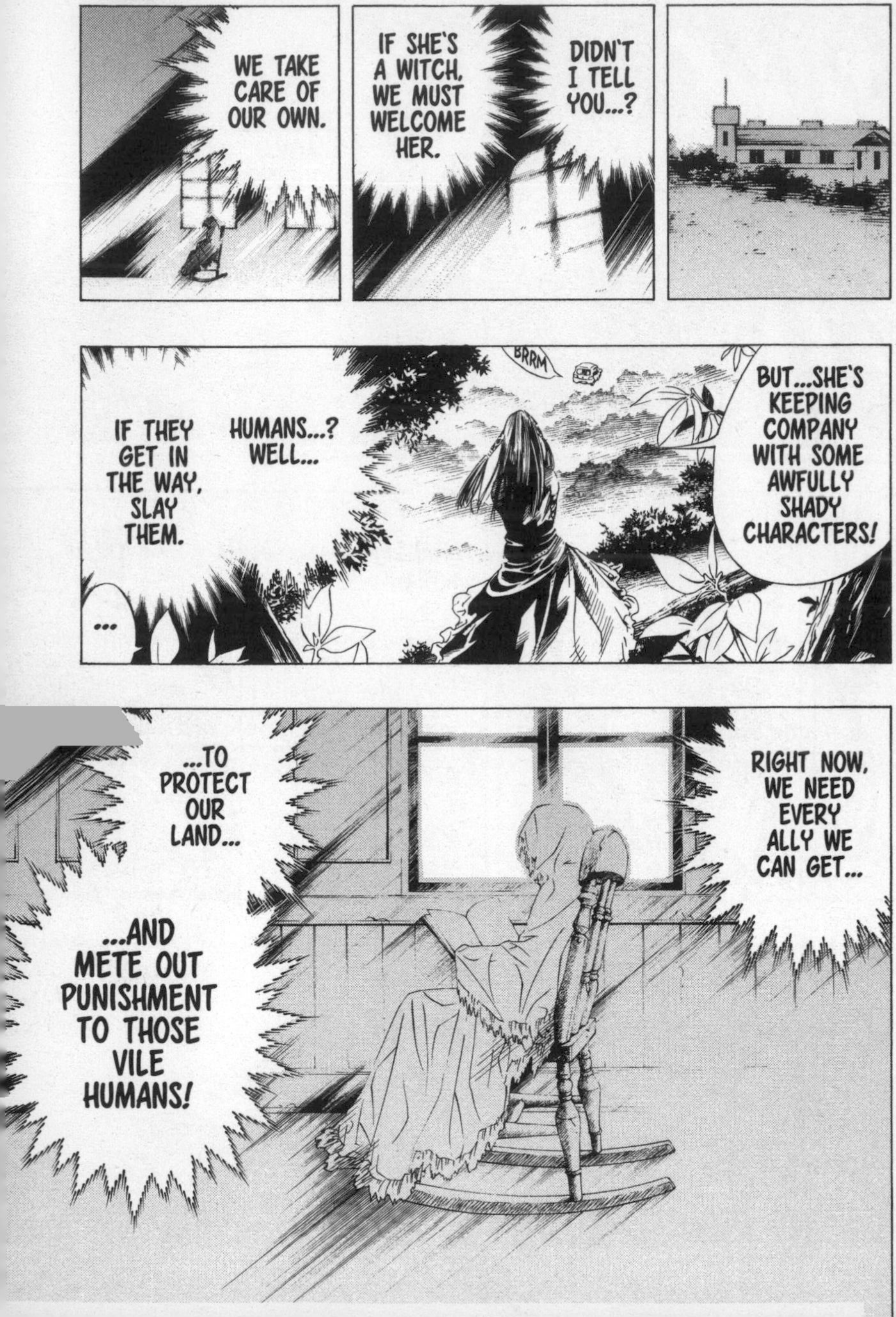
DIDN'T I TELL YOU...?
IF SHE'S A WITCH, WE MUST WELCOME HER.
WE TAKE CARE OF OUR OWN.
BRRM
BUT...SHE'S KEEPING COMPANY WITH SOME AWFULLY SHADY CHARACTERS!
HUMANS...? WELL...
IF THEY GET IN THE WAY, SLAY THEM.
...
RIGHT NOW, WE NEED EVERY ALLY WE CAN GET...
...TO PROTECT OUR LAND...
...AND METE OUT PUNISHMENT TO THOSE VILE HUMANS!

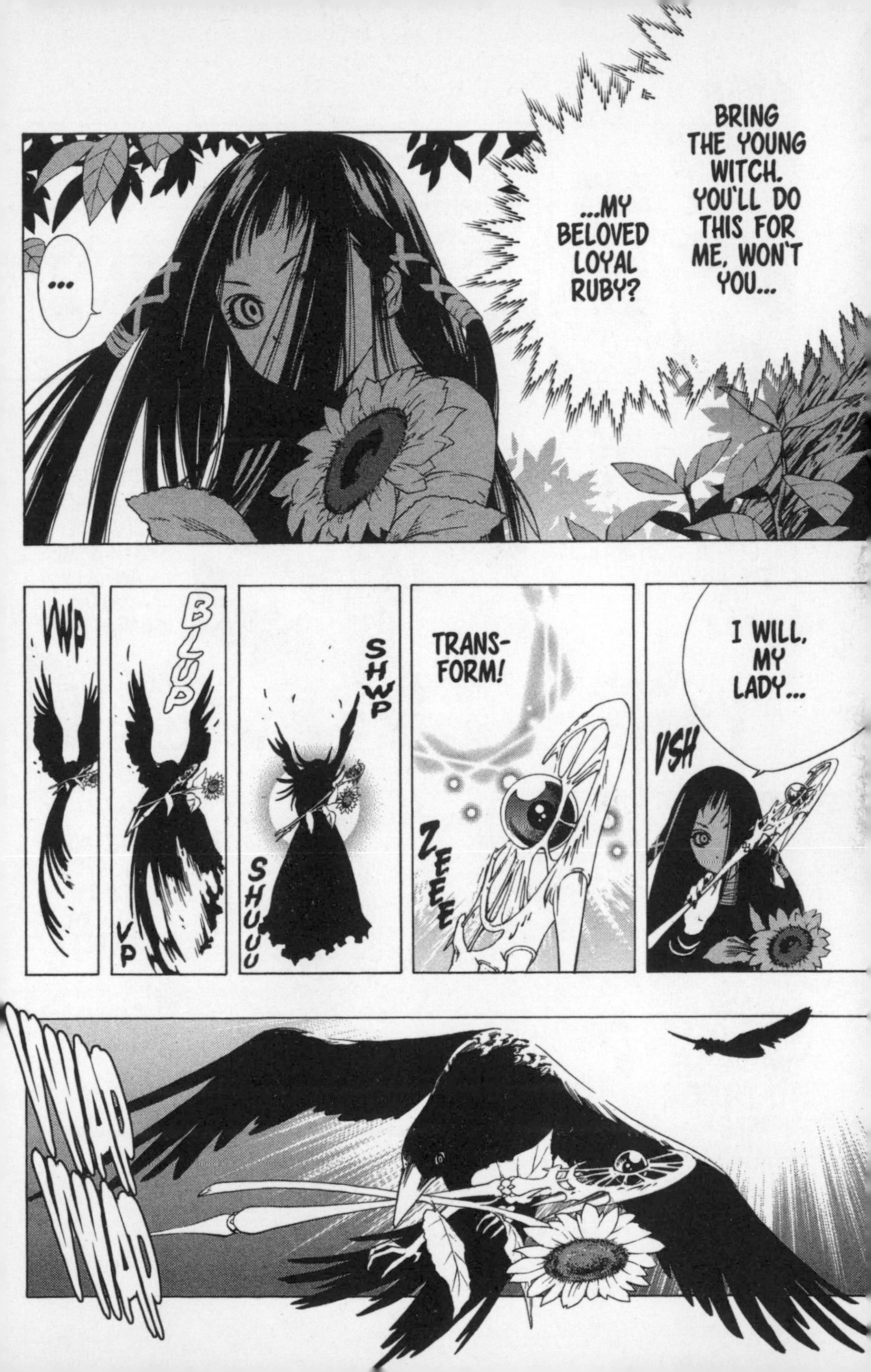
BRING THE YOUNG WITCH. YOU'LL DO THIS FOR ME, WON'T YOU...
...MY BELOVED LOYAL RUBY?
...
I WILL, MY LADY...
VSH
TRANS-FORM!
ZEEE
SHWP
SHUUU
BLUP
VP
VWP

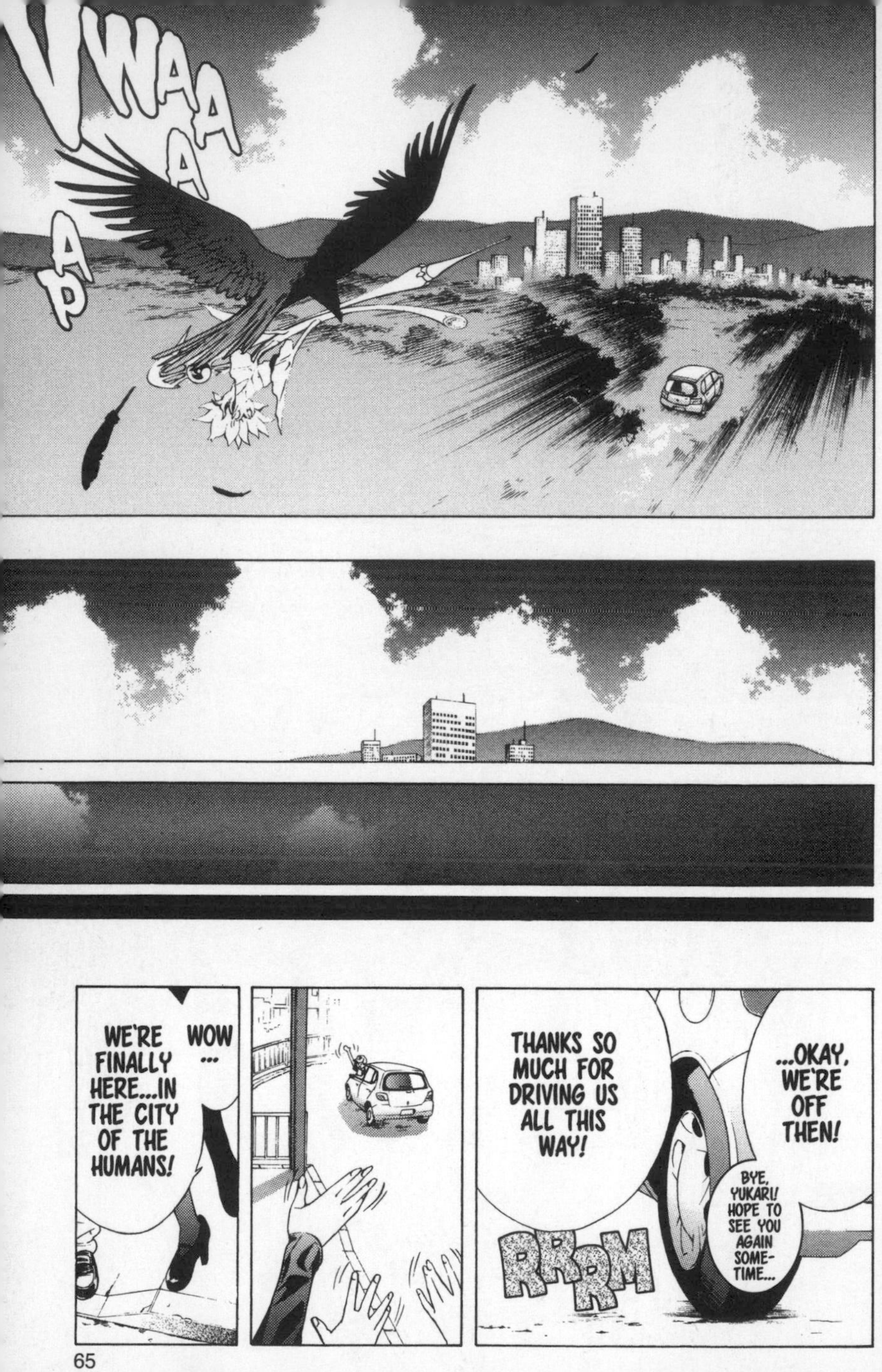
VWAAAAP
...OKAY, WE'RE OFF THEN!
THANKS SO MUCH FOR DRIVING US ALL THIS WAY!
BYE, YUKARI! HOPE TO SEE YOU AGAIN SOME-TIME...
RRRRM
WOW...
WE'RE FINALLY HERE...IN THE CITY OF THE HUMANS!

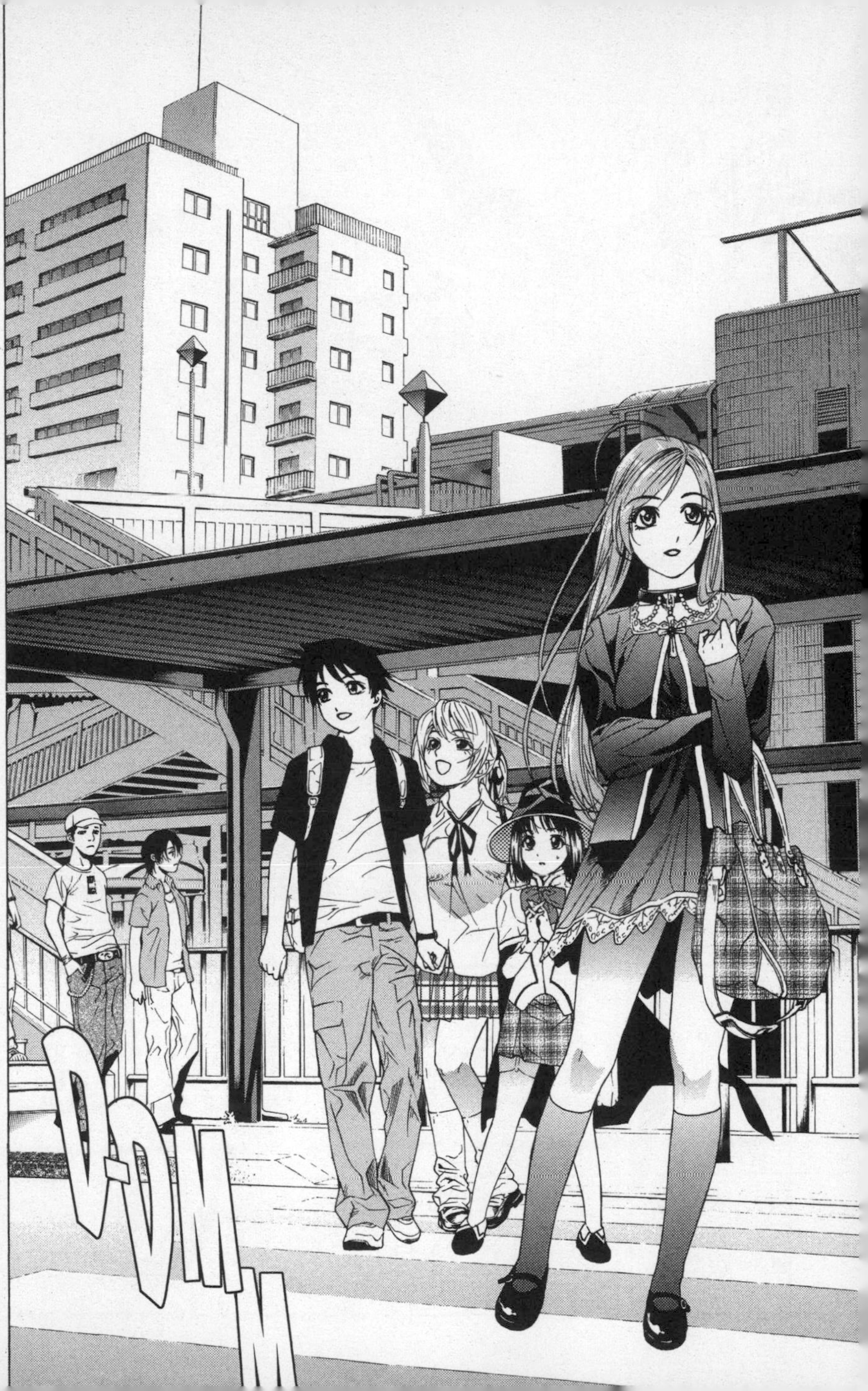
D-OMM

READ THIS WAY

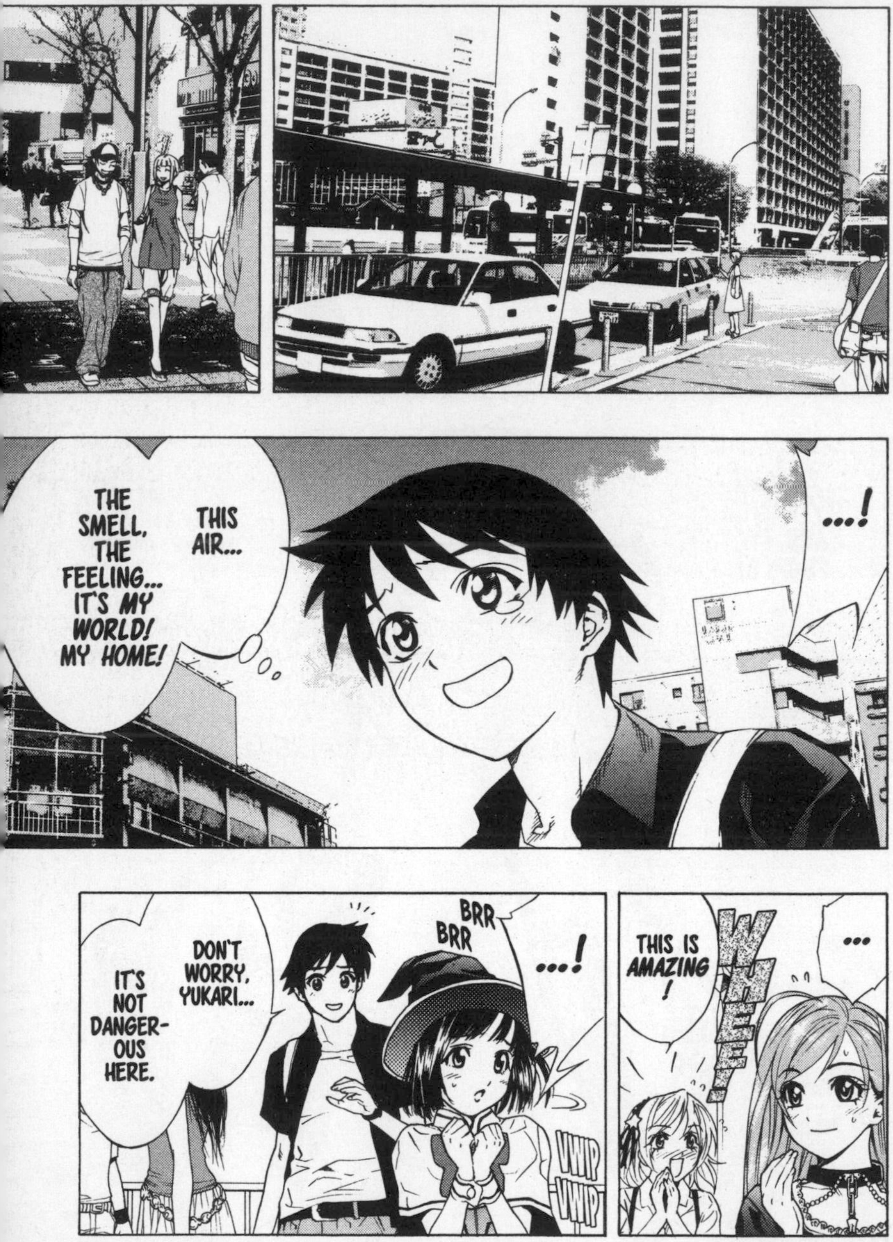

...!
THIS AIR...
THE SMELL, THE FEELING... IT'S *MY* WORLD! MY HOME!
...
THIS IS AMAZING!
...!
BRR BRR
DON'T WORRY, YUKARI...
IT'S NOT DANGER-OUS HERE.
VWIP VWIP

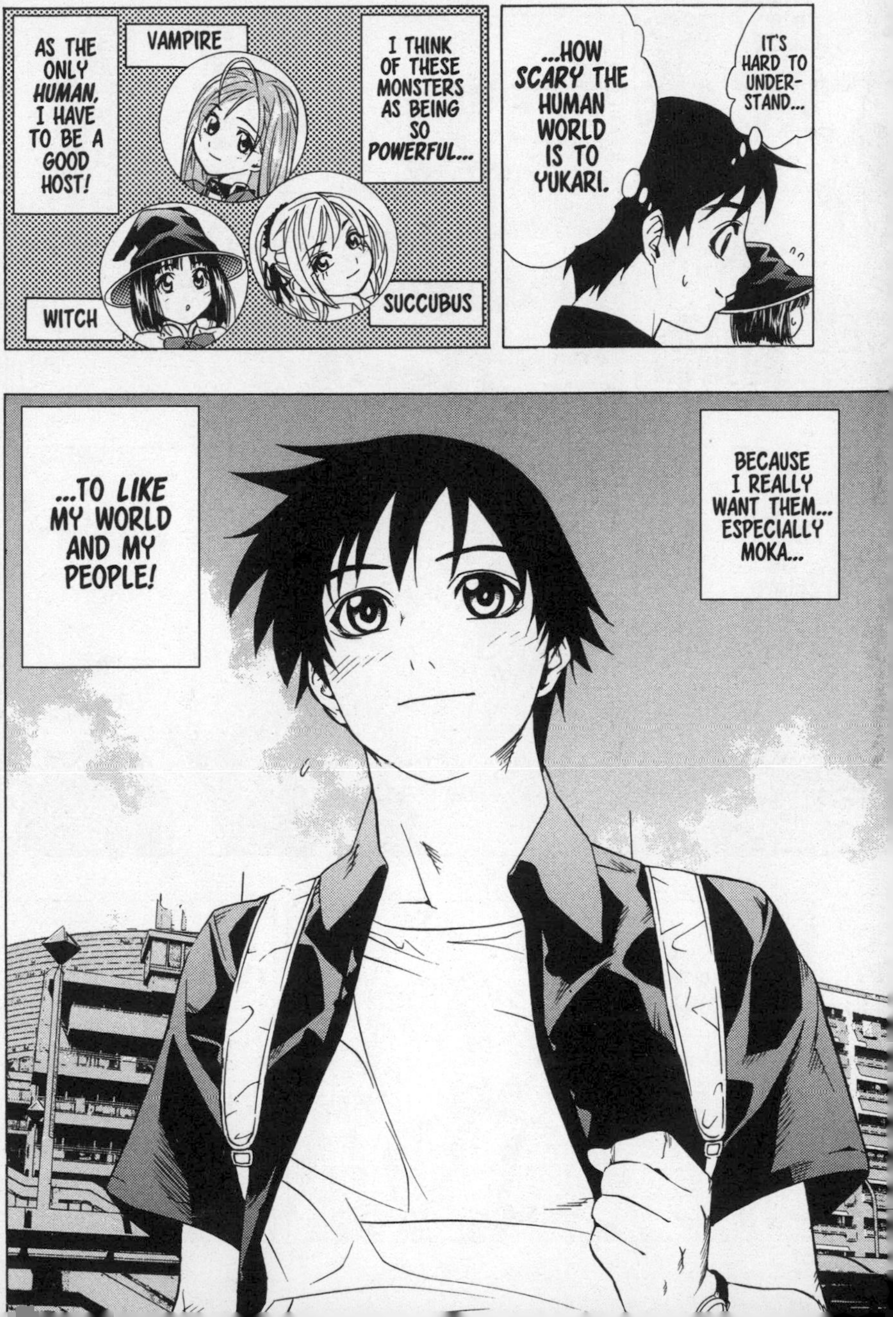
IT'S HARD TO UNDER-STAND...
...HOW SCARY THE HUMAN WORLD IS TO YUKARI.
I THINK OF THESE MONSTERS AS BEING SO POWERFUL...
VAMPIRE
SUCCUBUS
WITCH
AS THE ONLY HUMAN, I HAVE TO BE A GOOD HOST!
BECAUSE I REALLY WANT THEM... ESPECIALLY MOKA...
...TO LIKE MY WORLD AND MY PEOPLE!

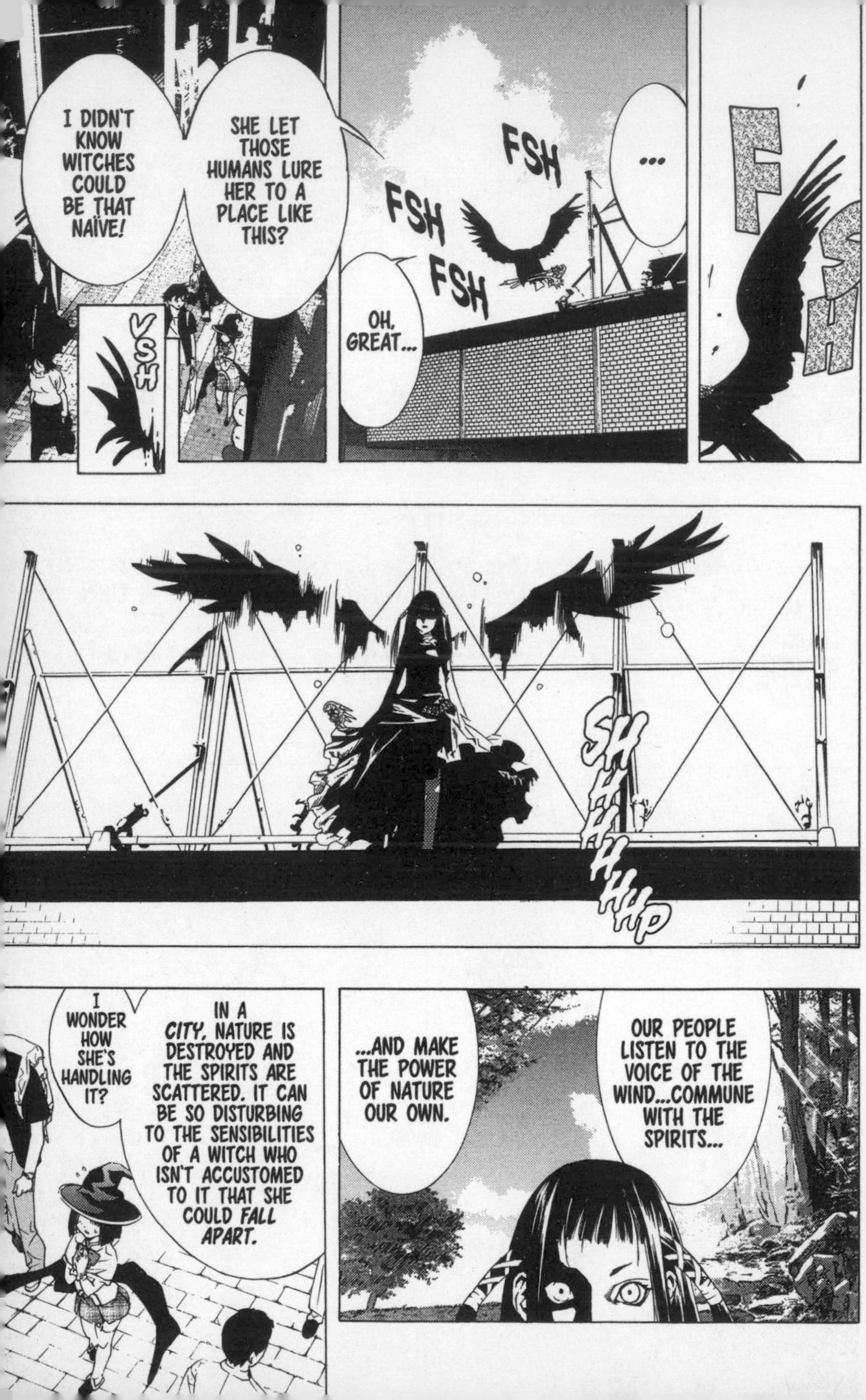
FSH
...
FSH
FSH
FSH
OH, GREAT...
SHE LET THOSE HUMANS LURE HER TO A PLACE LIKE THIS?
I DIDN'T KNOW WITCHES COULD BE THAT NAÏVE!
VSH
SHHHHHP
OUR PEOPLE LISTEN TO THE VOICE OF THE WIND...COMMUNE WITH THE SPIRITS...
...AND MAKE THE POWER OF NATURE OUR OWN.
IN A *CITY*, NATURE IS DESTROYED AND THE SPIRITS ARE SCATTERED. IT CAN BE SO DISTURBING TO THE SENSIBILITIES OF A WITCH WHO ISN'T ACCUSTOMED TO IT THAT SHE COULD *FALL APART*.
I WONDER HOW SHE'S HANDLING IT?

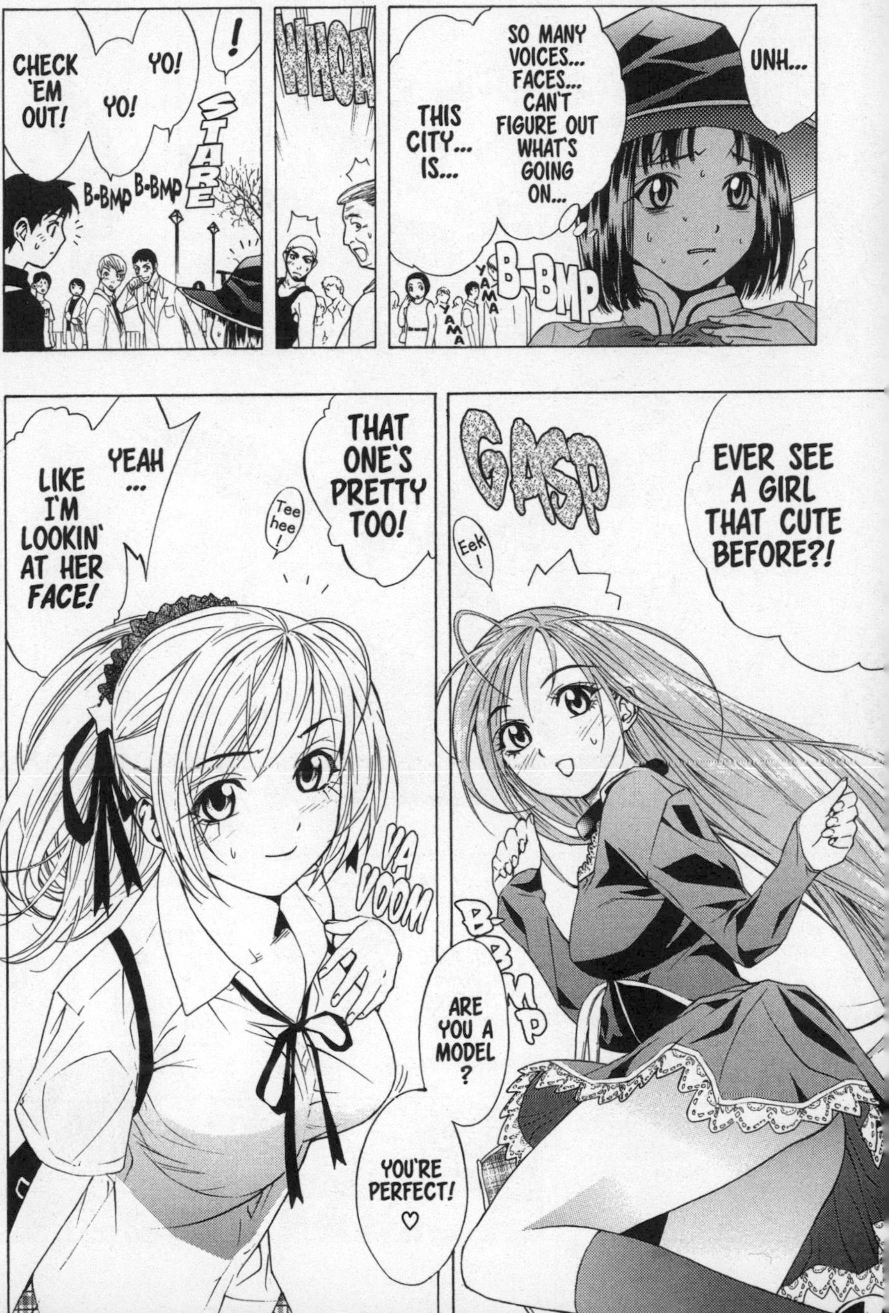
UNH...
SO MANY VOICES... FACES... CAN'T FIGURE OUT WHAT'S GOING ON...
THIS CITY... IS...
YAMA YAMA
B-BMP
WHOA
!
STARE
YO!
YO!
CHECK 'EM OUT!
B-BMP B-BMP
EVER SEE A GIRL THAT CUTE BEFORE?!
GASP
Eek!
BBMP
ARE YOU A MODEL?
YOU'RE PERFECT! ♡
THAT ONE'S PRETTY TOO!
Tee hee!
YEAH...
LIKE I'M LOOKIN' AT HER FACE!
VA VOOM

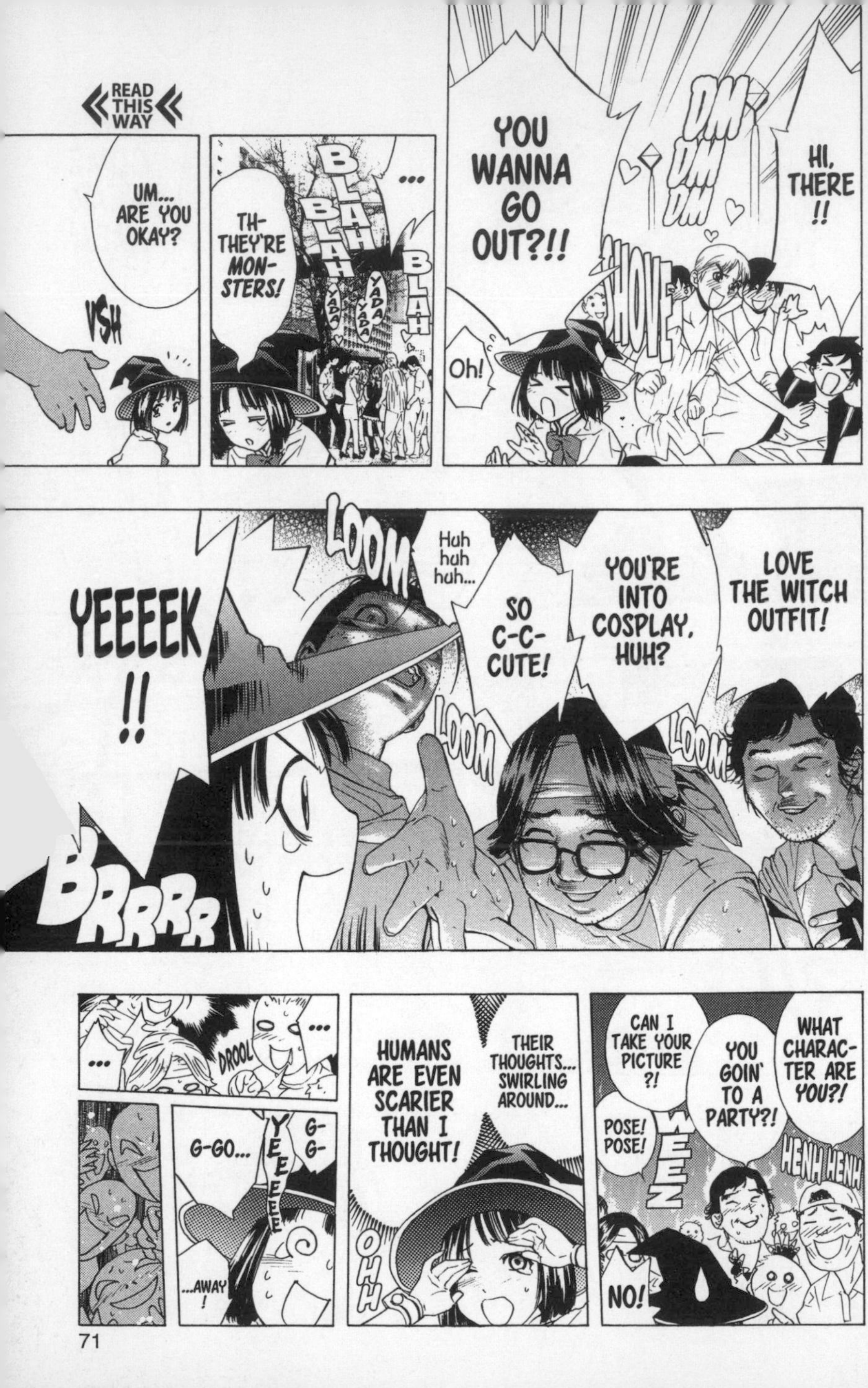
READ THIS WAY
HI, THERE !!
DM DM DM
YOU WANNA GO OUT?!!
SHOVE
Oh!
...
BLAH BLAH BLAH BLAH
YADA YADA YADA
TH-THEY'RE MONSTERS!
UM... ARE YOU OKAY?
VSH
LOVE THE WITCH OUTFIT!
YOU'RE INTO COSPLAY, HUH?
LOOM
SO C-C-CUTE!
Huh huh huh...
LOOM
LOOM
YEEEEK !!
BRRRRR
WHAT CHARACTER ARE YOU?!
HENH HENH
YOU GOIN' TO A PARTY?!
CAN I TAKE YOUR PICTURE ?!
WEEZ
POSE! POSE!
NO!
THEIR THOUGHTS... SWIRLING AROUND...
HUMANS ARE EVEN SCARIER THAN I THOUGHT!
OHH
...
DROOL
...
G-G-
YEEEEE
G-GO...
...AWAY!

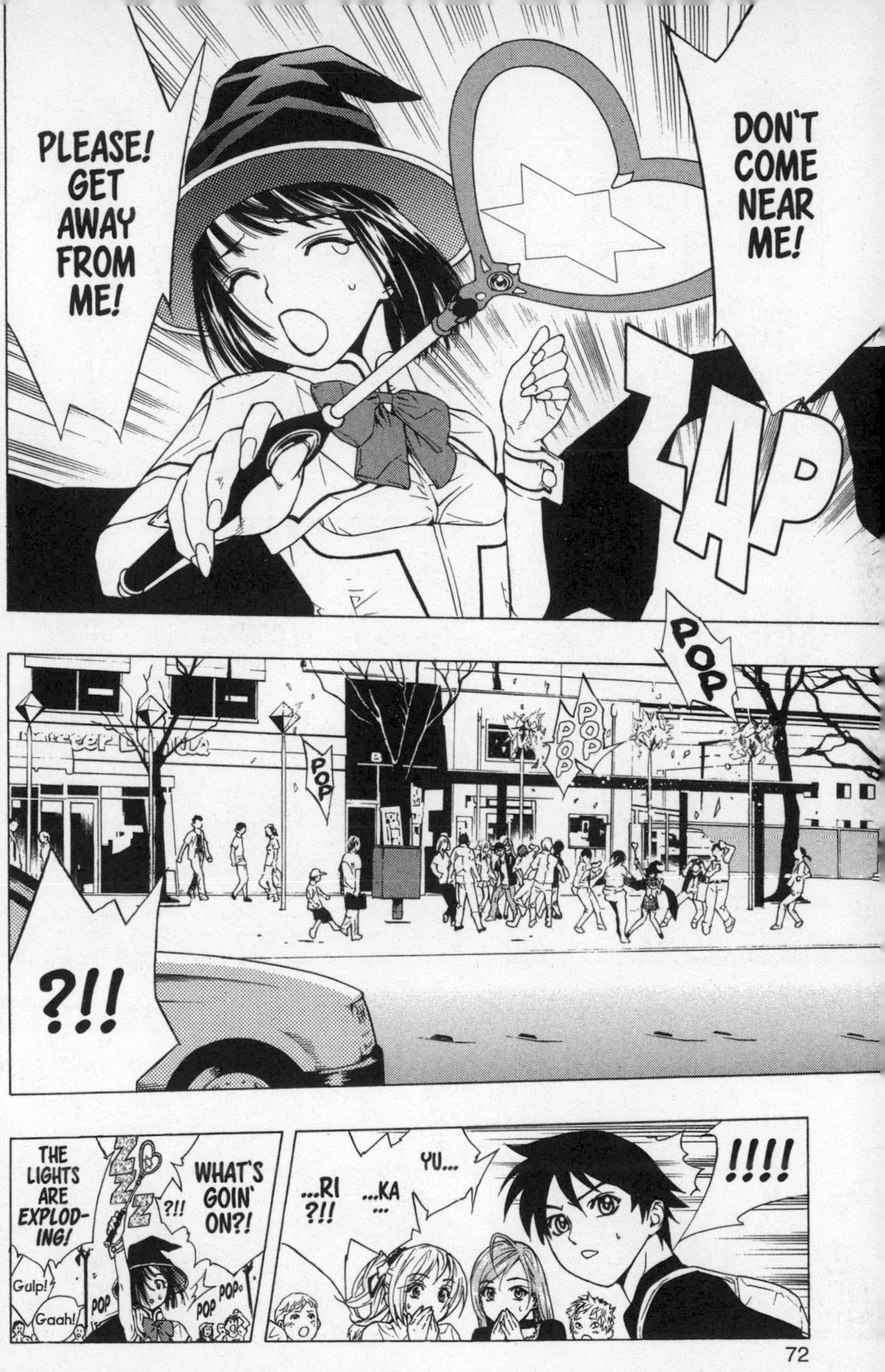
DON'T COME NEAR ME!
PLEASE! GET AWAY FROM ME!
ZAP
POP
POP POP POP POP
POP
?!!
!!!!
YU...
...KA...
...RI ?!!
WHAT'S GOIN' ON?!
?!!
THE LIGHTS ARE EXPLODING!
POP POP
POP
Gulp!
Gaah!

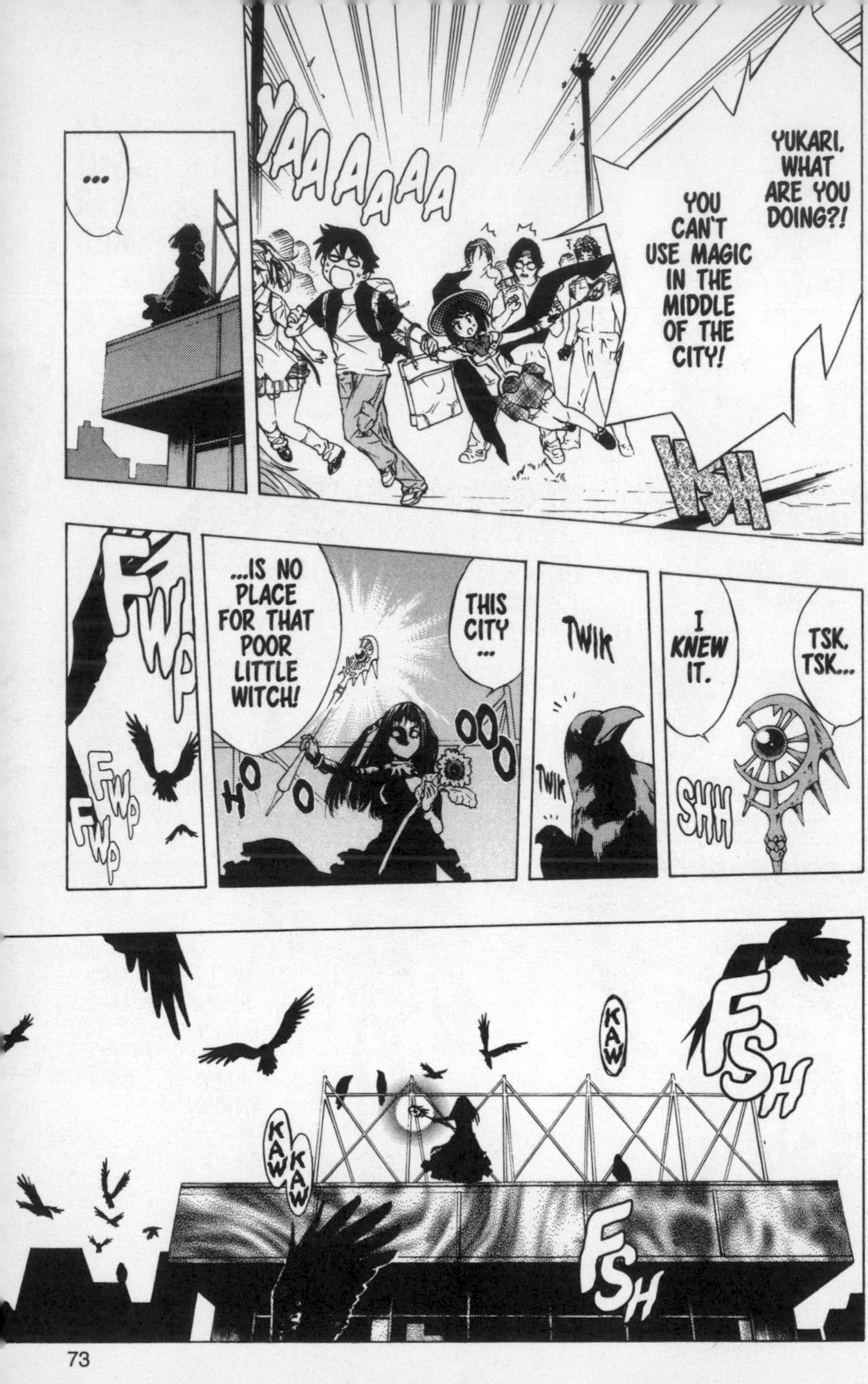
YUKARI, WHAT ARE YOU DOING?!
YOU CAN'T USE MAGIC IN THE MIDDLE OF THE CITY!
YAAAAAAAA
WHSH
...
TSK, TSK...
I KNEW IT.
SHH
TWIK
TWIK
THIS CITY...
...IS NO PLACE FOR THAT POOR LITTLE WITCH!
HOHOOOO
FWP
FWP
FWP
FSH
KAW
KAW KAW
FSH

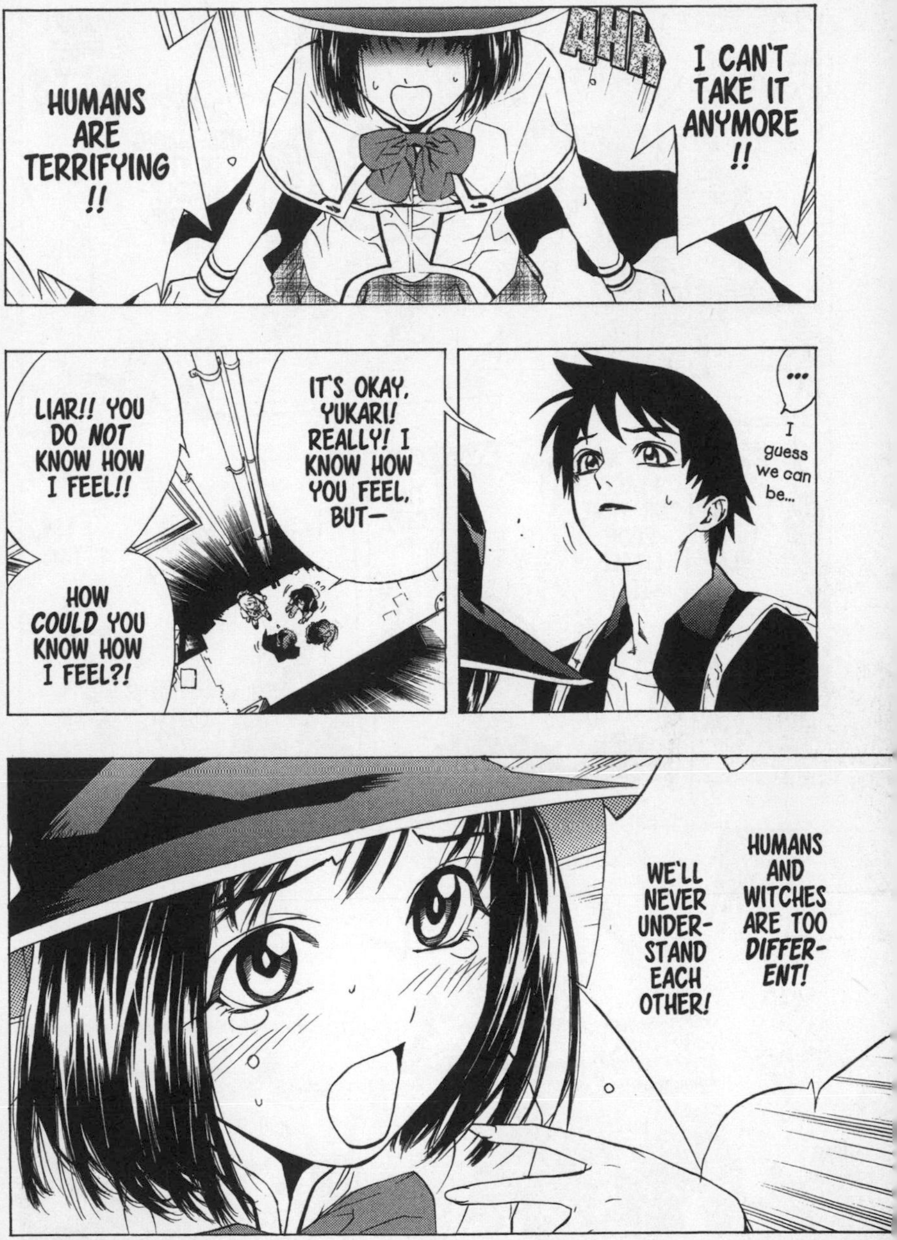
AHH
I CAN'T TAKE IT ANYMORE!!
HUMANS ARE TERRIFYING!!
...
I guess we can be...
IT'S OKAY, YUKARI! REALLY! I KNOW HOW YOU FEEL, BUT—
LIAR!! YOU DO *NOT* KNOW HOW I FEEL!!
HOW *COULD* YOU KNOW HOW I FEEL?!
HUMANS AND WITCHES ARE TOO *DIFFERENT!*
WE'LL NEVER UNDERSTAND EACH OTHER!

READ THIS WAY

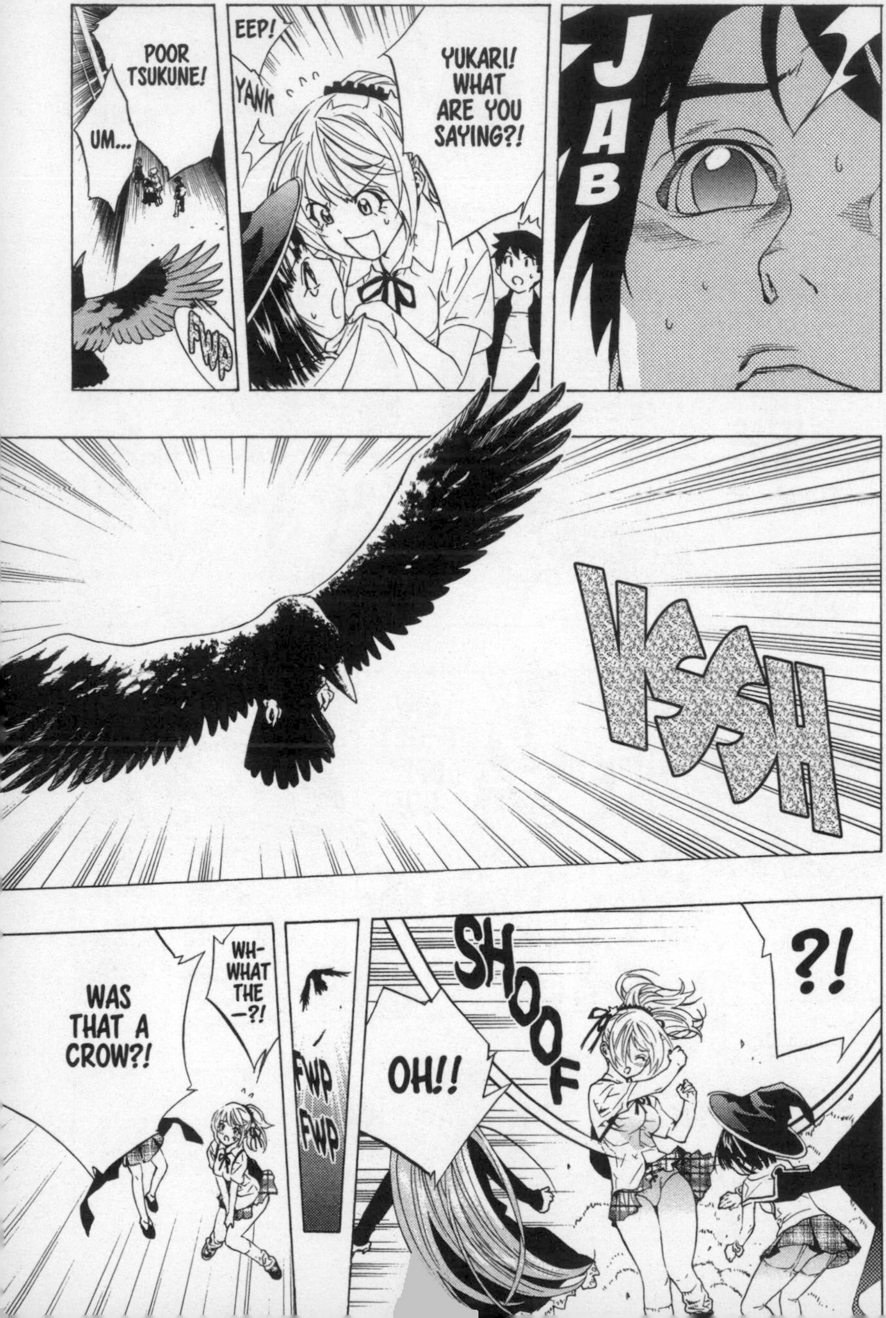
JAB
YUKARI! WHAT ARE YOU SAYING?!
EEP!
YANK
POOR TSUKUNE!
UM...
FWP
VSSH
?!
SHOOF
OH!!
FWP FWP
WH-WHAT THE—?!
WAS THAT A CROW?!

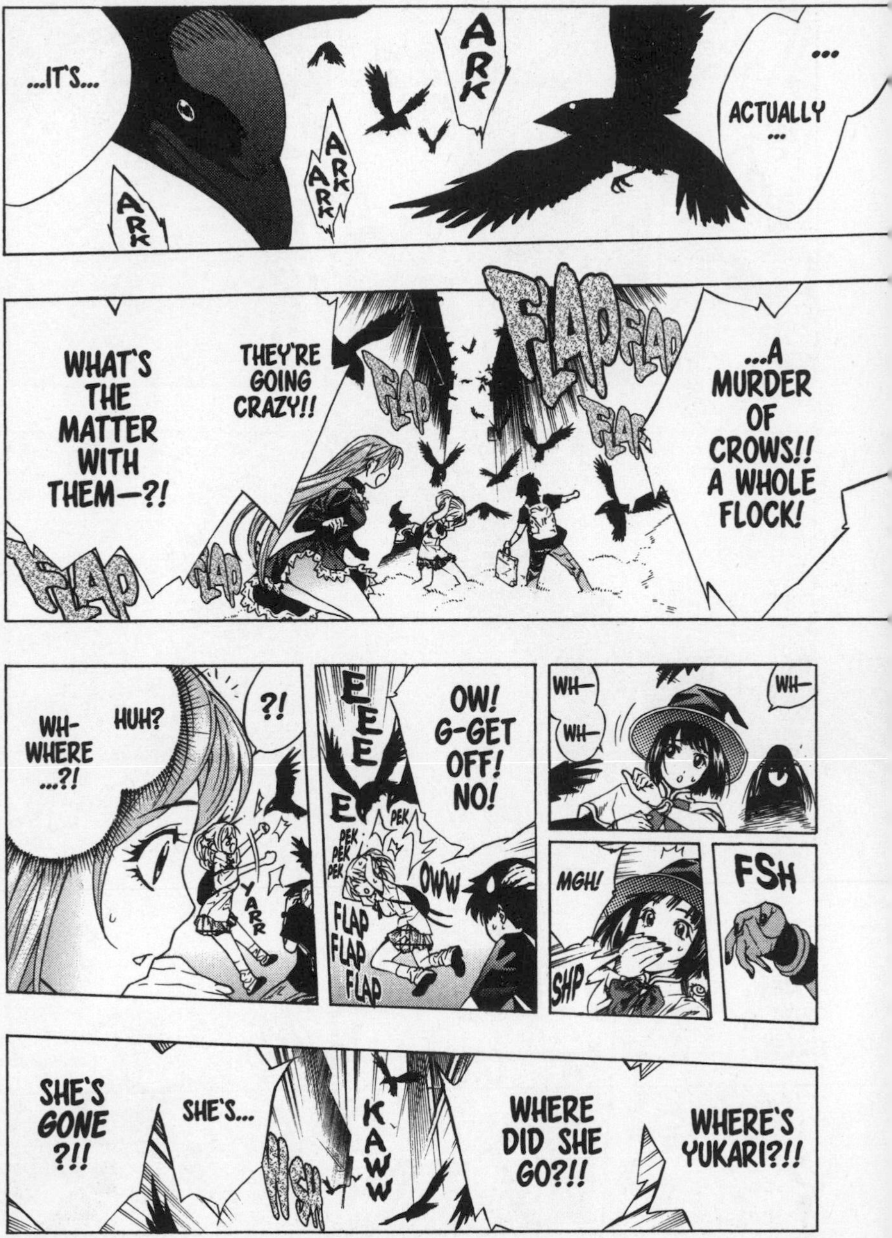
... ACTUALLY ...
ARK
ARK ARK
ARK
...IT'S...
...A MURDER OF CROWS!! A WHOLE FLOCK!
FLAP FLAP
FLAP
FLAP
THEY'RE GOING CRAZY!!
WHAT'S THE MATTER WITH THEM—?!
FLAP
FLAP
WH-
WH-
WH-
FSH
MGH!
SHP
OW! G-GET OFF! NO!
EEEE
PEK
PEK PEK PEK
OWW
FLAP FLAP FLAP
?!
HUH?
WH- WHERE ...?!
YARR
WHERE'S YUKARI?!!
WHERE DID SHE GO?!!
KAWW
SHE'S...
SHE'S GONE ?!!

READ THIS WAY

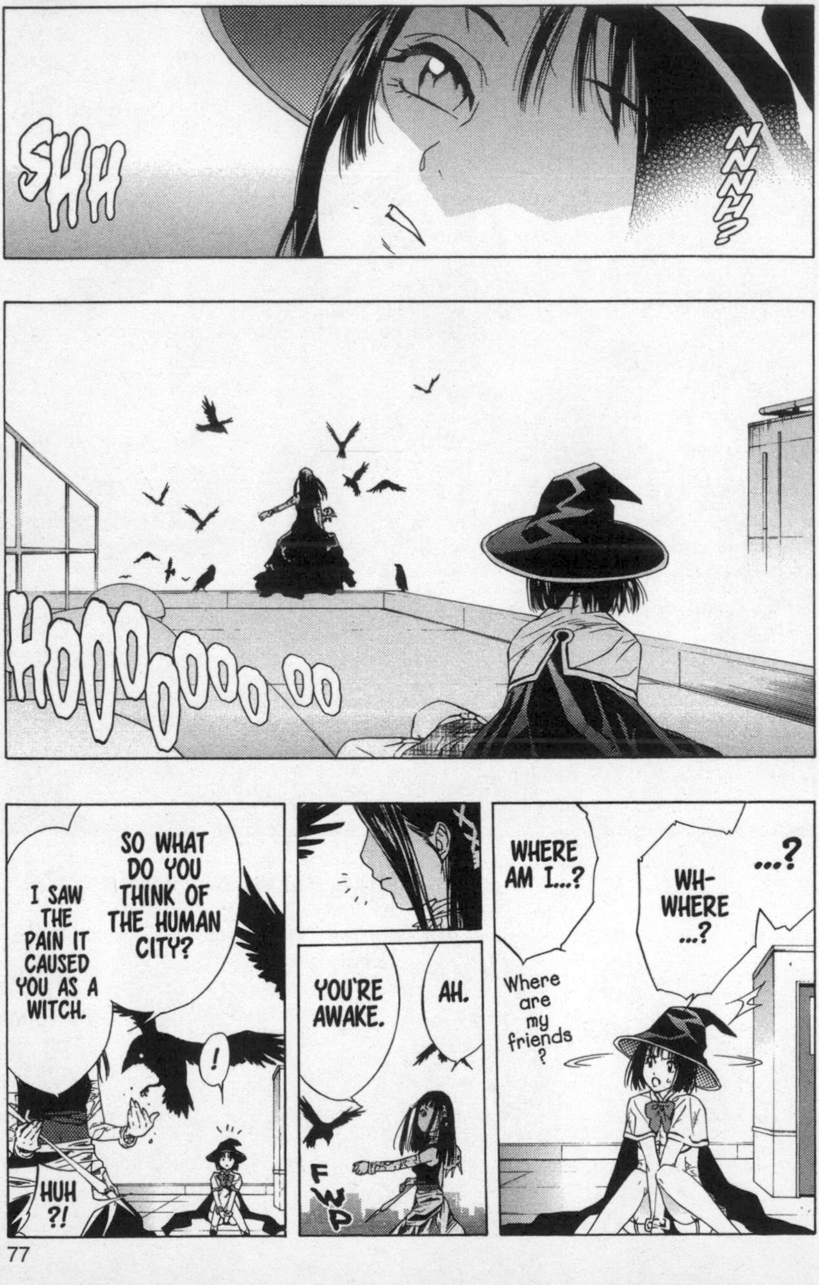
NNNH?
SHH
HOOOOOOO OO
...?
WH-WHERE ...?
WHERE AM I...?
Where are my friends?
AH.
YOU'RE AWAKE.
FWP
SO WHAT DO YOU THINK OF THE HUMAN CITY?
I SAW THE PAIN IT CAUSED YOU AS A WITCH.
!
HUH?!

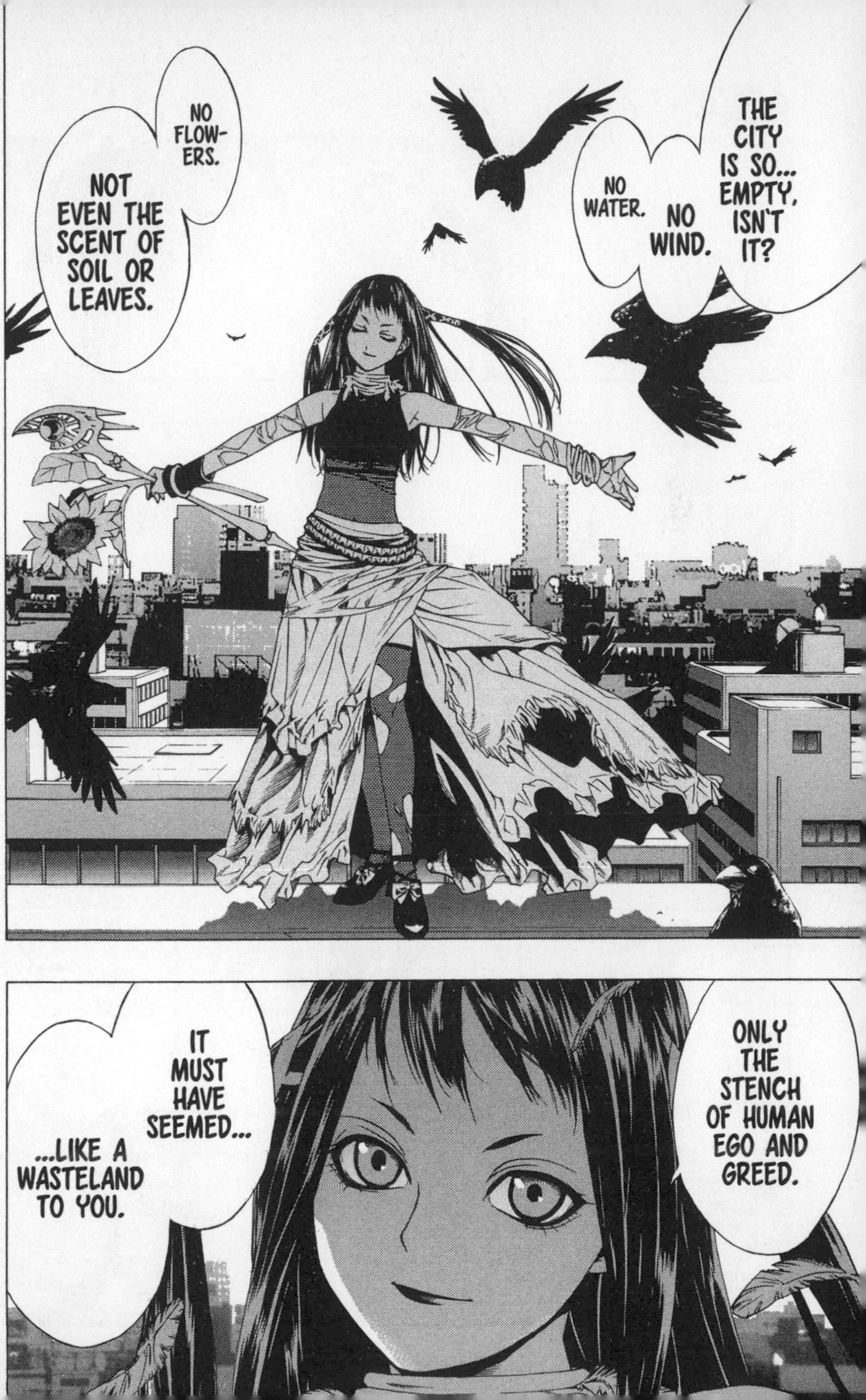
THE CITY IS SO... EMPTY, ISN'T IT?
NO WIND.
NO WATER.
NO FLOW-ERS.
NOT EVEN THE SCENT OF SOIL OR LEAVES.
ONLY THE STENCH OF HUMAN EGO AND GREED.
IT MUST HAVE SEEMED...
...LIKE A WASTELAND TO YOU.

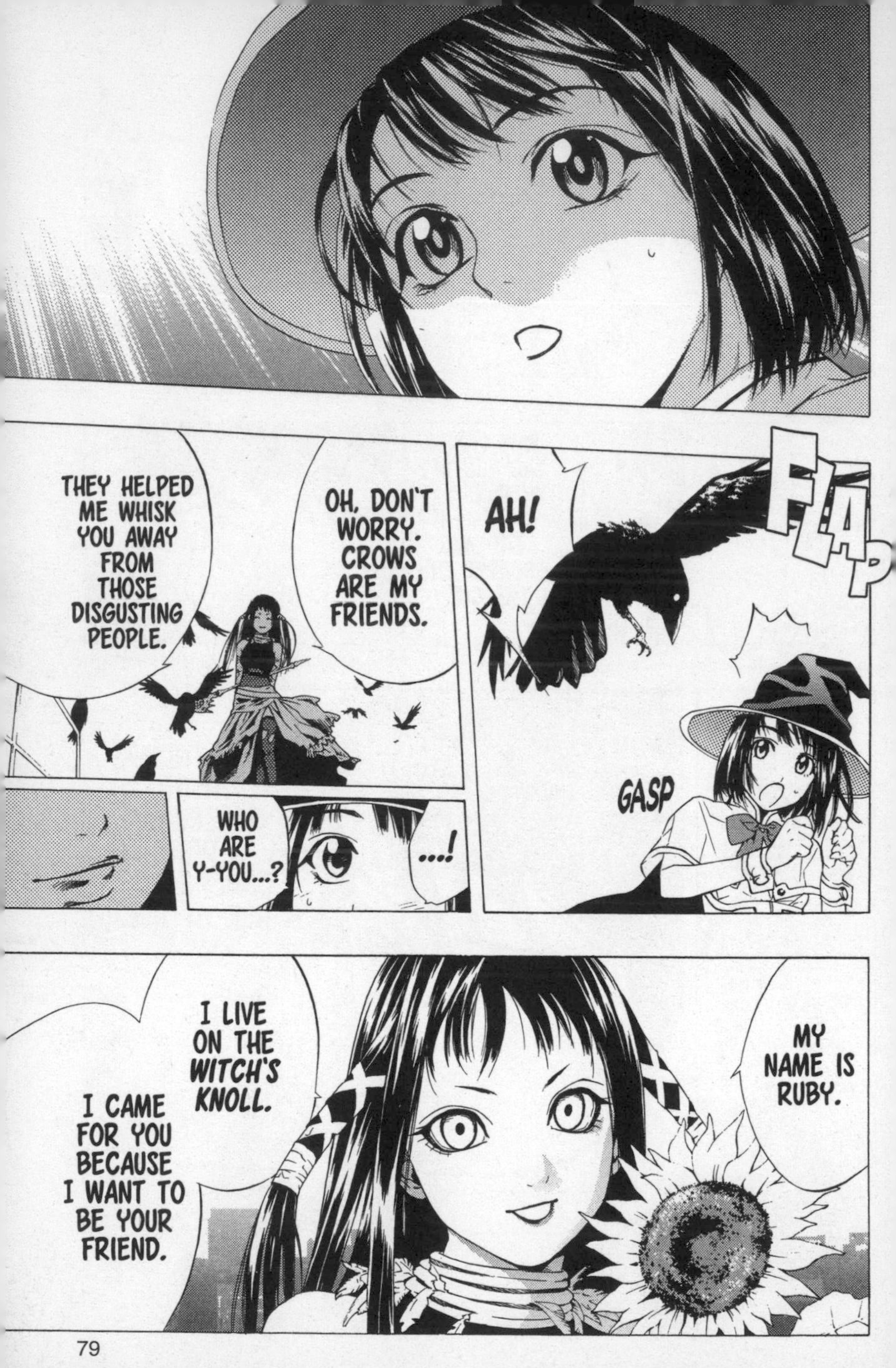
FLAP
AH!
GASP
OH, DON'T WORRY. CROWS ARE MY FRIENDS.
THEY HELPED ME WHISK YOU AWAY FROM THOSE DISGUSTING PEOPLE.
...!
WHO ARE Y-YOU...?
MY NAME IS RUBY.
I LIVE ON THE *WITCH'S* KNOLL.
I CAME FOR YOU BECAUSE I WANT TO BE YOUR FRIEND.

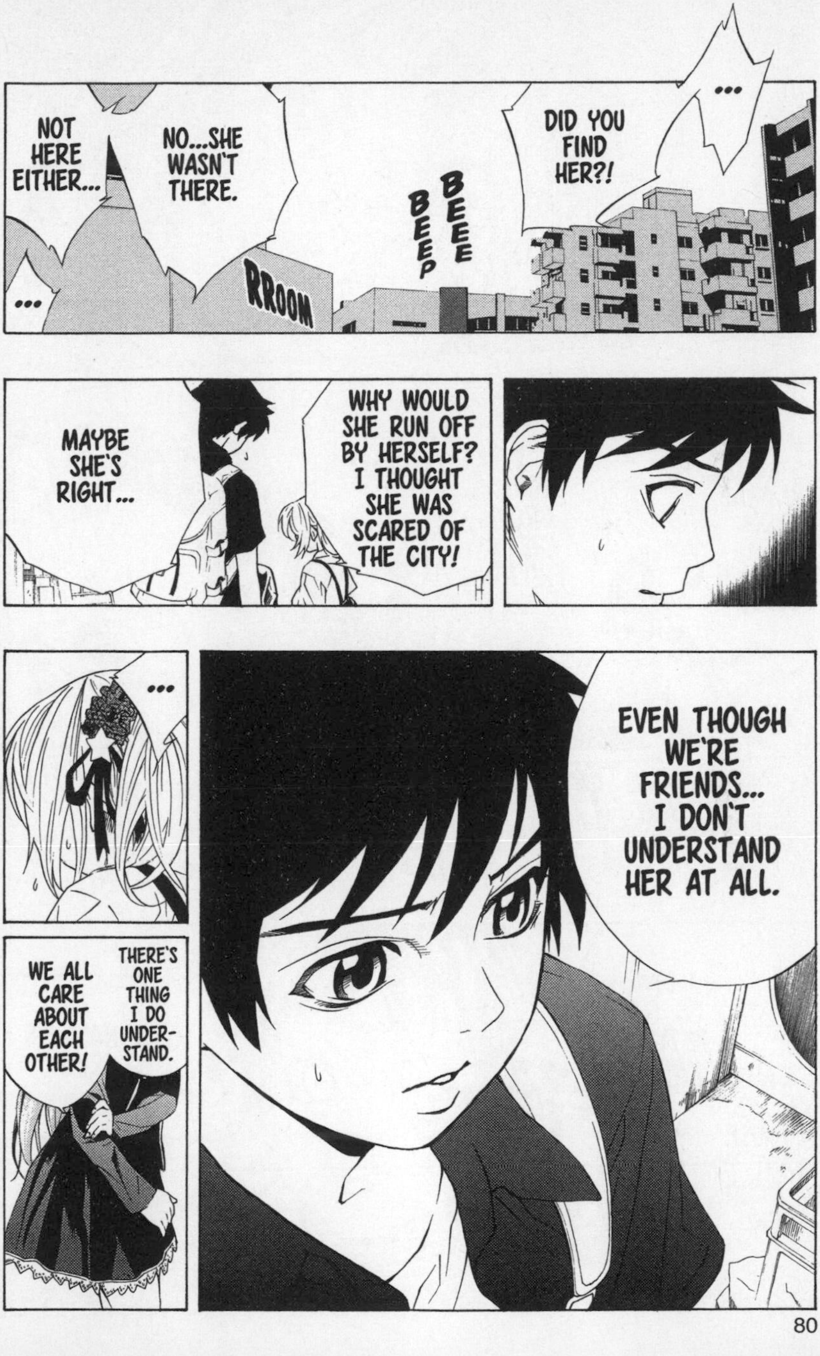
...
DID YOU FIND HER?!
BEEEE
BEEP
RROOM
NO...SHE WASN'T THERE.
NOT HERE EITHER...
...
WHY WOULD SHE RUN OFF BY HERSELF? I THOUGHT SHE WAS SCARED OF THE CITY!
MAYBE SHE'S RIGHT...
EVEN THOUGH WE'RE FRIENDS... I DON'T UNDERSTAND HER AT ALL.
...
THERE'S ONE THING I DO UNDER-STAND.
WE ALL CARE ABOUT EACH OTHER!

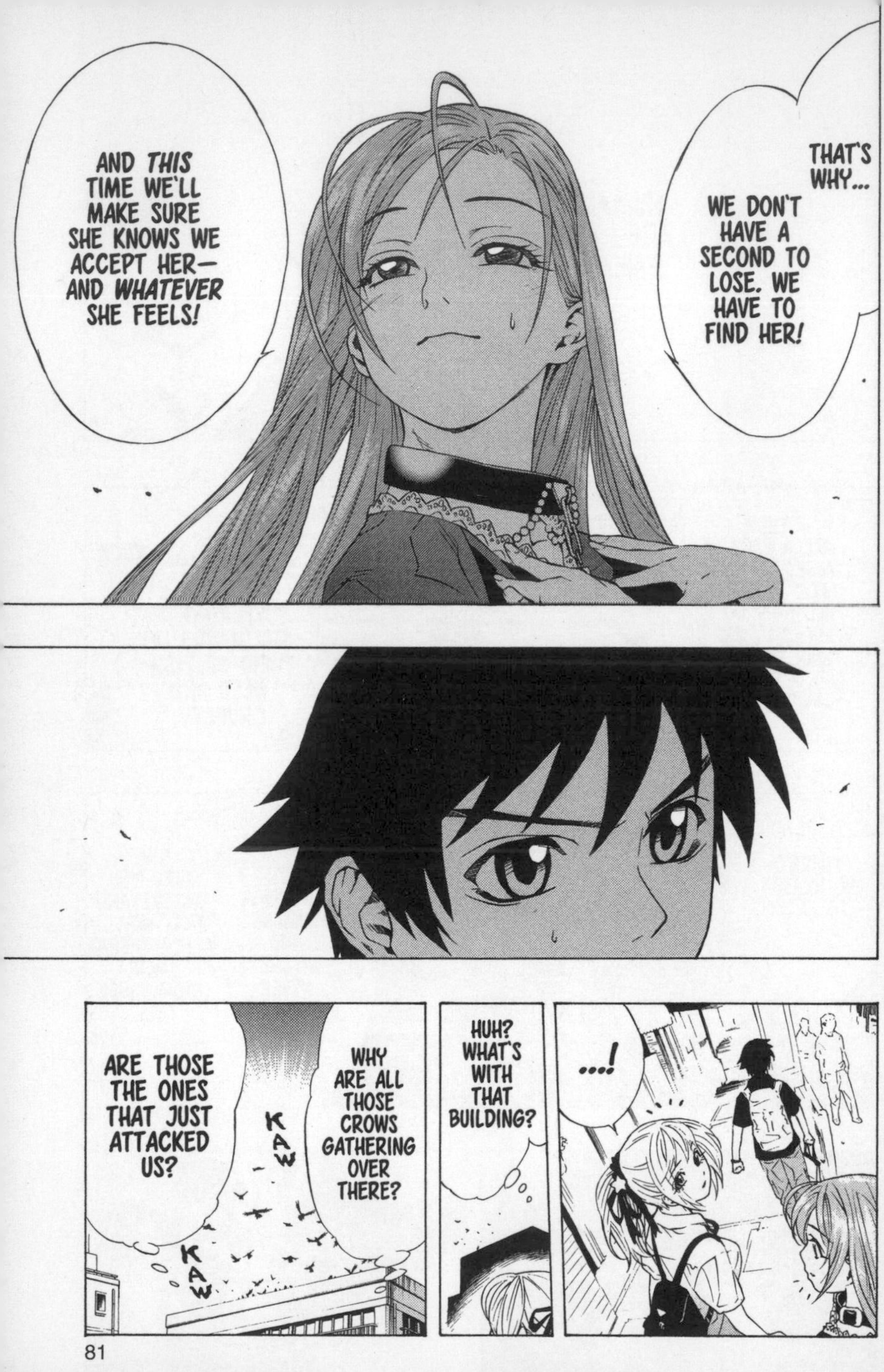
THAT'S WHY...
WE DON'T HAVE A SECOND TO LOSE. WE HAVE TO FIND HER!
AND THIS TIME WE'LL MAKE SURE SHE KNOWS WE ACCEPT HER—AND WHATEVER SHE FEELS!
...!
HUH? WHAT'S WITH THAT BUILDING?
WHY ARE ALL THOSE CROWS GATHERING OVER THERE?
KAW
ARE THOSE THE ONES THAT JUST ATTACKED US?
KAW

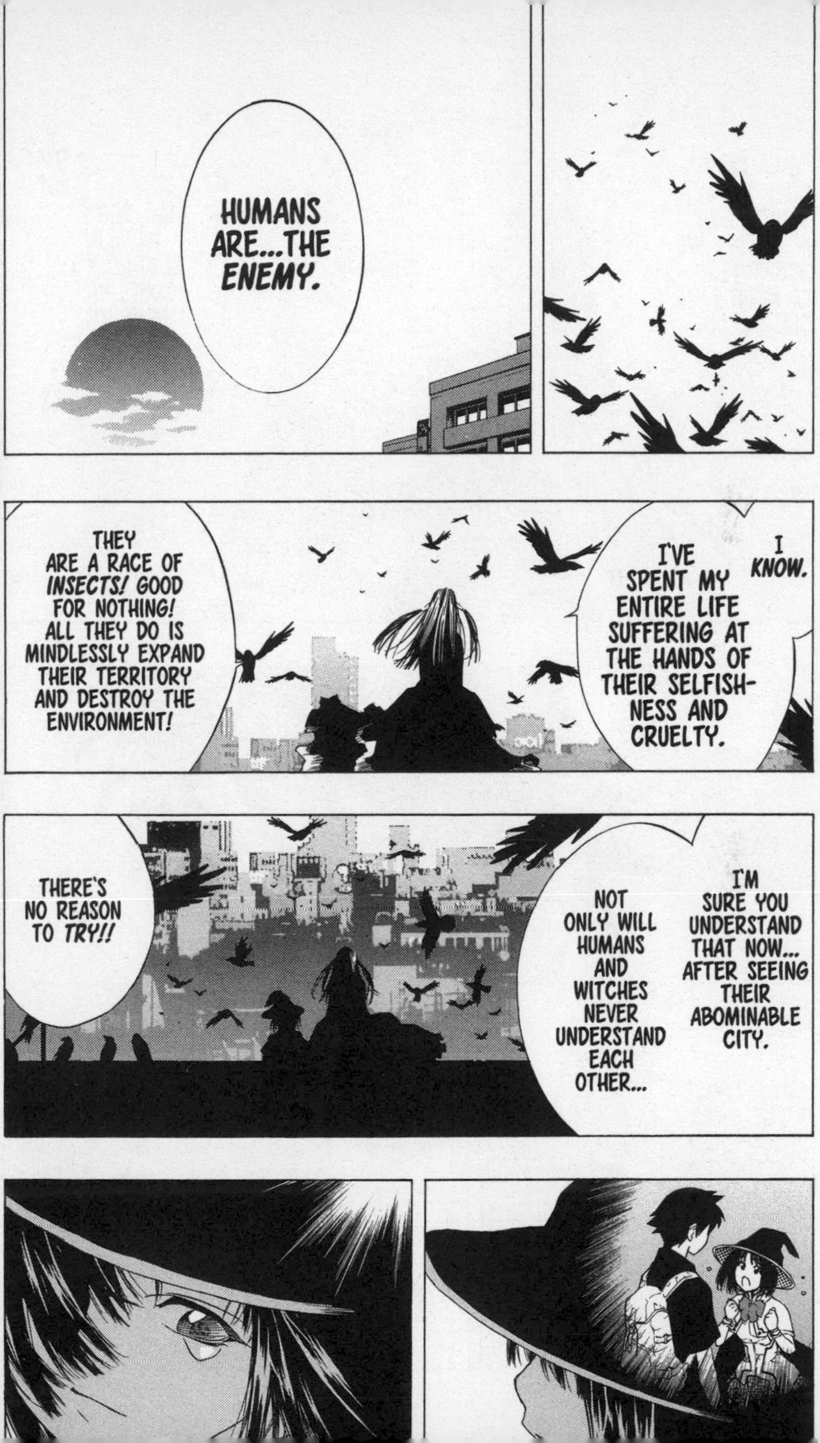
HUMANS ARE...THE *ENEMY.*
I KNOW.
I'VE SPENT MY ENTIRE LIFE SUFFERING AT THE HANDS OF THEIR SELFISHNESS AND CRUELTY.
THEY ARE A RACE OF *INSECTS!* GOOD FOR NOTHING! ALL THEY DO IS MINDLESSLY EXPAND THEIR TERRITORY AND DESTROY THE ENVIRONMENT!
I'M SURE YOU UNDERSTAND THAT NOW... AFTER SEEING THEIR ABOMINABLE CITY.
NOT ONLY WILL HUMANS AND WITCHES NEVER UNDERSTAND EACH OTHER...
THERE'S NO REASON TO *TRY!!*

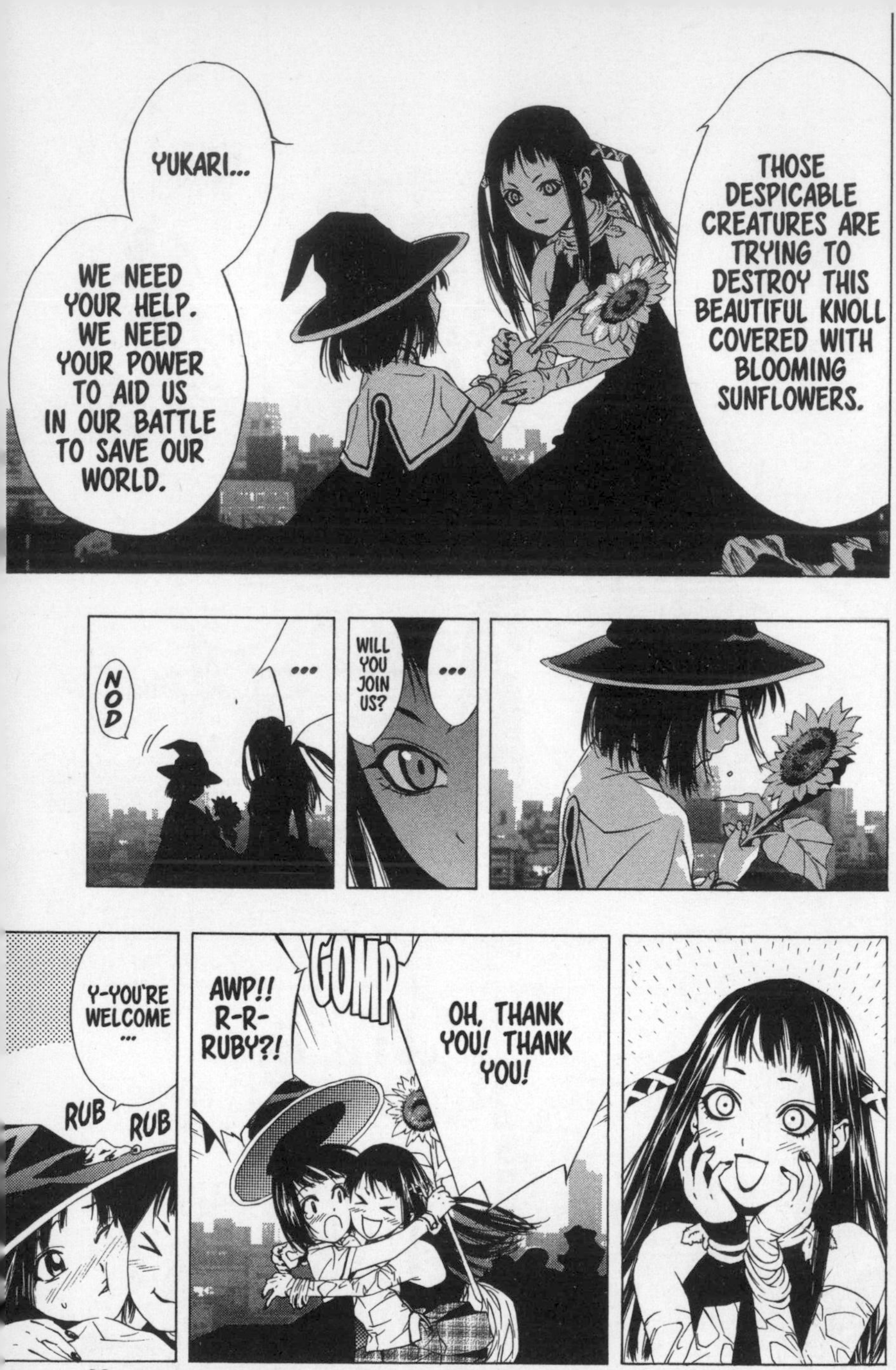
THOSE DESPICABLE CREATURES ARE TRYING TO DESTROY THIS BEAUTIFUL KNOLL COVERED WITH BLOOMING SUNFLOWERS.
YUKARI...
WE NEED YOUR HELP. WE NEED YOUR POWER TO AID US IN OUR BATTLE TO SAVE OUR WORLD.
WILL YOU JOIN US?
...
...
NOD
OH, THANK YOU! THANK YOU!
GOMP
AWP!! R-R-RUBY?!
Y-YOU'RE WELCOME ...
RUB RUB

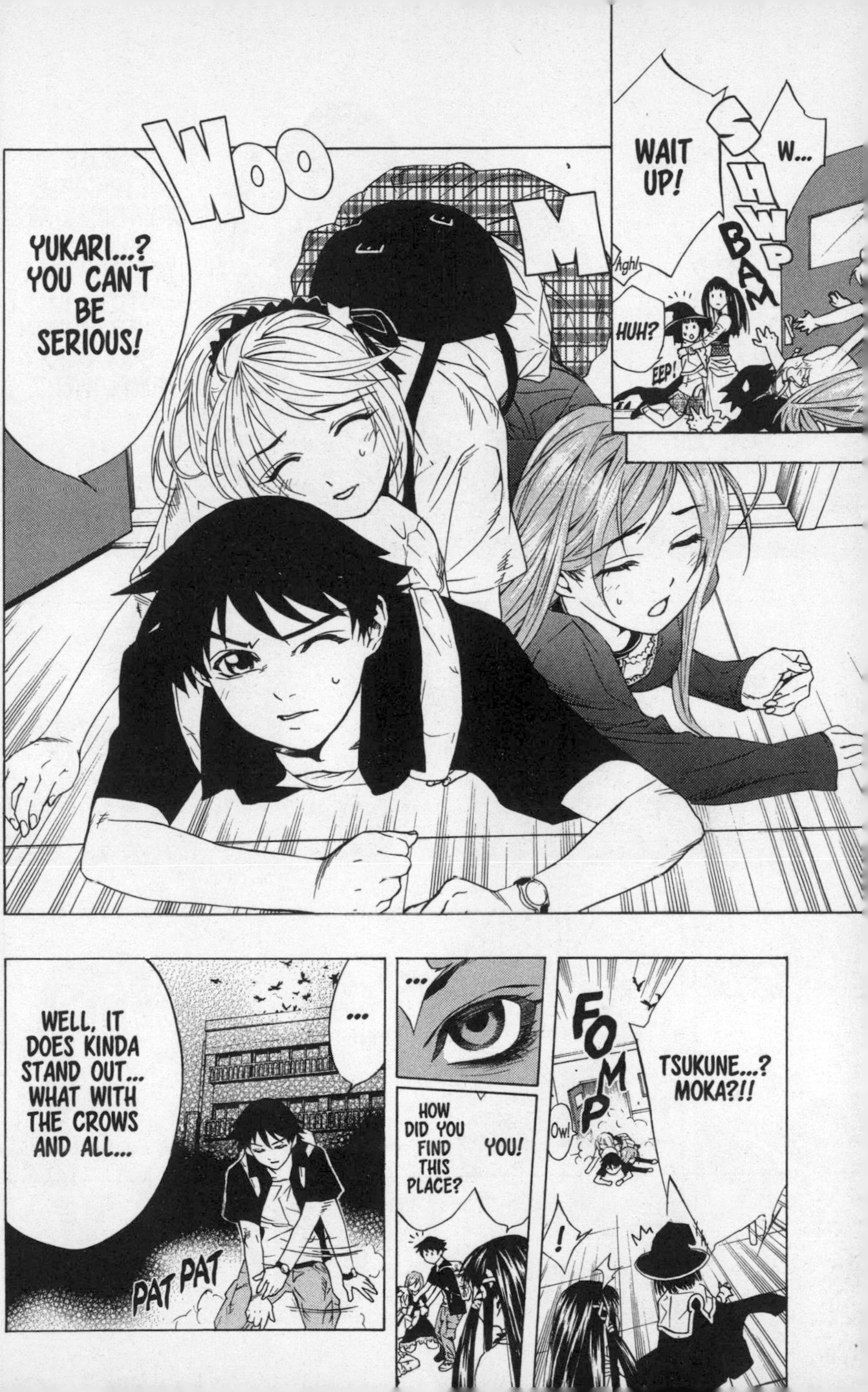
W...
SHWP
WAIT UP!
BAM
Aghl
HUH?
EEP!
WOOM
YUKARI...? YOU CAN'T BE SERIOUS!
FOMP
TSUKUNE...? MOKA?!!
Ow!
...
YOU!
HOW DID YOU FIND THIS PLACE?
!
...
WELL, IT DOES KINDA STAND OUT... WHAT WITH THE CROWS AND ALL...
PAT PAT

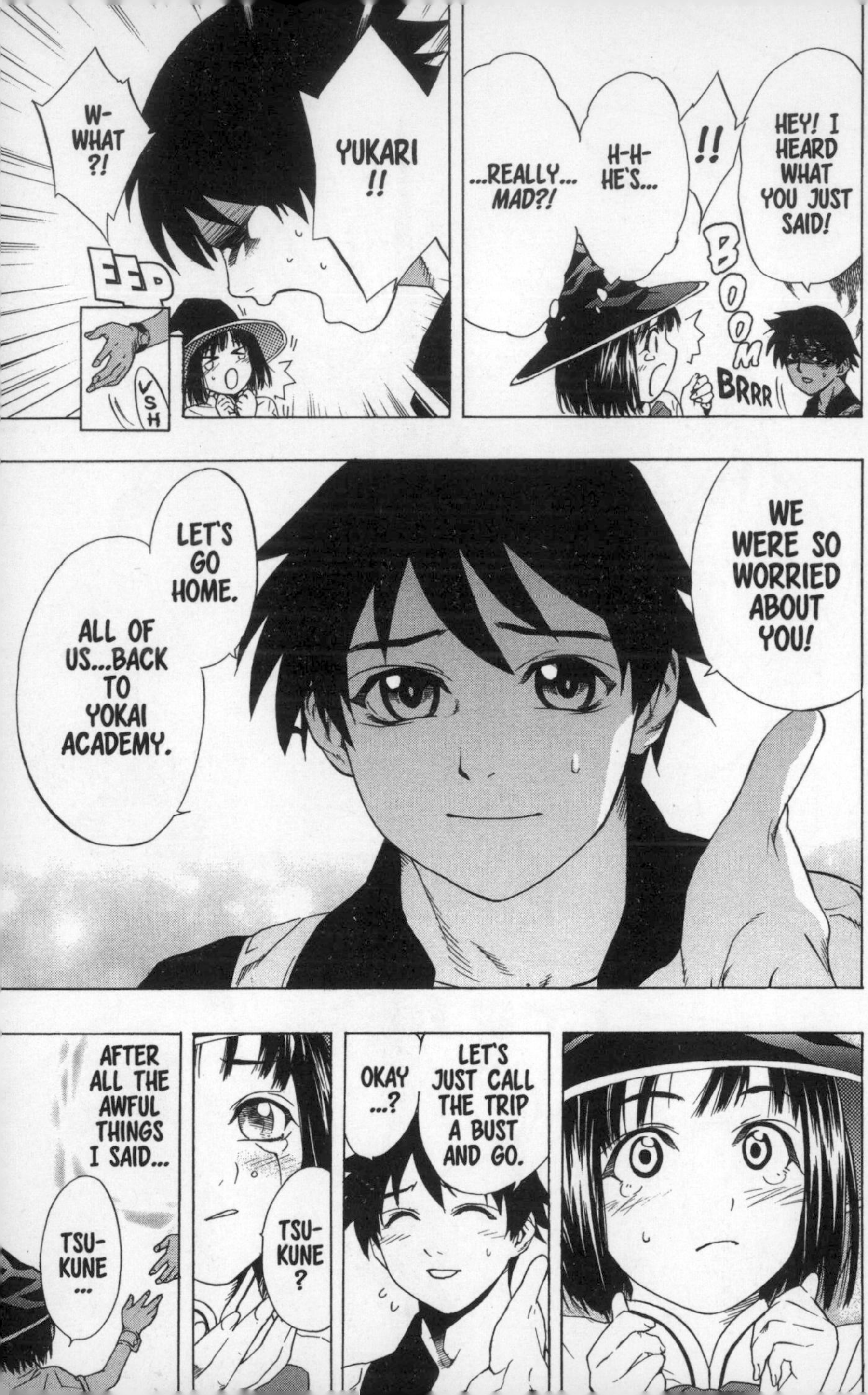

HEY! I HEARD WHAT YOU JUST SAID!
!!
BOOM
BRRR
H-H-HE'S...
...REALLY... MAD?!
YUKARI!!
W-WHAT?!
EEP
VSH
WE WERE SO WORRIED ABOUT YOU!
LET'S GO HOME.
ALL OF US...BACK TO YOKAI ACADEMY.
LET'S JUST CALL THE TRIP A BUST AND GO.
OKAY...?
TSU-KUNE?
AFTER ALL THE AWFUL THINGS I SAID...
TSU-KUNE...

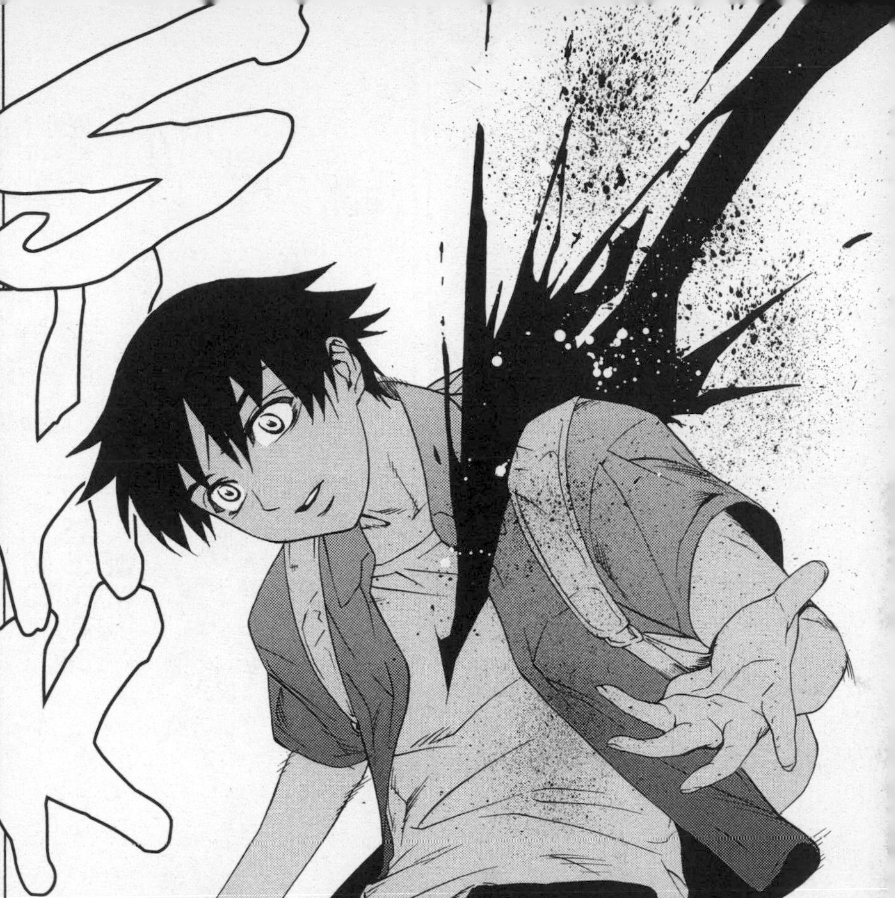

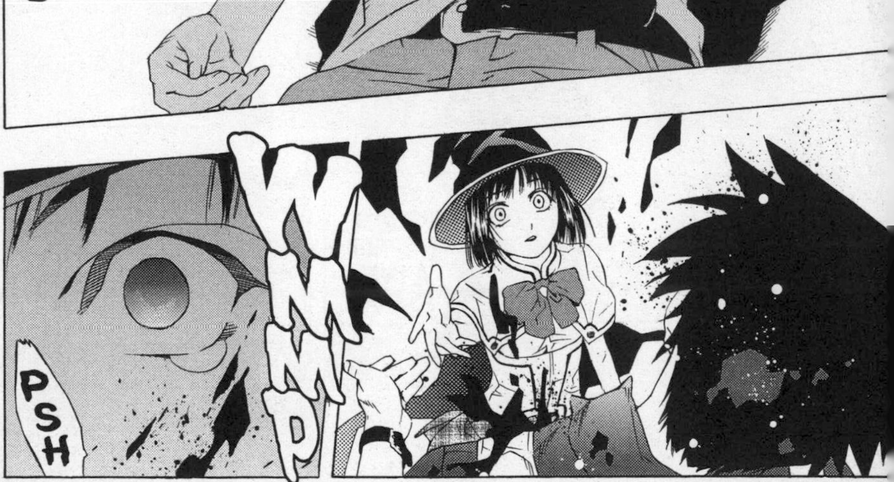
WMMP
PSH

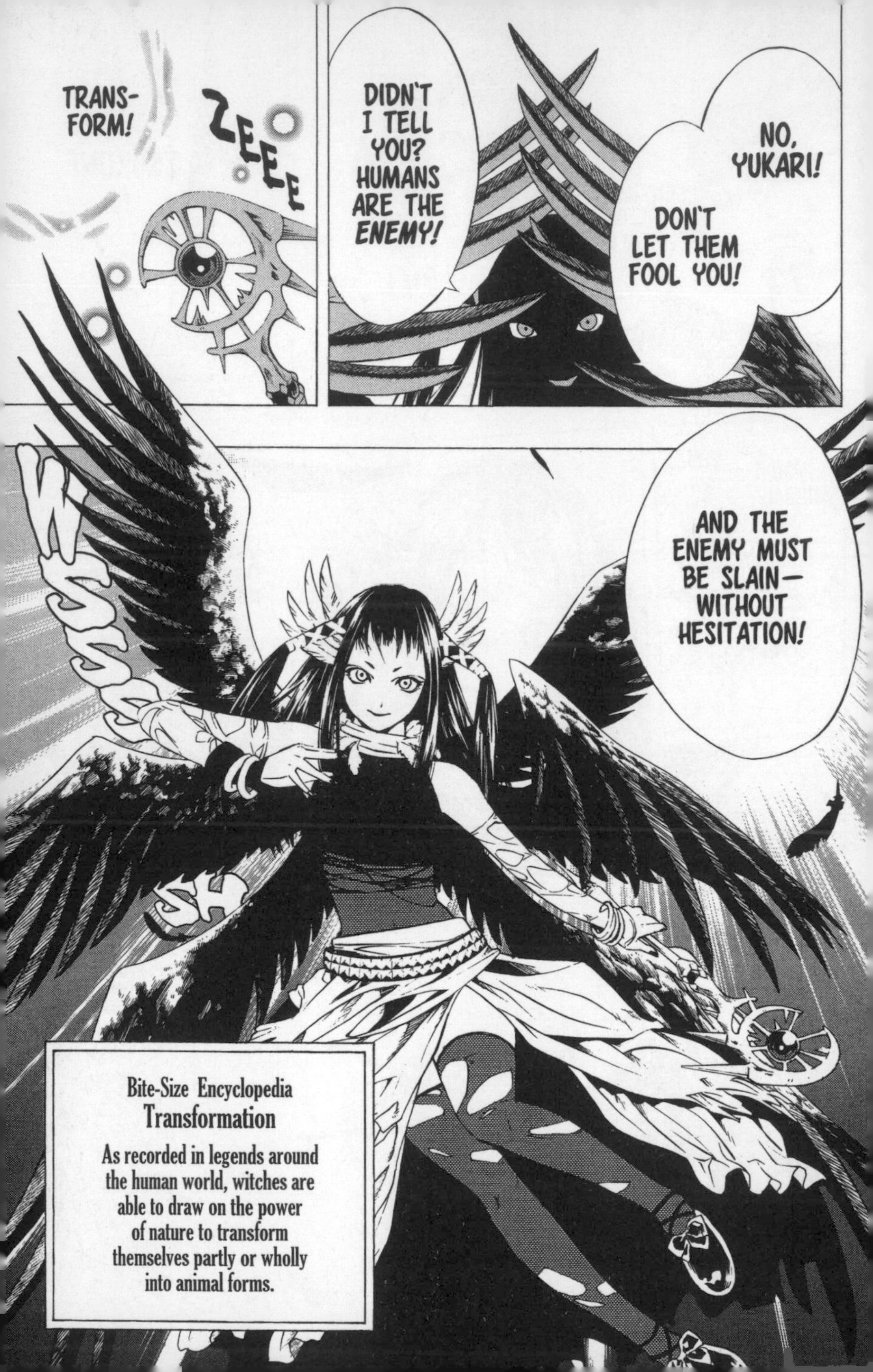
NO, YUKARI!
DON'T LET THEM FOOL YOU!
DIDN'T I TELL YOU? HUMANS ARE THE ENEMY!
TRANS-FORM!
ZEEEE
AND THE ENEMY MUST BE SLAIN—WITHOUT HESITATION!
Bite-Size Encyclopedia
Transformation
As recorded in legends around the human world, witches are able to draw on the power of nature to transform themselves partly or wholly into animal forms.

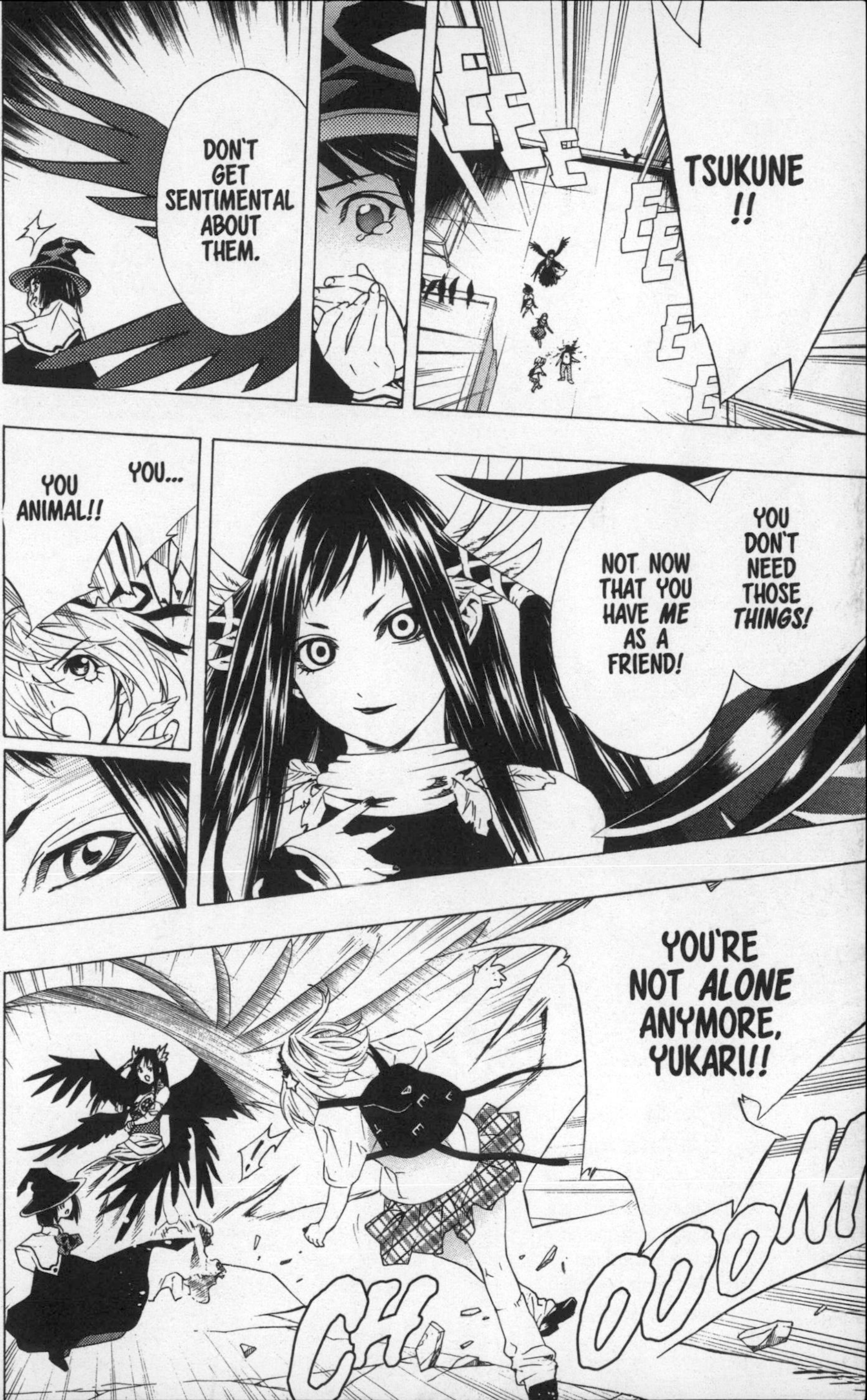
EEEEEEEEEEEE
TSUKUNE !!
DON'T GET SENTIMENTAL ABOUT THEM.
YOU DON'T NEED THOSE *THINGS!*
NOT NOW THAT YOU HAVE *ME* AS A FRIEND!
YOU...
YOU ANIMAL!!
YOU'RE NOT *ALONE* ANYMORE, YUKARI!!
CH OOOOM

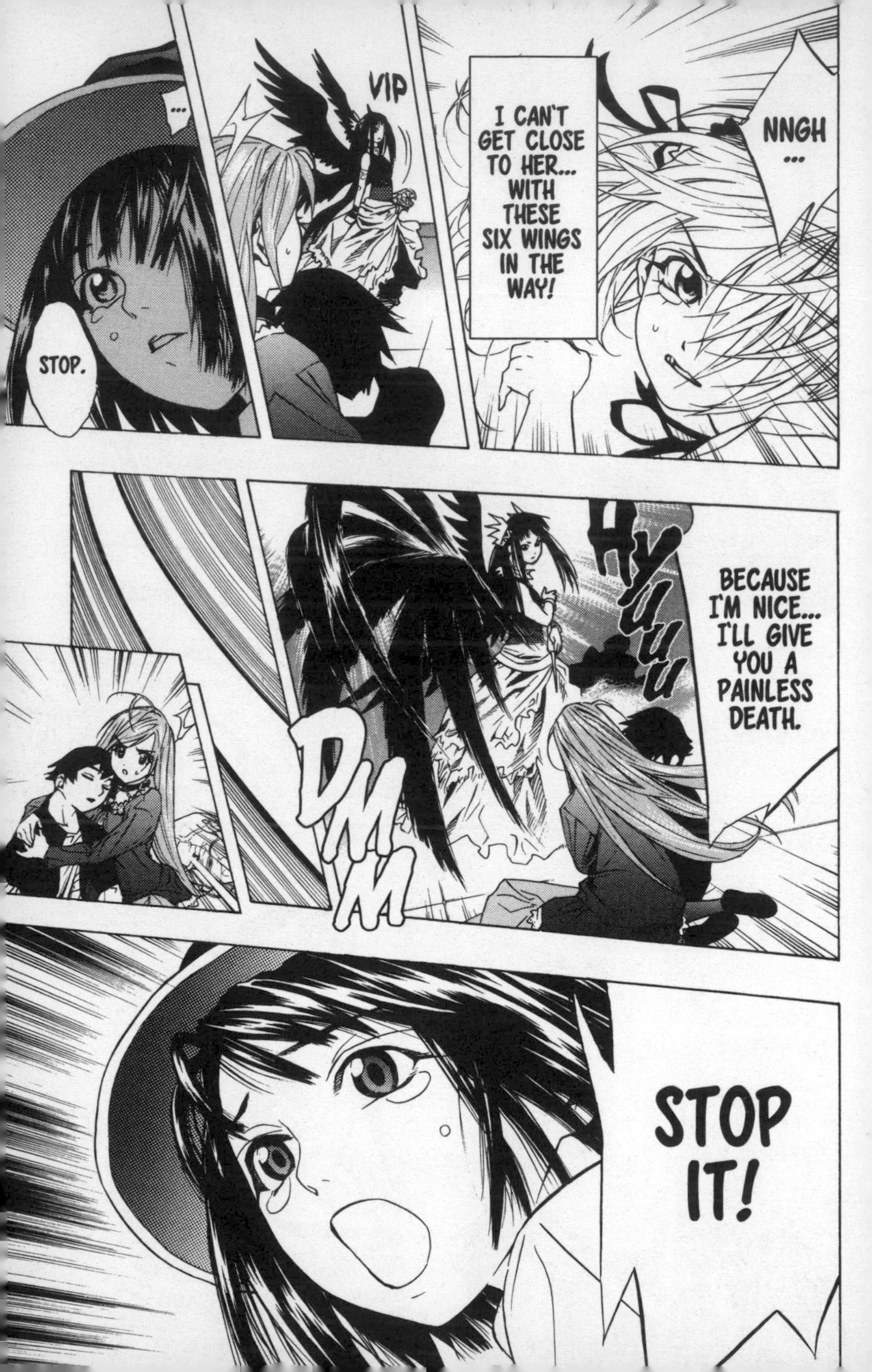
NNGH ...
I CAN'T GET CLOSE TO HER... WITH THESE SIX WINGS IN THE WAY!
VIP
...
STOP.
HYUUU
BECAUSE I'M NICE... I'LL GIVE YOU A PAINLESS DEATH.
DMM
STOP IT!

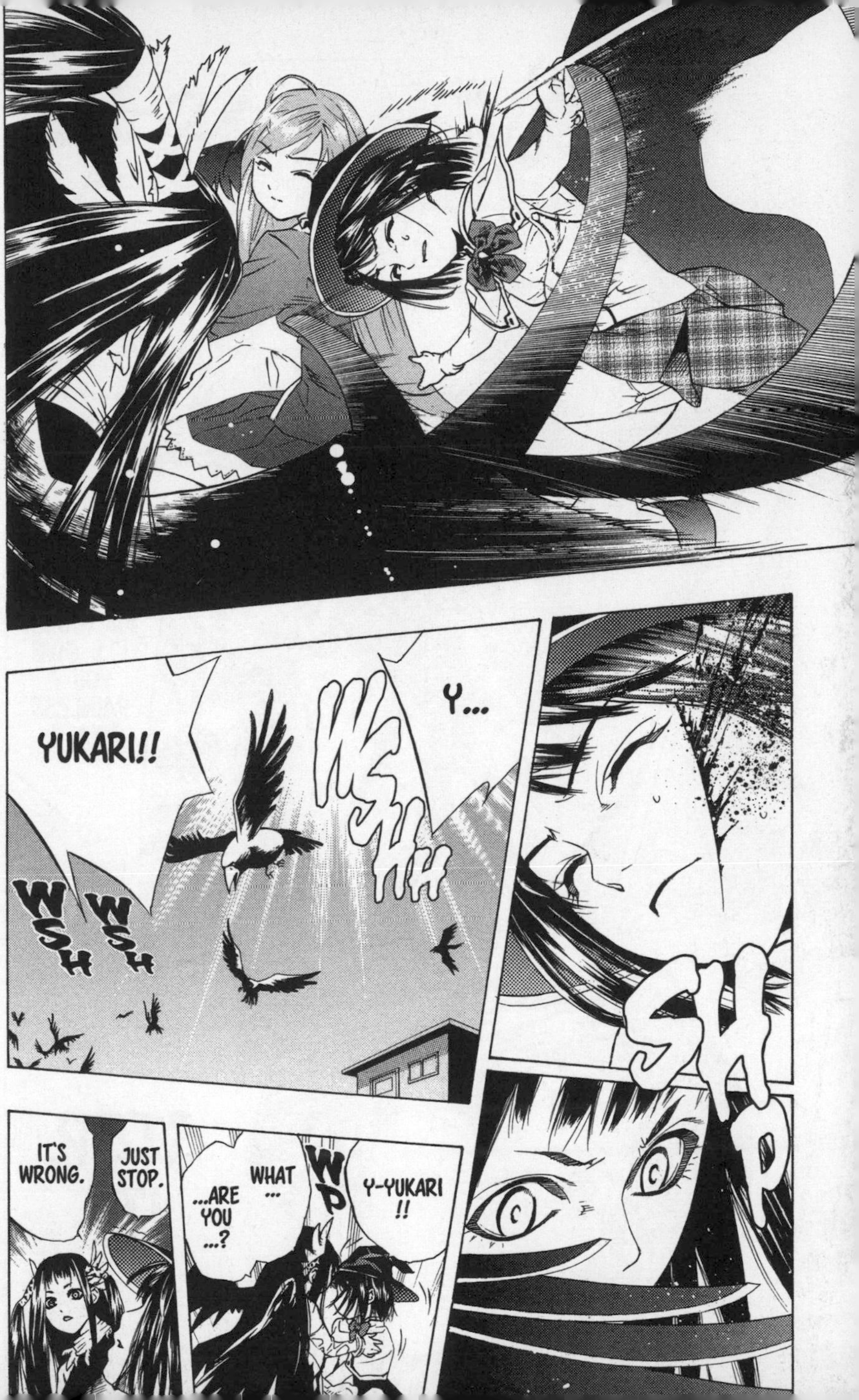
SHP
Y...
WSHHH
YUKARI!!
WSH WSH
Y-YUKARI !!
WP
WHAT ...
...ARE YOU ...?
JUST STOP.
IT'S WRONG.

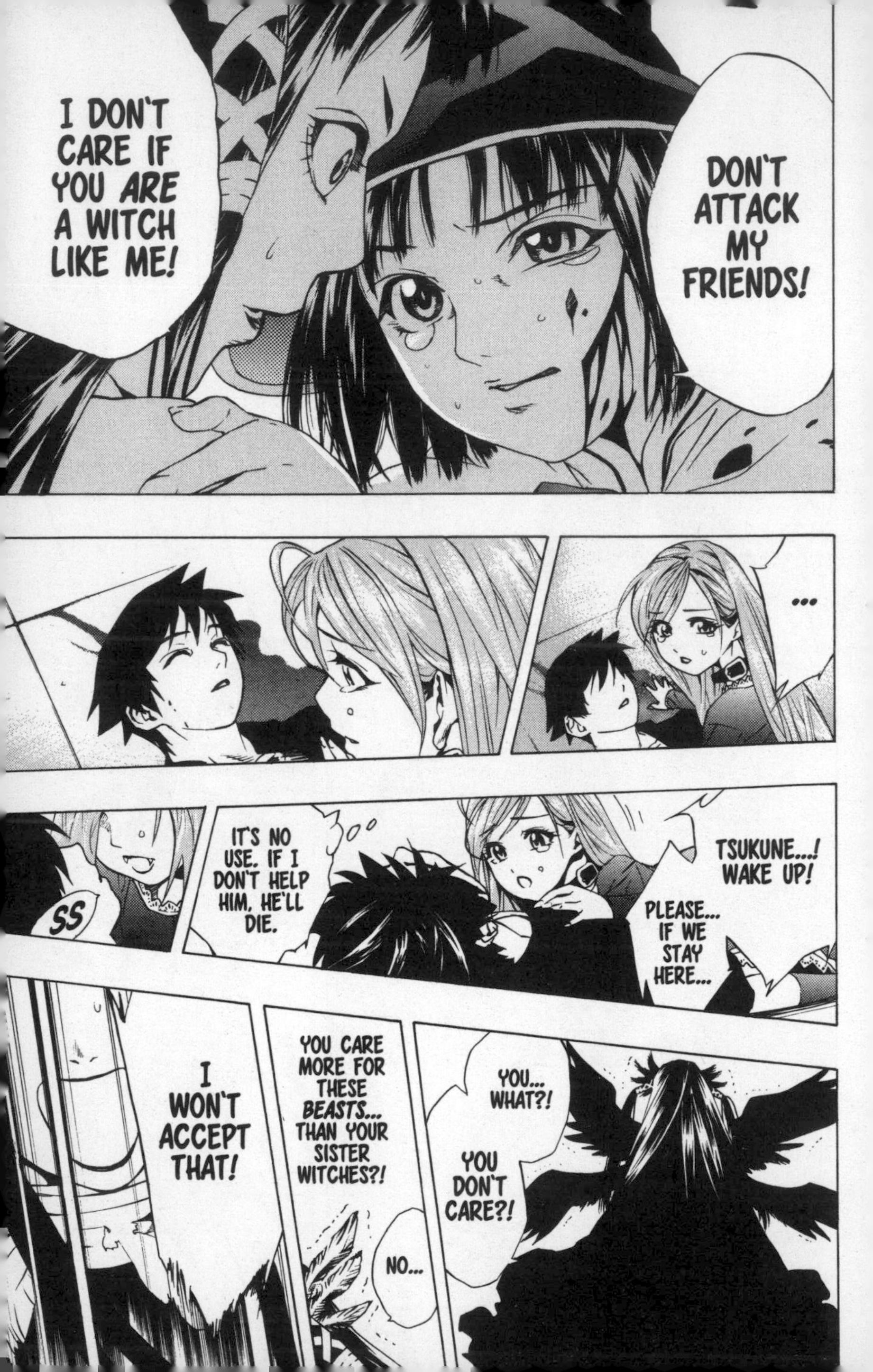
DON'T ATTACK MY FRIENDS!
I DON'T CARE IF YOU *ARE* A WITCH LIKE ME!
...
TSUKUNE...! WAKE UP!
PLEASE... IF WE STAY HERE...
IT'S NO USE. IF I DON'T HELP HIM, HE'LL DIE.
SS
YOU... WHAT?!
YOU DON'T CARE?!
NO...
YOU CARE MORE FOR THESE *BEASTS*... THAN YOUR SISTER WITCHES?!
I WON'T ACCEPT THAT!

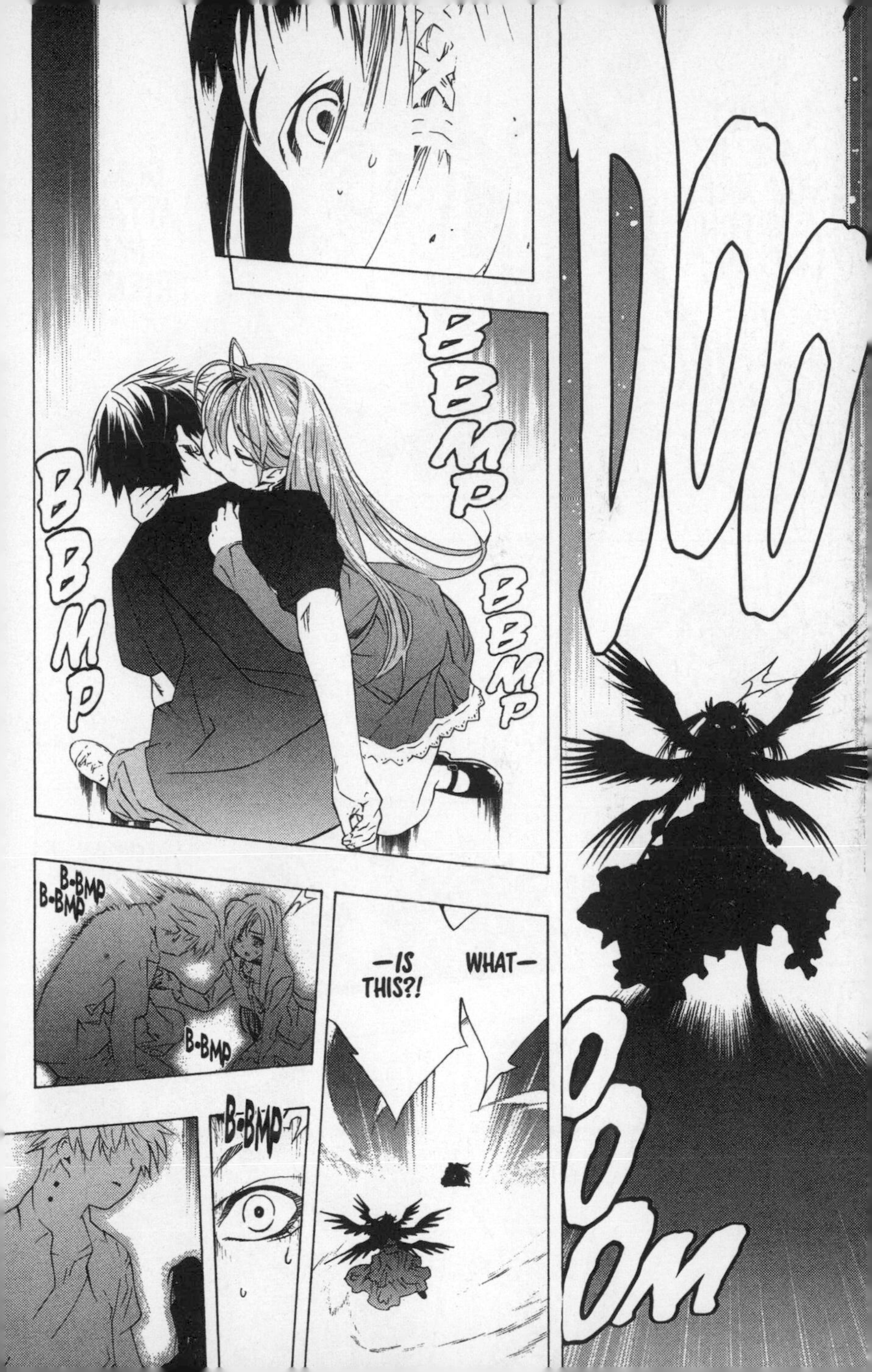
VOO
OOOOM
BBMP
BBMP
BBMP
WHAT—
—IS THIS?!
B-BMP
B-BMP
B-BMP
B-BMP

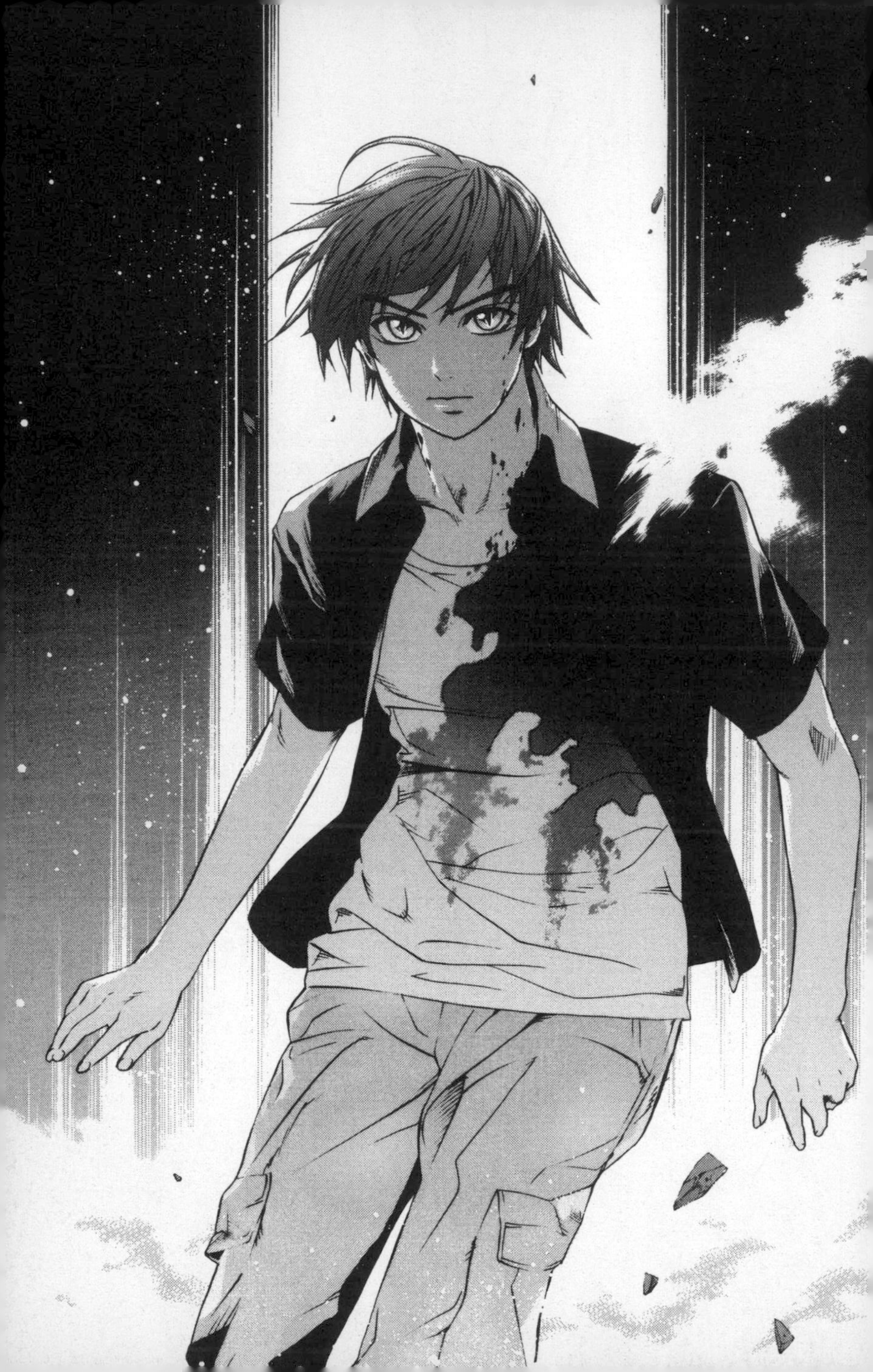

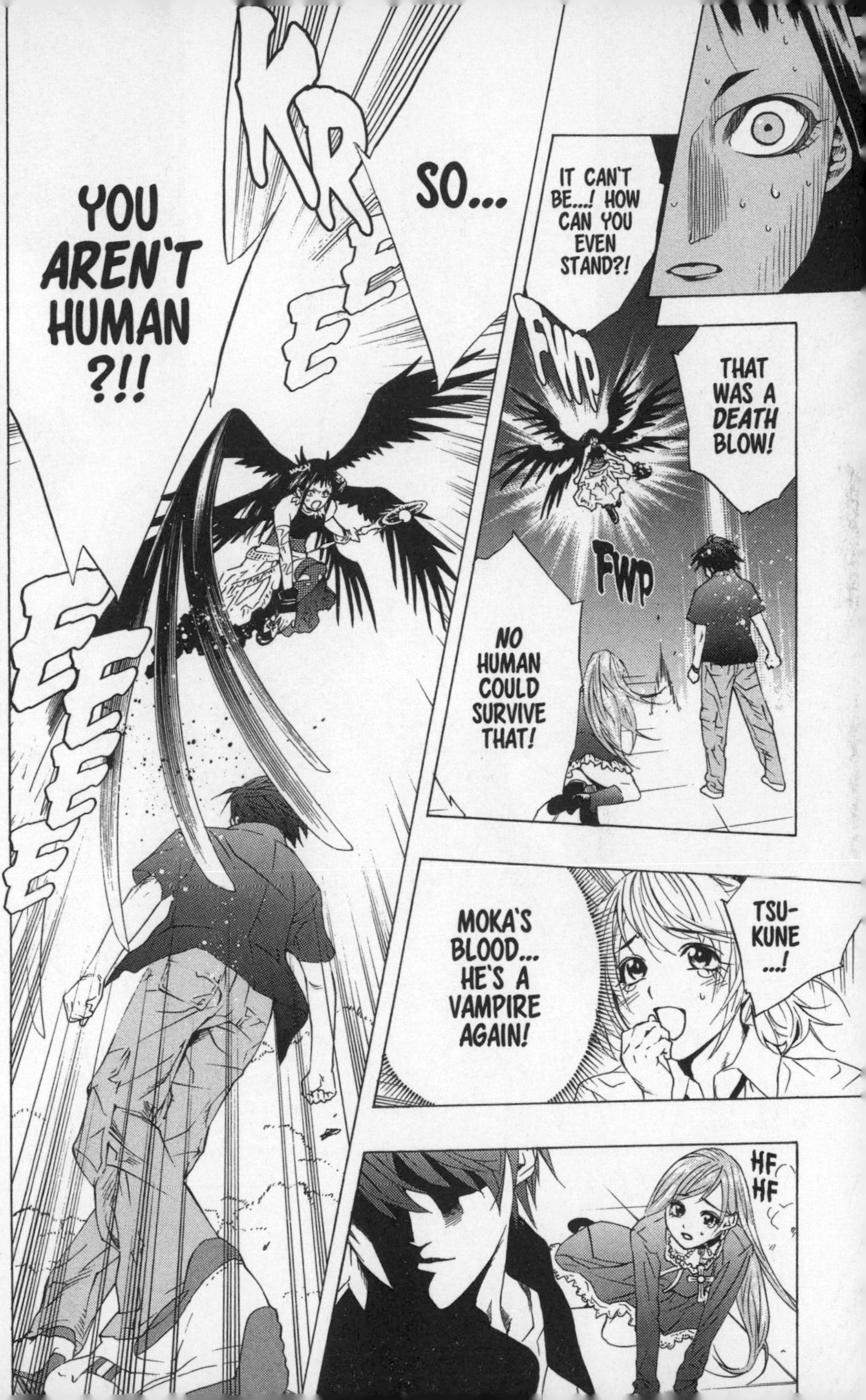
IT CAN'T BE...! HOW CAN YOU EVEN STAND?!
FWP
THAT WAS A DEATH BLOW!
FWP
NO HUMAN COULD SURVIVE THAT!
TSU-KUNE ...!
MOKA'S BLOOD... HE'S A VAMPIRE AGAIN!
HF HF
KREEE
SO...
YOU AREN'T HUMAN ?!!
EEEEE

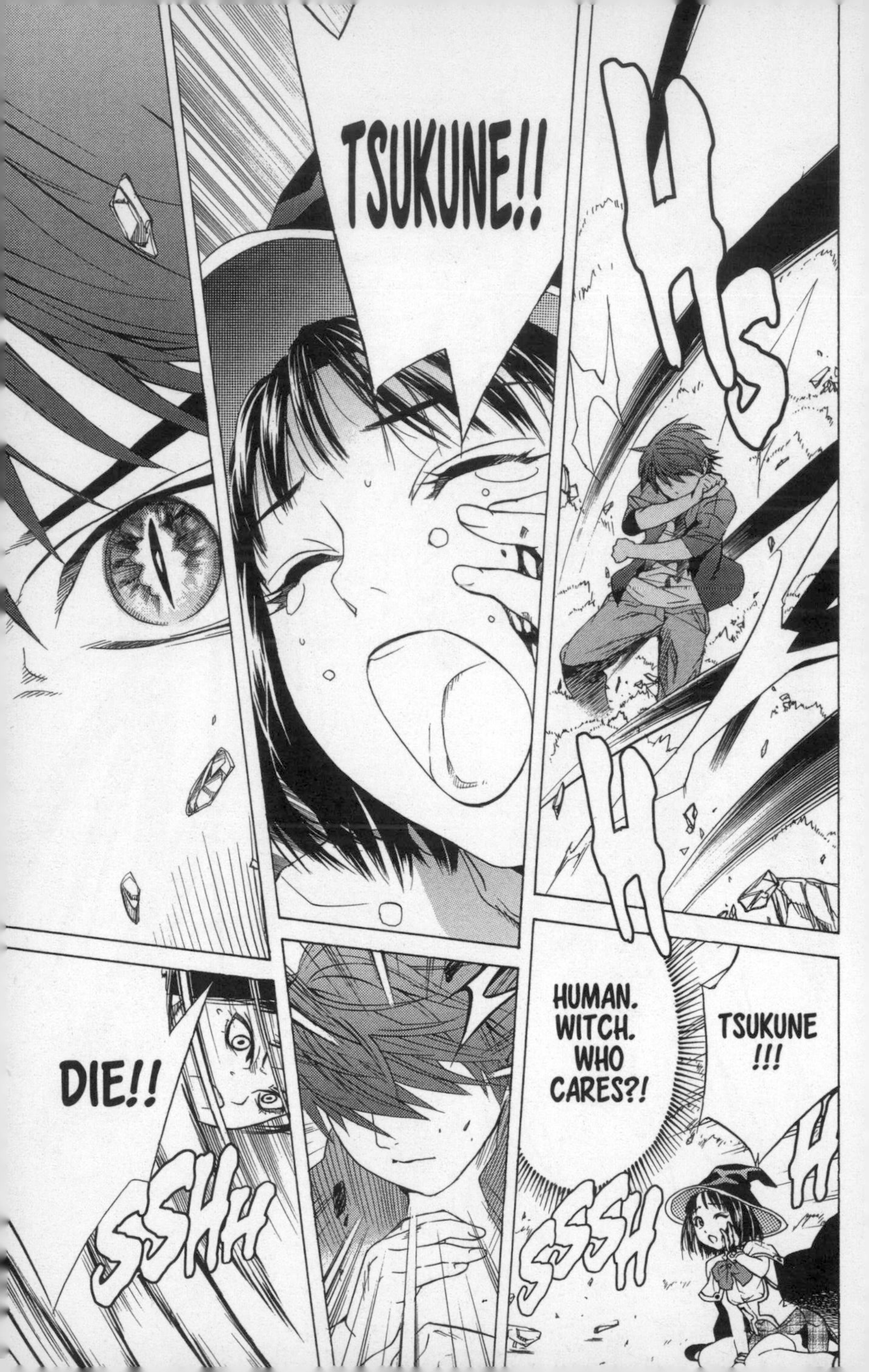
TSUKUNE!!
TSUKUNE !!!
HUMAN. WITCH. WHO CARES?!
SSSH
DIE!!
SSHH

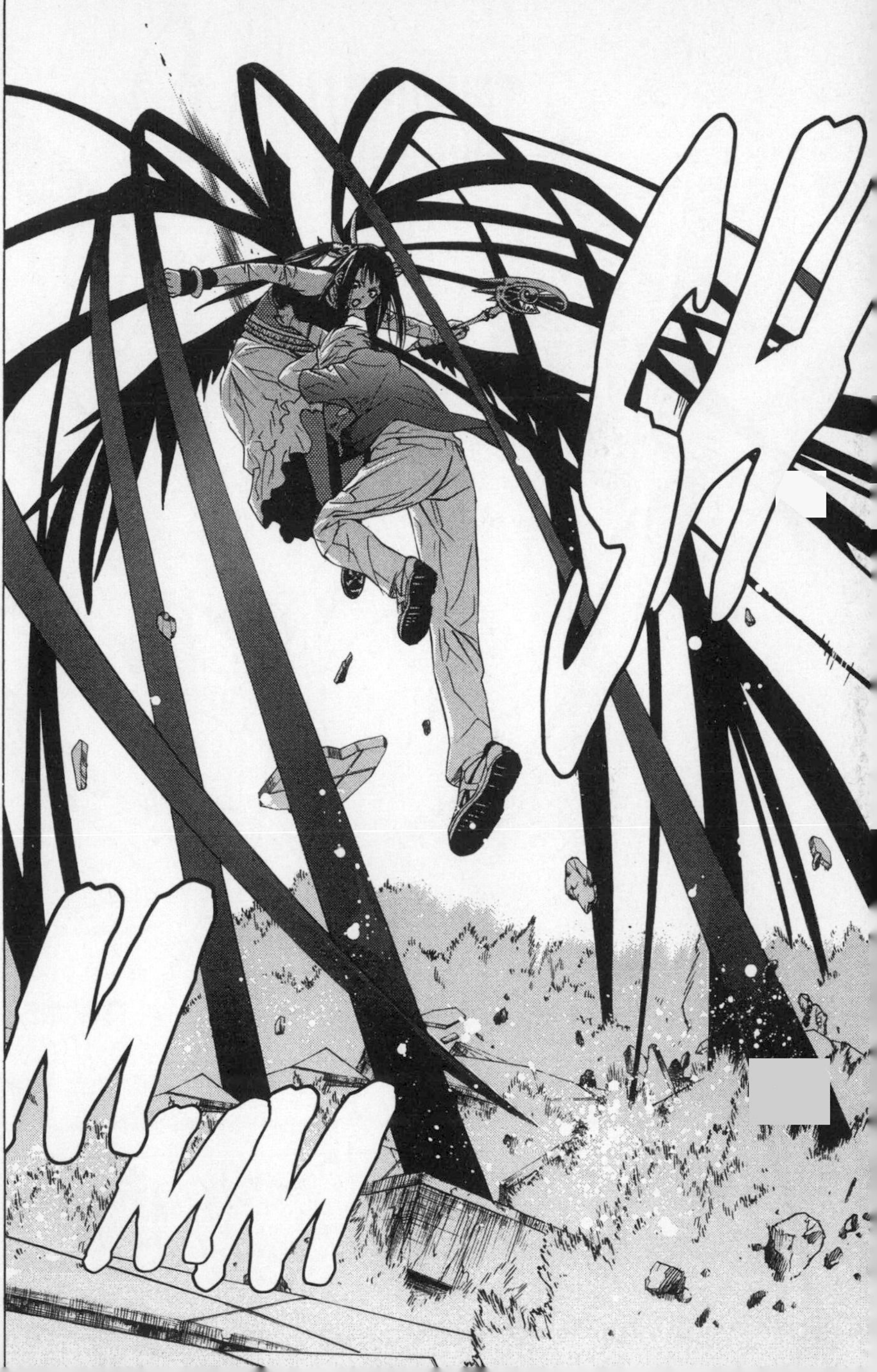
MMM

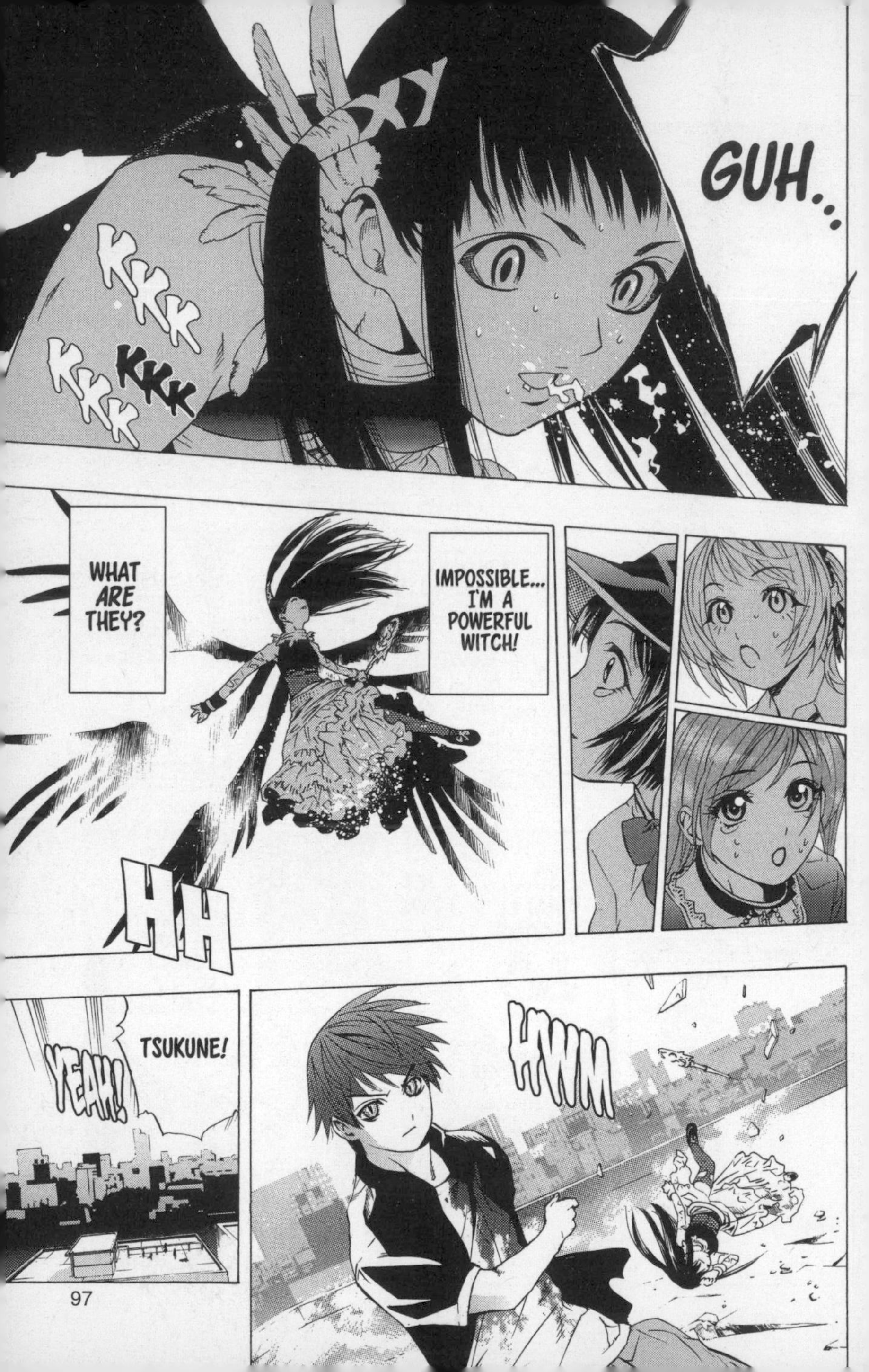
GUH...
KKK
KKK
KKK
IMPOSSIBLE... I'M A POWERFUL WITCH!
WHAT ARE THEY?
HH
HWM
TSUKUNE!
YEAH!!

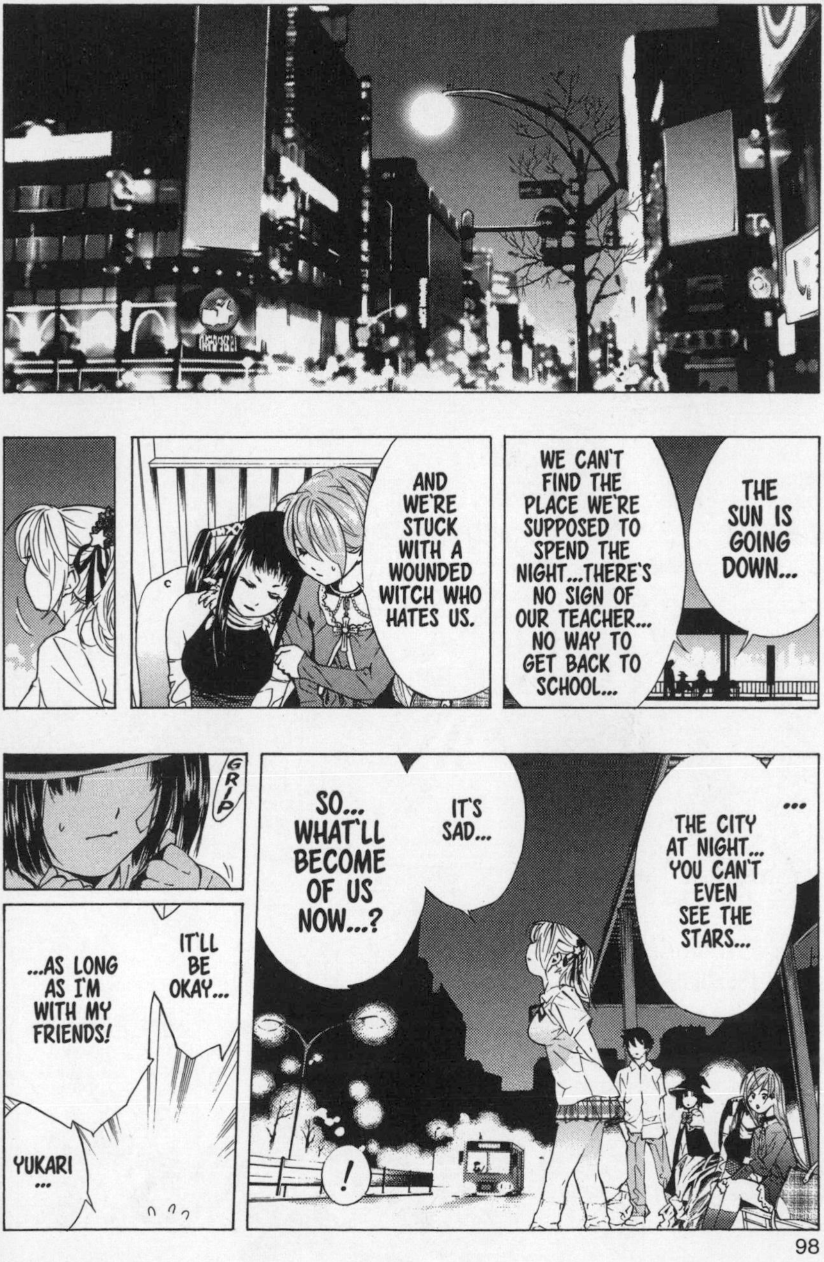
THE SUN IS GOING DOWN...
WE CAN'T FIND THE PLACE WE'RE SUPPOSED TO SPEND THE NIGHT...THERE'S NO SIGN OF OUR TEACHER... NO WAY TO GET BACK TO SCHOOL...
AND WE'RE STUCK WITH A WOUNDED WITCH WHO HATES US.
...
THE CITY AT NIGHT... YOU CAN'T EVEN SEE THE STARS...
IT'S SAD...
SO... WHAT'LL BECOME OF US NOW...?
!
GRIP
IT'LL BE OKAY...
...AS LONG AS I'M WITH MY FRIENDS!
YUKARI ...

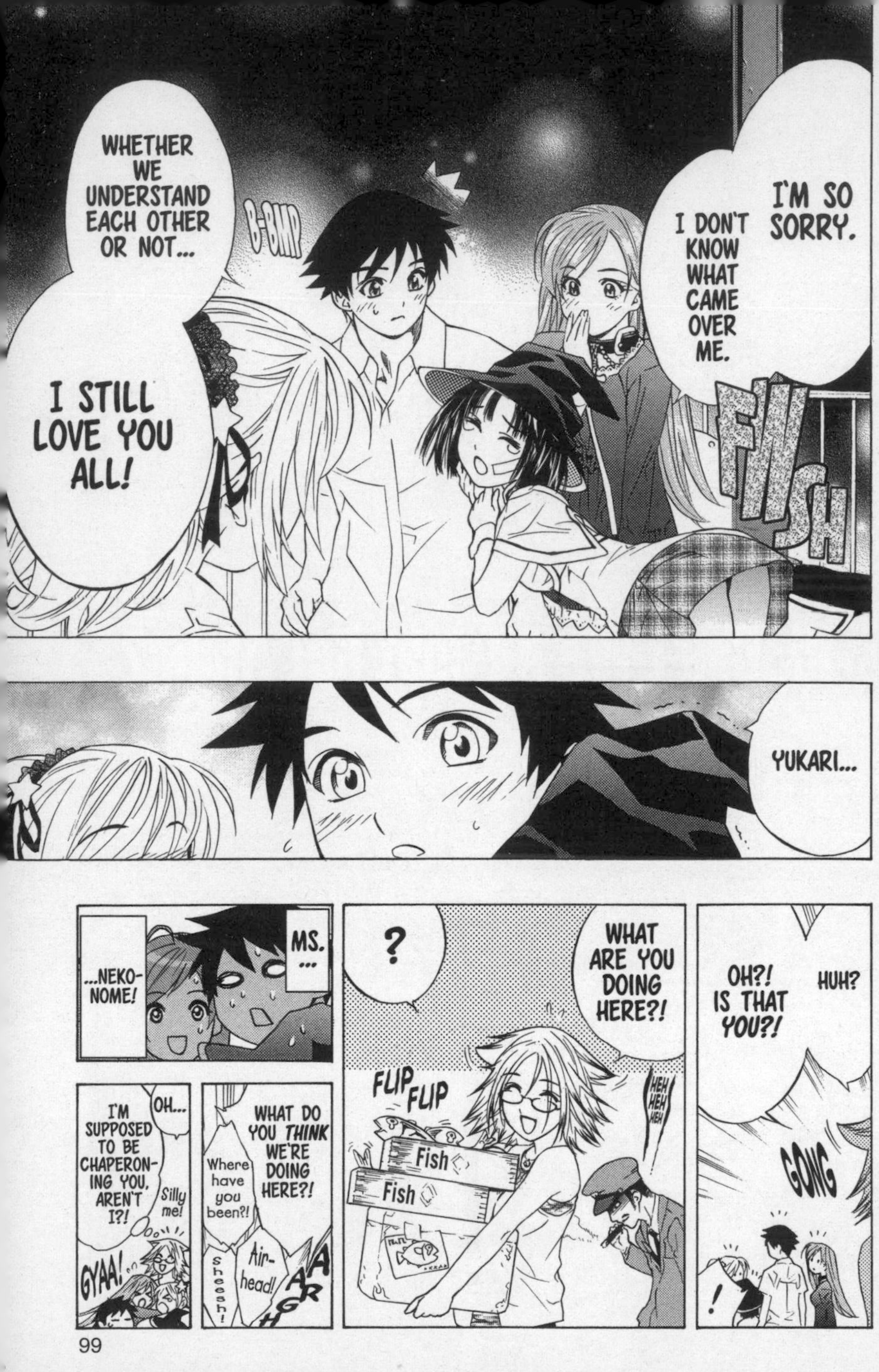
I'M SO SORRY.
I DON'T KNOW WHAT CAME OVER ME.
FWISH
B-BMP
WHETHER WE UNDERSTAND EACH OTHER OR NOT...
I STILL LOVE YOU ALL!
YUKARI...
HUH?
OH?! IS THAT YOU?!
GONG
WHAT ARE YOU DOING HERE?!
?
FLIP FLIP
HEH HEH HEH
MS. ...
...NEKO-NOME!
WHAT DO YOU THINK WE'RE DOING HERE?!
Where have you been?!
Air-head!
AARGH
Sheesh!
OH...
I'M SUPPOSED TO BE CHAPERONING YOU, AREN'T I?!
Silly me!
GYAA!

15: Can't We All Just Get Along?

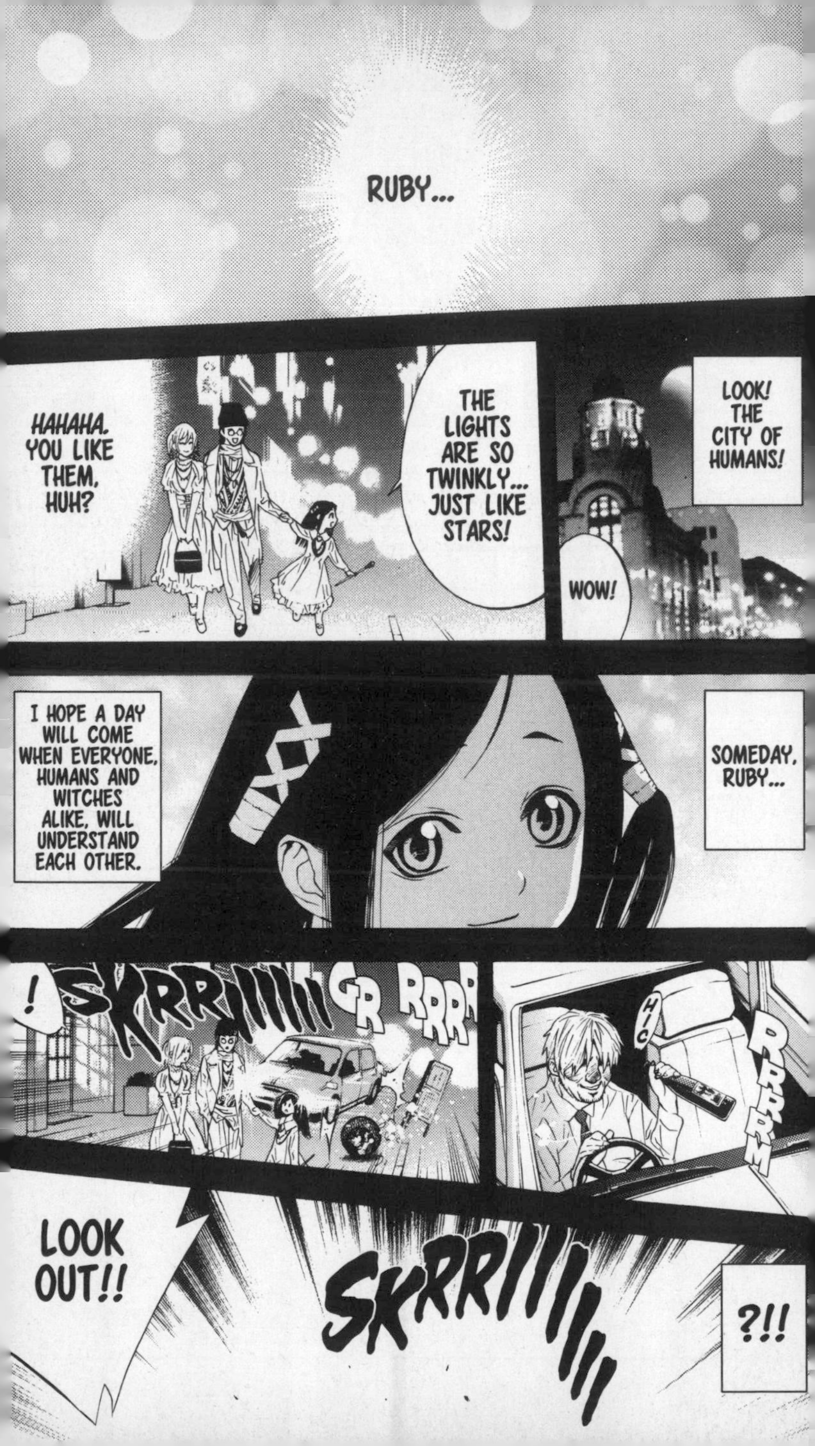
RUBY...
LOOK! THE CITY OF HUMANS!
WOW!
THE LIGHTS ARE SO TWINKLY... JUST LIKE STARS!
HAHAHA. YOU LIKE THEM, HUH?
SOMEDAY, RUBY...
I HOPE A DAY WILL COME WHEN EVERYONE, HUMANS AND WITCHES ALIKE, WILL UNDERSTAND EACH OTHER.
HIC
RRRRM
GR RRRR
SKRRIIIII
!
?!!
SKRRIIIIII
LOOK OUT!!

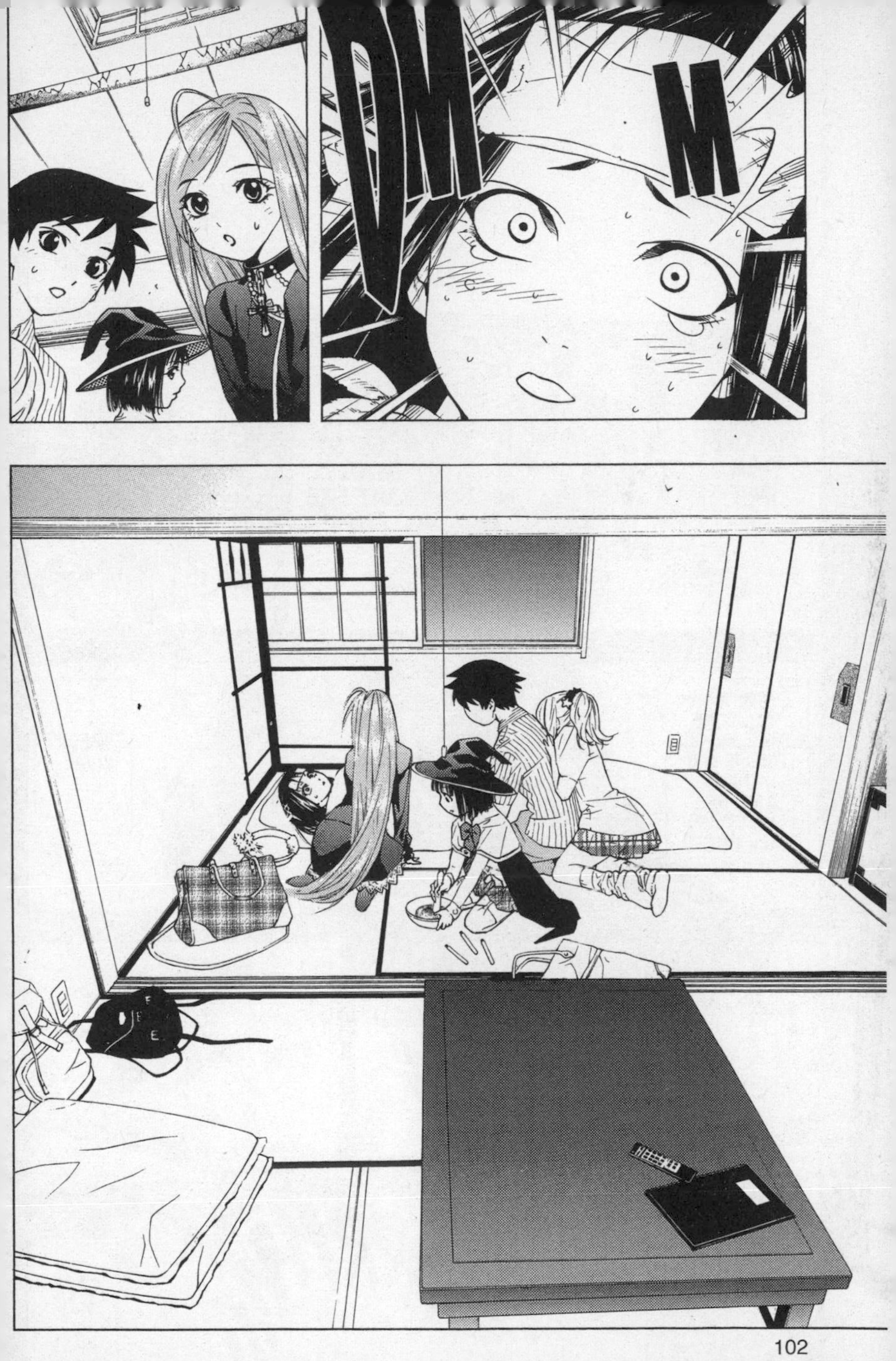
DM
M

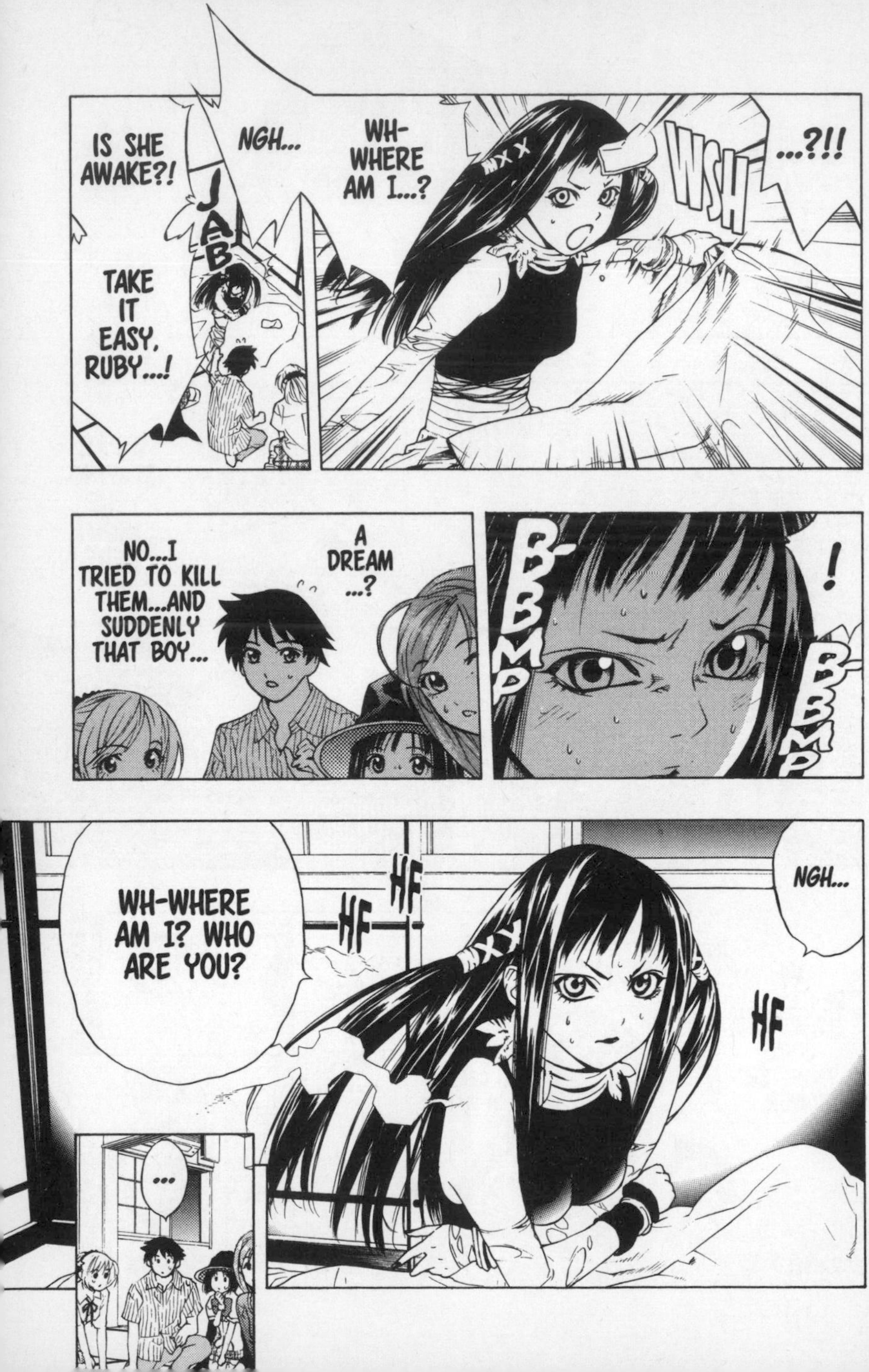
...?!!
WSH
WH-WHERE AM I...?
NGH...
IS SHE AWAKE?!
JAB
TAKE IT EASY, RUBY...!
!
B-BMP
BMP
A DREAM ...?
NO...I TRIED TO KILL THEM...AND SUDDENLY THAT BOY...
NGH...
HF
HF
HF
WH-WHERE AM I? WHO ARE YOU?
...

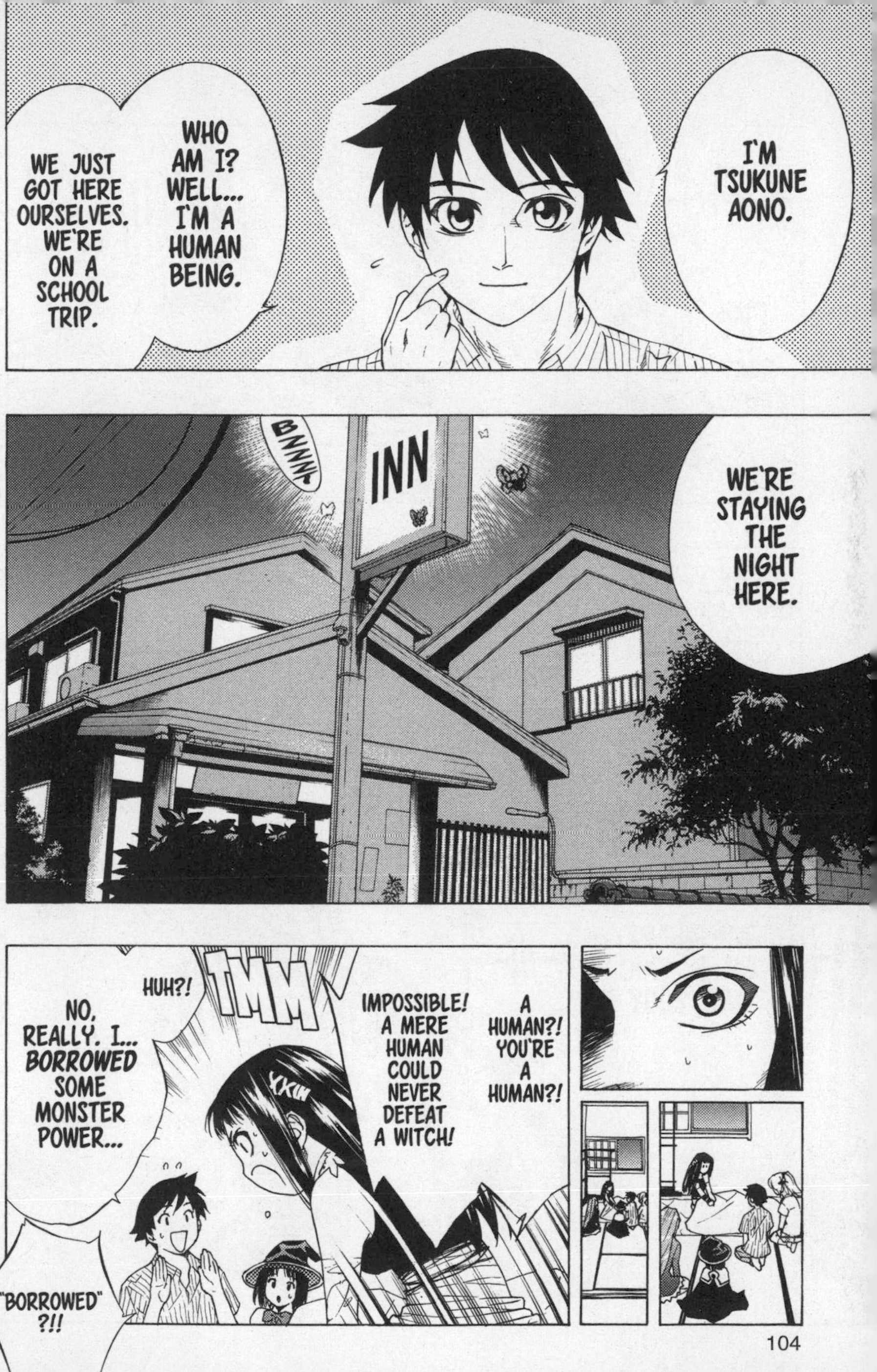
I'M TSUKUNE AONO.
WHO AM I? WELL... I'M A HUMAN BEING.
WE JUST GOT HERE OURSELVES. WE'RE ON A SCHOOL TRIP.
WE'RE STAYING THE NIGHT HERE.
INN
A HUMAN?! YOU'RE A HUMAN?!
IMPOSSIBLE! A MERE HUMAN COULD NEVER DEFEAT A WITCH!
TMM
HUH?!
NO, REALLY. I... BORROWED SOME MONSTER POWER...
"BORROWED"?!!

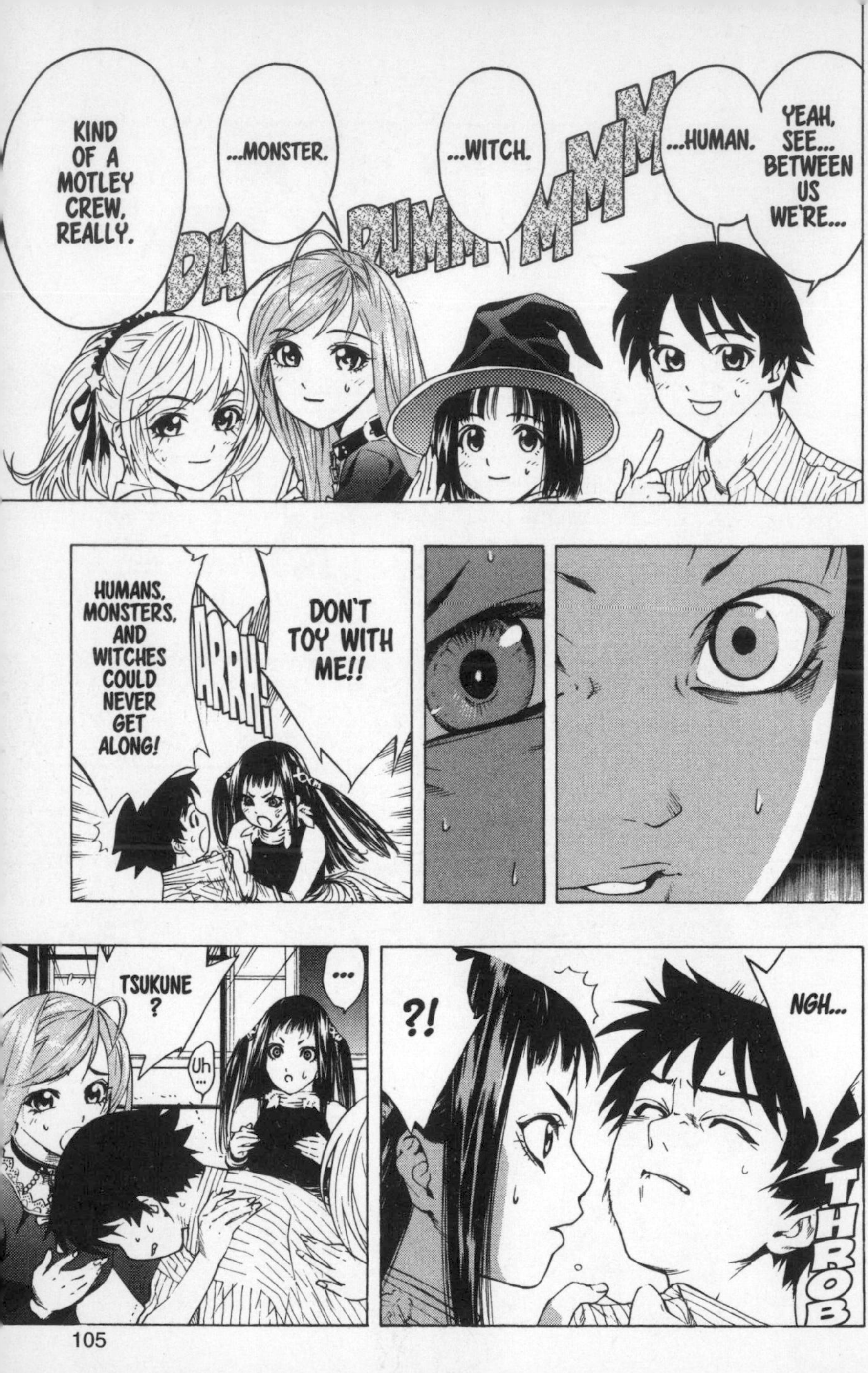
YEAH, SEE... BETWEEN US WE'RE...
...HUMAN.
...WITCH.
...MONSTER.
KIND OF A MOTLEY CREW, REALLY.
DA DUMMMMMM
DON'T TOY WITH ME!!
ARRH!
HUMANS, MONSTERS, AND WITCHES COULD NEVER GET ALONG!
NGH...
THROB
?!
...
TSUKUNE?
Uh...

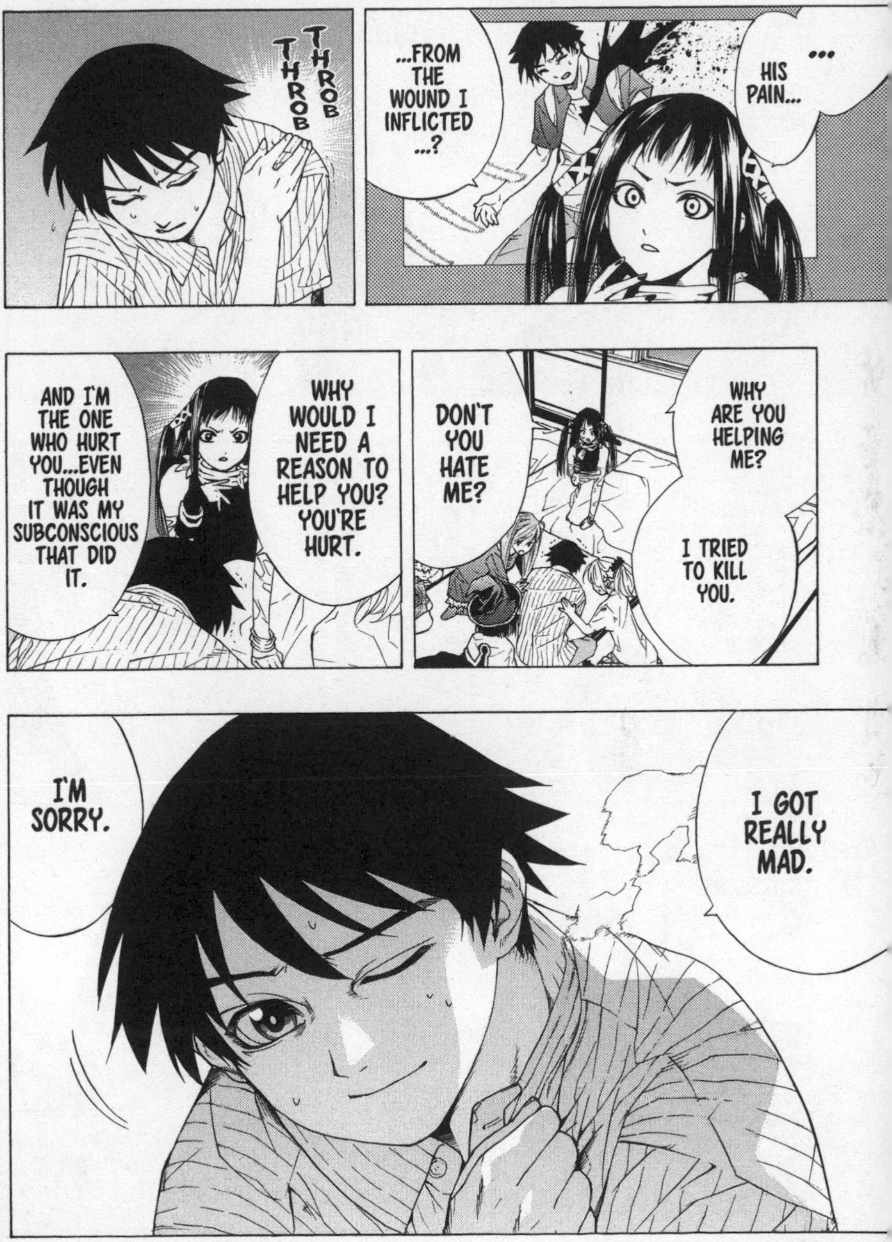
...
HIS PAIN...
...FROM THE WOUND I INFLICTED ...?
THROB THROB
WHY ARE YOU HELPING ME?
I TRIED TO KILL YOU.
DON'T YOU HATE ME?
WHY WOULD I NEED A REASON TO HELP YOU? YOU'RE HURT.
AND I'M THE ONE WHO HURT YOU...EVEN THOUGH IT WAS MY SUBCONSCIOUS THAT DID IT.
I GOT REALLY MAD.
I'M SORRY.

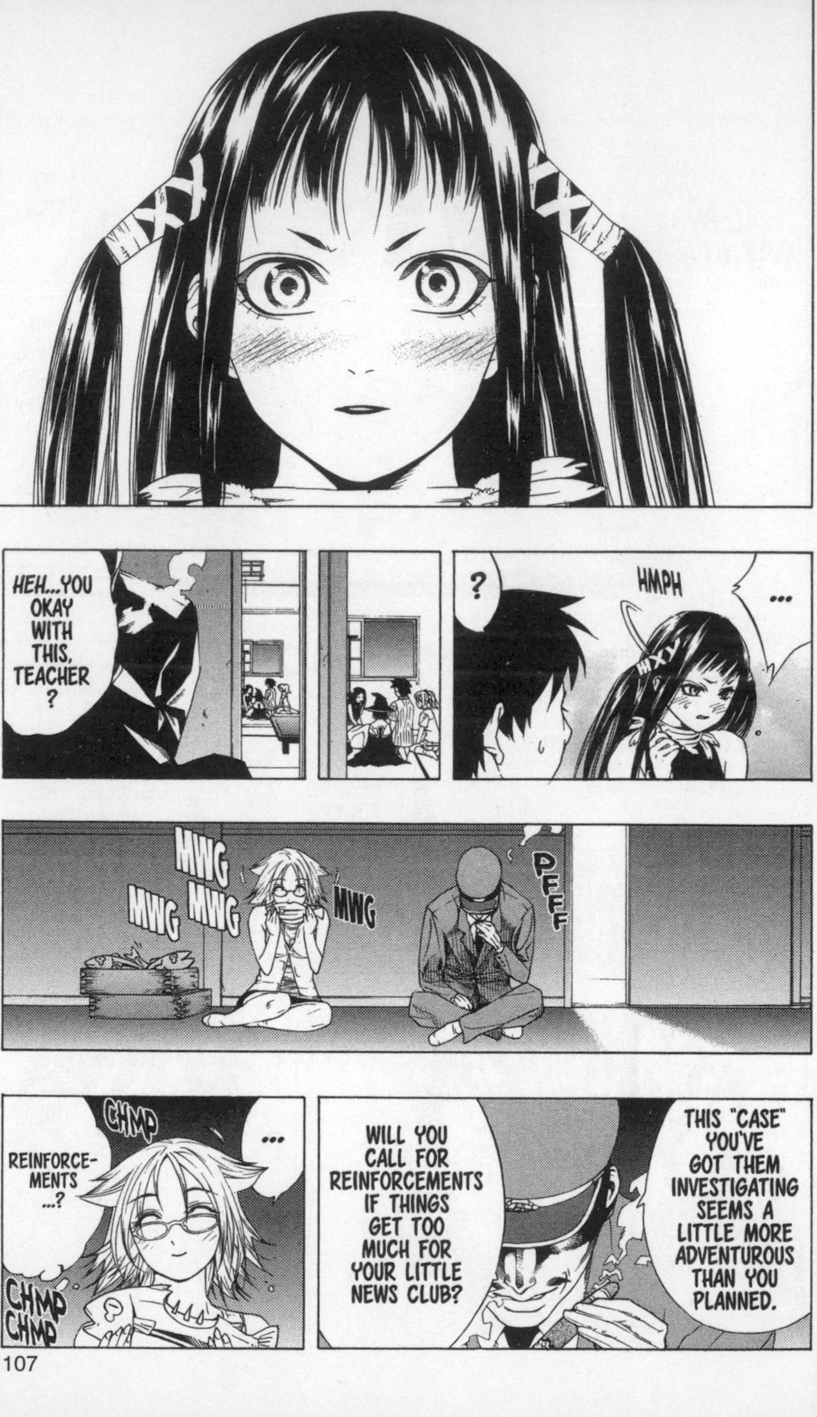
...
HMPH
?
HEH...YOU OKAY WITH THIS, TEACHER?
PFFF
MWG
MWG MWG
MWG
THIS "CASE" YOU'VE GOT THEM INVESTIGATING SEEMS A LITTLE MORE ADVENTUROUS THAN YOU PLANNED.
WILL YOU CALL FOR REINFORCEMENTS IF THINGS GET TOO MUCH FOR YOUR LITTLE NEWS CLUB?
CHMP
...
REINFORCE-MENTS ...?
CHMP CHMP

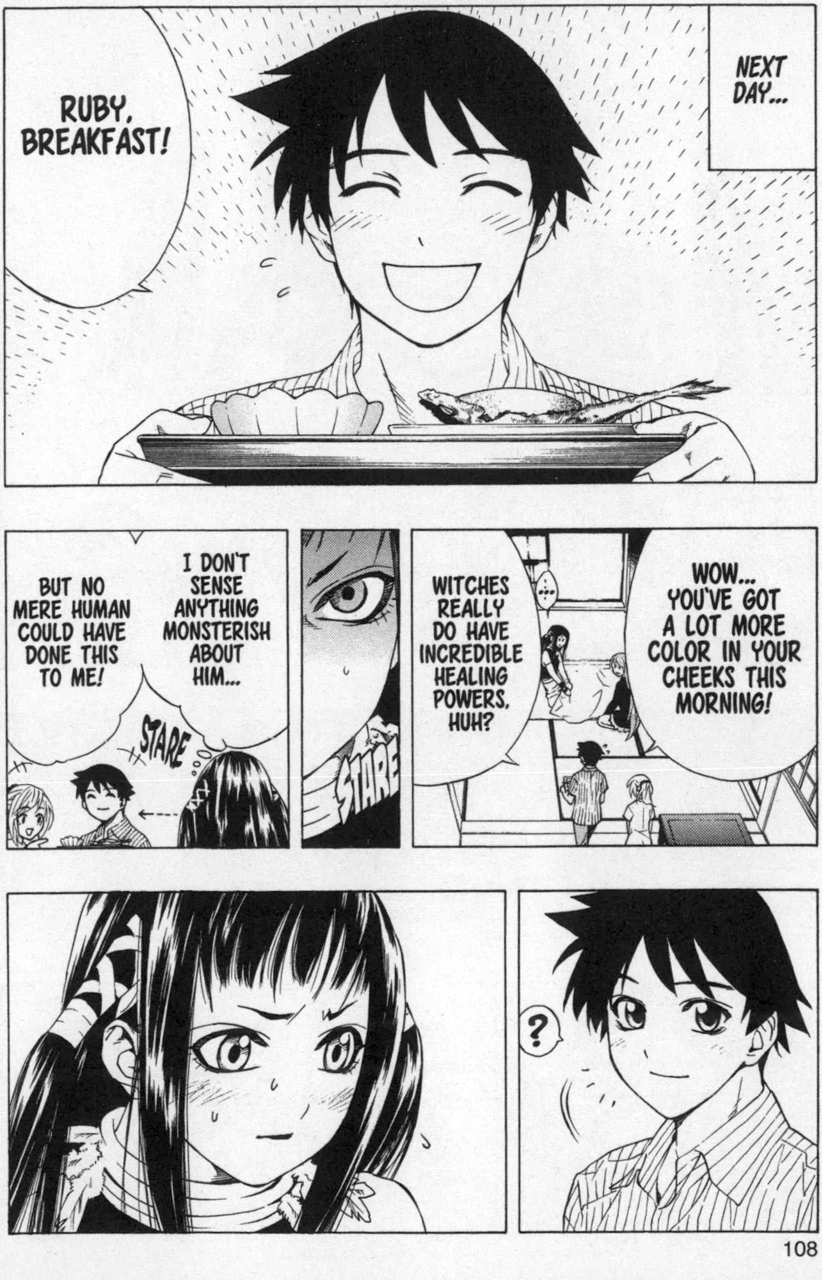
NEXT DAY...
RUBY, BREAKFAST!
WOW... YOU'VE GOT A LOT MORE COLOR IN YOUR CHEEKS THIS MORNING!
WITCHES REALLY DO HAVE INCREDIBLE HEALING POWERS, HUH?
STARE
I DON'T SENSE ANYTHING MONSTERISH ABOUT HIM...
BUT NO MERE HUMAN COULD HAVE DONE THIS TO ME!
STARE
?

READ THIS WAY

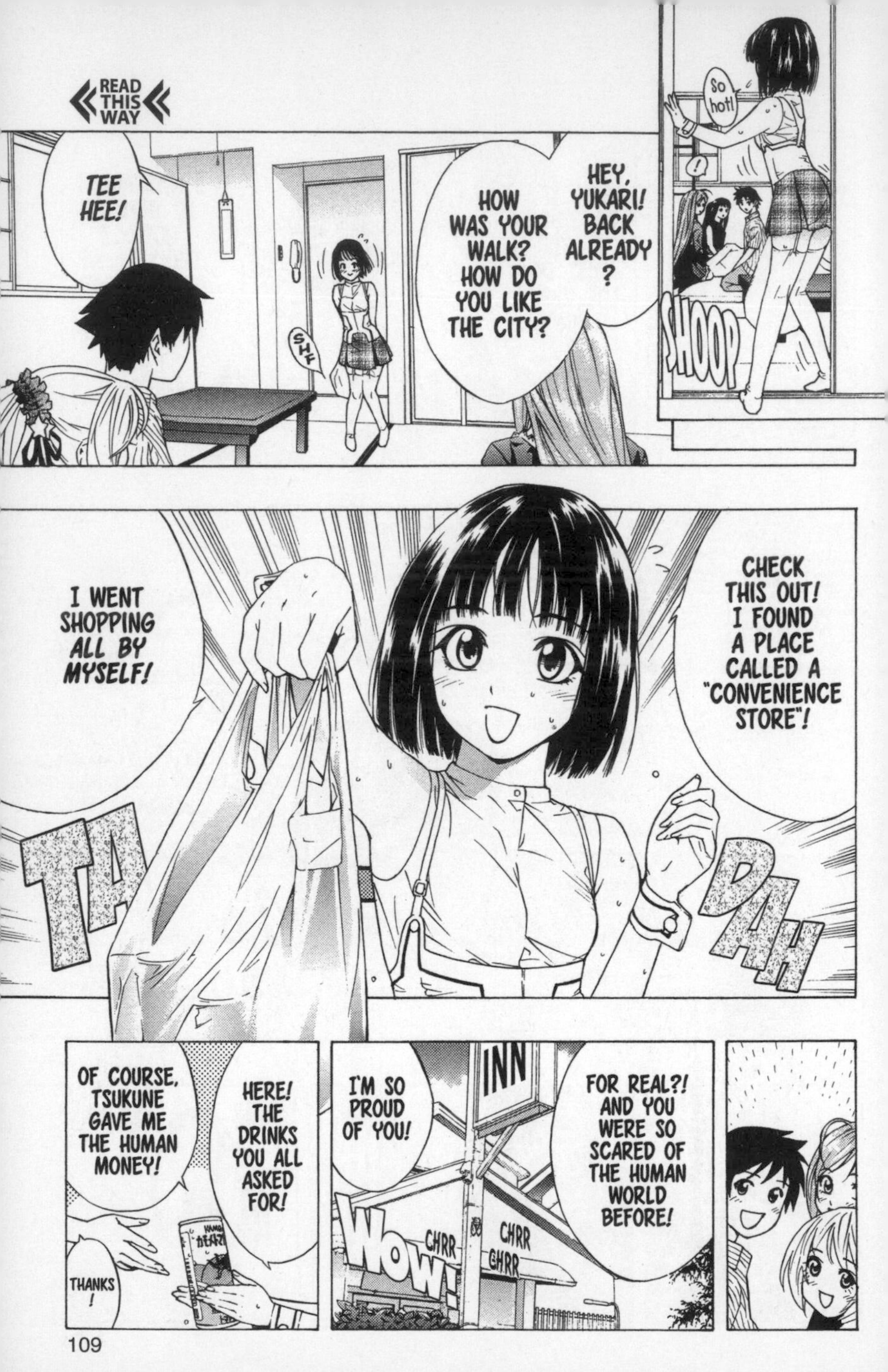

So hot!
!
SHOOP
HEY, YUKARI! BACK ALREADY?
HOW WAS YOUR WALK? HOW DO YOU LIKE THE CITY?
SHF
TEE HEE!
CHECK THIS OUT! I FOUND A PLACE CALLED A "CONVENIENCE STORE"!
I WENT SHOPPING ALL BY MYSELF!
TA
DAH
FOR REAL?! AND YOU WERE SO SCARED OF THE HUMAN WORLD BEFORE!
I'M SO PROUD OF YOU!
INN
WOW!
CHRR
CHRR
CHRR
HERE! THE DRINKS YOU ALL ASKED FOR!
OF COURSE, TSUKUNE GAVE ME THE HUMAN MONEY!
THANKS!

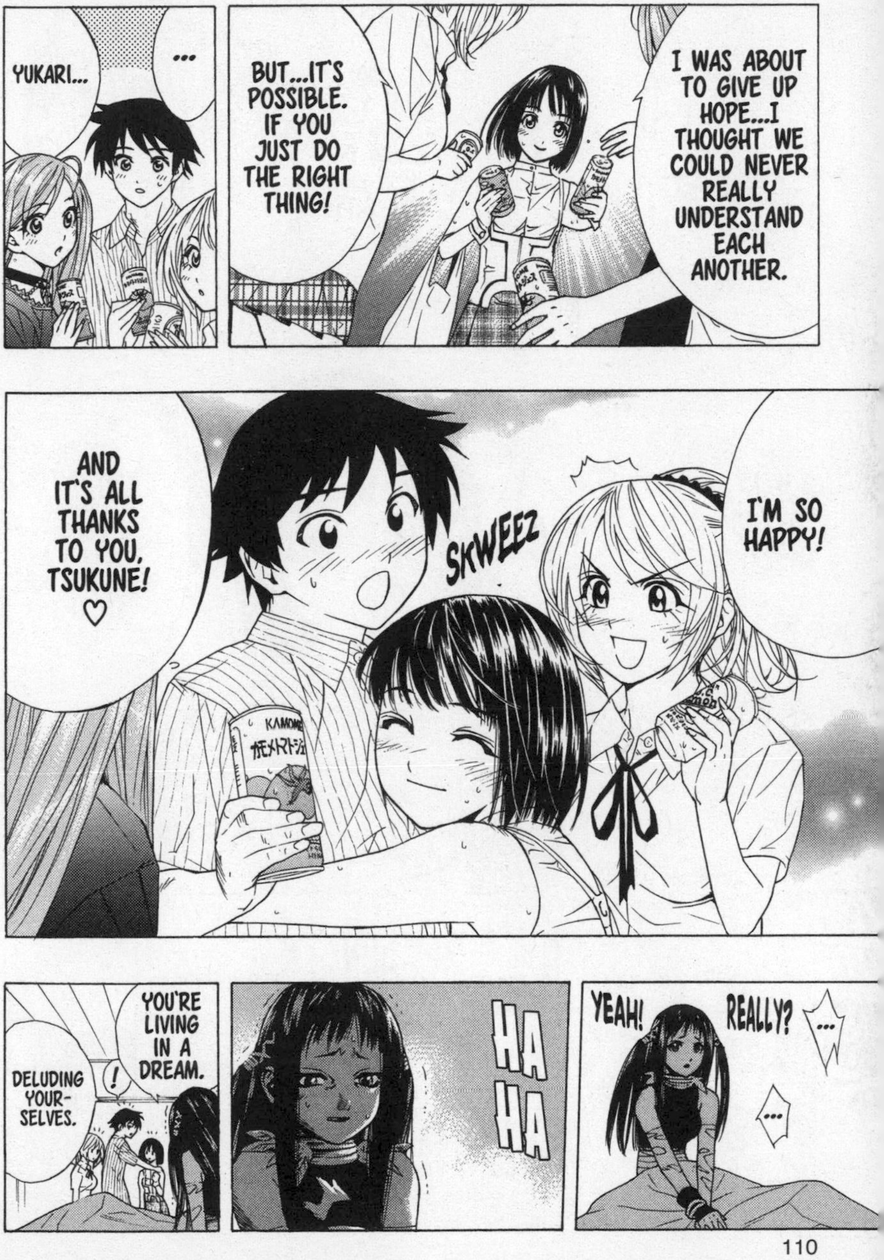
I WAS ABOUT TO GIVE UP HOPE...I THOUGHT WE COULD NEVER REALLY UNDERSTAND EACH ANOTHER.
BUT...IT'S POSSIBLE. IF YOU JUST DO THE RIGHT THING!
...
YUKARI...
I'M SO HAPPY!
SKWEEZ
AND IT'S ALL THANKS TO YOU, TSUKUNE! ♡
...
REALLY?
YEAH!
...
HA HA
YOU'RE LIVING IN A DREAM.
!
DELUDING YOUR-SELVES.

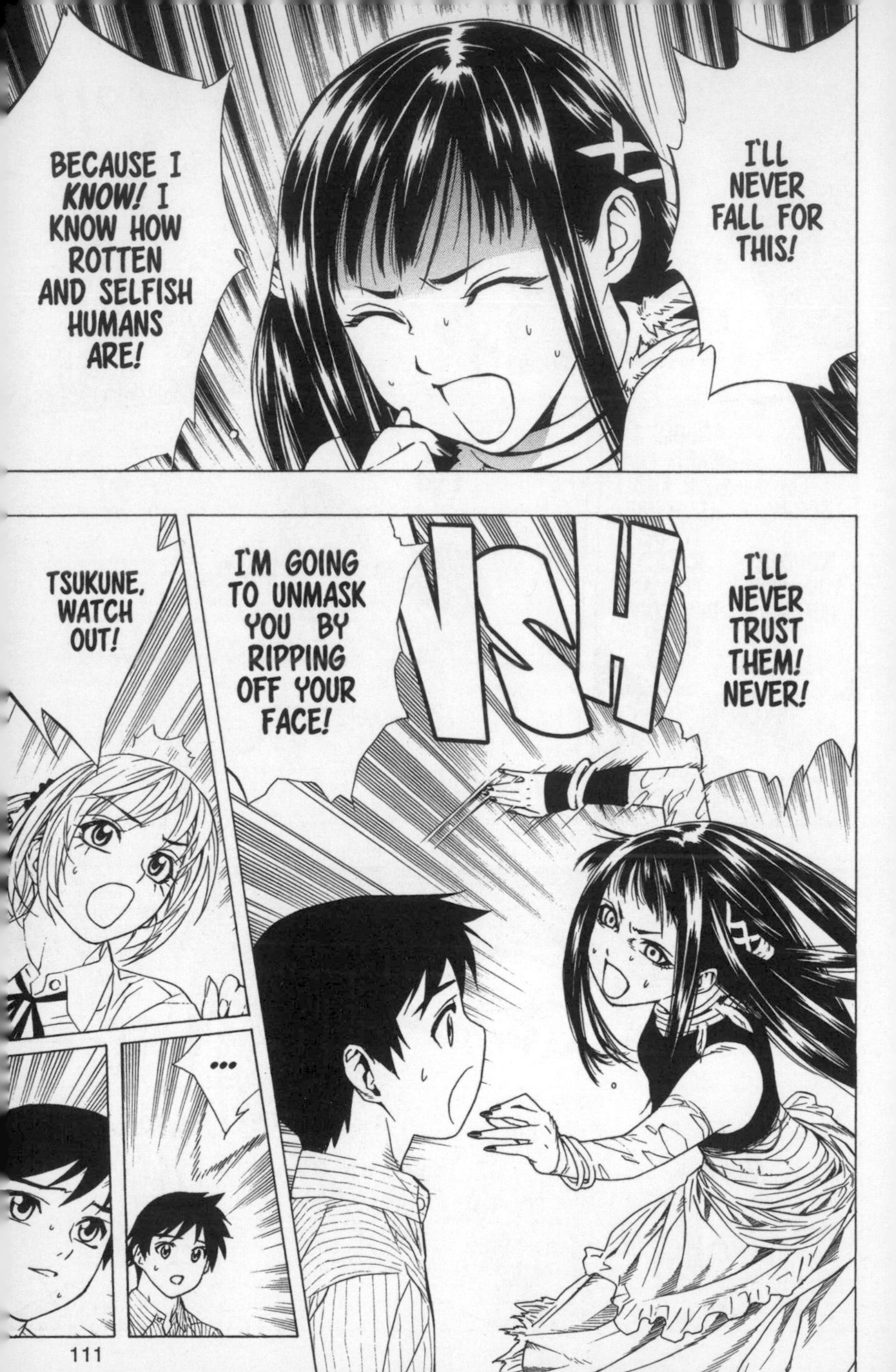
I'LL NEVER FALL FOR THIS!
BECAUSE I KNOW! I KNOW HOW ROTTEN AND SELFISH HUMANS ARE!
I'LL NEVER TRUST THEM! NEVER!
VSH
I'M GOING TO UNMASK YOU BY RIPPING OFF YOUR FACE!
TSUKUNE, WATCH OUT!
...

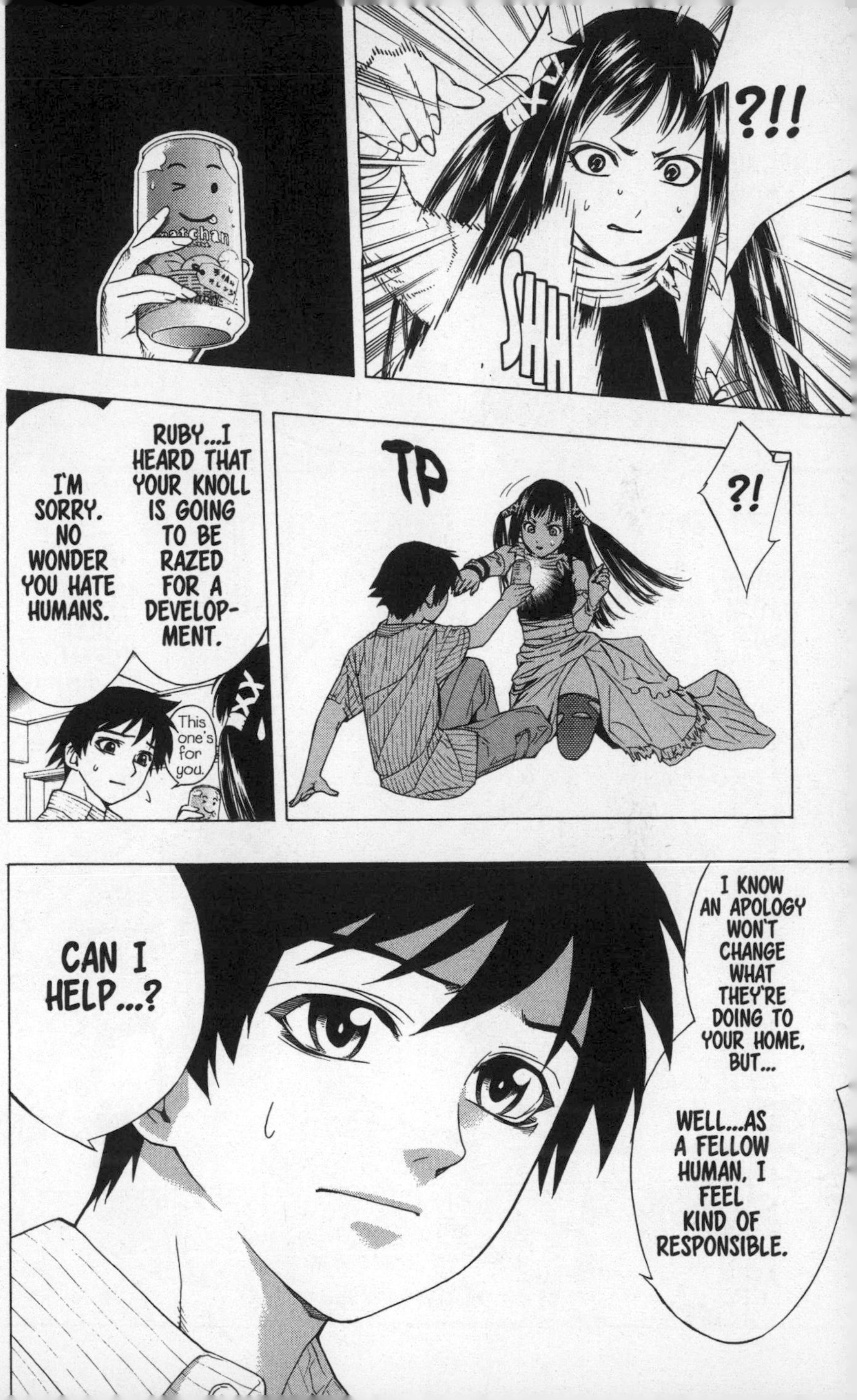
?!!
SHH
TP
?!
RUBY...I HEARD THAT YOUR KNOLL IS GOING TO BE RAZED FOR A DEVELOP-MENT.
I'M SORRY. NO WONDER YOU HATE HUMANS.
This one's for you.
I KNOW AN APOLOGY WON'T CHANGE WHAT THEY'RE DOING TO YOUR HOME, BUT...
WELL...AS A FELLOW HUMAN, I FEEL KIND OF RESPONSIBLE.
CAN I HELP...?

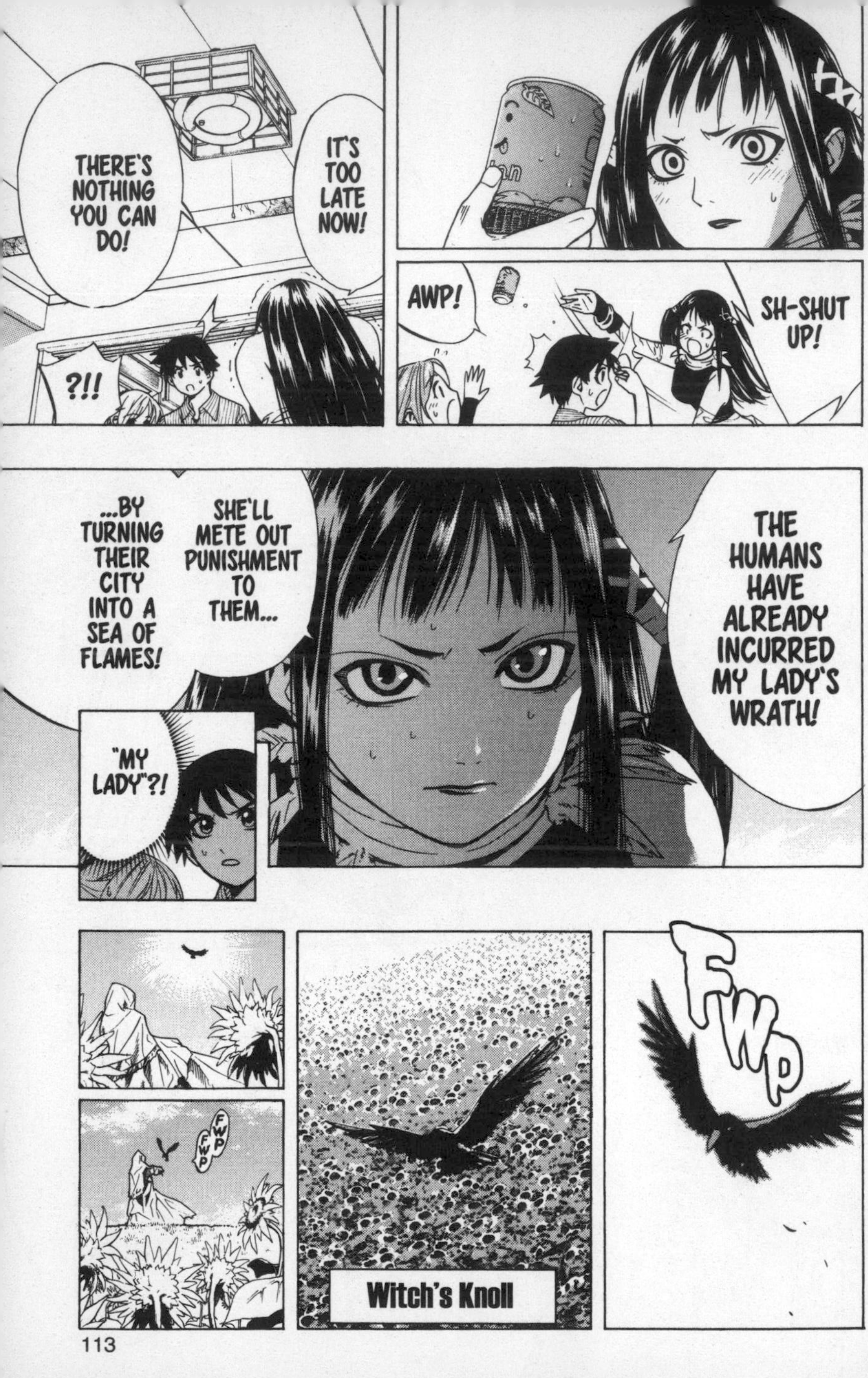
SH-SHUT UP!
AWP!
IT'S TOO LATE NOW!
THERE'S NOTHING YOU CAN DO!
?!!
THE HUMANS HAVE ALREADY INCURRED MY LADY'S WRATH!
SHE'LL METE OUT PUNISHMENT TO THEM...
...BY TURNING THEIR CITY INTO A SEA OF FLAMES!
"MY LADY"?!
FWP
Witch's Knoll
FWP
FWP

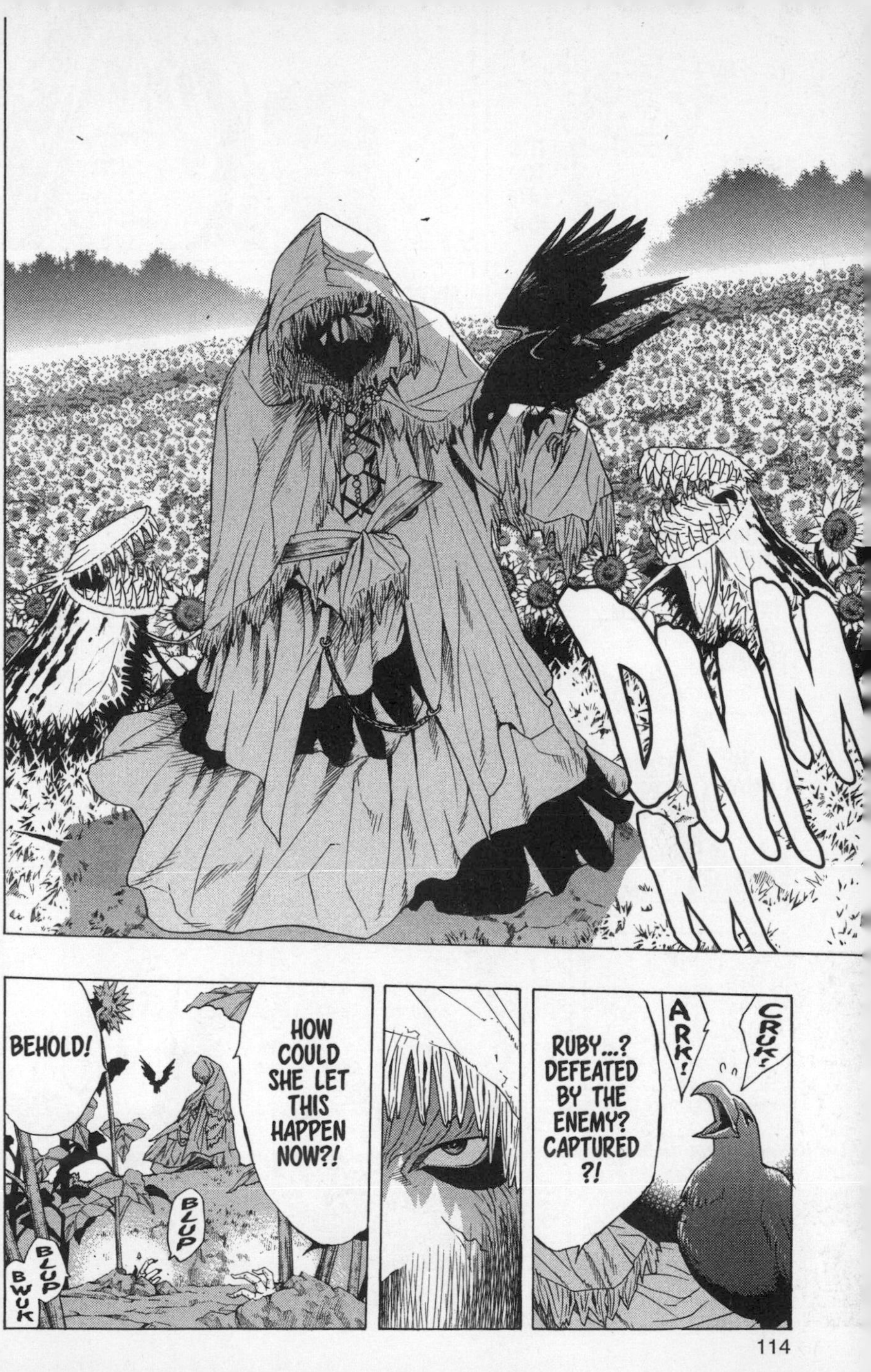
DMM
CRUK!
ARK!
RUBY...? DEFEATED BY THE ENEMY? CAPTURED?!
HOW COULD SHE LET THIS HAPPEN NOW?!
BEHOLD!
BLUP
BLUP
BWUK

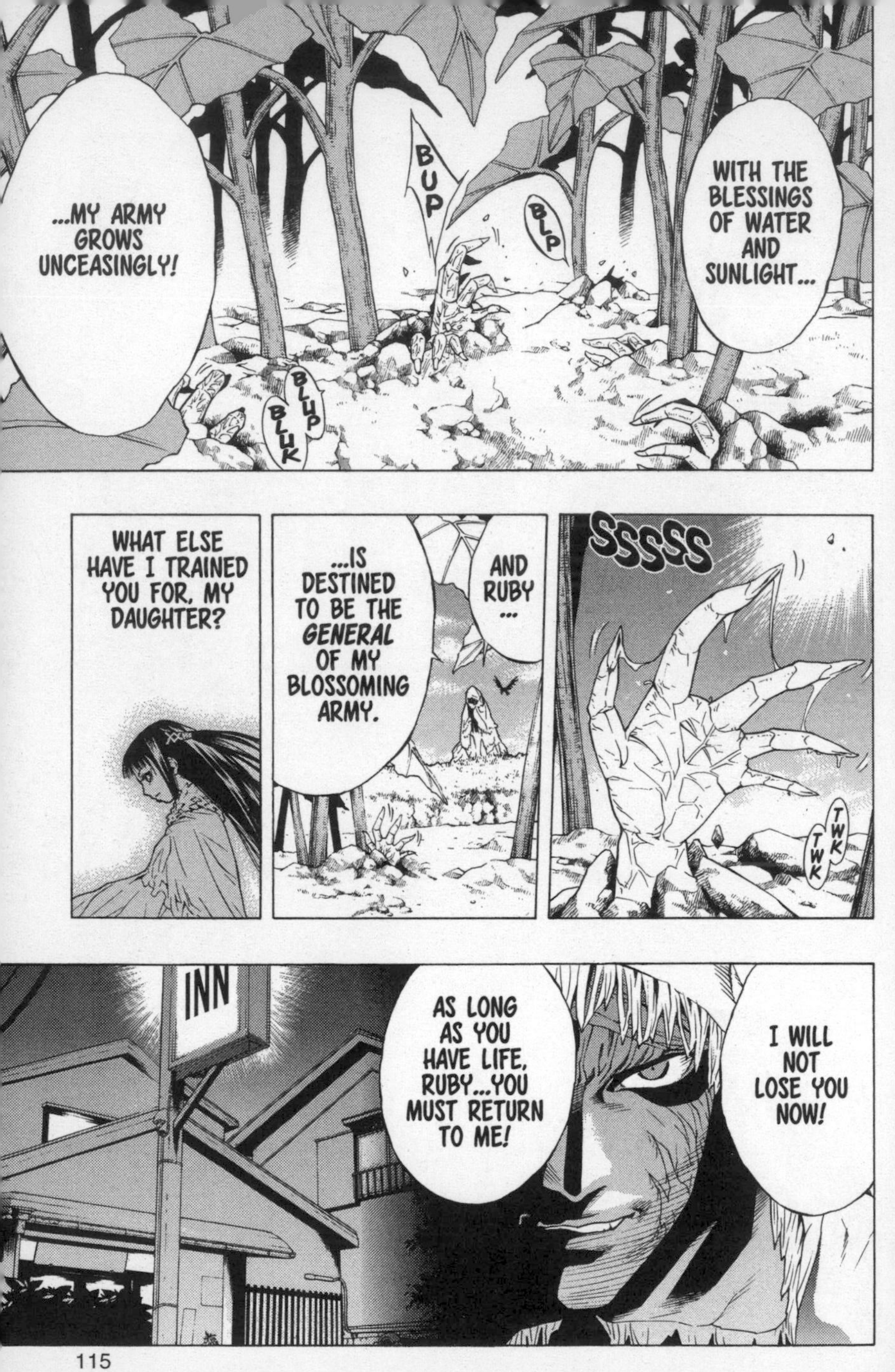
WITH THE BLESSINGS OF WATER AND SUNLIGHT...
BLP
BUP
BLUP
BLUK
...MY ARMY GROWS UNCEASINGLY!
SSSSS
TWK
TWK
AND RUBY ...
...IS DESTINED TO BE THE *GENERAL* OF MY BLOSSOMING ARMY.
WHAT ELSE HAVE I TRAINED YOU FOR, MY DAUGHTER?
I WILL NOT LOSE YOU NOW!
AS LONG AS YOU HAVE LIFE, RUBY...YOU MUST RETURN TO ME!
INN

THEY'RE HEALING QUICKLY...IS IT BECAUSE THEY'RE TAKING CARE OF ME?

MY WOUNDS...

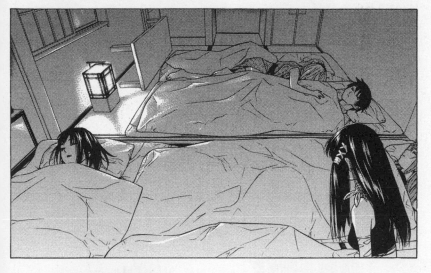

TPP

CAN I HELP?

•••

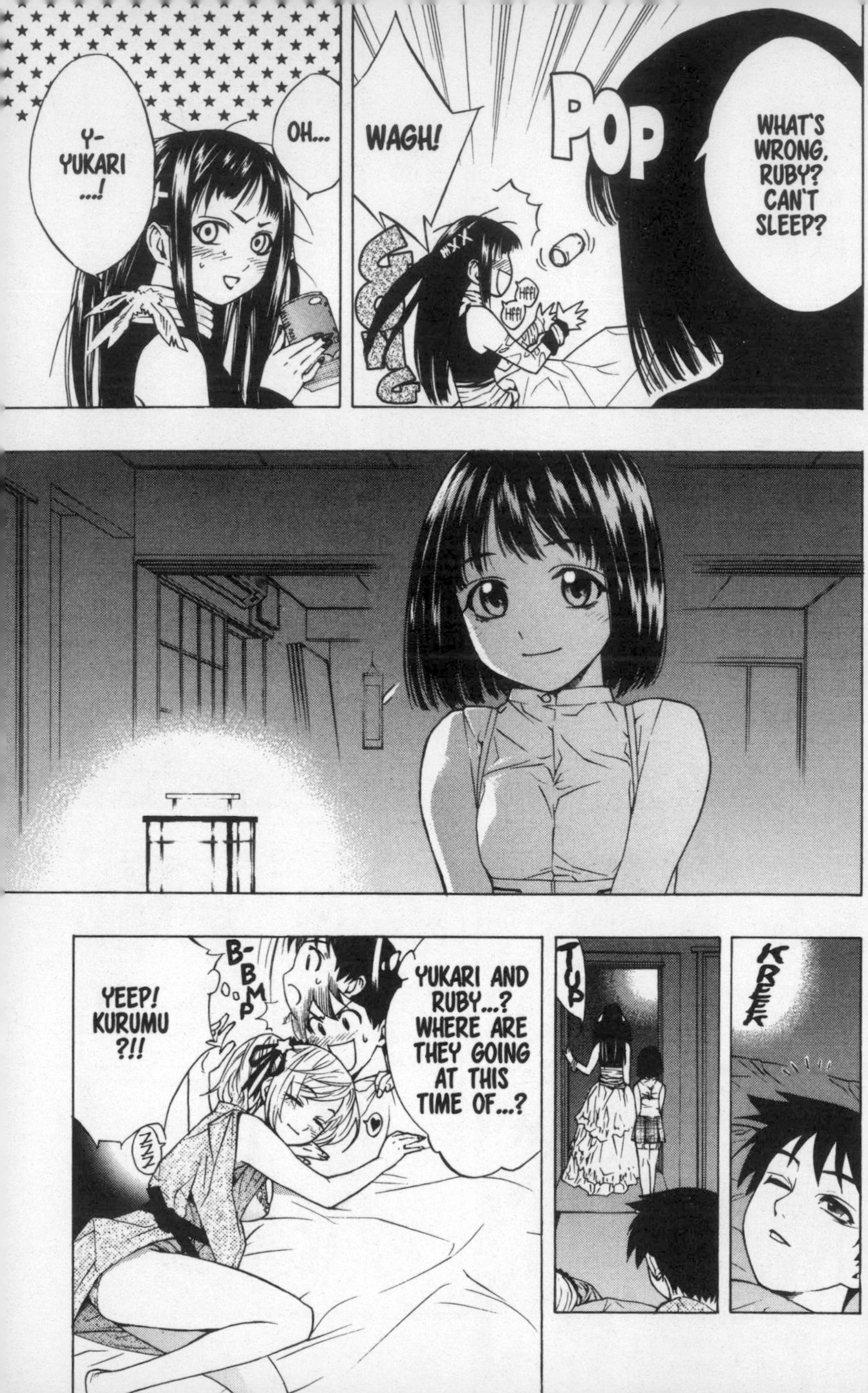
POP
WHAT'S WRONG, RUBY? CAN'T SLEEP?
WAGH!
Hffl
Hffl
OH...
Y-YUKARI ...!
KREEK
TUP
YUKARI AND RUBY...? WHERE ARE THEY GOING AT THIS TIME OF...?
B-BMP
YEEP! KURUMU ?!!
ZZZ

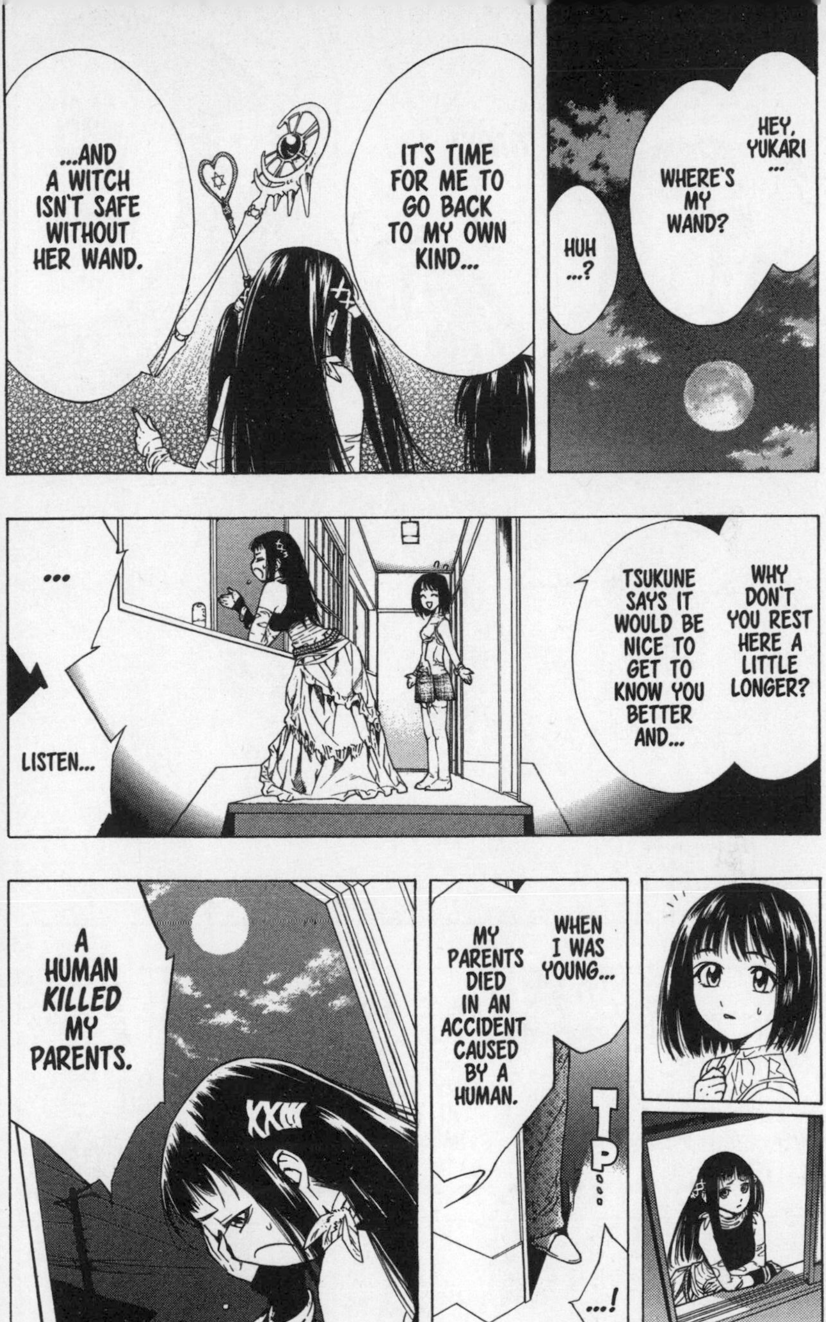
HEY, YUKARI ...
WHERE'S MY WAND?
HUH ...?
IT'S TIME FOR ME TO GO BACK TO MY OWN KIND...
...AND A WITCH ISN'T SAFE WITHOUT HER WAND.
WHY DON'T YOU REST HERE A LITTLE LONGER?
TSUKUNE SAYS IT WOULD BE NICE TO GET TO KNOW YOU BETTER AND...
...
LISTEN...
WHEN I WAS YOUNG...
MY PARENTS DIED IN AN ACCIDENT CAUSED BY A HUMAN.
TP...
...!
A HUMAN KILLED MY PARENTS.

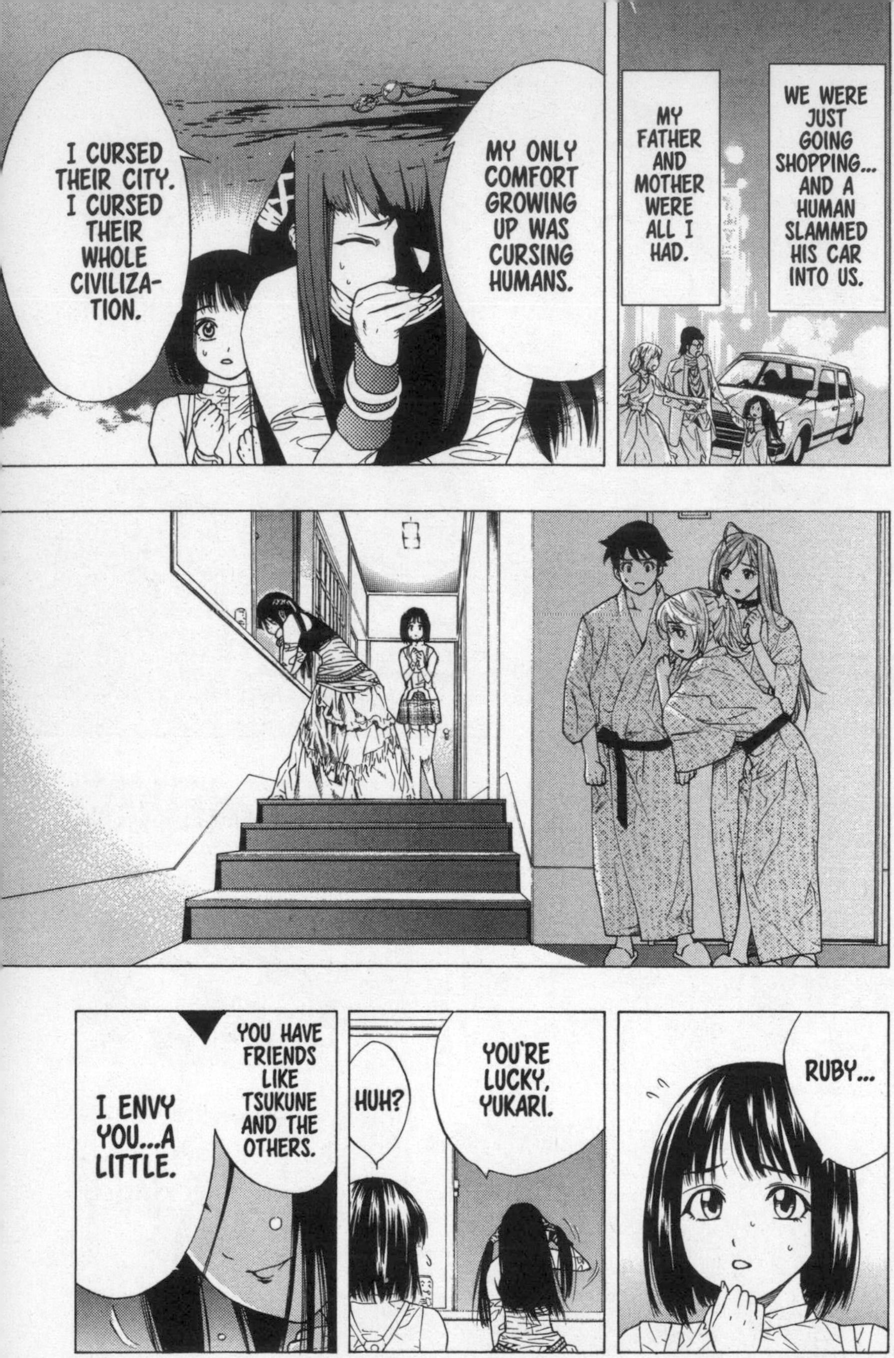
WE WERE JUST GOING SHOPPING... AND A HUMAN SLAMMED HIS CAR INTO US.
MY FATHER AND MOTHER WERE ALL I HAD.
MY ONLY COMFORT GROWING UP WAS CURSING HUMANS.
I CURSED THEIR CITY. I CURSED THEIR WHOLE CIVILIZA-TION.
RUBY...
YOU'RE LUCKY, YUKARI.
HUH?
YOU HAVE FRIENDS LIKE TSUKUNE AND THE OTHERS.
I ENVY YOU...A LITTLE.

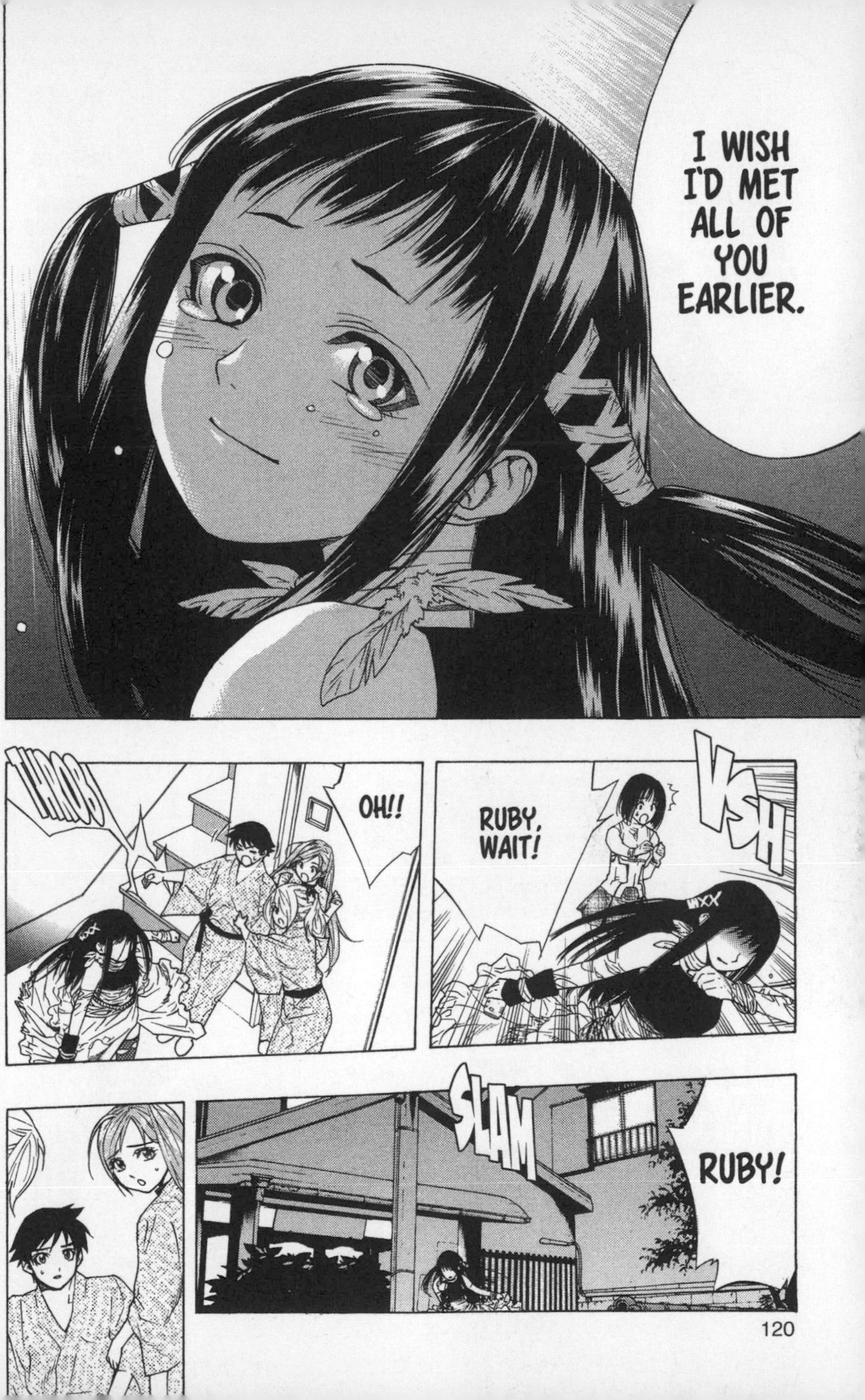
I WISH I'D MET ALL OF YOU EARLIER.
VSH
RUBY, WAIT!
OH!!
THROB
SLAM
RUBY!

READ THIS WAY

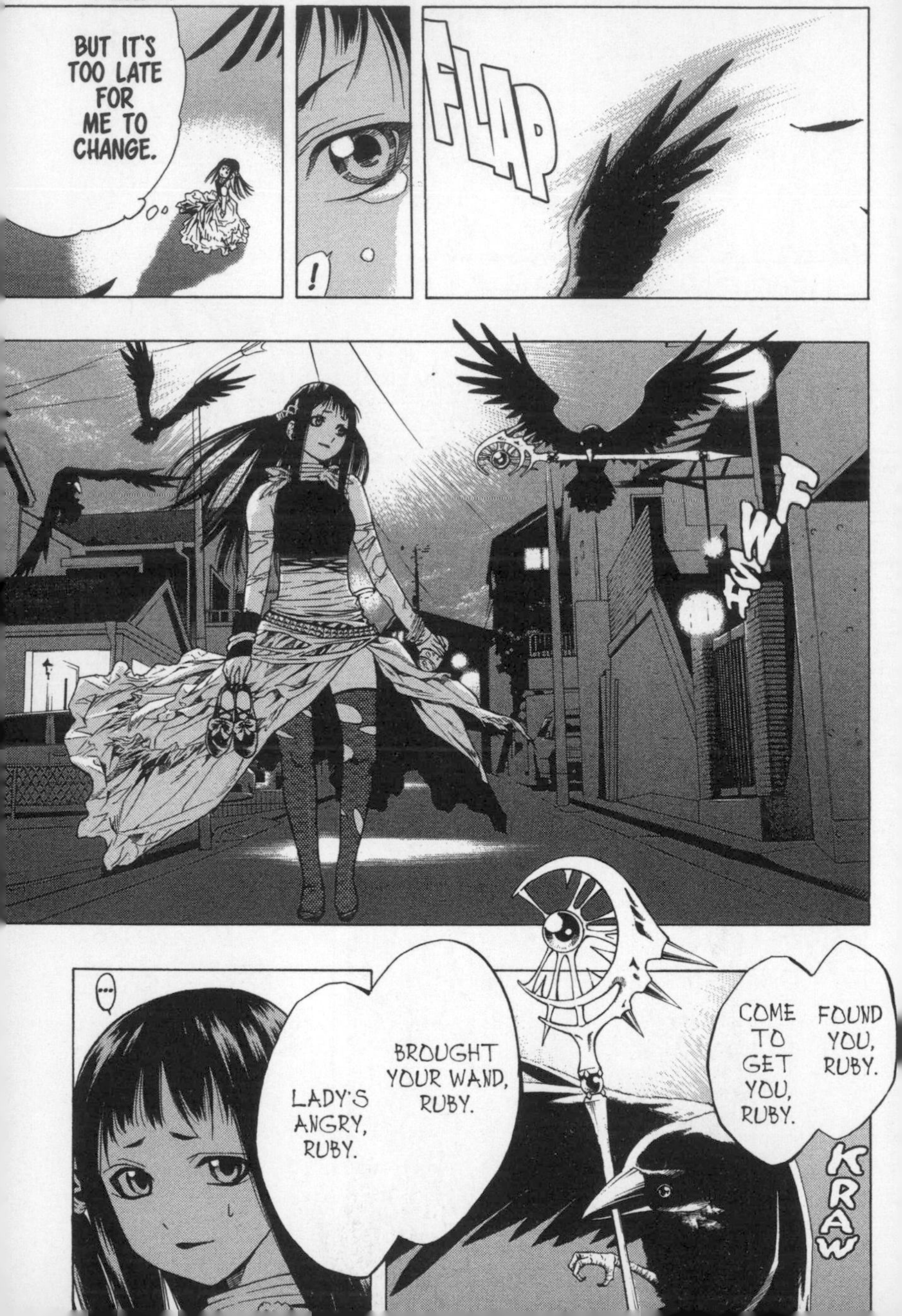
FLAP
!
BUT IT'S TOO LATE FOR ME TO CHANGE.
FWSH
KRAW
FOUND YOU, RUBY.
COME TO GET YOU, RUBY.
BROUGHT YOUR WAND, RUBY.
LADY'S ANGRY, RUBY.
...

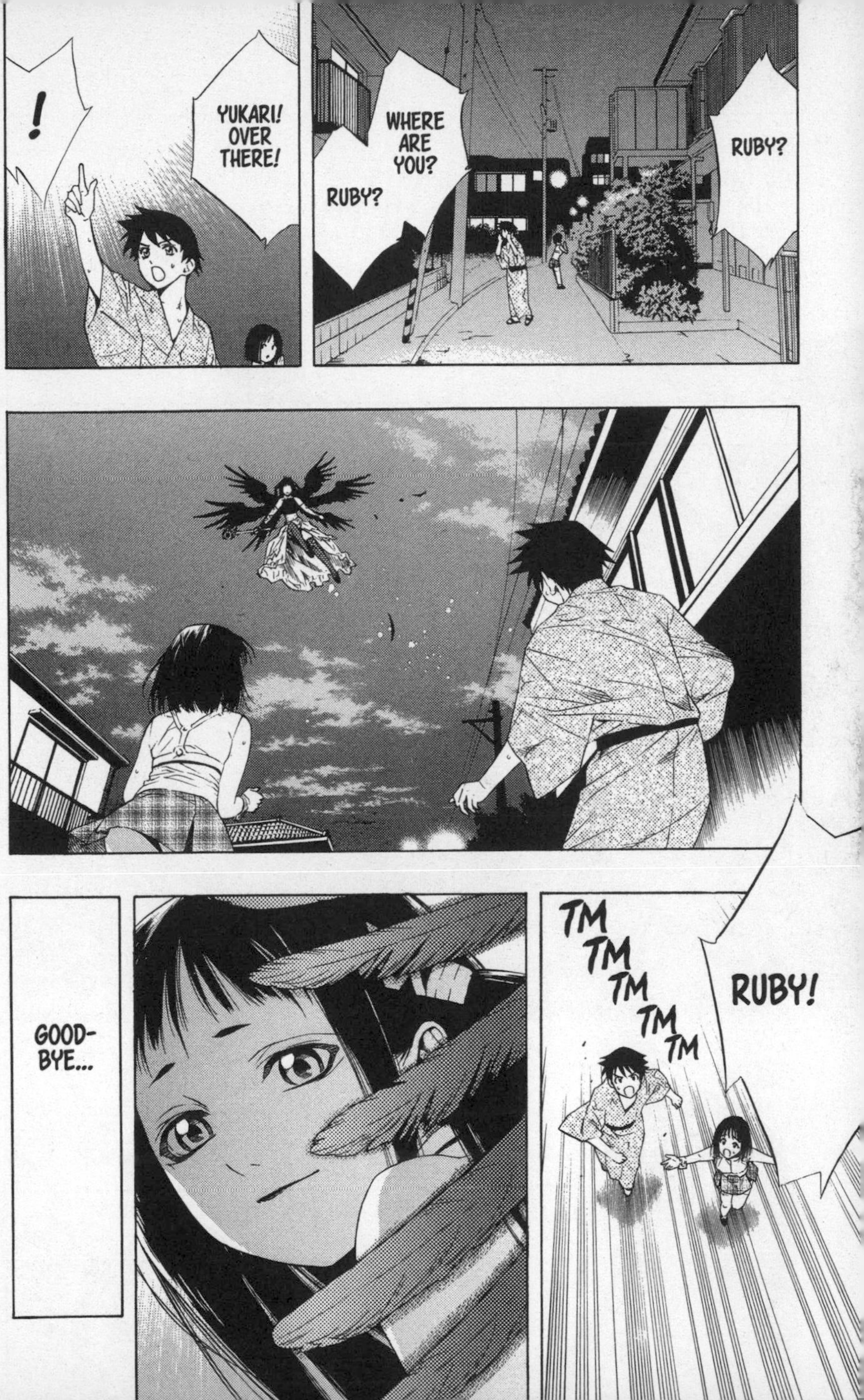
RUBY?
WHERE ARE YOU?
RUBY?
YUKARI! OVER THERE!
!
RUBY!
TM TM TM TM TM
GOOD-BYE...

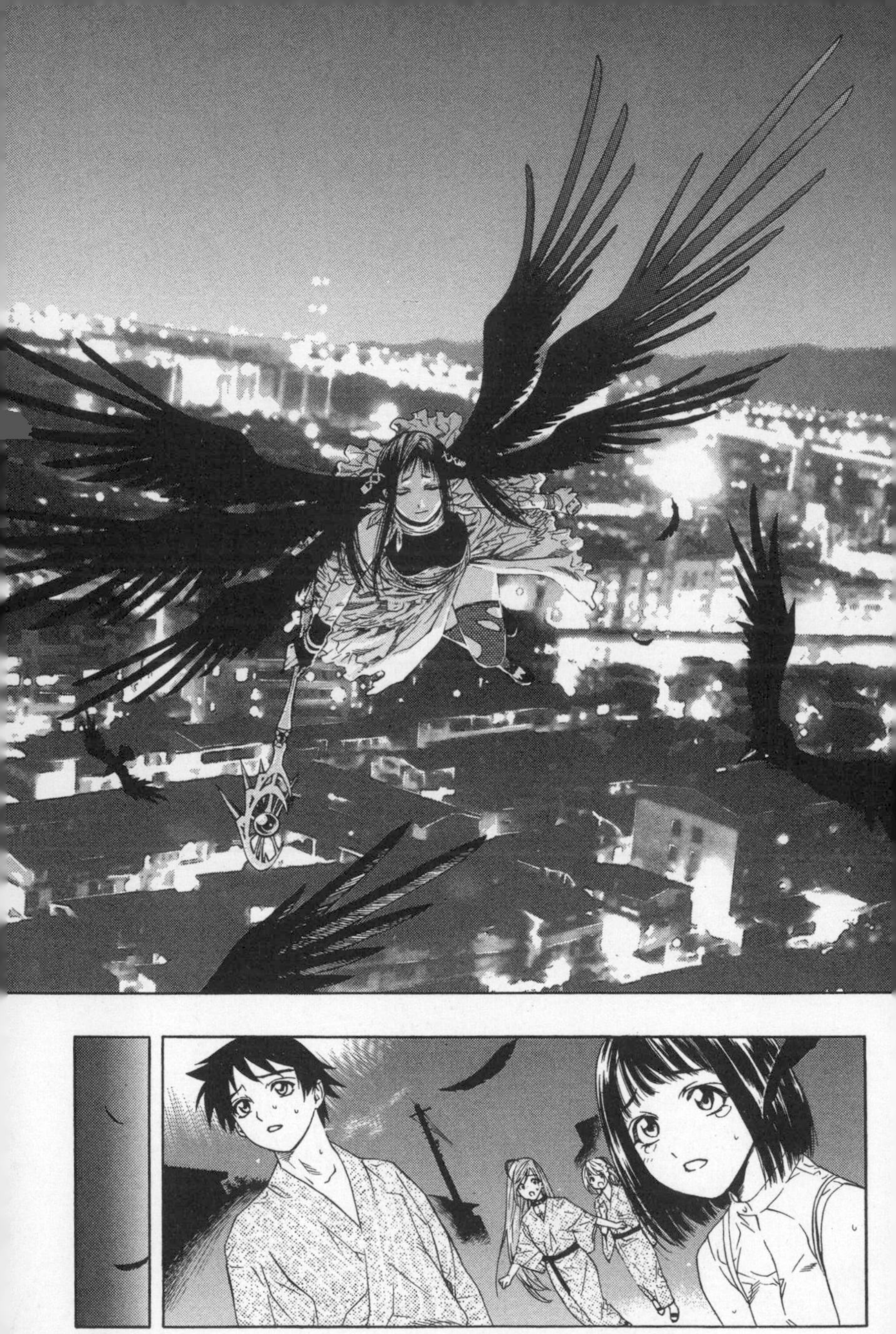

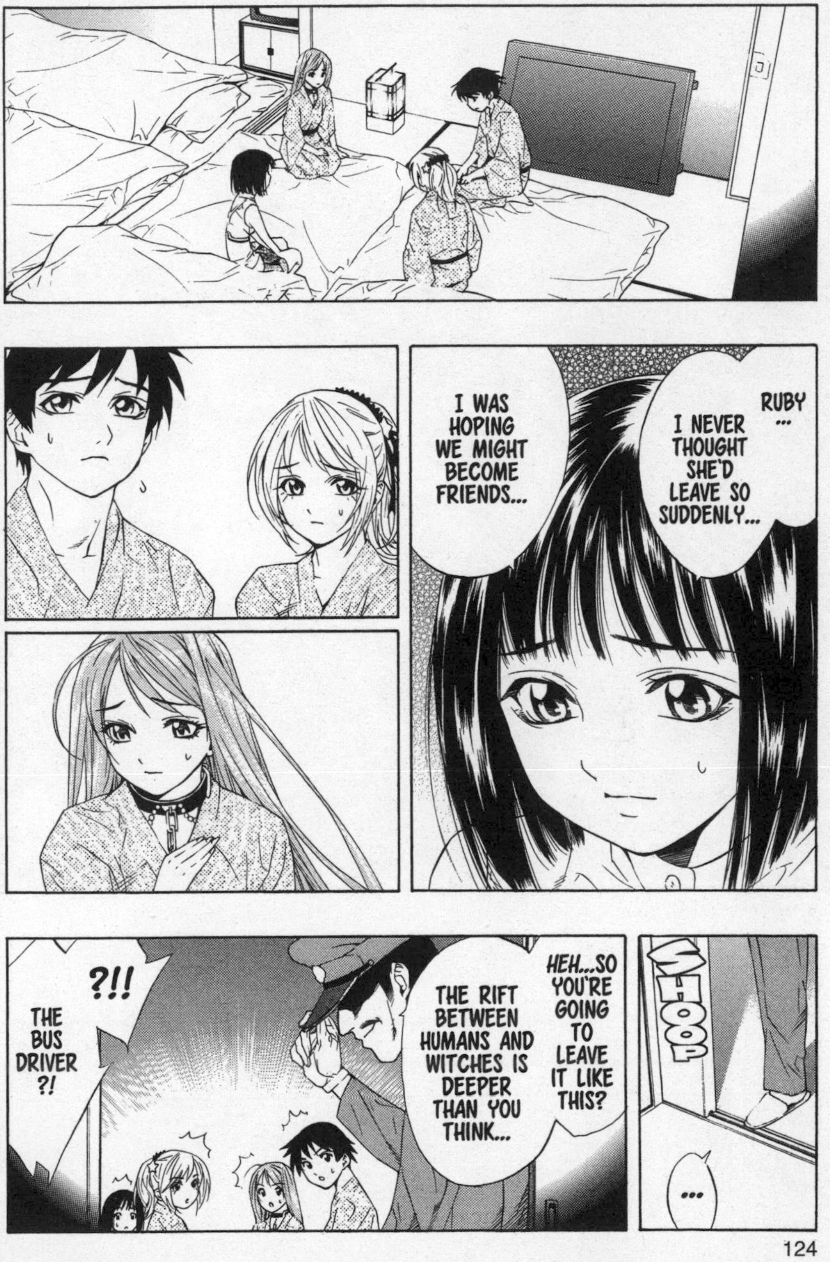
RUBY... I NEVER THOUGHT SHE'D LEAVE SO SUDDENLY...
I WAS HOPING WE MIGHT BECOME FRIENDS...
SHOOP
...
HEH...SO YOU'RE GOING TO LEAVE IT LIKE THIS?
THE RIFT BETWEEN HUMANS AND WITCHES IS DEEPER THAN YOU THINK...
?!!
THE BUS DRIVER ?!

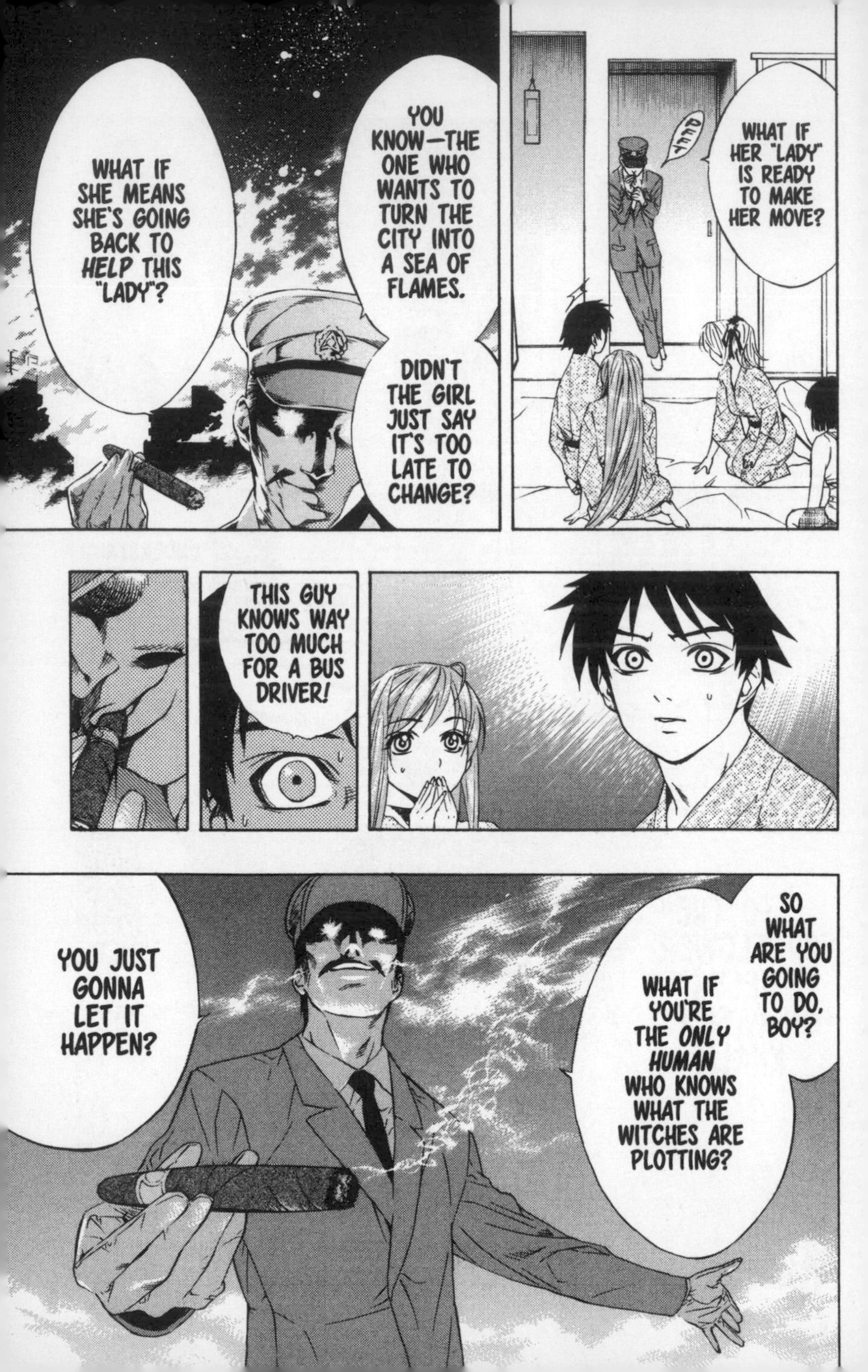
WHAT IF HER "LADY" IS READY TO MAKE HER MOVE?
YOU KNOW—THE ONE WHO WANTS TO TURN THE CITY INTO A SEA OF FLAMES.
DIDN'T THE GIRL JUST SAY IT'S TOO LATE TO CHANGE?
WHAT IF SHE MEANS SHE'S GOING BACK TO *HELP* THIS "LADY"?
THIS GUY KNOWS WAY TOO MUCH FOR A BUS DRIVER!
SO WHAT ARE YOU GOING TO DO, BOY?
WHAT IF YOU'RE THE *ONLY HUMAN* WHO KNOWS WHAT THE WITCHES ARE PLOTTING?
YOU JUST GONNA LET IT HAPPEN?

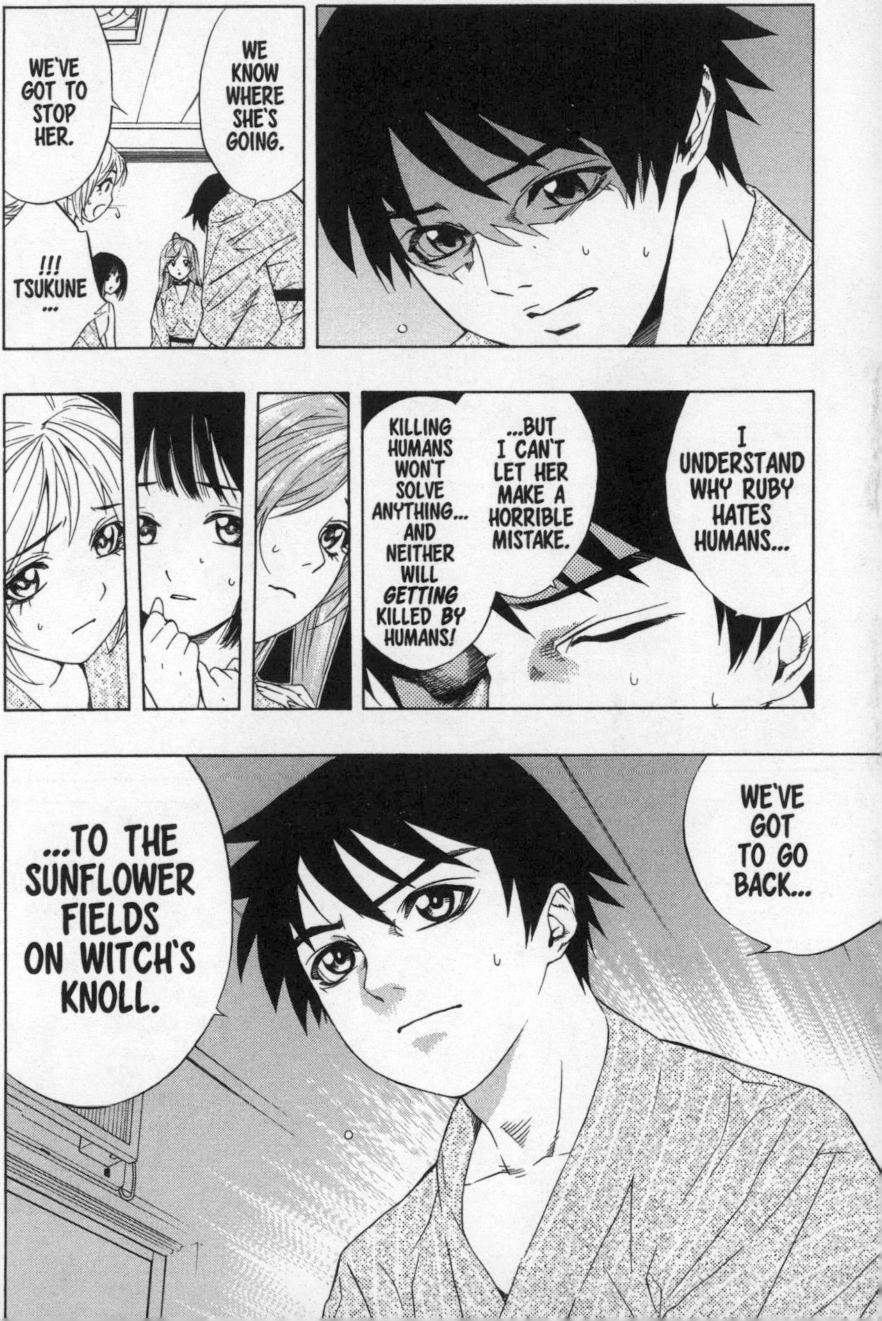
WE KNOW WHERE SHE'S GOING.
WE'VE GOT TO STOP HER.
!!! TSUKUNE...
I UNDERSTAND WHY RUBY HATES HUMANS...
...BUT I CAN'T LET HER MAKE A HORRIBLE MISTAKE.
KILLING HUMANS WON'T SOLVE ANYTHING... AND NEITHER WILL GETTING KILLED BY HUMANS!
WE'VE GOT TO GO BACK...
...TO THE SUNFLOWER FIELDS ON WITCH'S KNOLL.

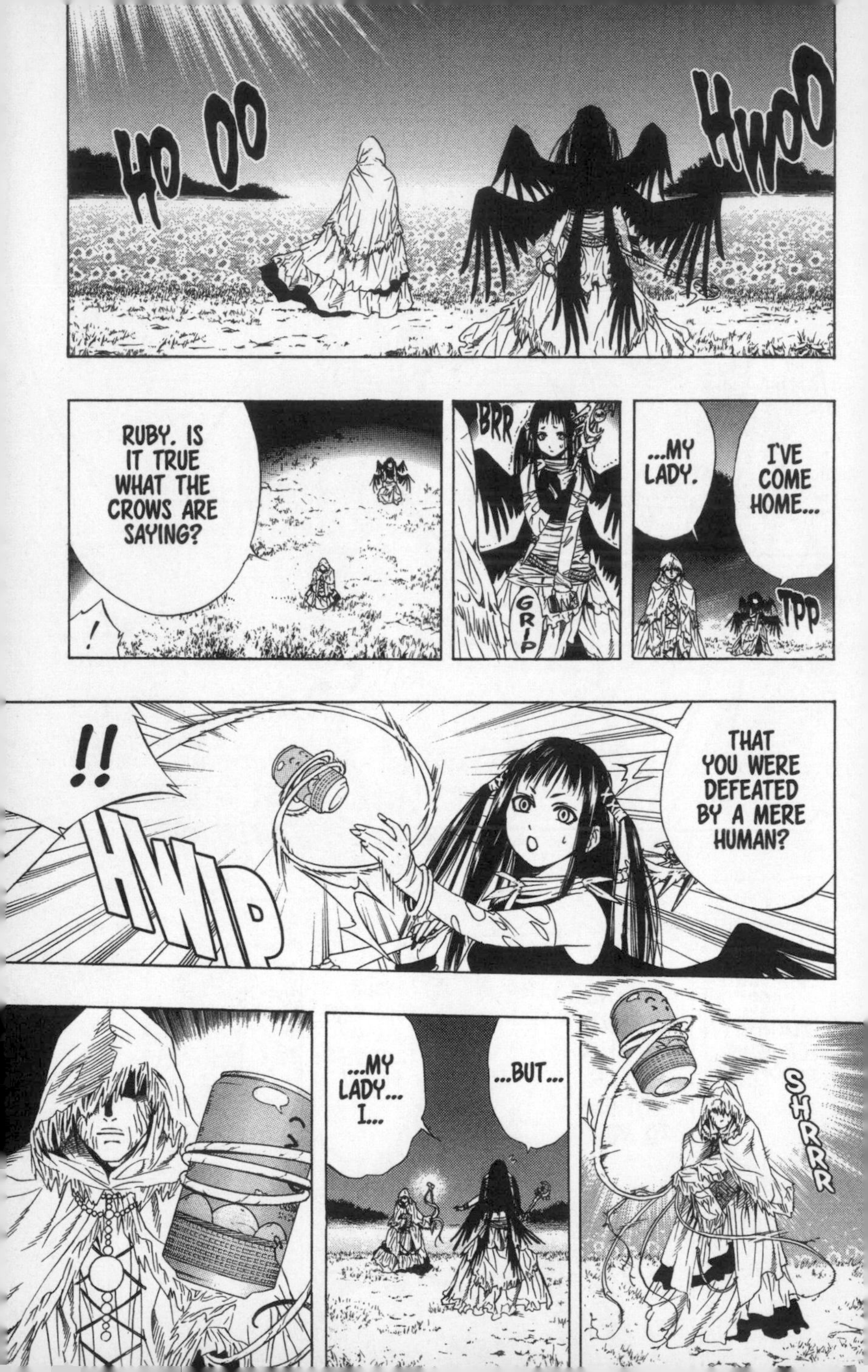
HWOO
HO OO
I'VE COME HOME...
...MY LADY.
TPP
BRR
GRIP
RUBY. IS IT TRUE WHAT THE CROWS ARE SAYING?
!
THAT YOU WERE DEFEATED BY A MERE HUMAN?
!!
HWIP
SHRRR
...BUT...
...MY LADY... I...

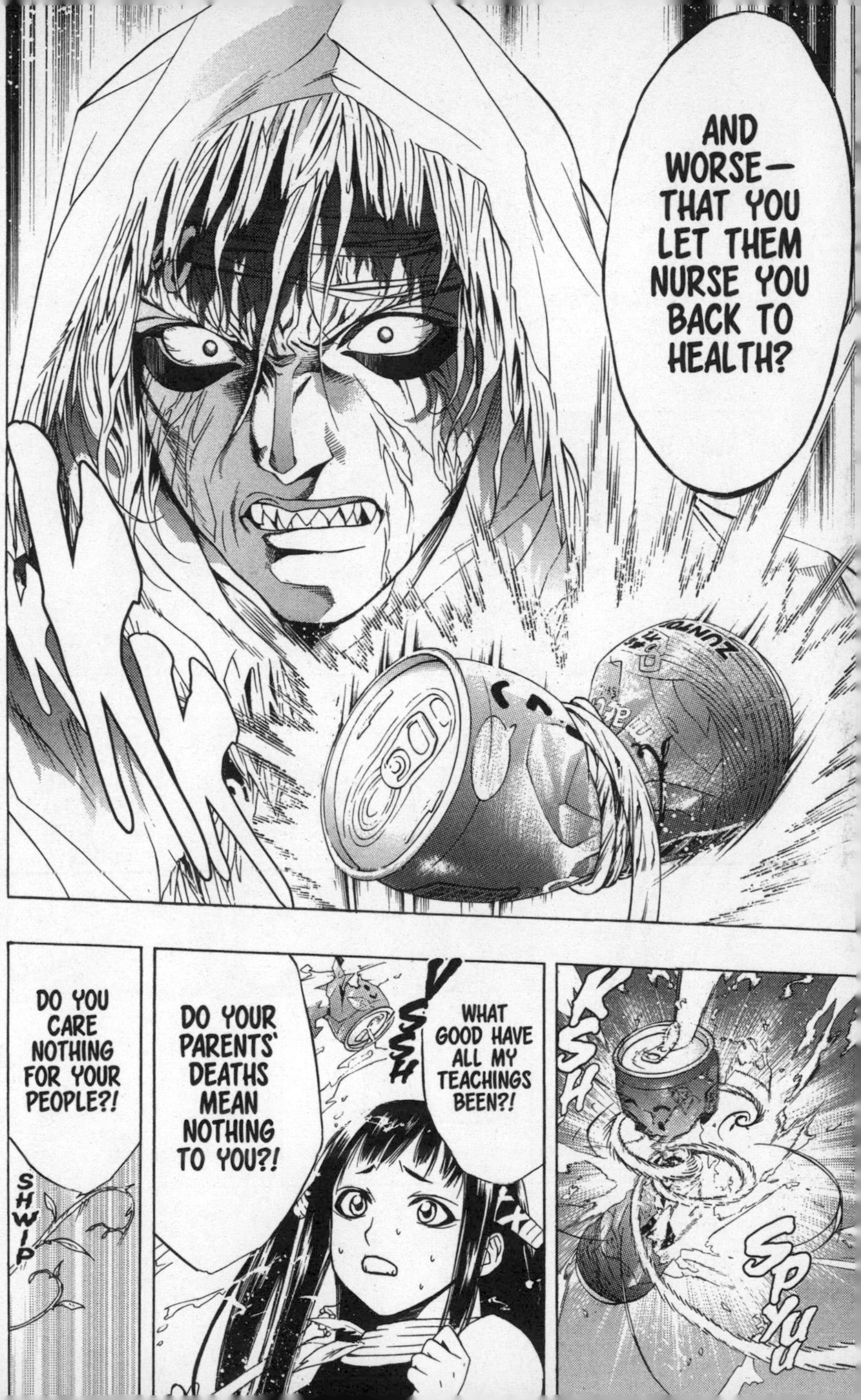
AND WORSE—THAT YOU LET THEM NURSE YOU BACK TO HEALTH?
SPYU
WHAT GOOD HAVE ALL MY TEACHINGS BEEN?!
DO YOUR PARENTS' DEATHS MEAN NOTHING TO YOU?!
DO YOU CARE NOTHING FOR YOUR PEOPLE?!
SHWIP

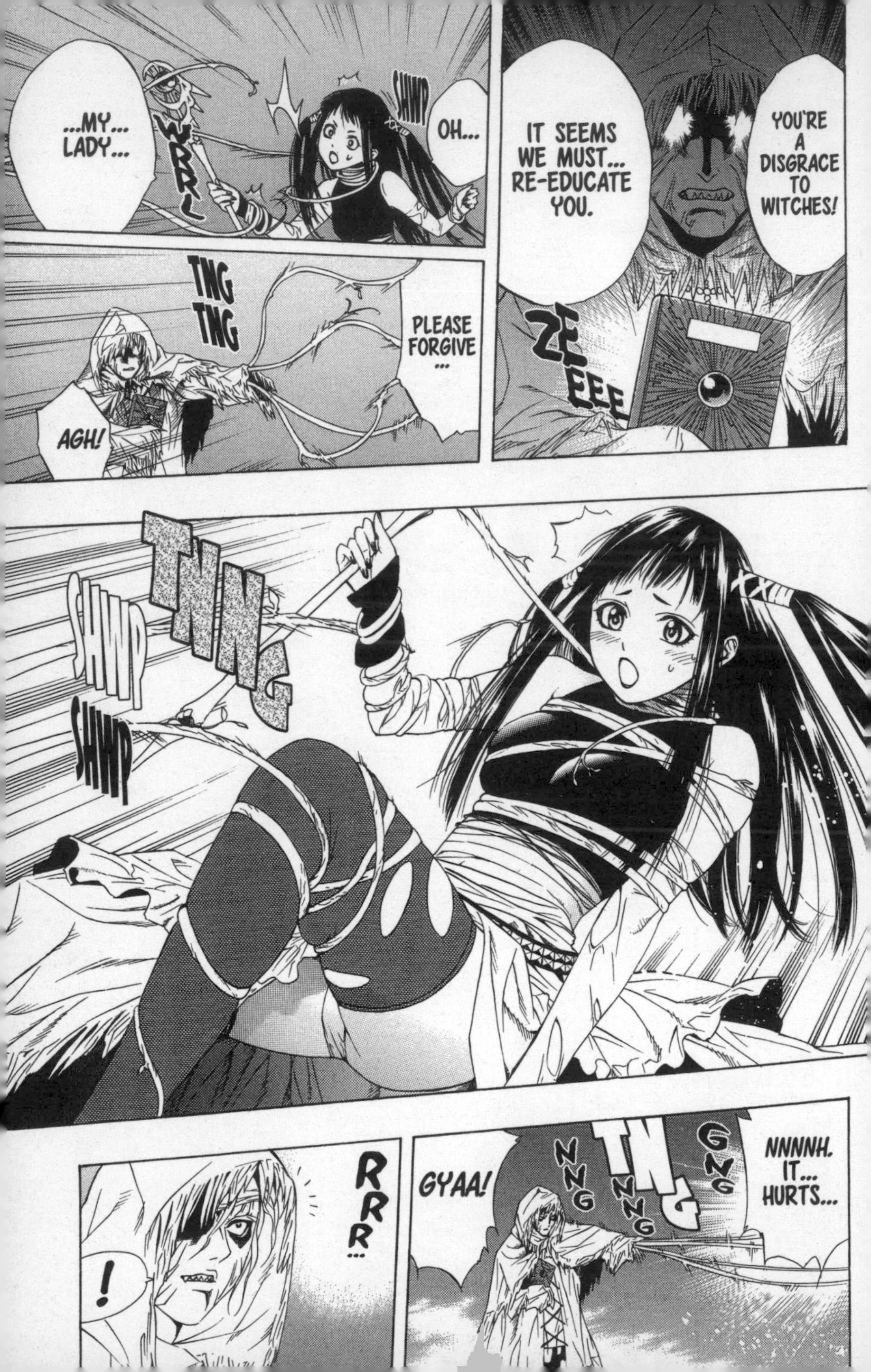
YOU'RE A DISGRACE TO WITCHES!
IT SEEMS WE MUST... RE-EDUCATE YOU.
ZEEEE
OH...
SHWP
...MY... LADY...
WRRL
PLEASE FORGIVE ...
TNG TNG
AGH!
TNNG
SHWP
SHWP
NNNNH. IT... HURTS...
GNG
TNG
NNG
NNNG
GYAA!
RRR...
!

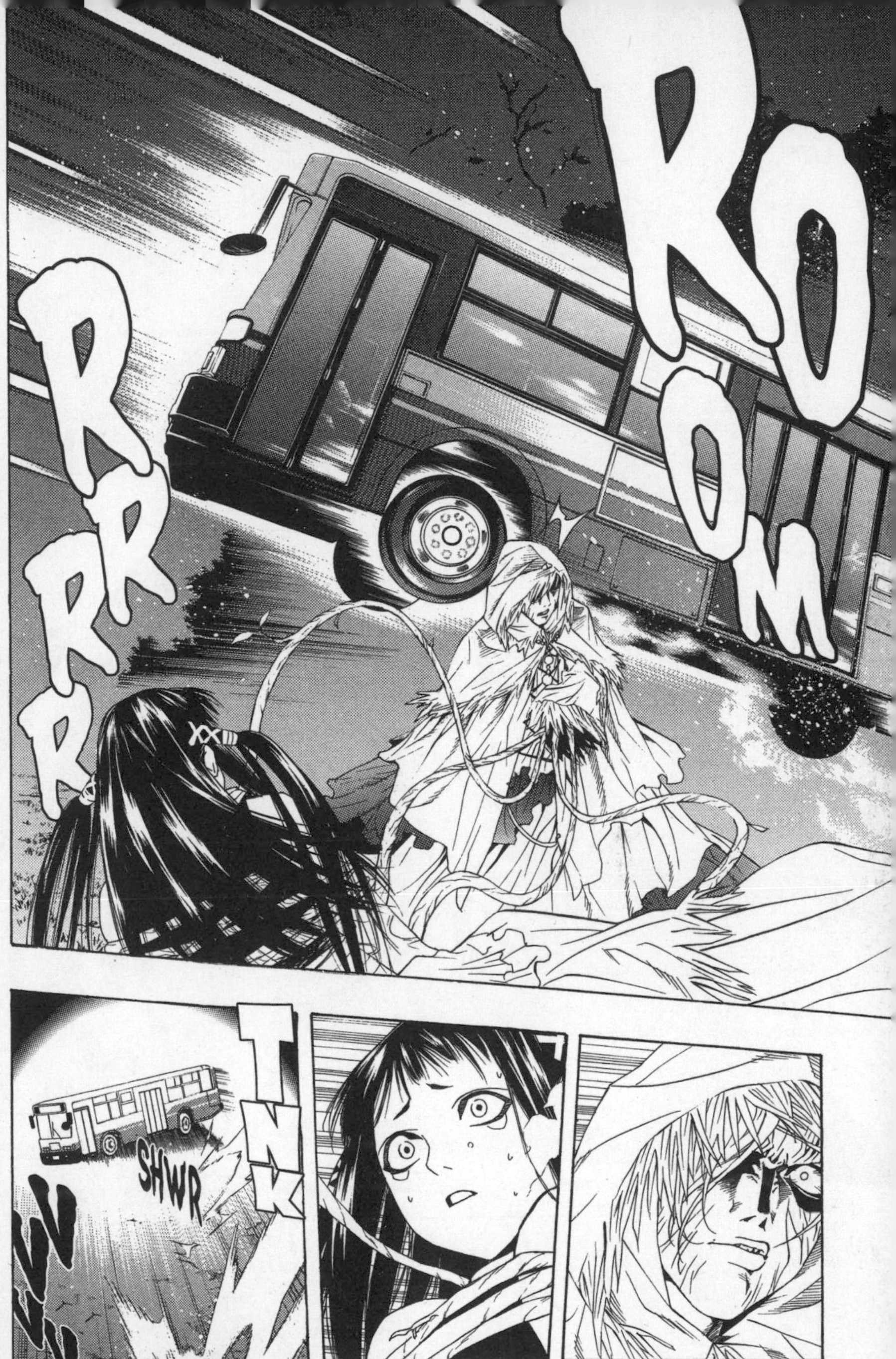
ROOM
RRRRR
TINK
SHWR

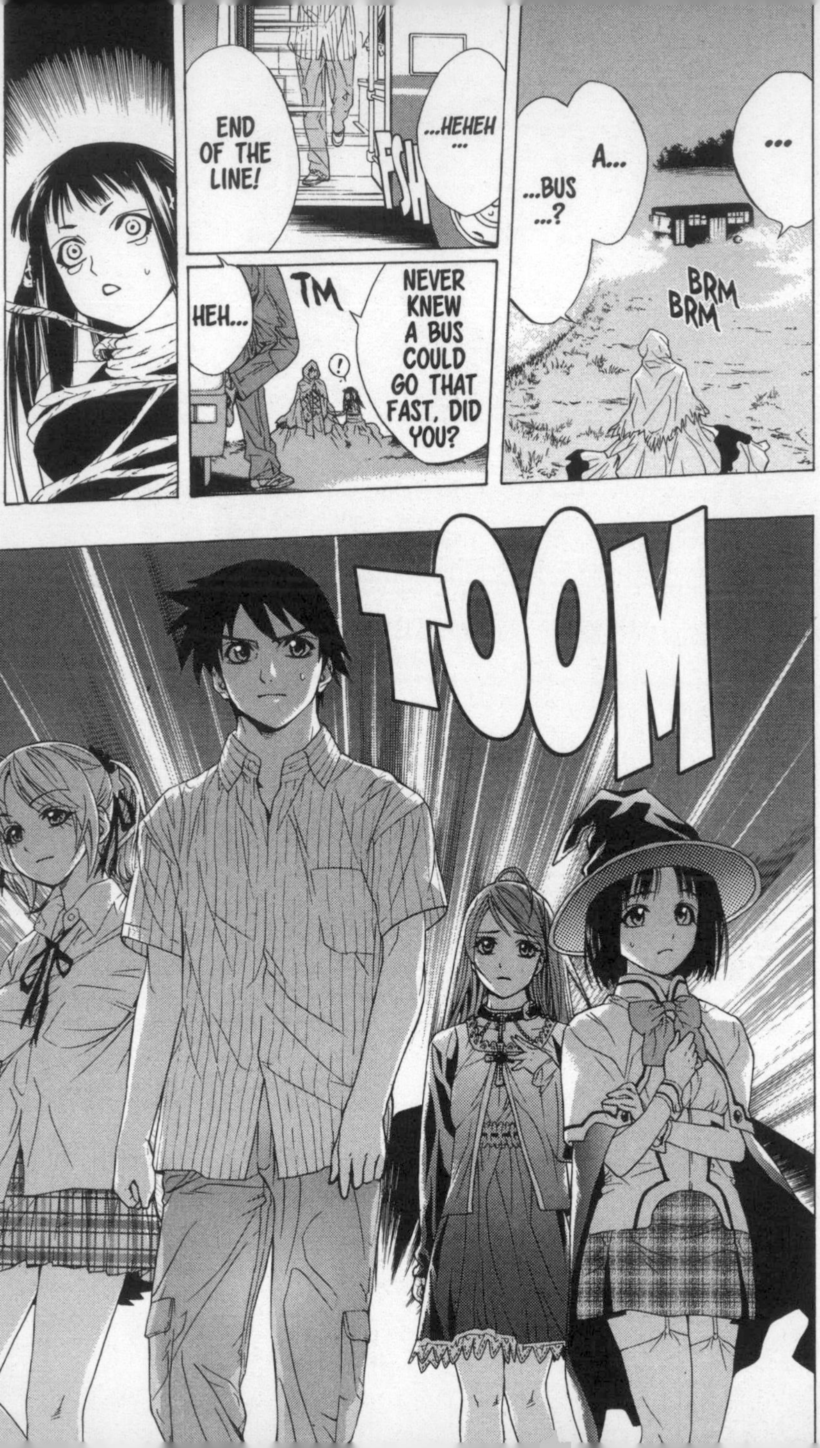
...
A... ...BUS ...?
BRM BRM
...HEHEH ...
FSH
END OF THE LINE!
NEVER KNEW A BUS COULD GO THAT FAST, DID YOU?
TM
!
HEH...
TOOM

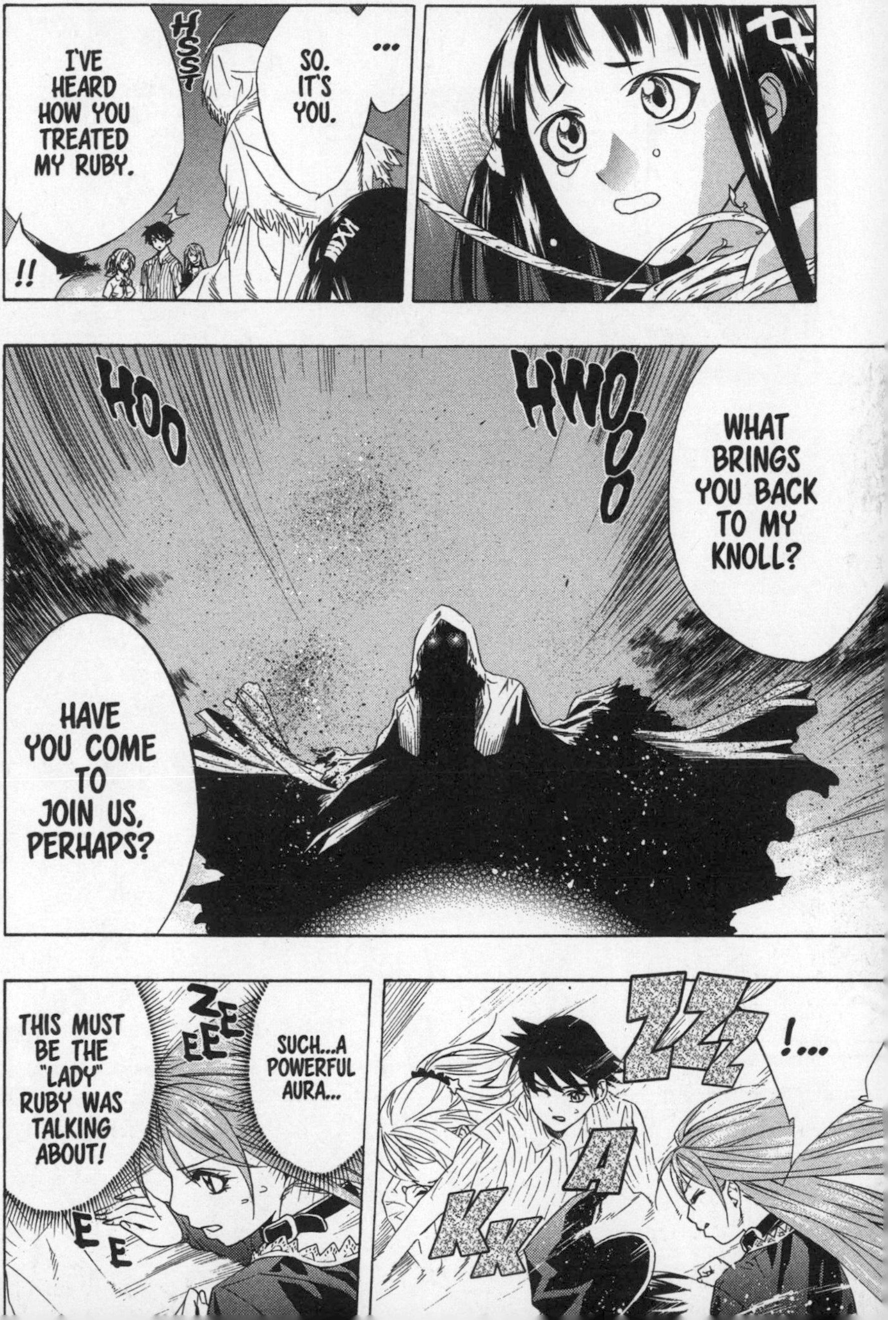
...
SO. IT'S YOU.
HSST
I'VE HEARD HOW YOU TREATED MY RUBY.
!!
WHAT BRINGS YOU BACK TO MY KNOLL?
HWOOOO
HOO
HAVE YOU COME TO JOIN US, PERHAPS?
!...
ZZZ
AKK
SUCH...A POWERFUL AURA...
ZEEE
THIS MUST BE THE "LADY" RUBY WAS TALKING ABOUT!
EE

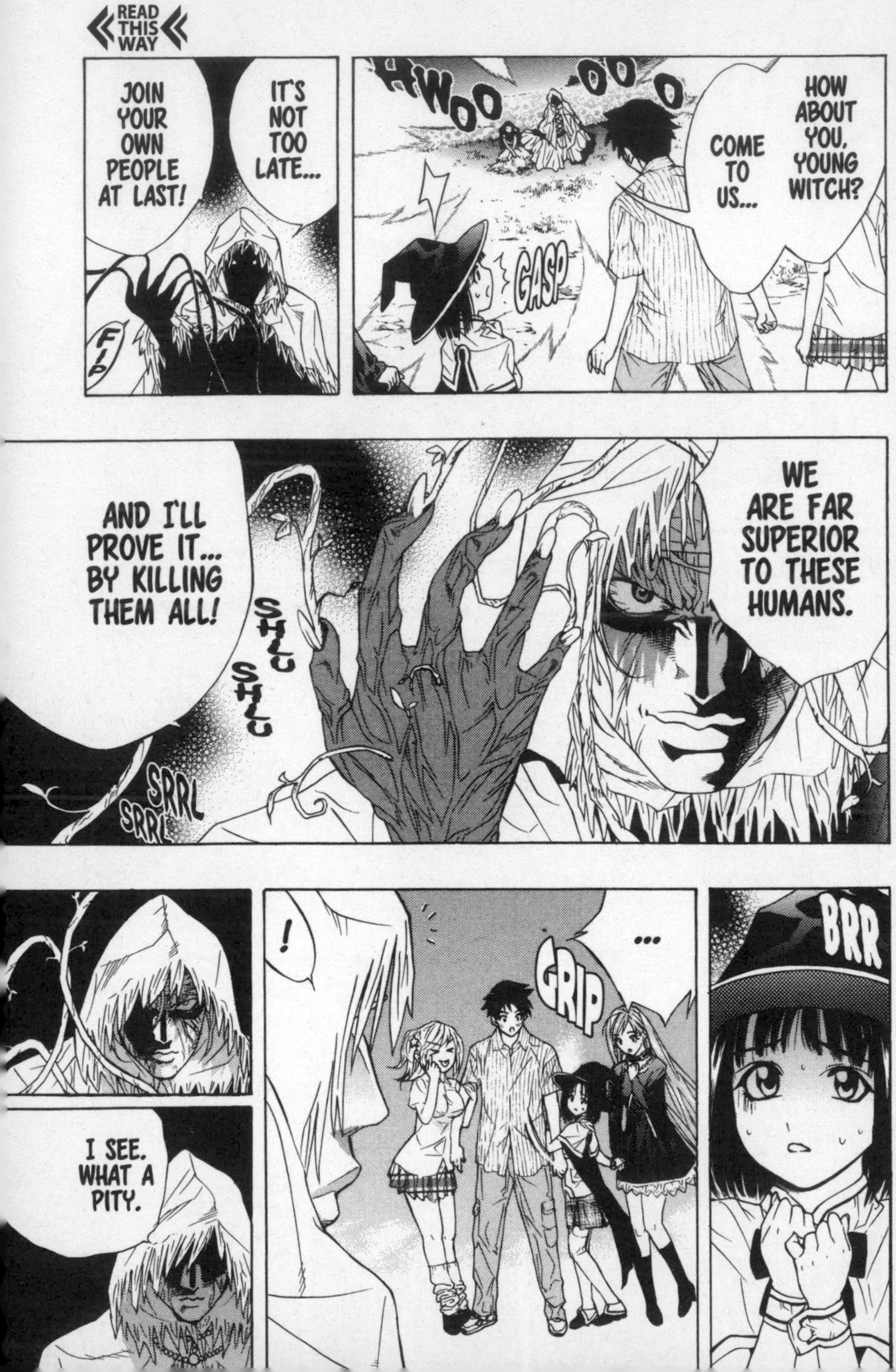
READ THIS WAY
HOW ABOUT YOU, YOUNG WITCH?
COME TO US...
HWOO-OO-O
GASP
IT'S NOT TOO LATE...
JOIN YOUR OWN PEOPLE AT LAST!
FLIP
WE ARE FAR SUPERIOR TO THESE HUMANS.
AND I'LL PROVE IT... BY KILLING THEM ALL!
SHLU SHLU
SRRL SRRL
BRR
...
GRIP
!
I SEE. WHAT A PITY.

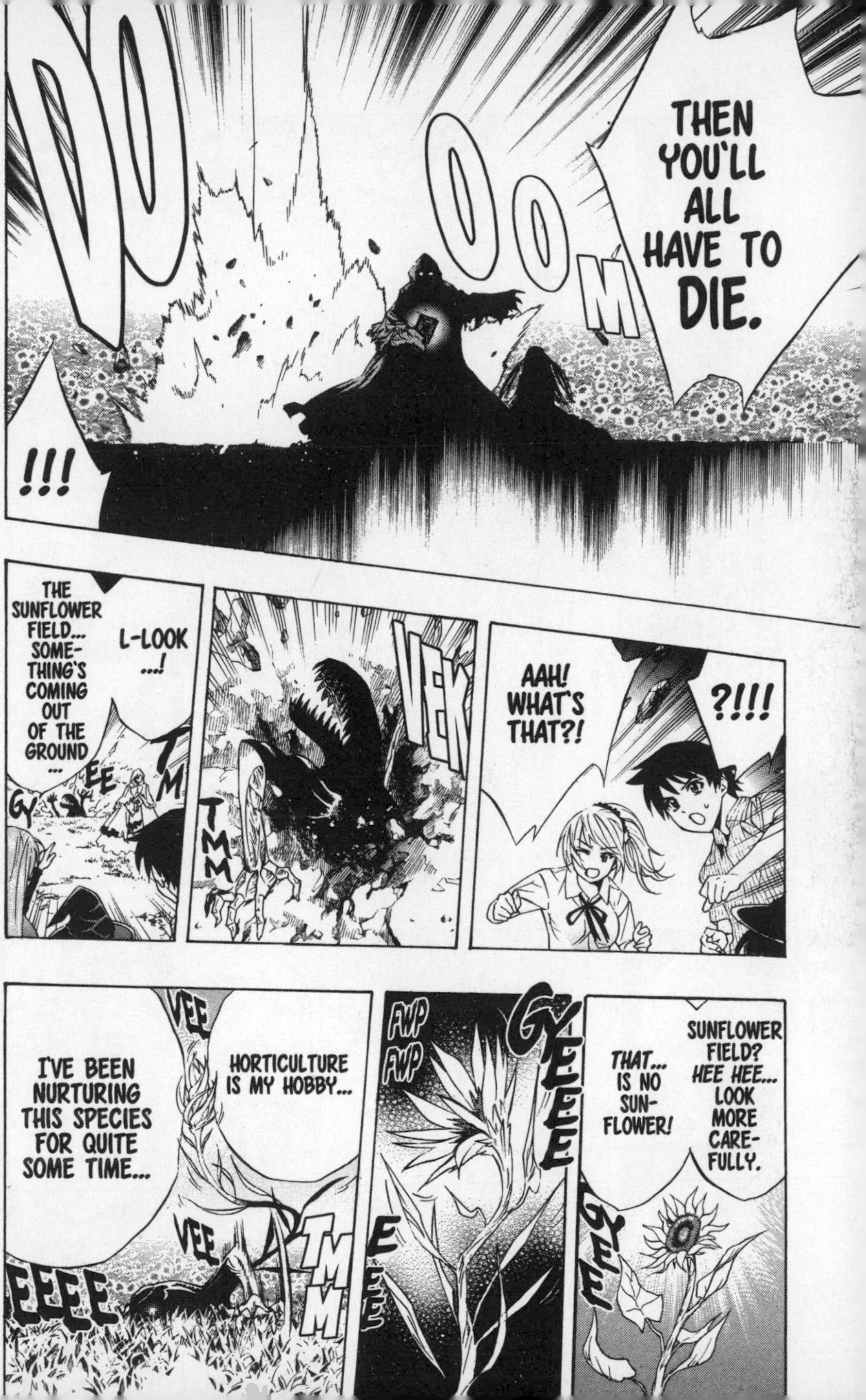
THEN YOU'LL ALL HAVE TO DIE.
DOOOM
!!!
?!!!
AAH! WHAT'S THAT?!
VEK
TMM
L-LOOK ...!
THE SUNFLOWER FIELD... SOME-THING'S COMING OUT OF THE GROUND ...
TMM
GYEE
SUNFLOWER FIELD? HEE HEE... LOOK MORE CARE-FULLY.
THAT... IS NO SUN-FLOWER!
GYEE
GYEEEEE
FWP FWP
EEEE
HORTICULTURE IS MY HOBBY...
I'VE BEEN NURTURING THIS SPECIES FOR QUITE SOME TIME...
VEE
VEE
TMM
EEEE

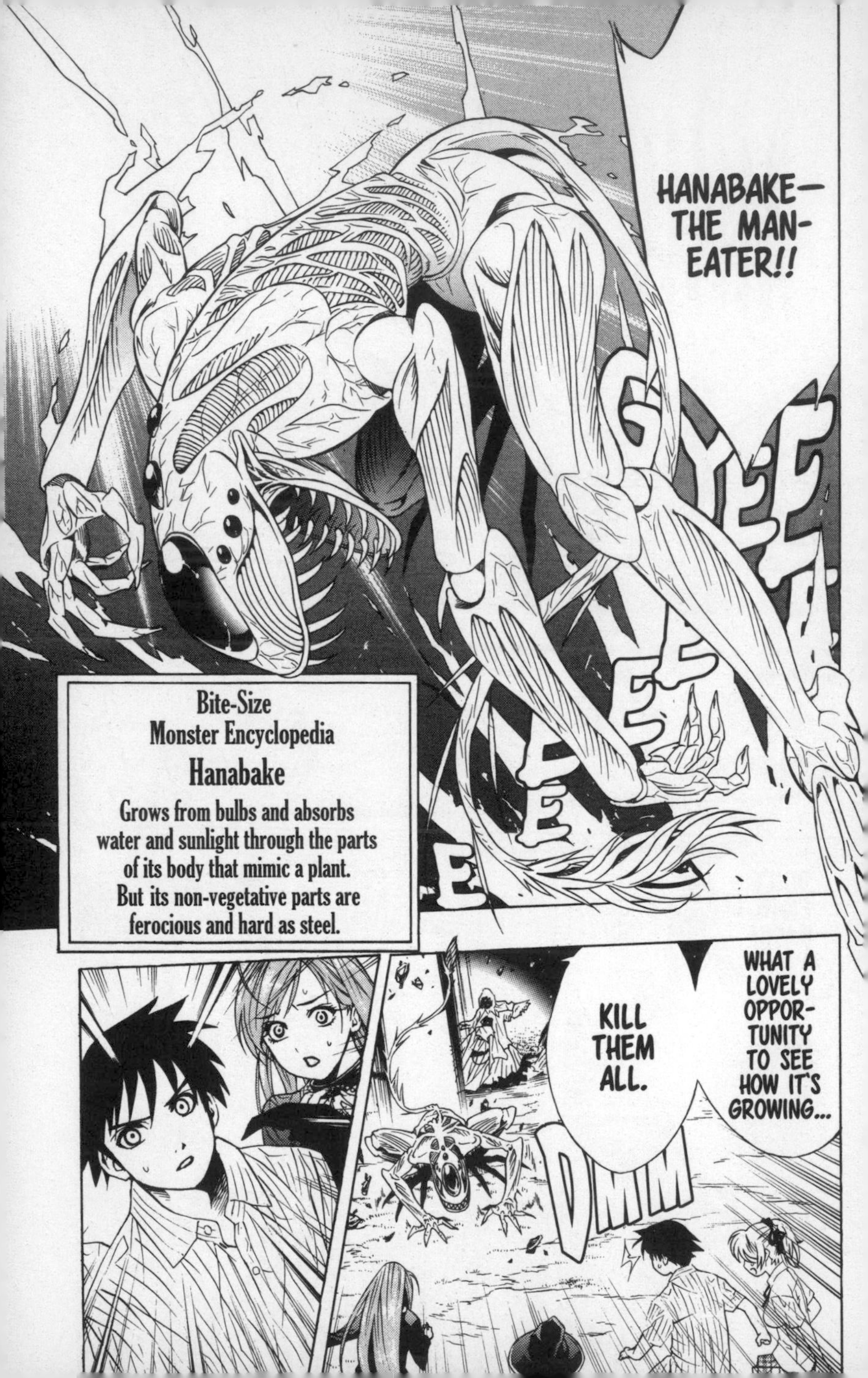
HANABAKE—THE MAN-EATER!!
GYEEEEEEEEE
Bite-Size Monster Encyclopedia
Hanabake
Grows from bulbs and absorbs water and sunlight through the parts of its body that mimic a plant. But its non-vegetative parts are ferocious and hard as steel.
WHAT A LOVELY OPPORTUNITY TO SEE HOW IT'S GROWING...
KILL THEM ALL.
DMMM

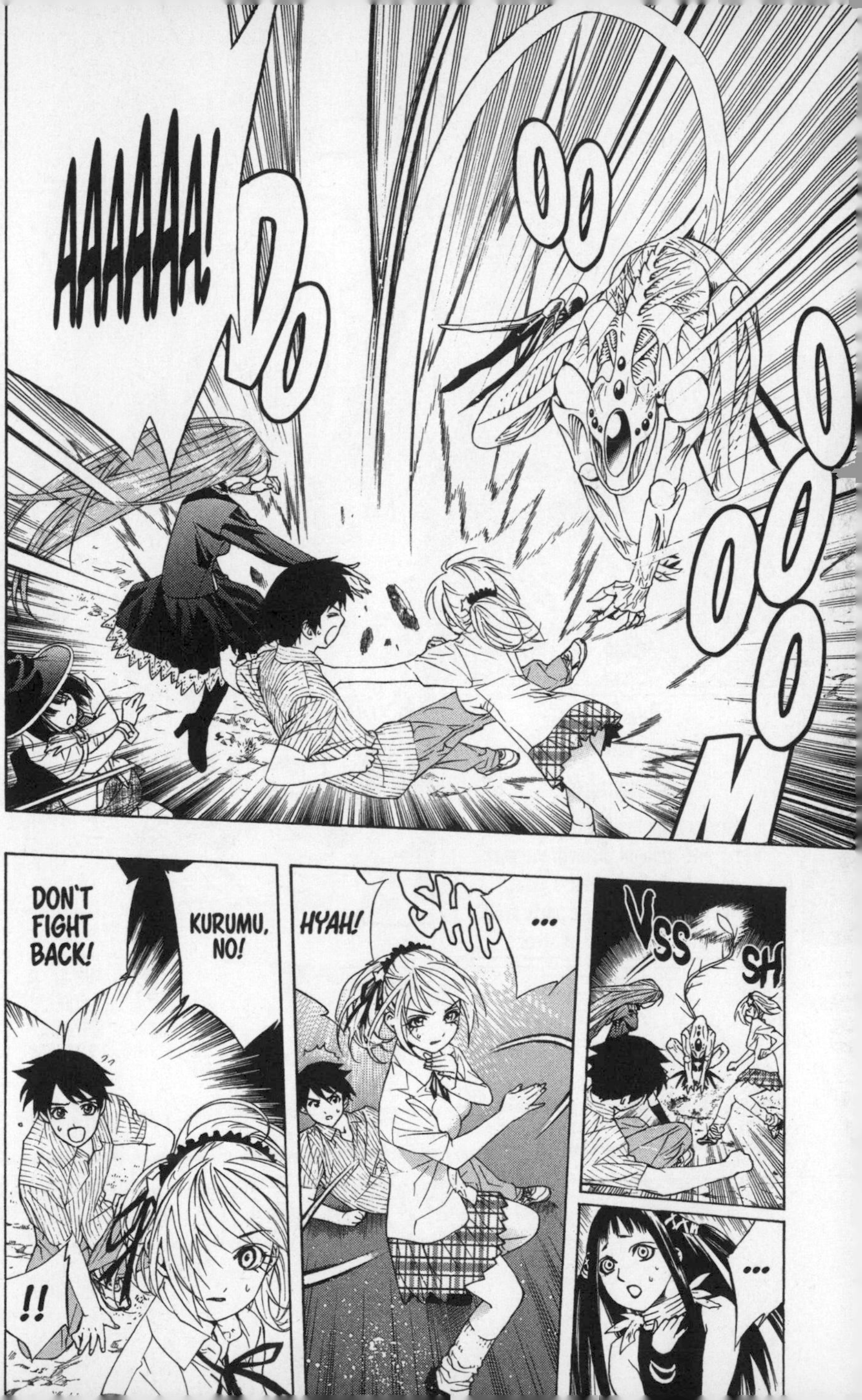
AAAAA!
DOOOOOOOOOM
VSS
SH
...
...
SHP
HYAH!
KURUMU, NO!
DON'T FIGHT BACK!
!!

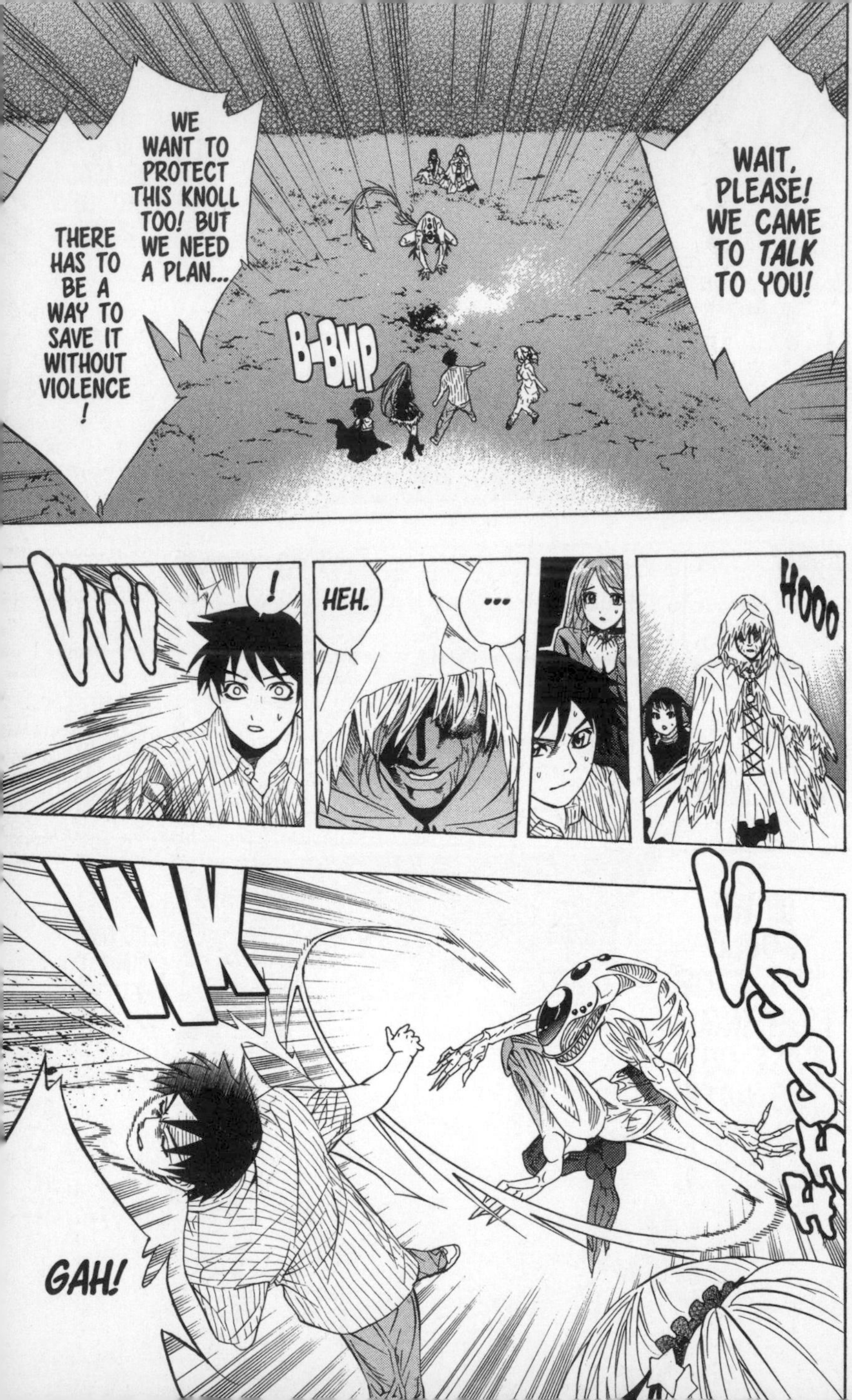
WAIT, PLEASE! WE CAME TO *TALK* TO YOU!
WE WANT TO PROTECT THIS KNOLL TOO! BUT WE NEED A PLAN...
THERE HAS TO BE A WAY TO SAVE IT WITHOUT VIOLENCE!
B-BMP
HOOO
...
HEH.
!
GAH!

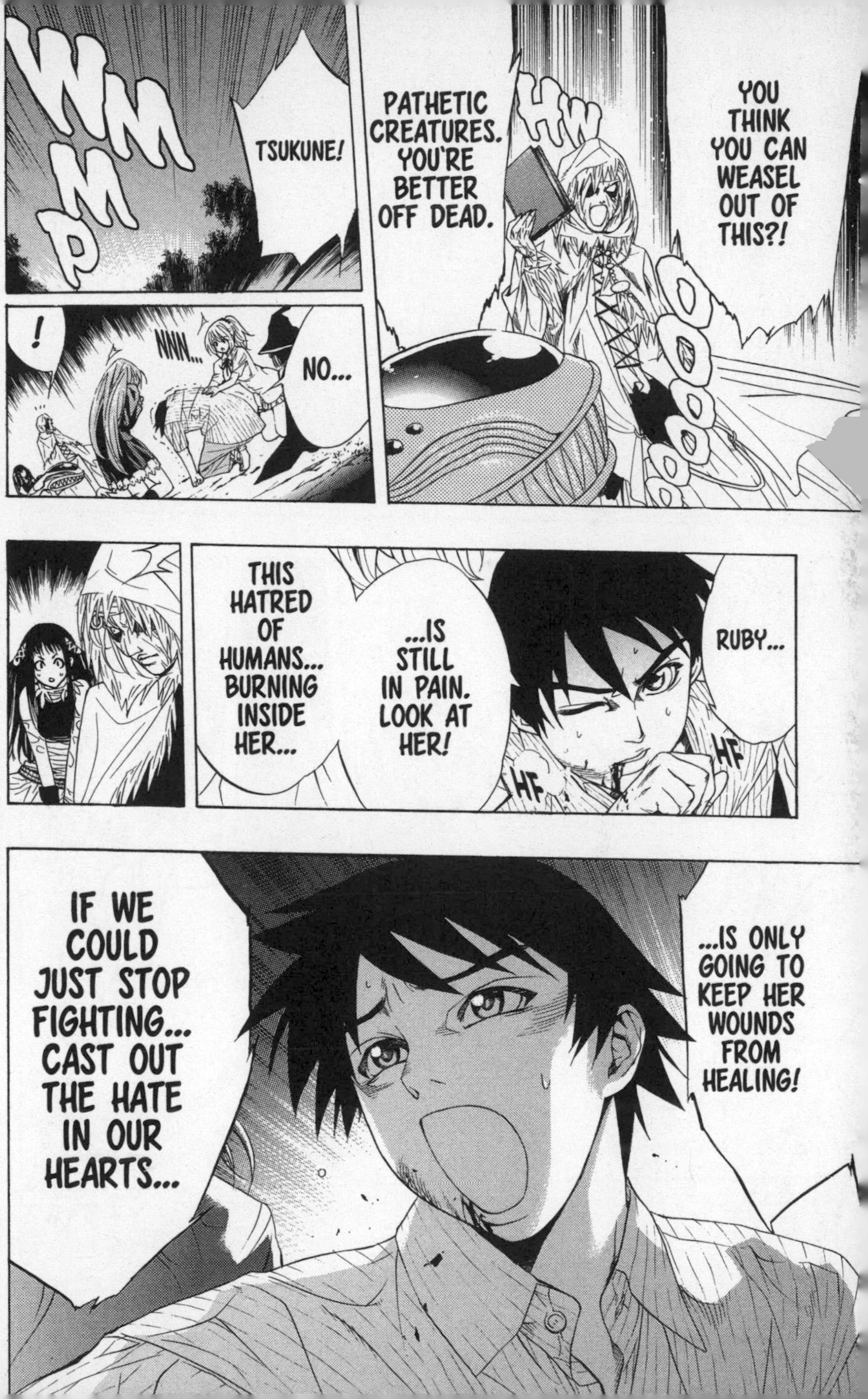
YOU THINK YOU CAN WEASEL OUT OF THIS?!
HW
PATHETIC CREATURES. YOU'RE BETTER OFF DEAD.
TSUKUNE!
WMMP
NO...
NNN...
!
RUBY...
HF
HF
...IS STILL IN PAIN. LOOK AT HER!
THIS HATRED OF HUMANS... BURNING INSIDE HER...
...IS ONLY GOING TO KEEP HER WOUNDS FROM HEALING!
IF WE COULD JUST STOP FIGHTING... CAST OUT THE HATE IN OUR HEARTS...

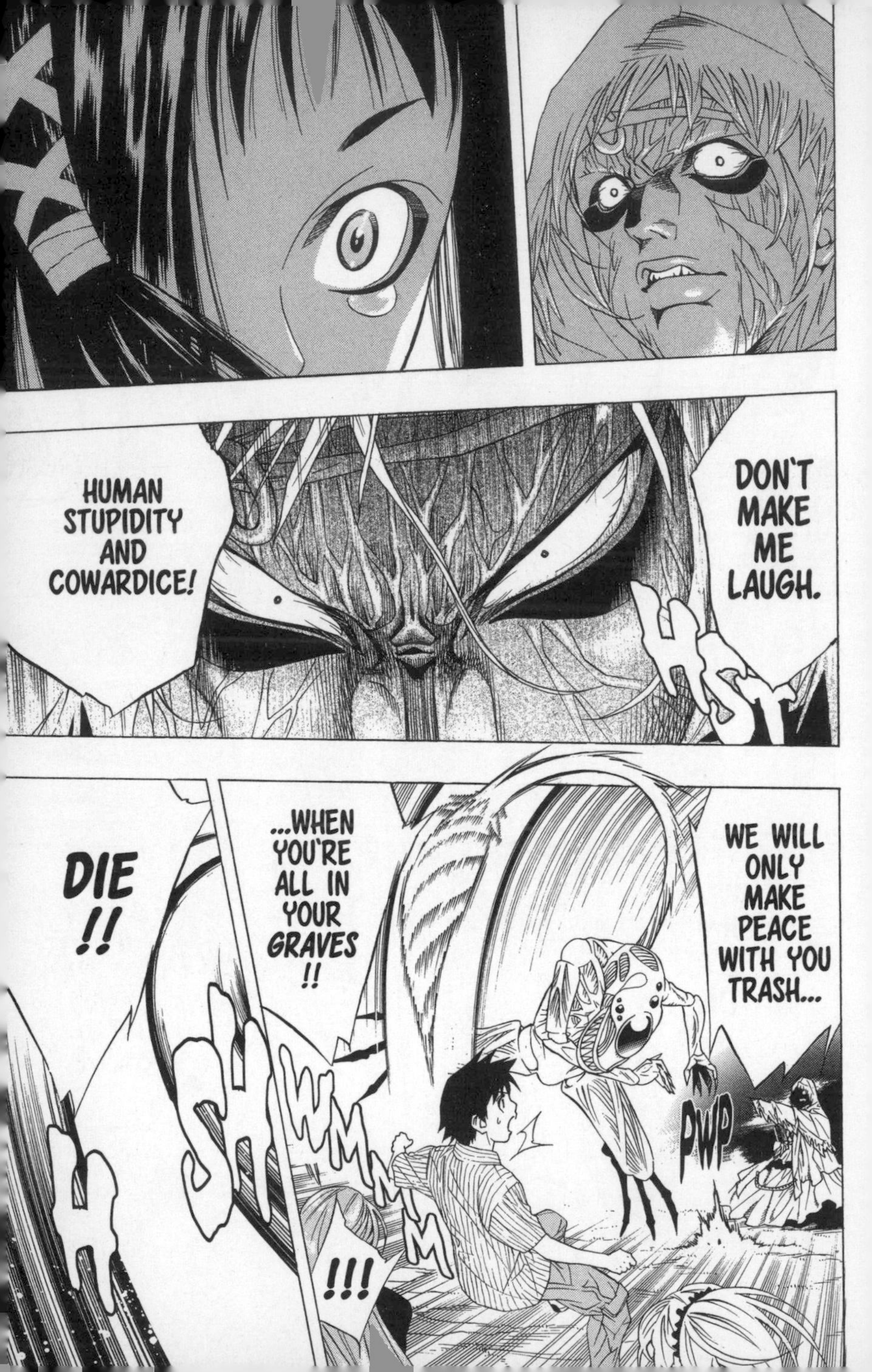
DON'T MAKE ME LAUGH.
HUMAN STUPIDITY AND COWARDICE!
WE WILL ONLY MAKE PEACE WITH YOU TRASH...
...WHEN YOU'RE ALL IN YOUR GRAVES!!
PWP
!!!
DIE!!

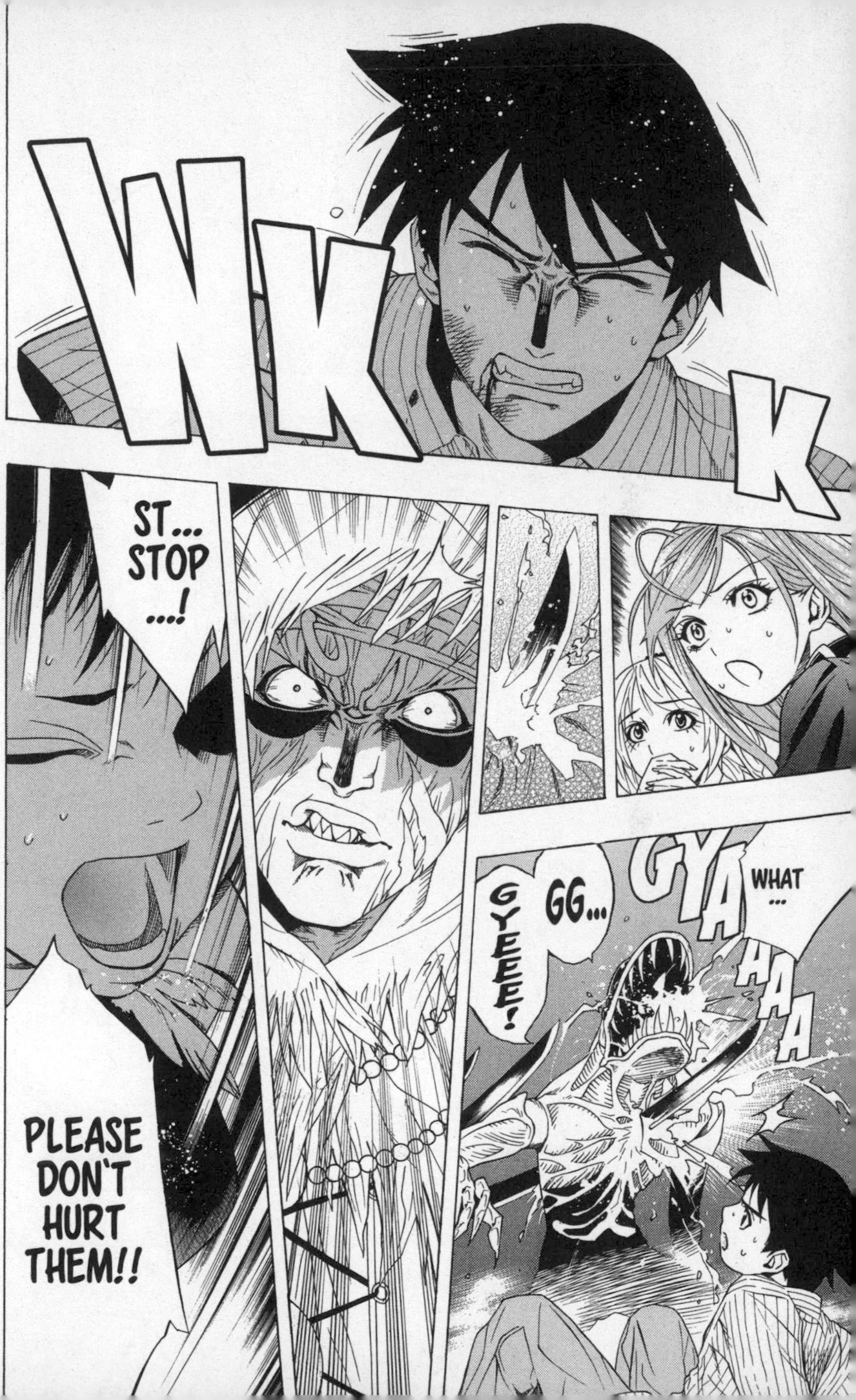
WKK
K
WHAT ...
GYAAAA
GG...
GYEEEE!
ST... STOP ...!
PLEASE DON'T HURT THEM!!

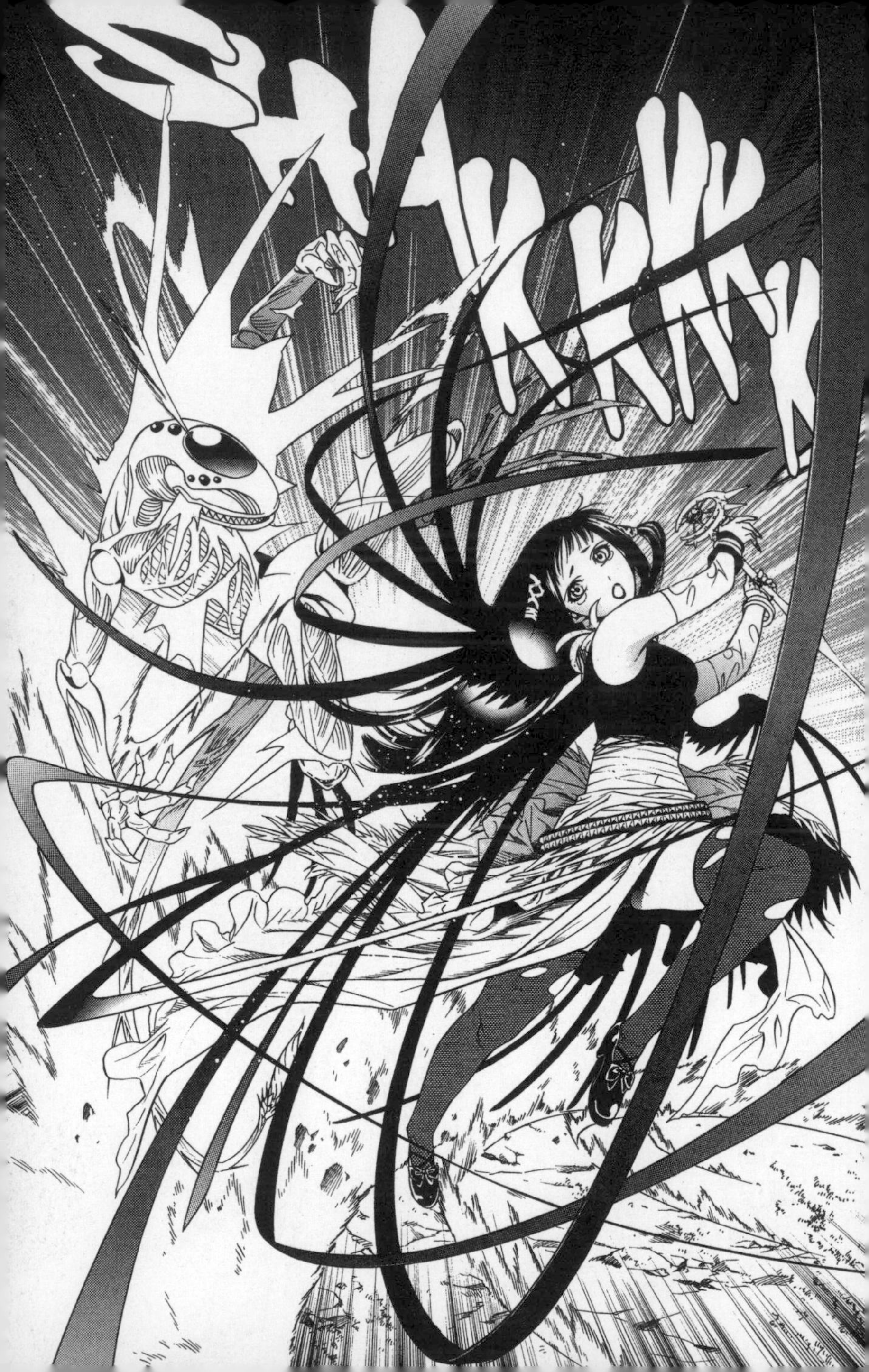

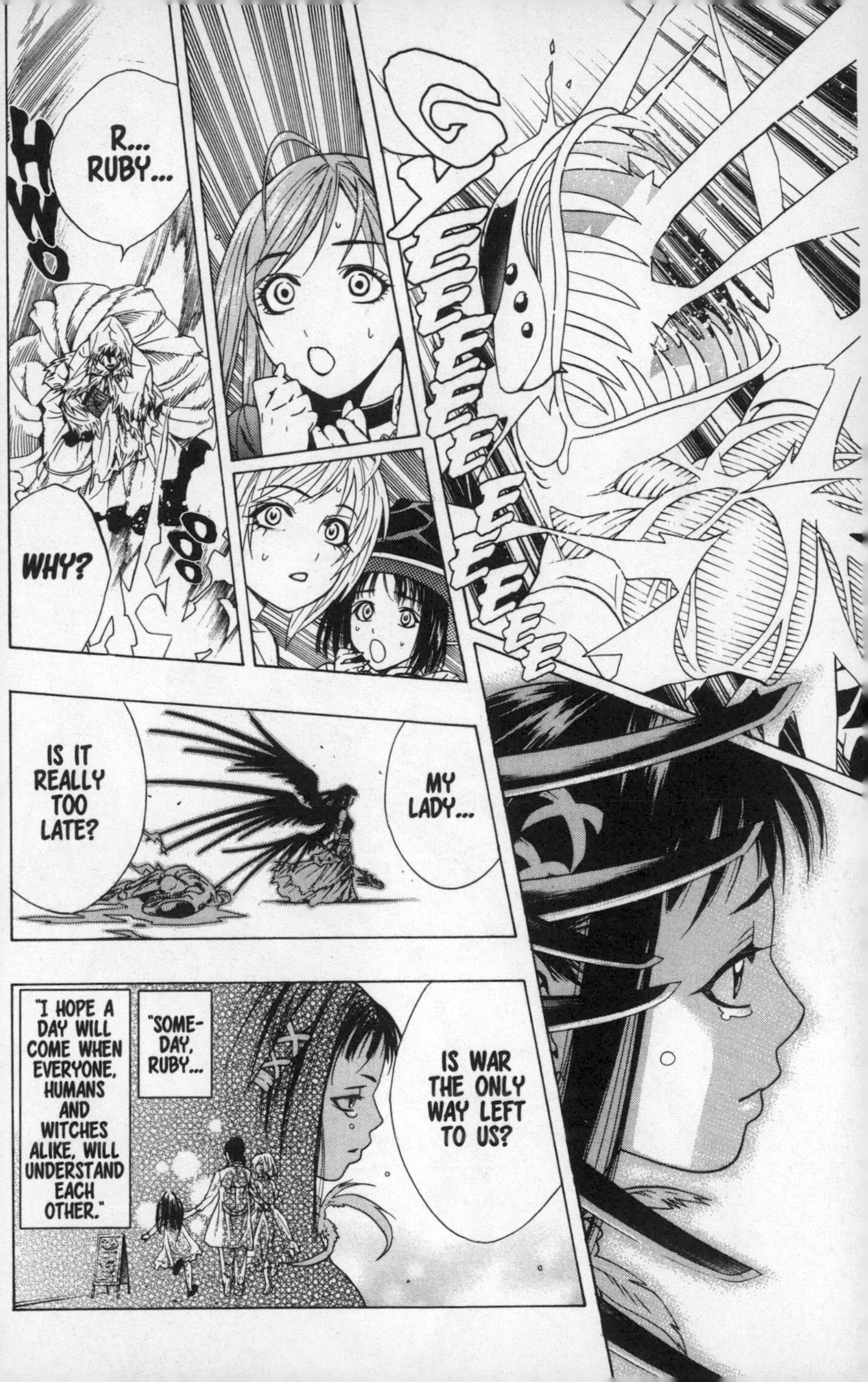
GYEEEEEEEEEEEEE
R... RUBY...
WHY?
HWOOOOO
MY LADY...
IS IT REALLY TOO LATE?
IS WAR THE ONLY WAY LEFT TO US?
"SOME-DAY, RUBY...
"I HOPE A DAY WILL COME WHEN EVERYONE, HUMANS AND WITCHES ALIKE, WILL UNDERSTAND EACH OTHER."

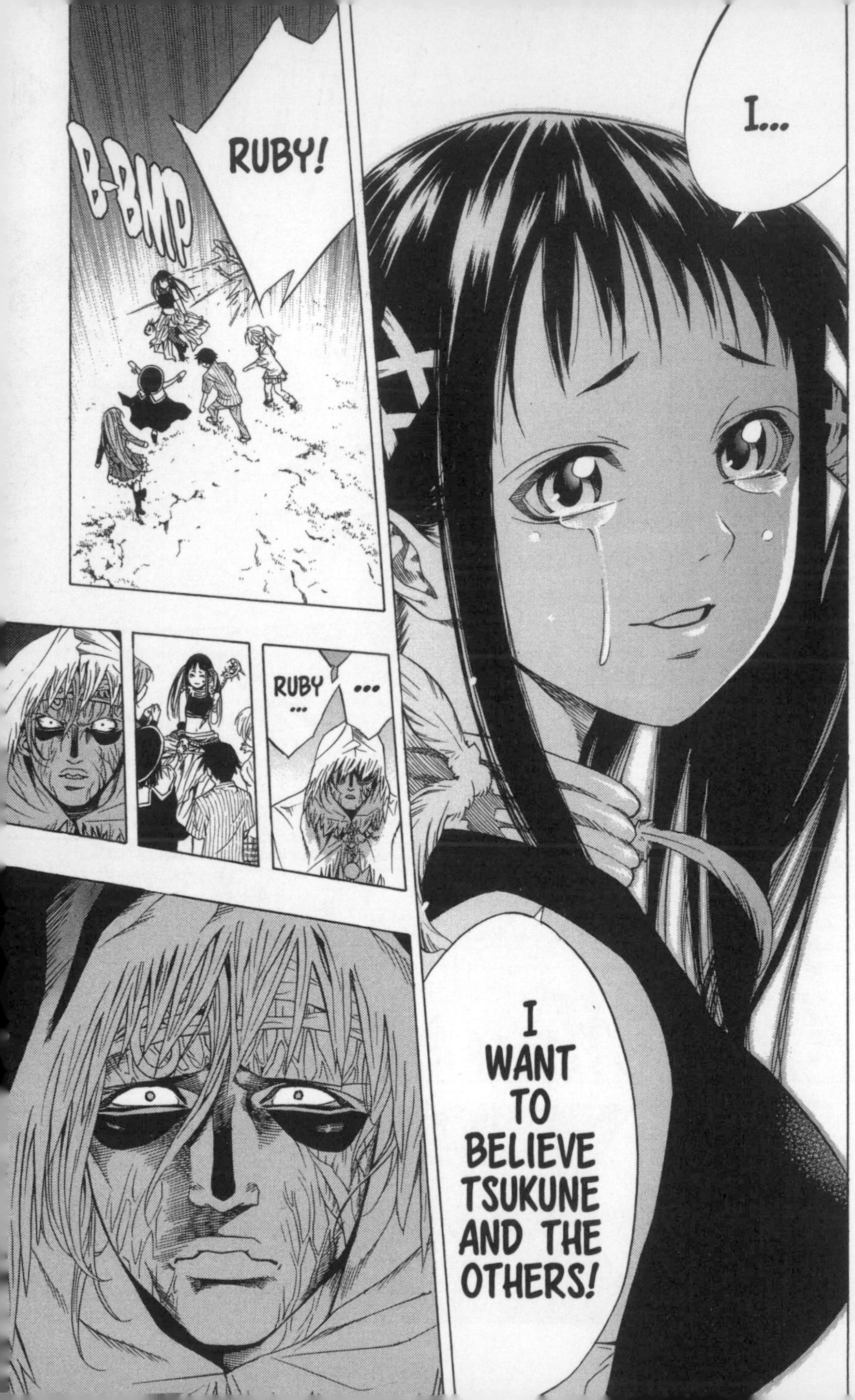
I...
I WANT TO BELIEVE TSUKUNE AND THE OTHERS!
RUBY!
B-BMP
...
RUBY ...

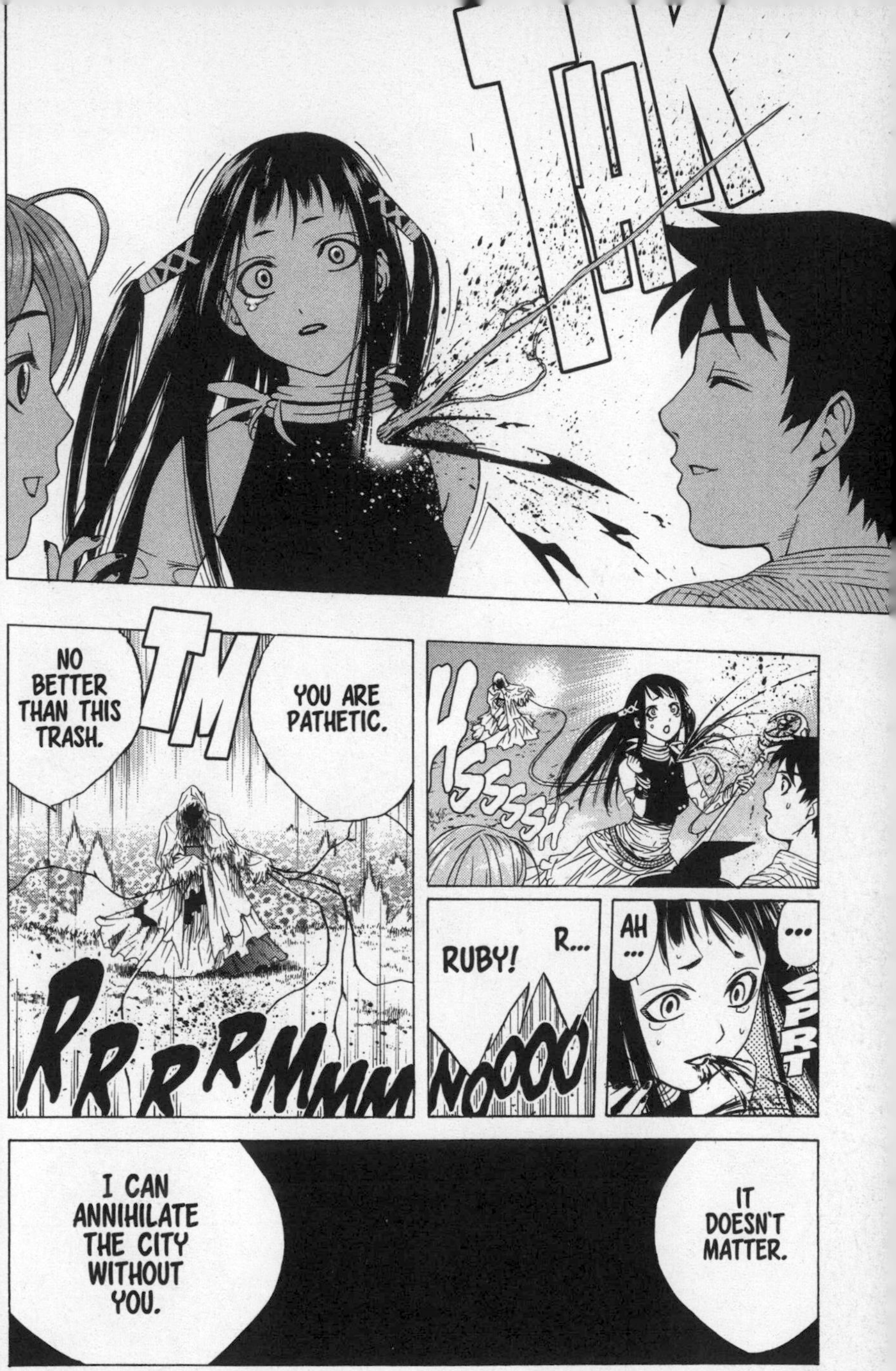
THK
HSSSSH
...
SPRT
AH ...
R...
RUBY!
NOOOO
YOU ARE PATHETIC.
TM
NO BETTER THAN THIS TRASH.
RRRRMMMM
IT DOESN'T MATTER.
I CAN ANNIHILATE THE CITY WITHOUT YOU.

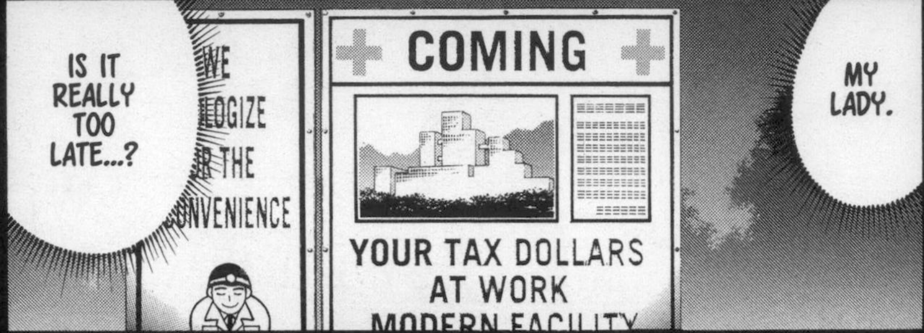
MY LADY.
COMING
YOUR TAX DOLLARS
AT WORK
MODERN FACILITY
IS IT REALLY TOO LATE...?

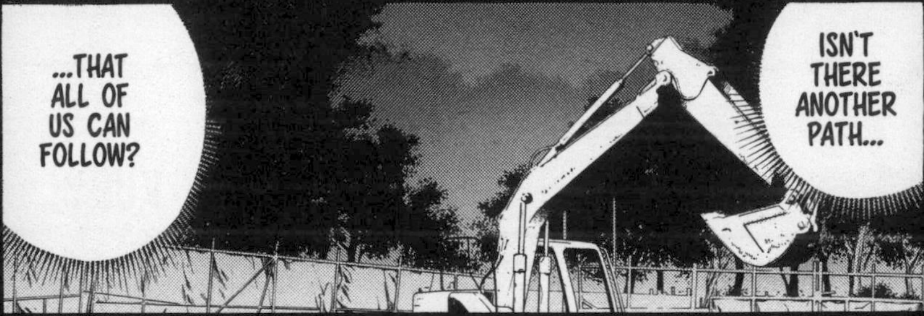
ISN'T THERE ANOTHER PATH...
...THAT ALL OF US CAN FOLLOW?

16: Witch's Knoll

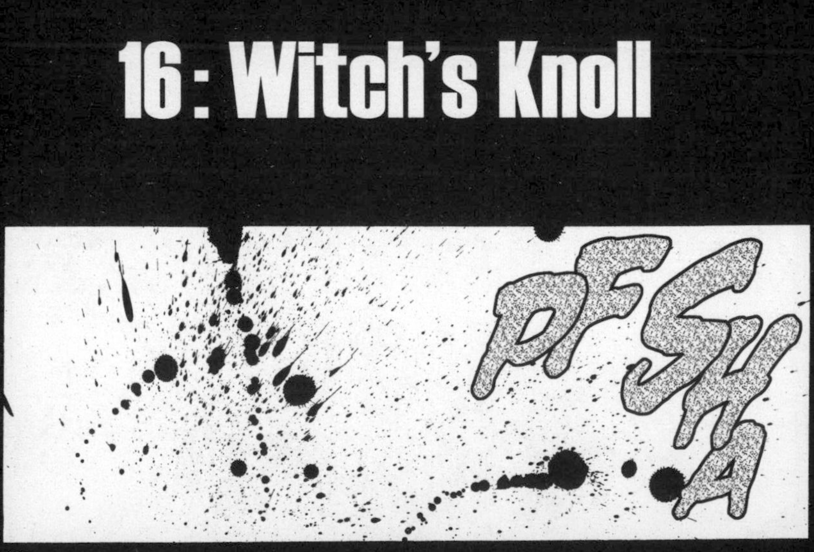
PFSHA

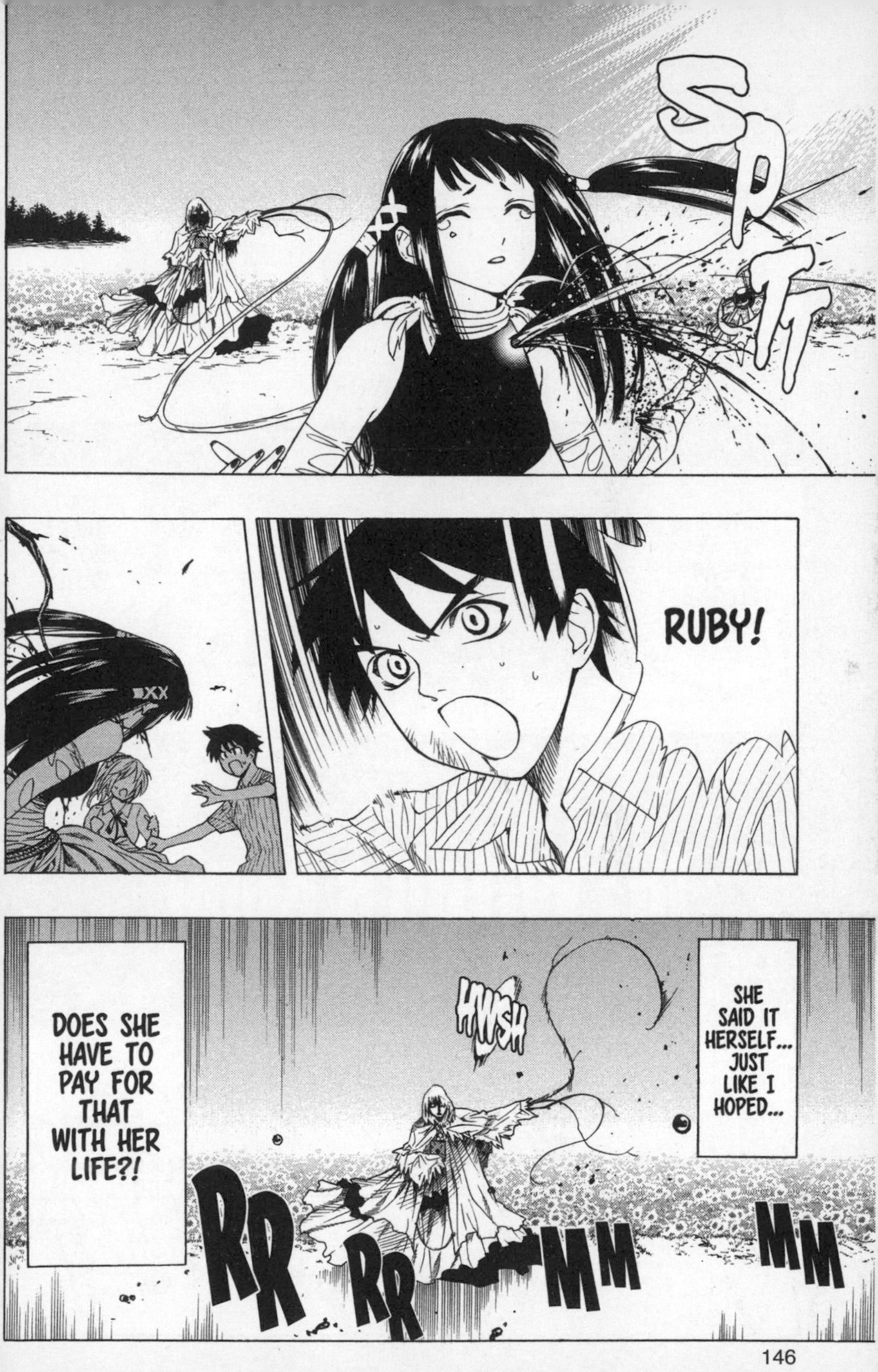
SPTT
RUBY!
SHE SAID IT HERSELF... JUST LIKE I HOPED...
HWSH
DOES SHE HAVE TO PAY FOR THAT WITH HER LIFE?!
RRRRMMMM

READ THIS WAY

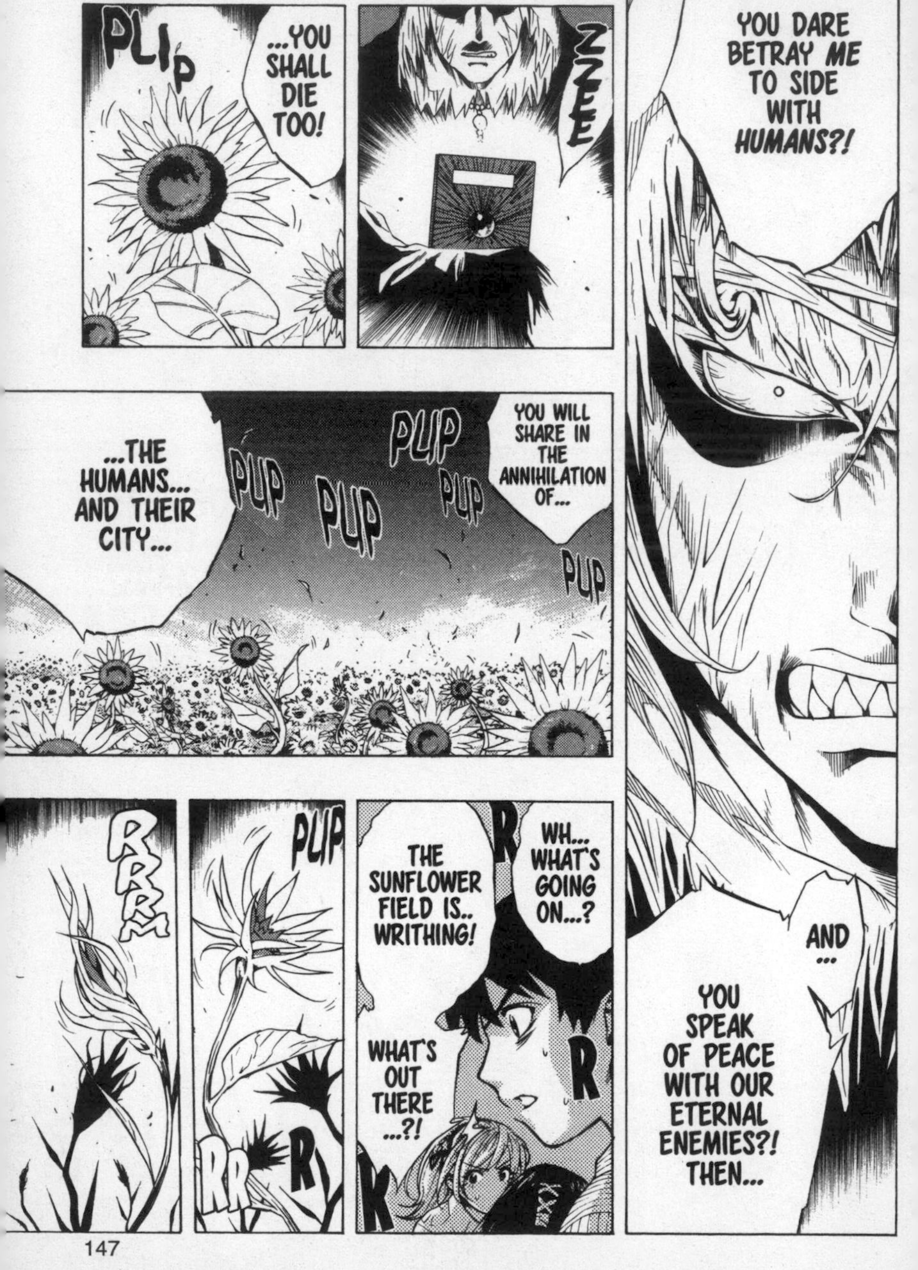

YOU DARE BETRAY ME TO SIDE WITH HUMANS?!
AND...
YOU SPEAK OF PEACE WITH OUR ETERNAL ENEMIES?! THEN...
ZZEEE
...YOU SHALL DIE TOO!
PLIP
YOU WILL SHARE IN THE ANNIHILATION OF...
PUP
PUP
PUP
PUP
PUP
...THE HUMANS... AND THEIR CITY...
R
WH... WHAT'S GOING ON...?
THE SUNFLOWER FIELD IS.. WRITHING!
R
WHAT'S OUT THERE ...?!
K
PLIP
R
RR
RRRM

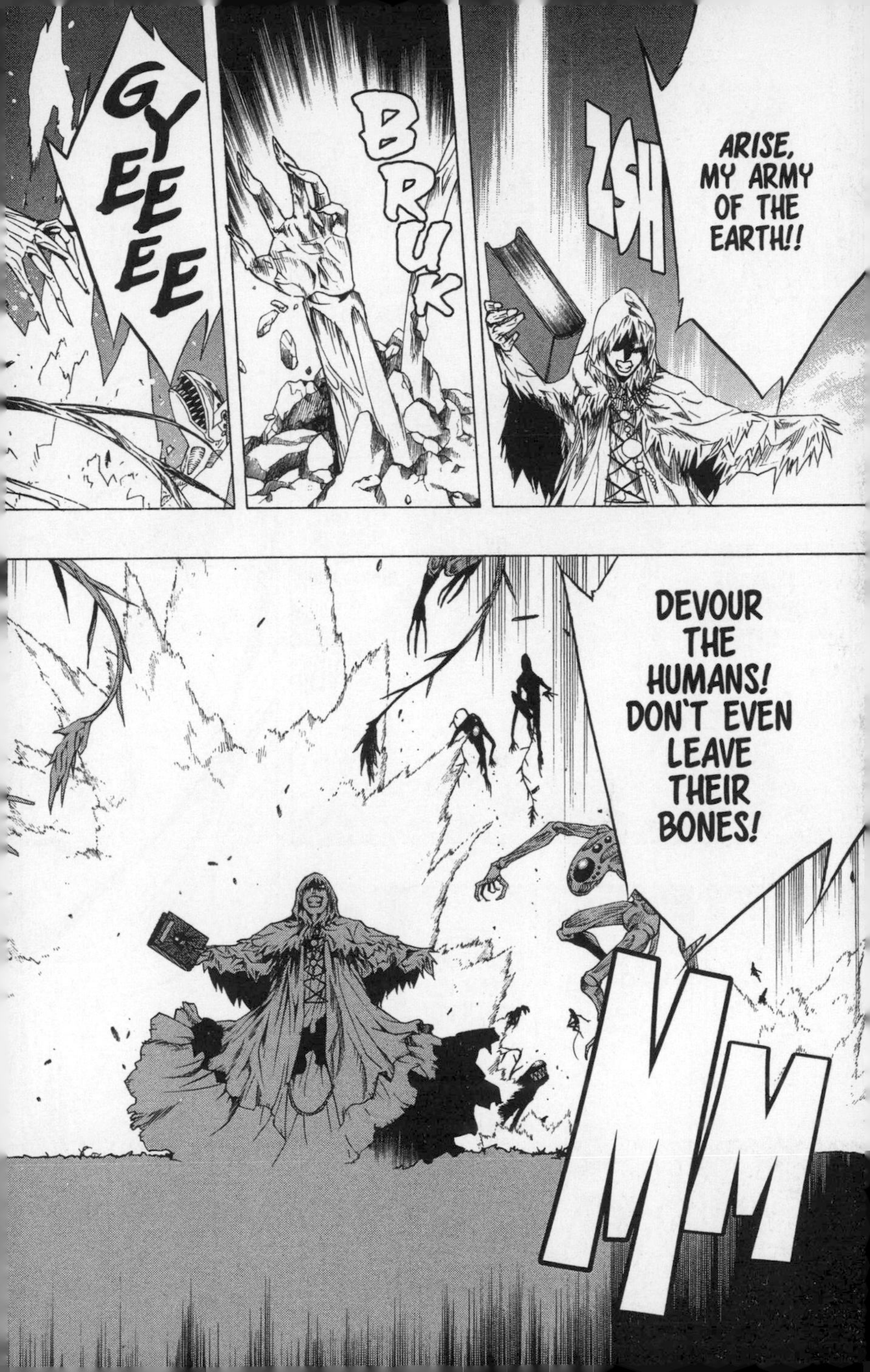
ZSH
ARISE, MY ARMY OF THE EARTH!!
BRUK
GYEEEE
DEVOUR THE HUMANS! DON'T EVEN LEAVE THEIR BONES!
MM

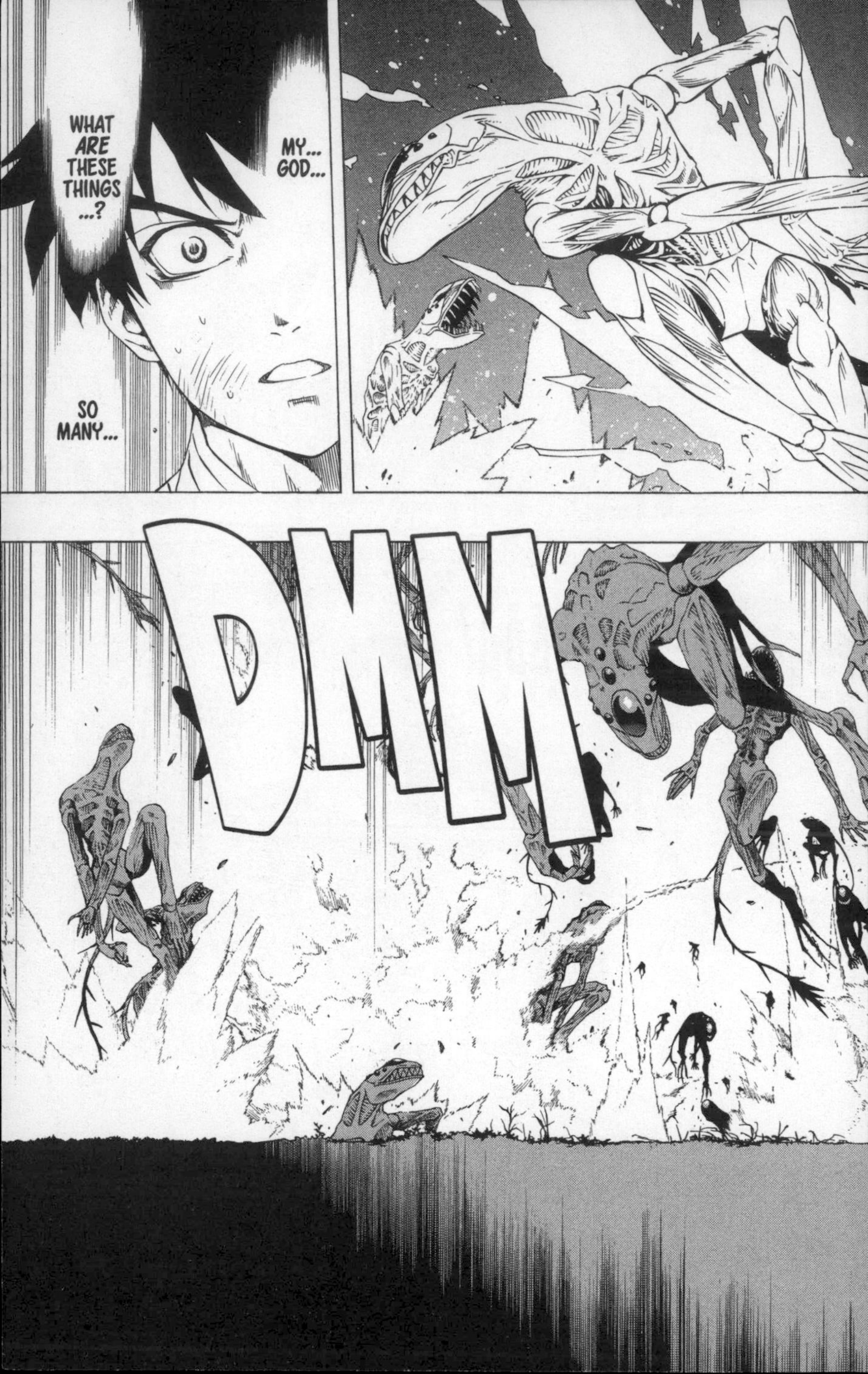
MY... GOD...
WHAT ARE THESE THINGS ...?
SO MANY...
DMM

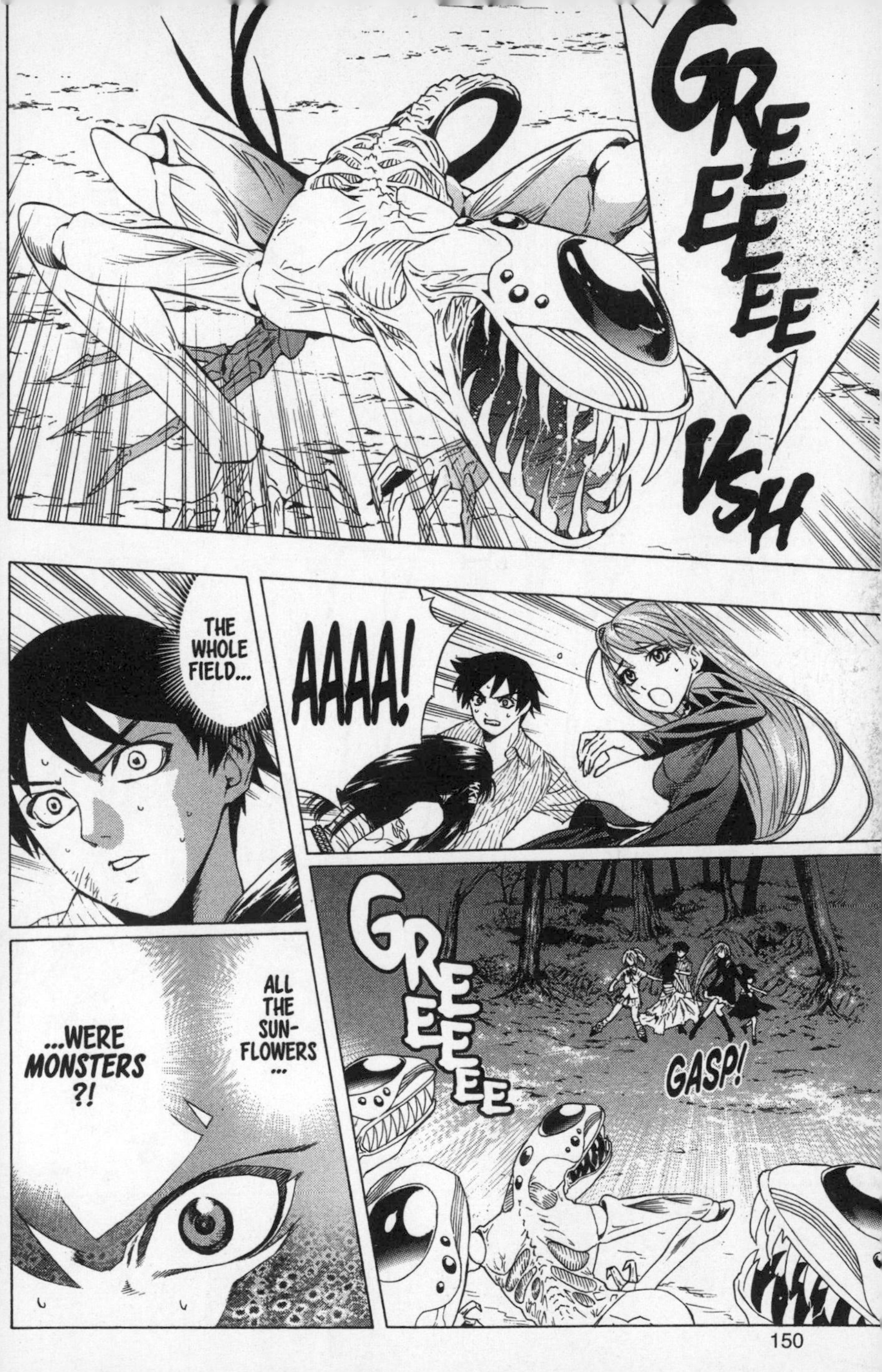
GREEEEEE
VSH
AAAA!
THE WHOLE FIELD...
GREEEEE
GASP!
ALL THE SUN-FLOWERS...
...WERE MONSTERS?!

READ THIS WAY

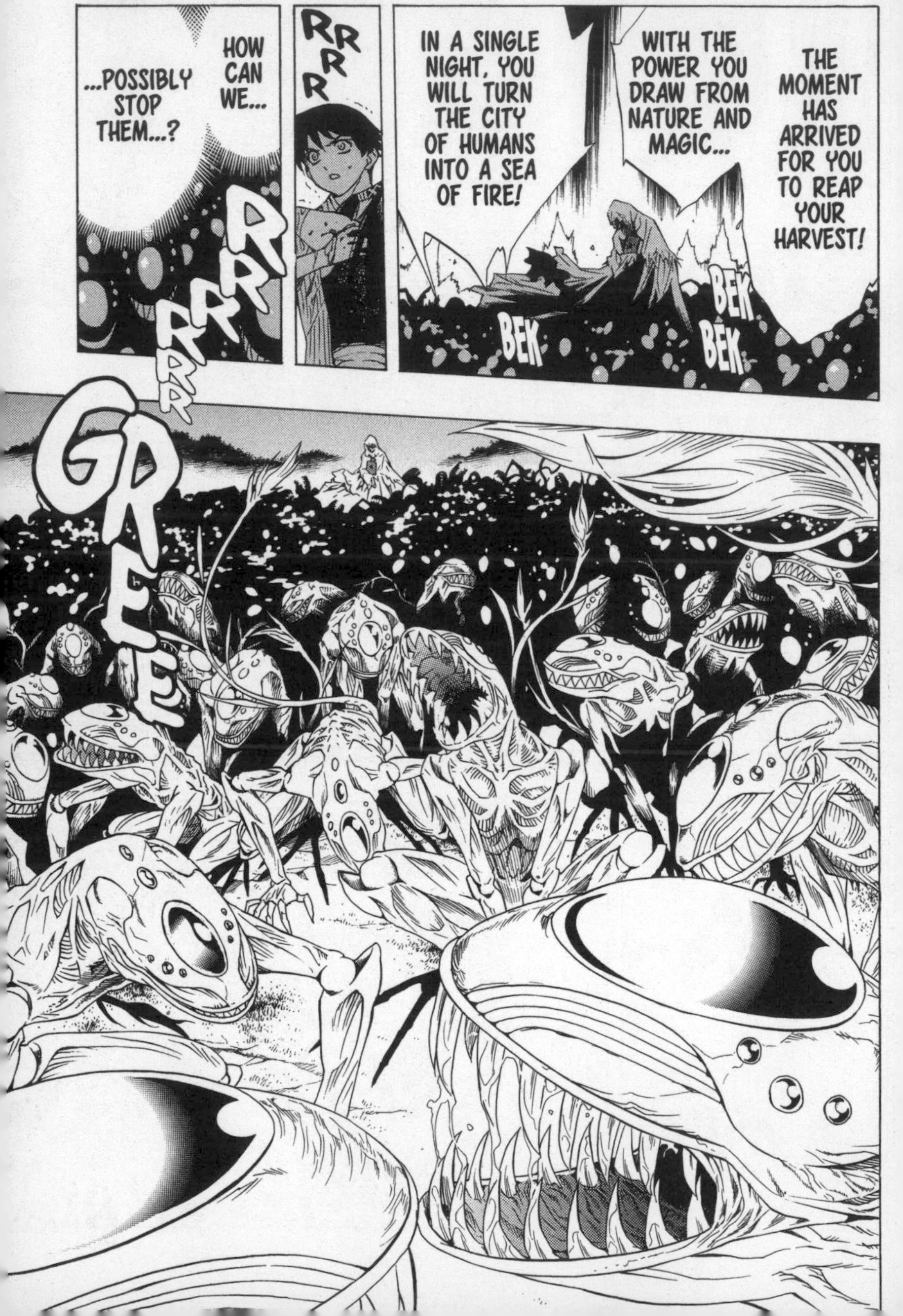
THE MOMENT HAS ARRIVED FOR YOU TO REAP YOUR HARVEST!
WITH THE POWER YOU DRAW FROM NATURE AND MAGIC...
IN A SINGLE NIGHT, YOU WILL TURN THE CITY OF HUMANS INTO A SEA OF FIRE!
BEK
BEK
BEK
RRRR
HOW CAN WE...
...POSSIBLY STOP THEM...?
RRRRRR
GREEE

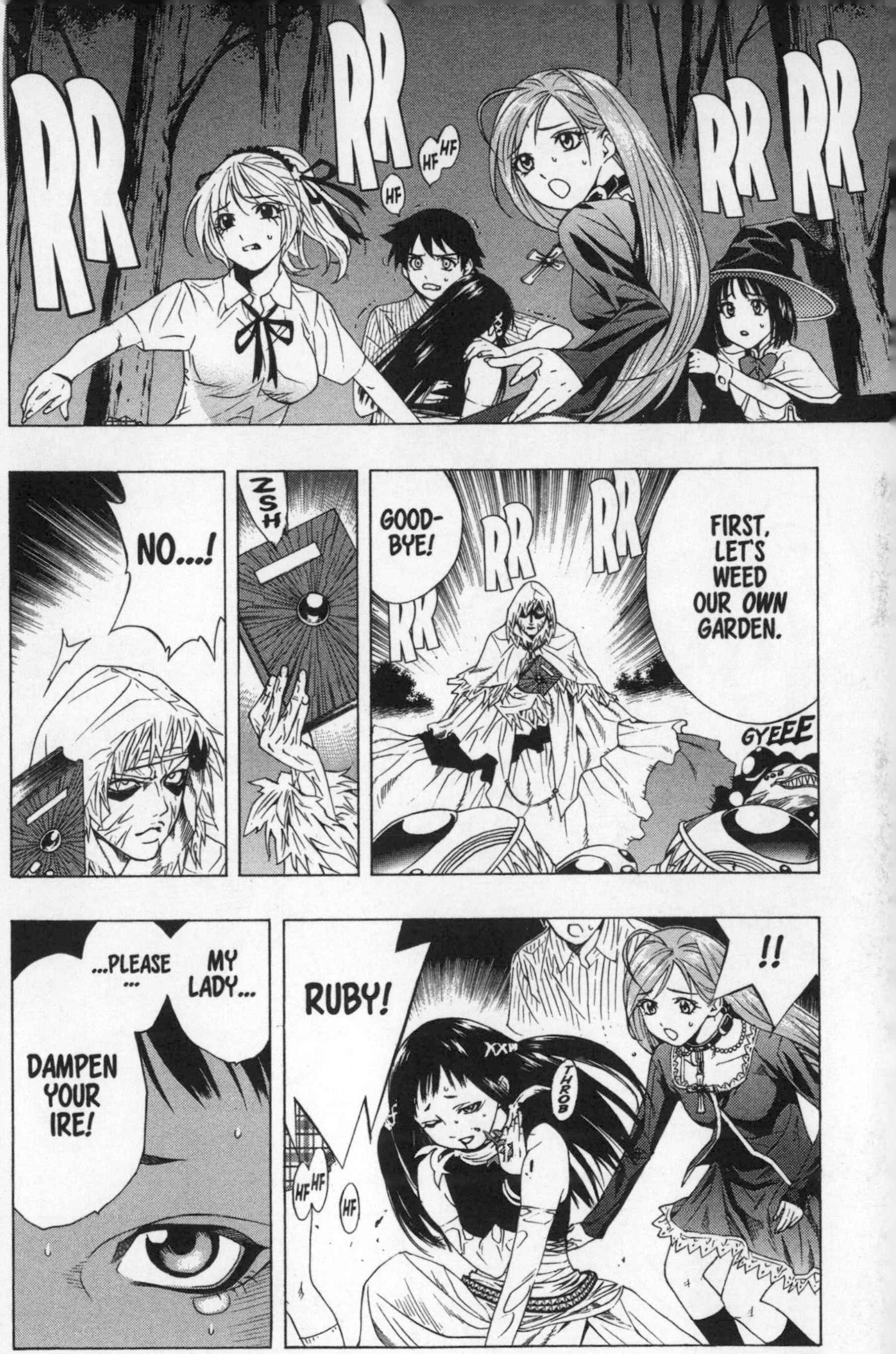
RR RR
HF HF
HF
RR
RR
FIRST, LET'S WEED OUR OWN GARDEN.
GYEEE
RR
RR
GOOD-BYE!
ZSH
NO...!
!!
RUBY!
THROB
HF HF
HF
MY LADY...
...PLEASE ...
DAMPEN YOUR IRE!

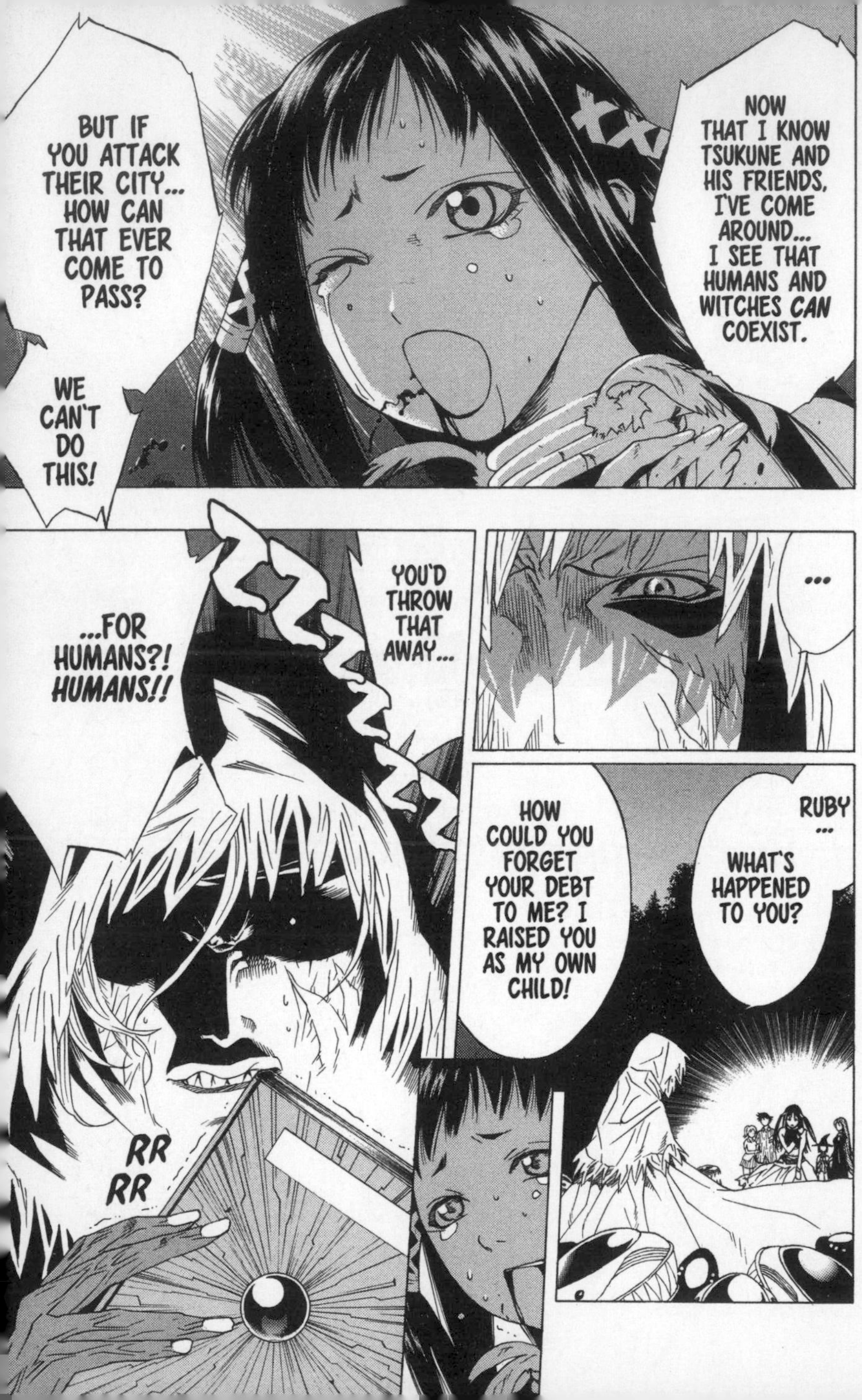
NOW THAT I KNOW TSUKUNE AND HIS FRIENDS, I'VE COME AROUND... I SEE THAT HUMANS AND WITCHES *CAN* COEXIST.
BUT IF YOU ATTACK THEIR CITY... HOW CAN THAT EVER COME TO PASS?
WE CAN'T DO THIS!
...
RUBY...
WHAT'S HAPPENED TO YOU?
HOW COULD YOU FORGET YOUR DEBT TO ME? I RAISED YOU AS MY OWN CHILD!
YOU'D THROW THAT AWAY...
...FOR HUMANS?! *HUMANS!!*
RR RR

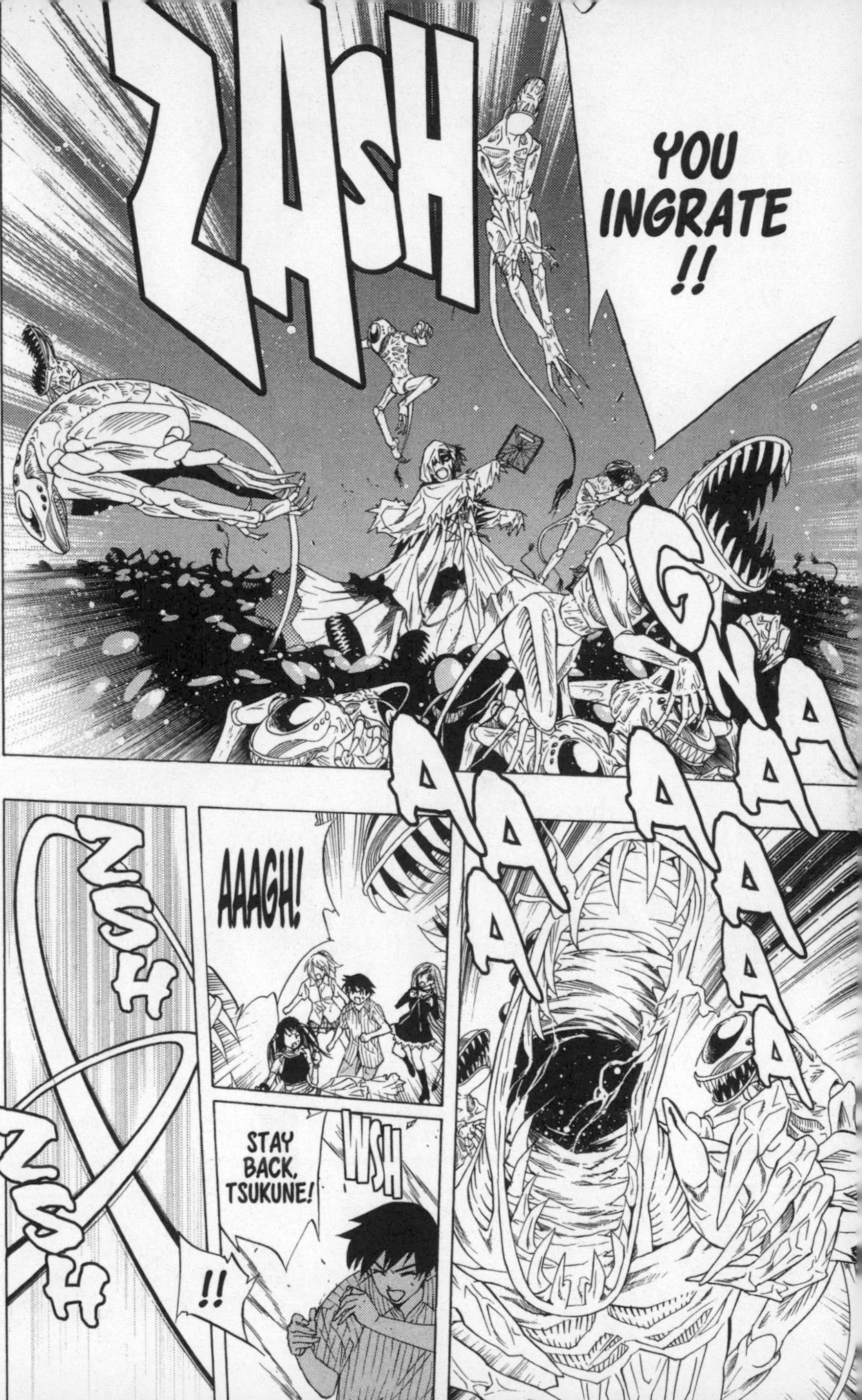
ZASH
YOU INGRATE!!
GNAAAAAAAA
AAAAA
AAAGH!
STAY BACK, TSUKUNE!
WSH
!!
ZSH
ZSH

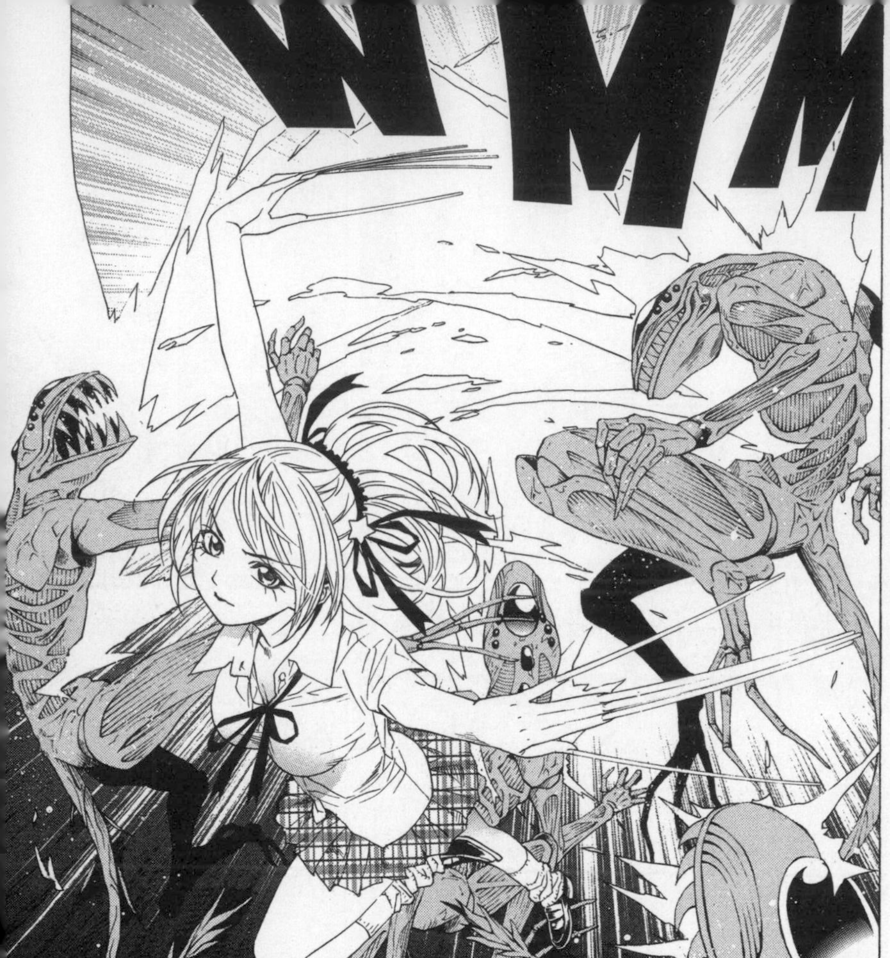
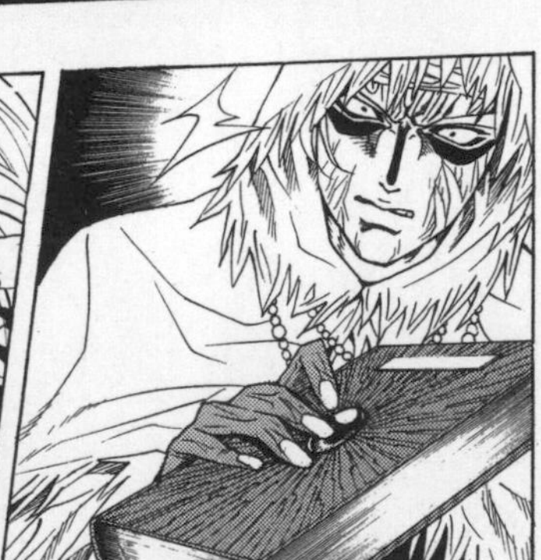
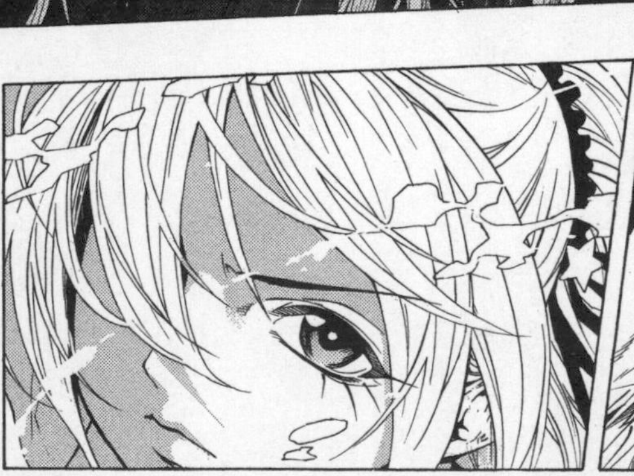

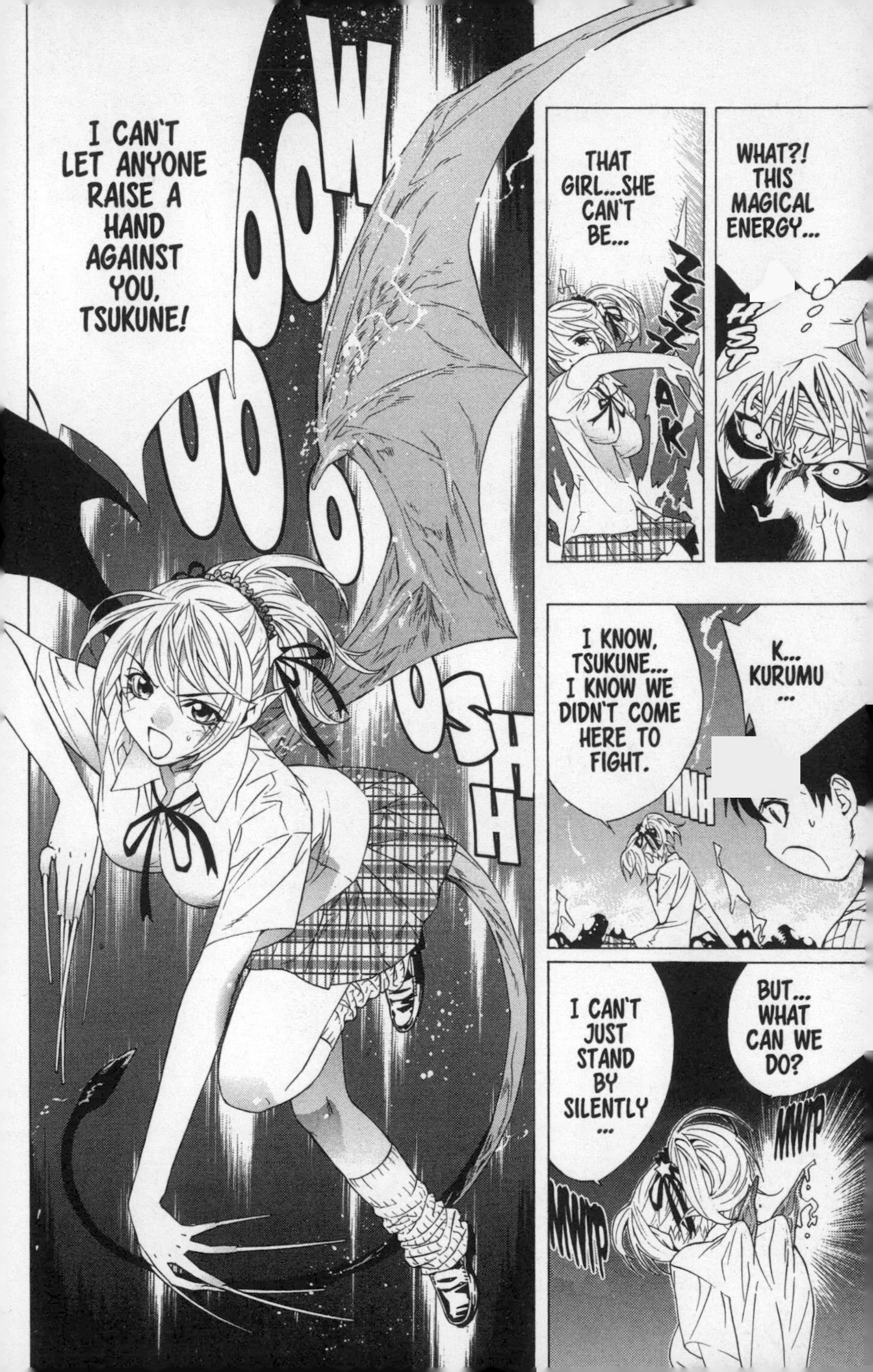
WHAT?! THIS MAGICAL ENERGY...
HSST
THAT GIRL...SHE CAN'T BE...
K... KURUMU...
I KNOW, TSUKUNE... I KNOW WE DIDN'T COME HERE TO FIGHT.
BUT... WHAT CAN WE DO?
MWIP
I CAN'T JUST STAND BY SILENTLY...
MWIP
I CAN'T LET ANYONE RAISE A HAND AGAINST YOU, TSUKUNE!

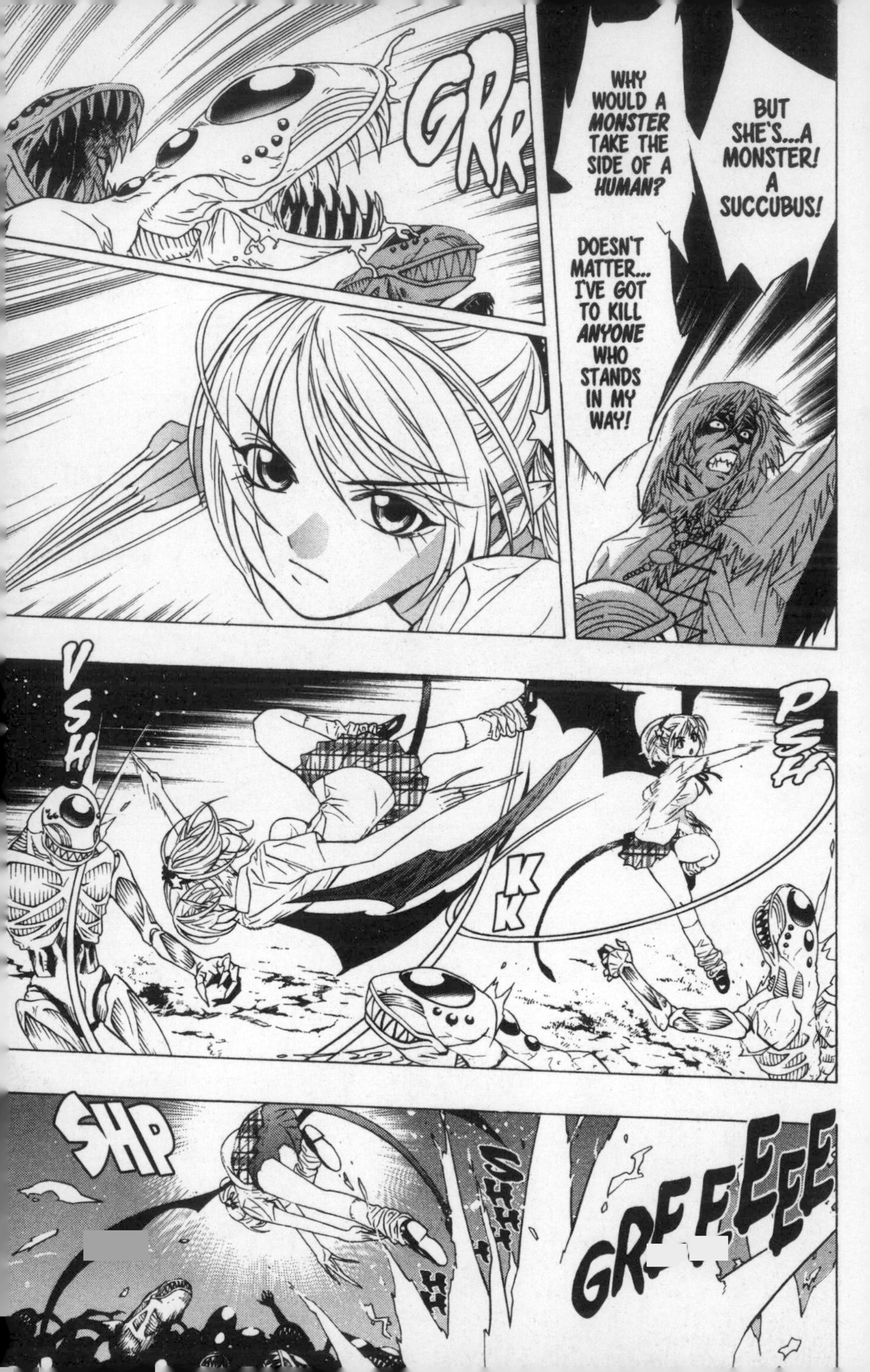
BUT SHE'S...A MONSTER! A SUCCUBUS!
WHY WOULD A MONSTER TAKE THE SIDE OF A HUMAN?
DOESN'T MATTER... I'VE GOT TO KILL ANYONE WHO STANDS IN MY WAY!
GRR
PSH
KK
VSH
SHP

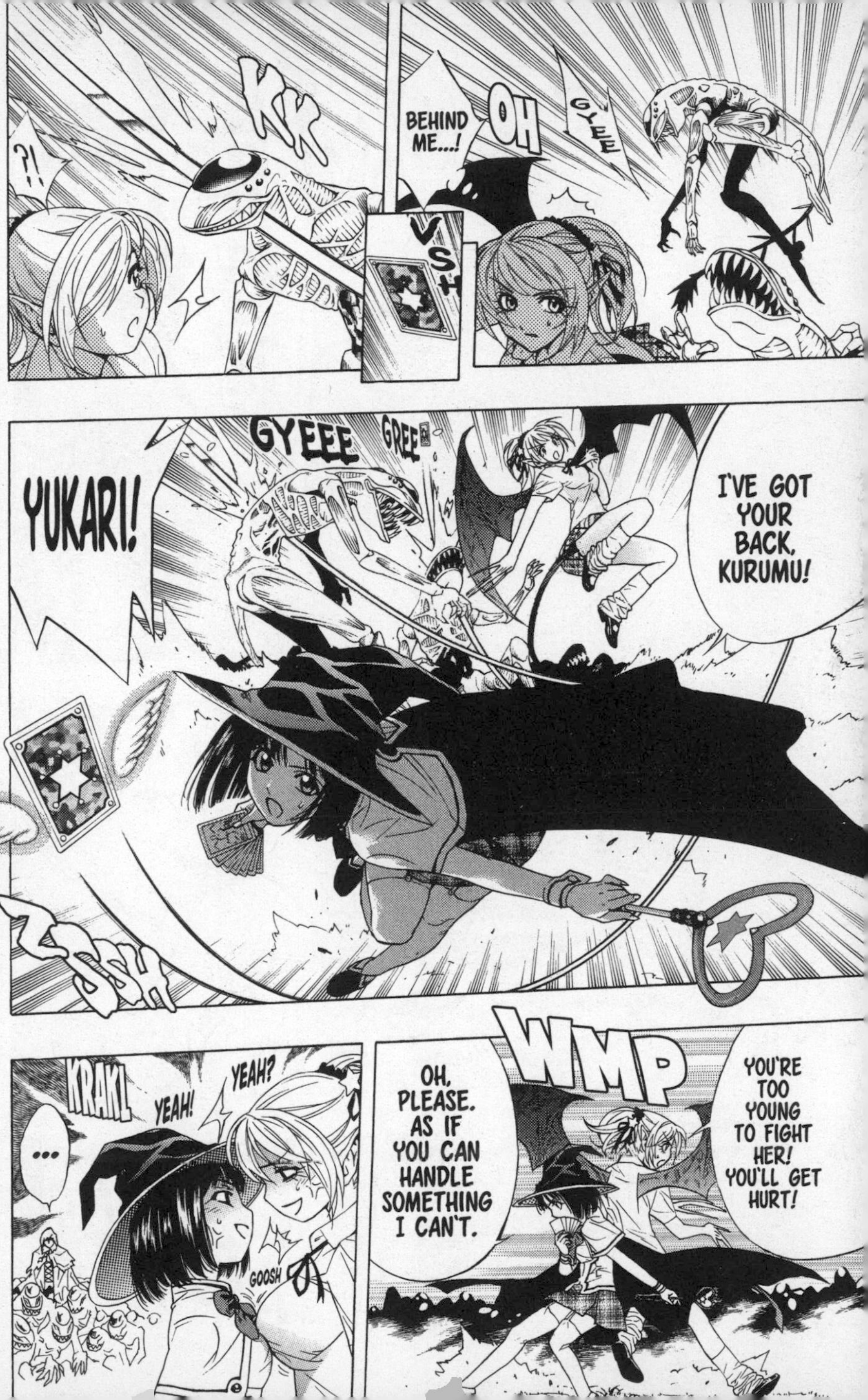
GYEEE
OH
BEHIND ME...!
VSH
KK
?!!
I'VE GOT YOUR BACK, KURUMU!
GREE
GYEEE
YUKARI!
ZSSH
WMP
YOU'RE TOO YOUNG TO FIGHT HER! YOU'LL GET HURT!
OH, PLEASE. AS IF YOU CAN HANDLE SOMETHING I CAN'T.
YEAH?
YEAH!
KRAKL
...
GOOSH

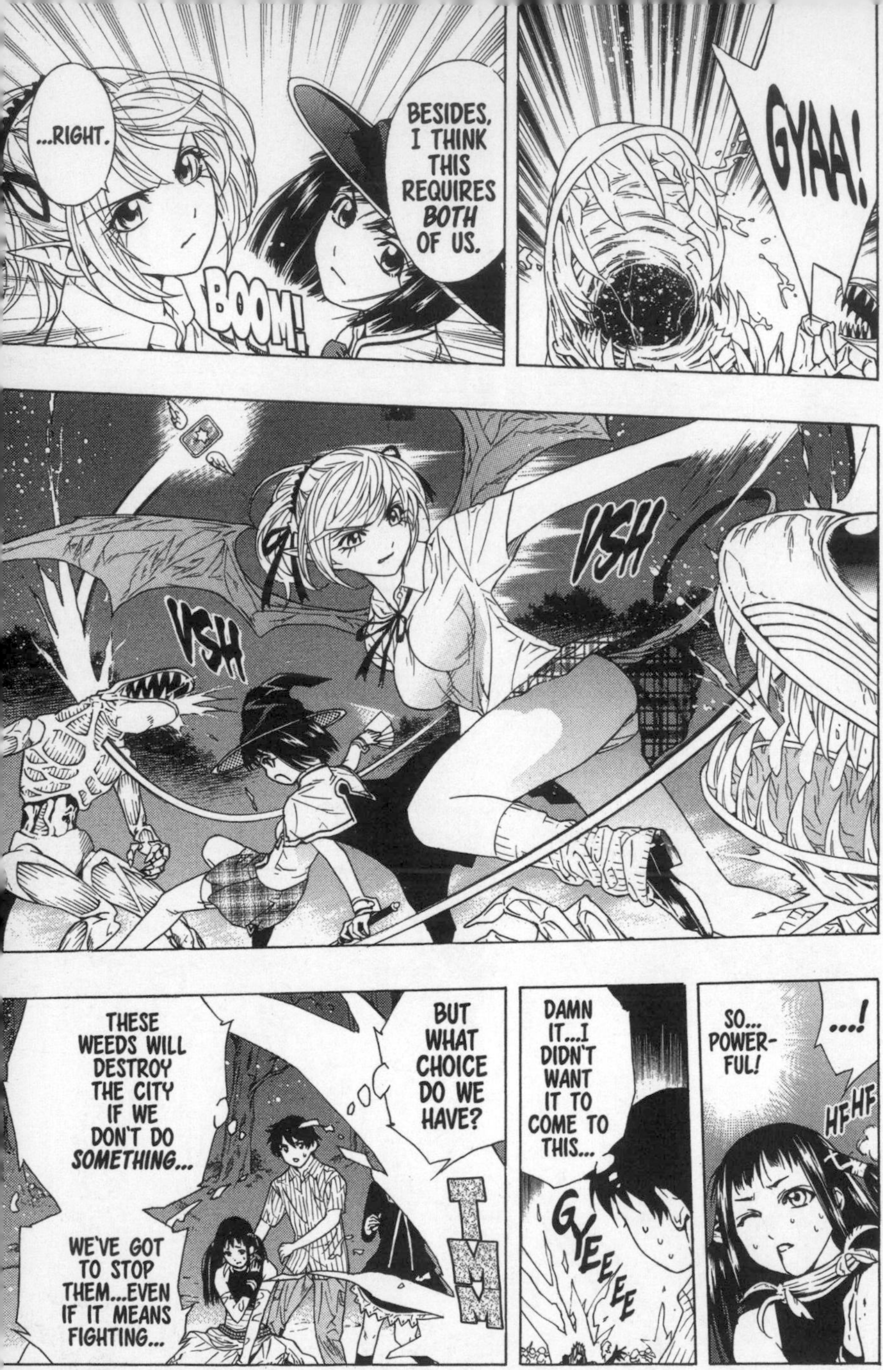
GYAA!
BESIDES, I THINK THIS REQUIRES *BOTH* OF US.
...RIGHT.
BOOM!
VSH
VSH
...!
SO... POWER-FUL!
HF HF
DAMN IT...I DIDN'T WANT IT TO COME TO THIS...
GYEEEEE
BUT WHAT CHOICE DO WE HAVE?
THESE WEEDS WILL DESTROY THE CITY IF WE DON'T DO *SOMETHING*...
TMM
WE'VE GOT TO STOP THEM...EVEN IF IT MEANS FIGHTING...

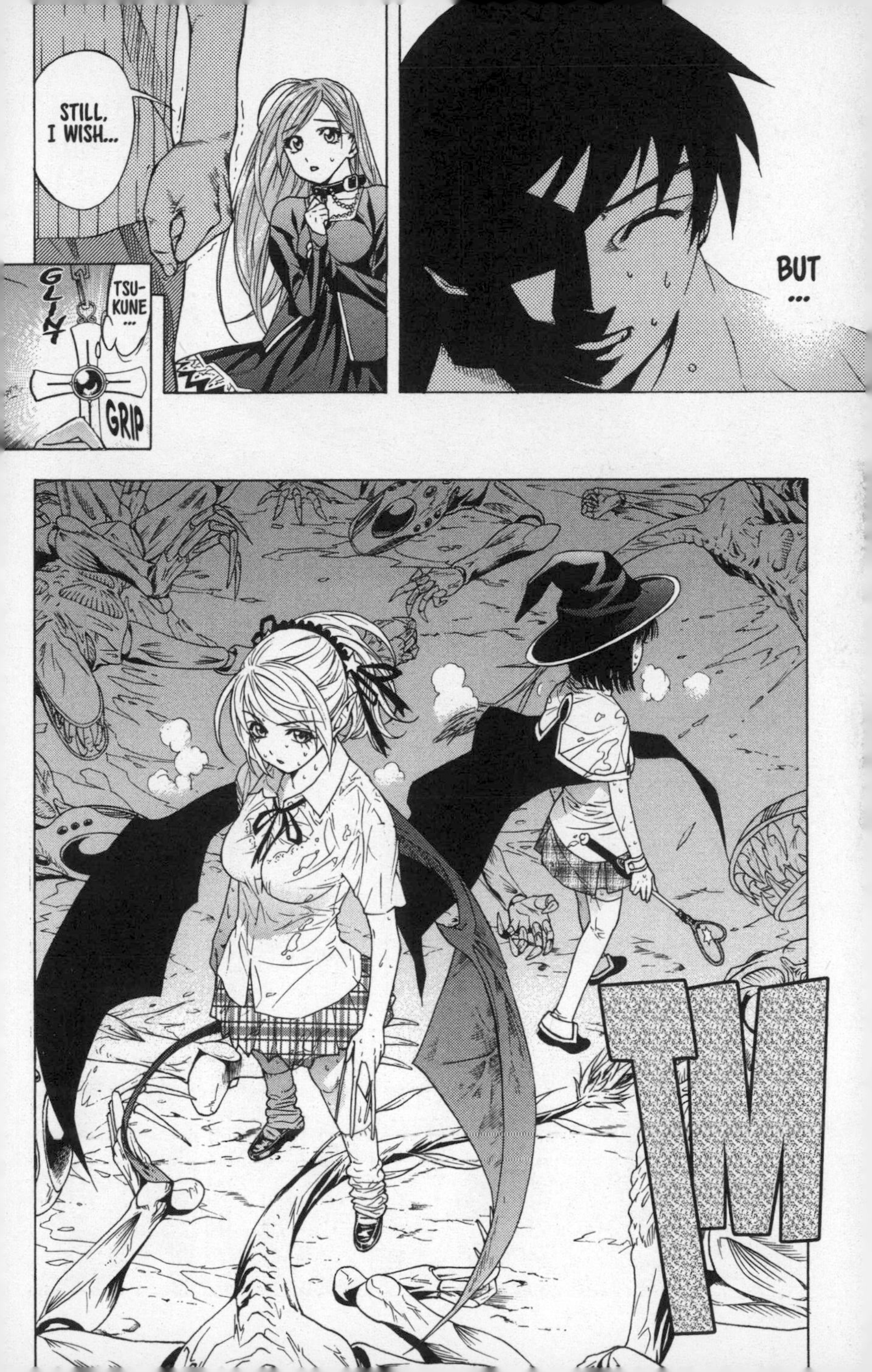
BUT ...
STILL, I WISH...
TSU-KUNE ...
GLINT
GRIP
TM

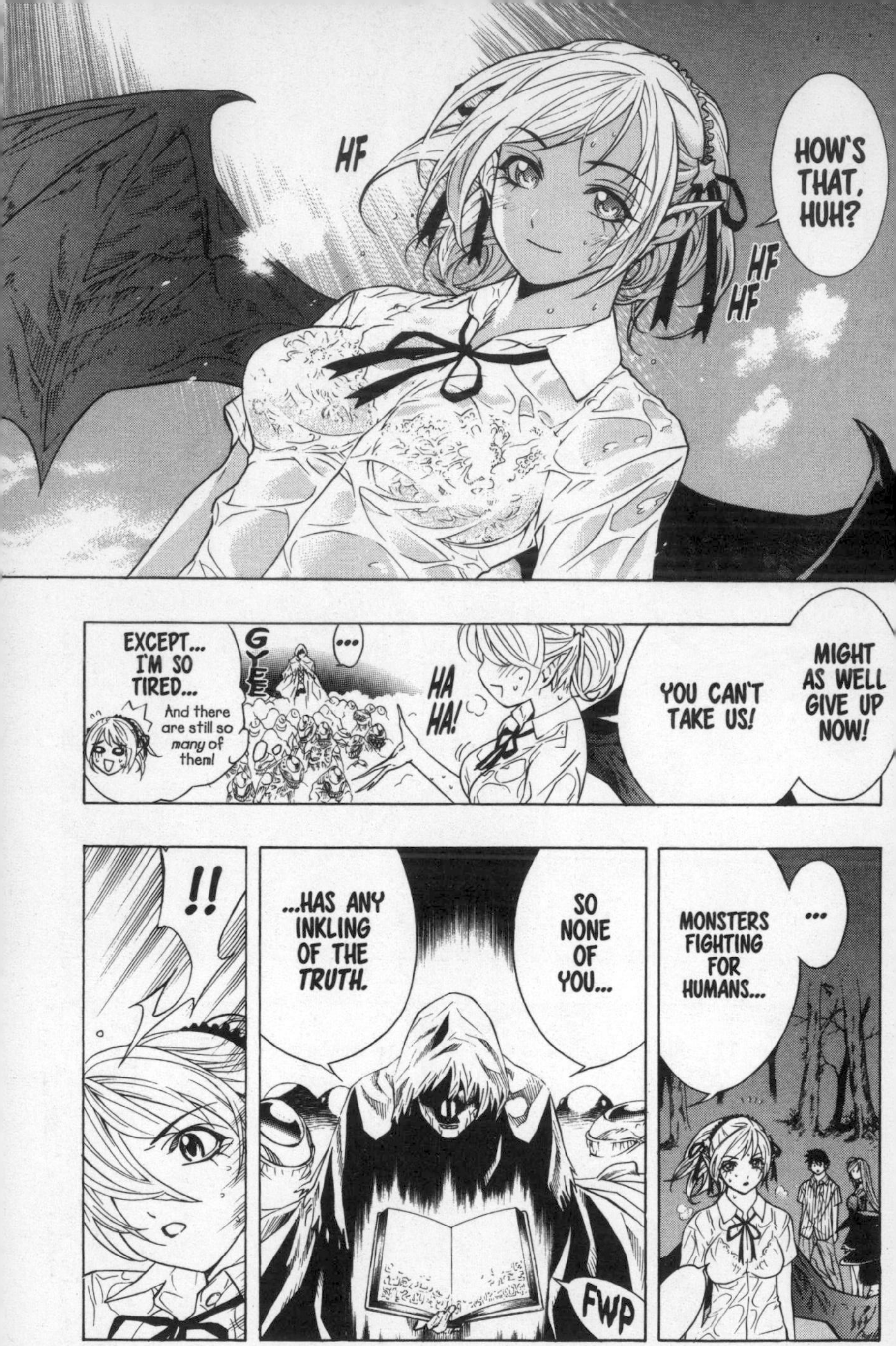
HOW'S THAT, HUH?
HF HF
HF
MIGHT AS WELL GIVE UP NOW!
YOU CAN'T TAKE US!
HA HA!
...
GYEE
EXCEPT... I'M SO TIRED...
And there are still so *many* of them!
...
MONSTERS FIGHTING FOR HUMANS...
SO NONE OF YOU...
...HAS ANY INKLING OF THE *TRUTH.*
FWP
!!

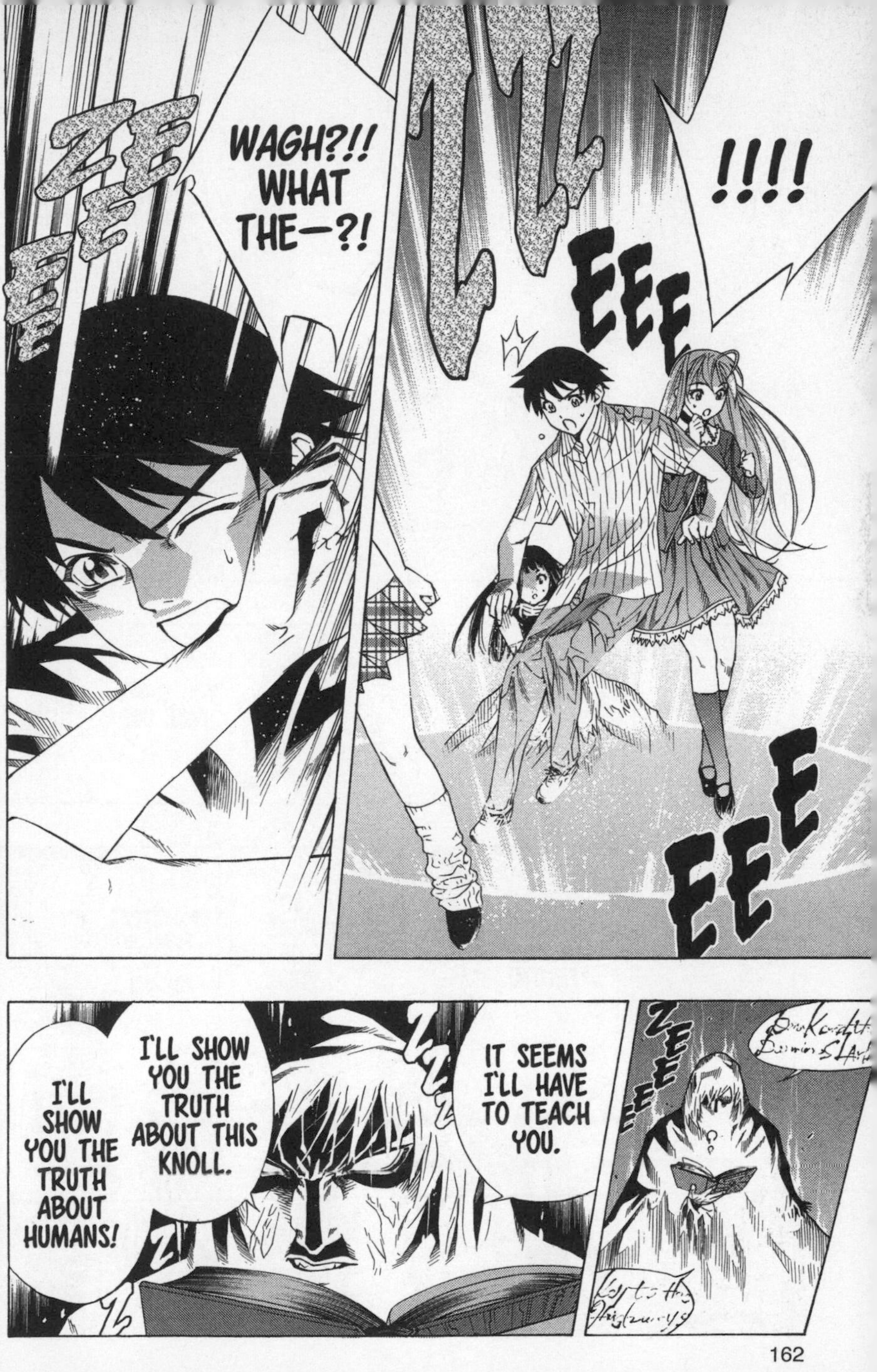
!!!!
EEE
EEE
ZEEE
WAGH?!! WHAT THE—?!
ZEEE
IT SEEMS I'LL HAVE TO TEACH YOU.
I'LL SHOW YOU THE TRUTH ABOUT THIS KNOLL.
I'LL SHOW YOU THE TRUTH ABOUT HUMANS!

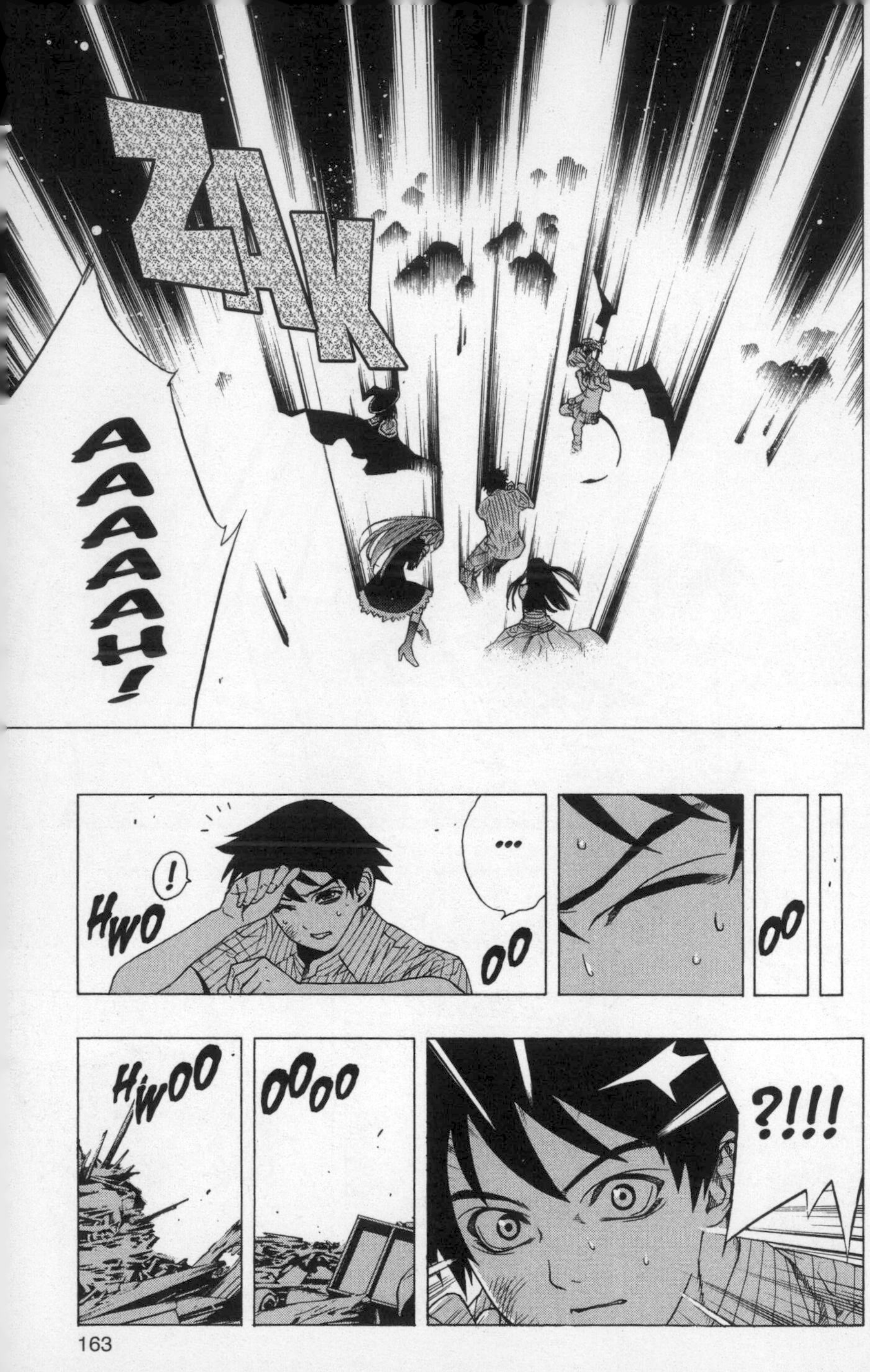
ZAK
AAAAAH!
OO
...
!
HWO
OO
?!!!
OOOO
HWOO

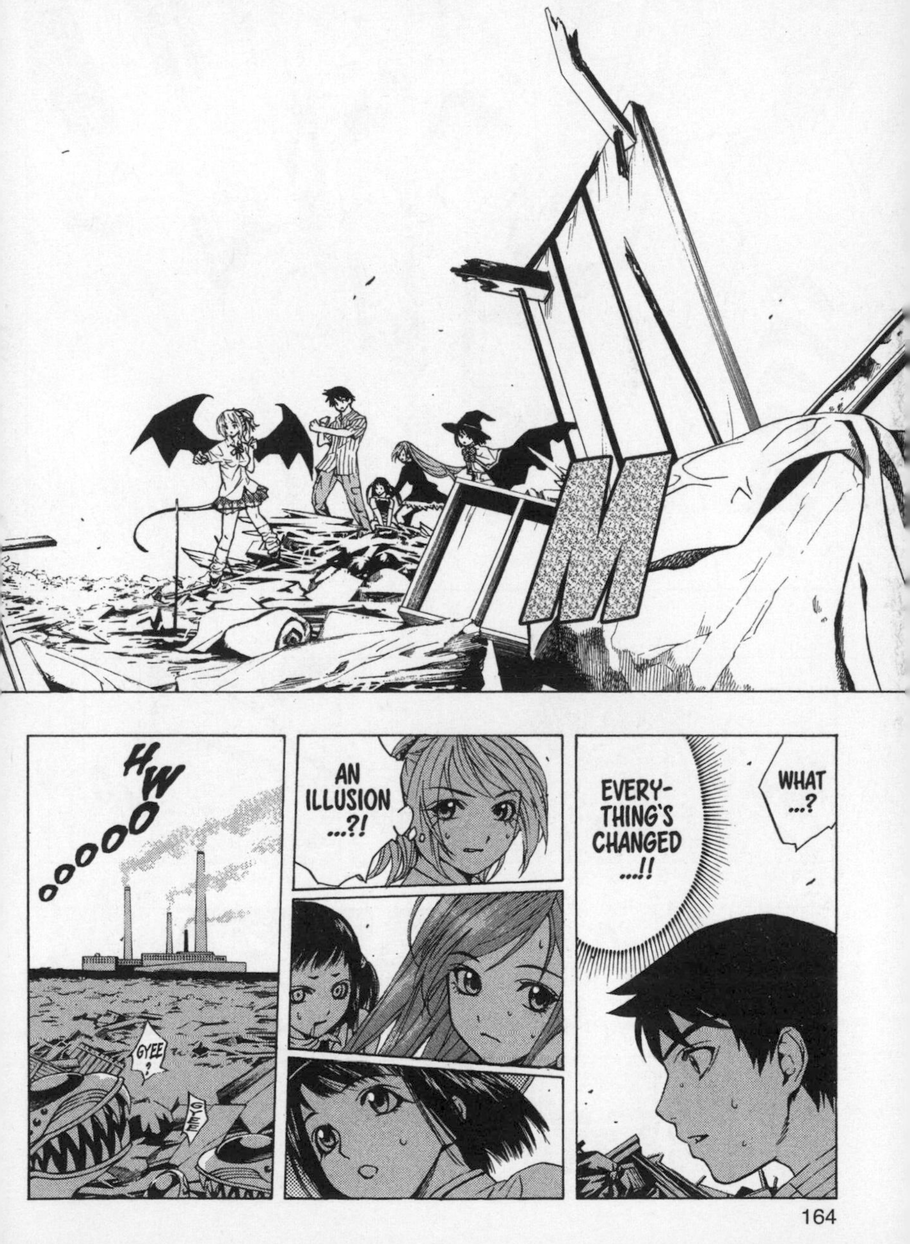
WHAT ...?
EVERY-THING'S CHANGED ...!!
AN ILLUSION ...?!
HWOOOOOO
GYEE ?
GYEE

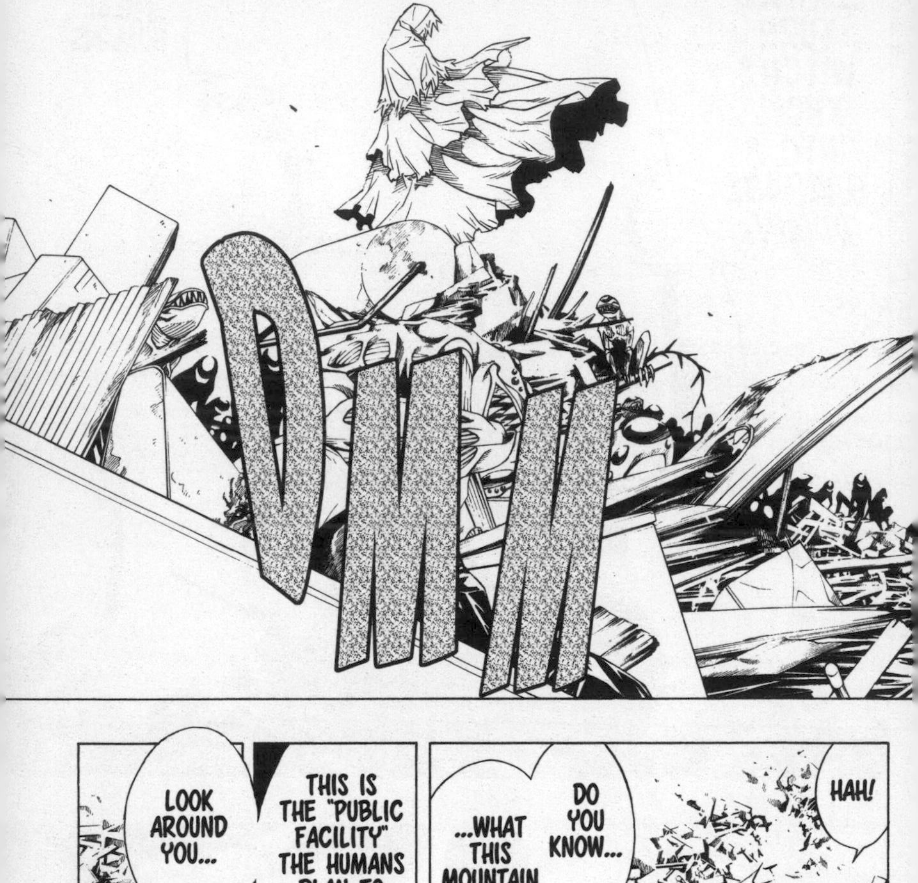
DMM

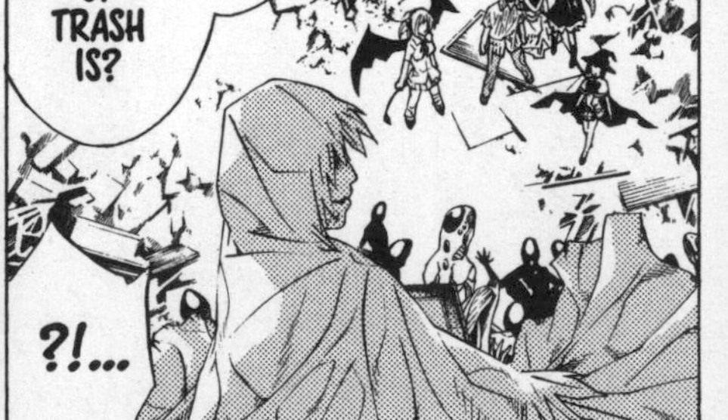
HAH!
DO YOU KNOW...
...WHAT THIS MOUNTAIN OF TRASH IS?
?!...

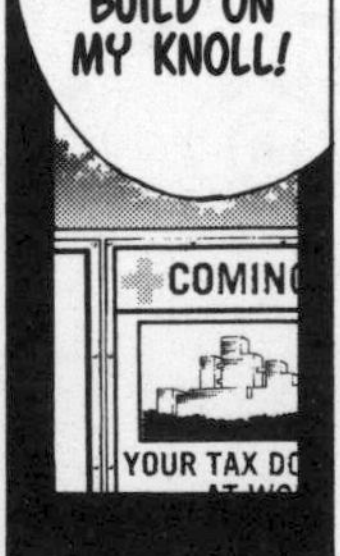
THIS IS THE "PUBLIC FACILITY" THE HUMANS PLAN TO BUILD ON MY KNOLL!

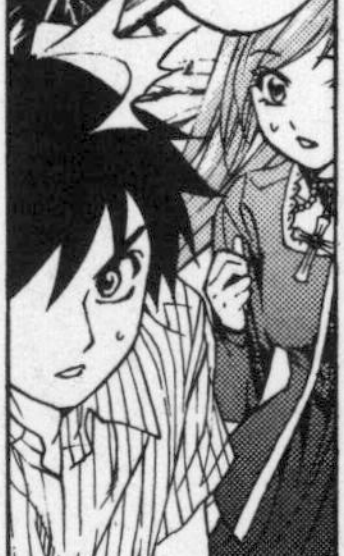
LOOK AROUND YOU...

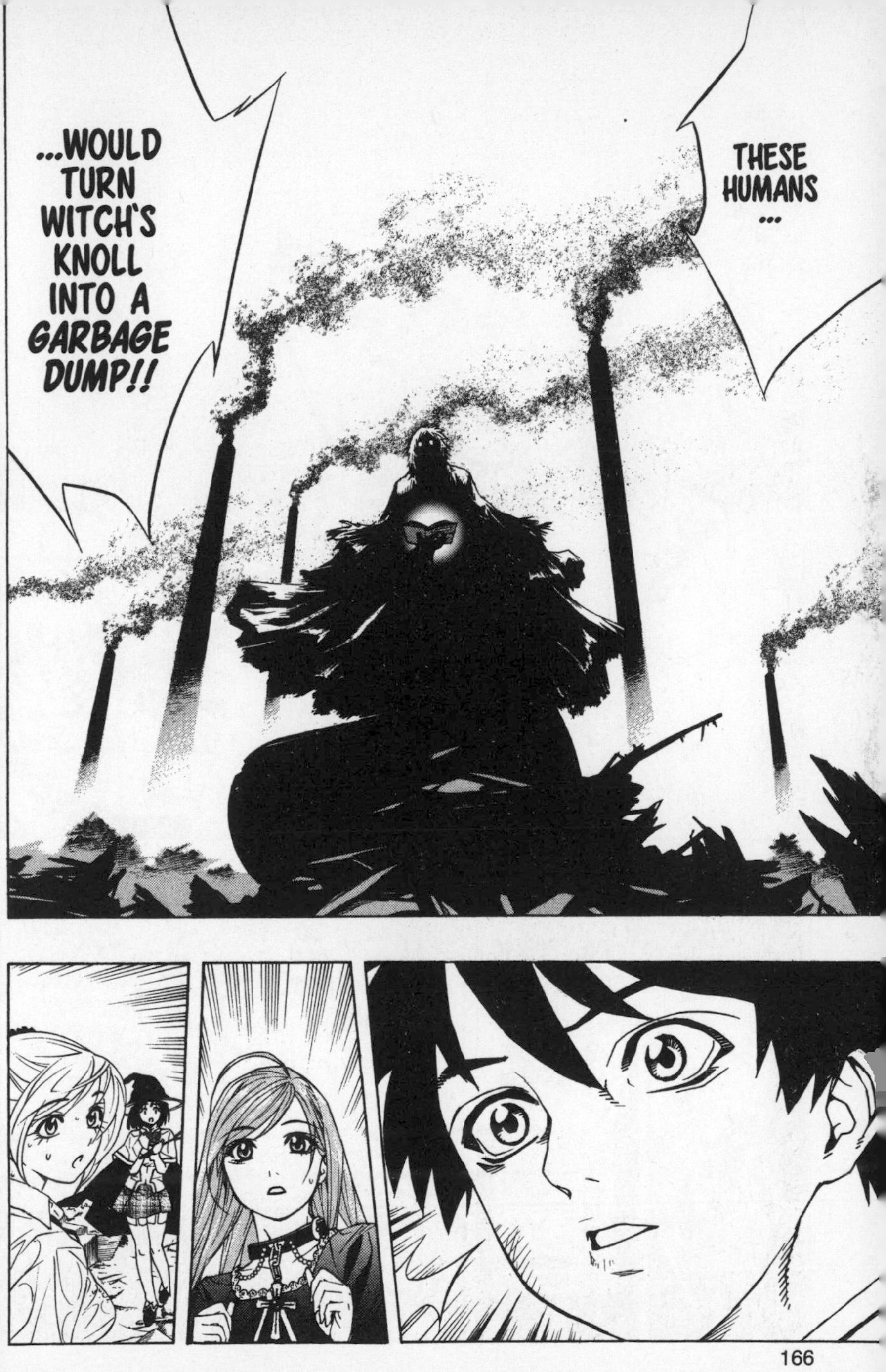
THESE HUMANS ...
...WOULD TURN WITCH'S KNOLL INTO A GARBAGE DUMP!!

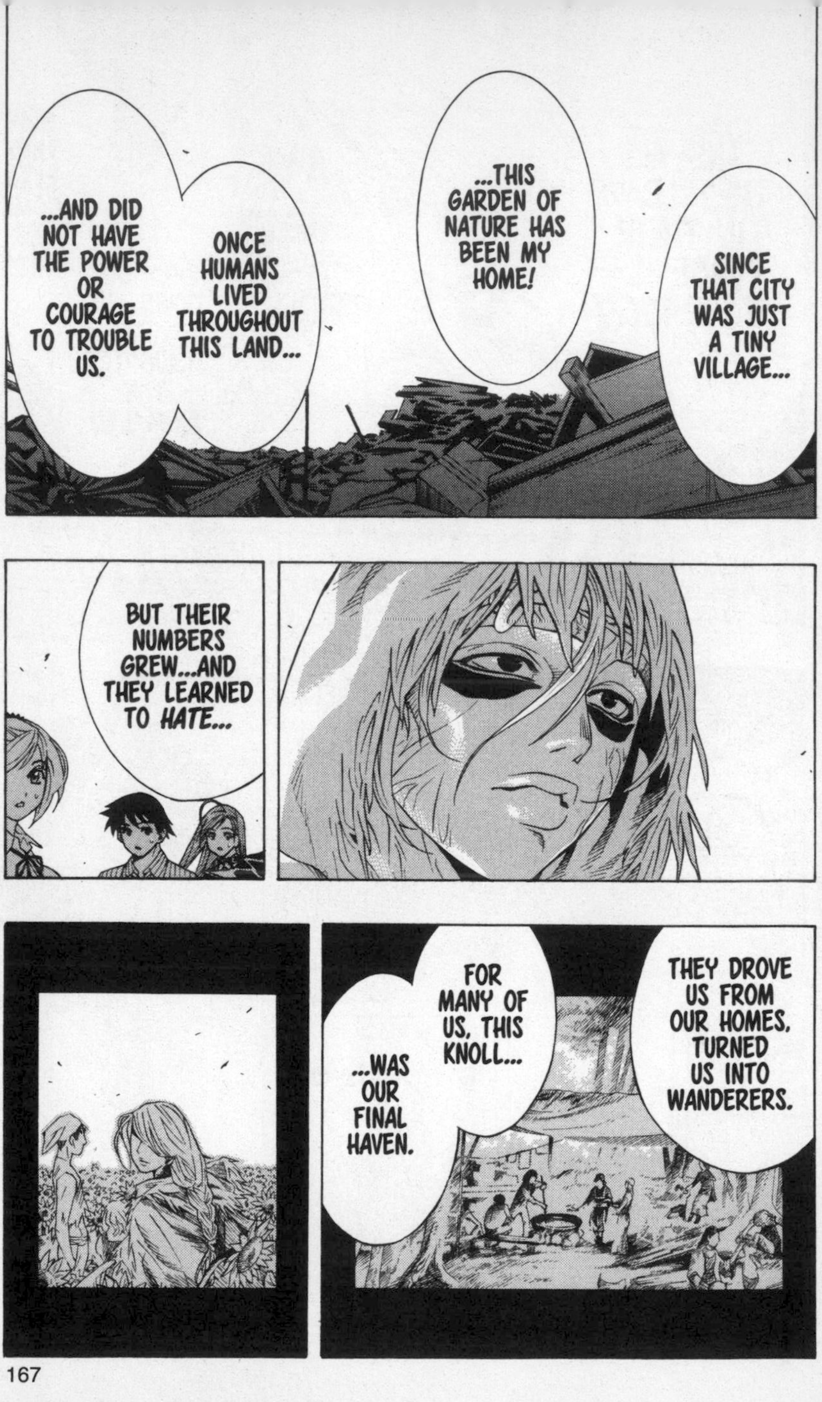
SINCE THAT CITY WAS JUST A TINY VILLAGE...
...THIS GARDEN OF NATURE HAS BEEN MY HOME!
ONCE HUMANS LIVED THROUGHOUT THIS LAND...
...AND DID NOT HAVE THE POWER OR COURAGE TO TROUBLE US.
BUT THEIR NUMBERS GREW...AND THEY LEARNED TO *HATE*...
THEY DROVE US FROM OUR HOMES, TURNED US INTO WANDERERS.
FOR MANY OF US, THIS KNOLL...
...WAS OUR FINAL HAVEN.

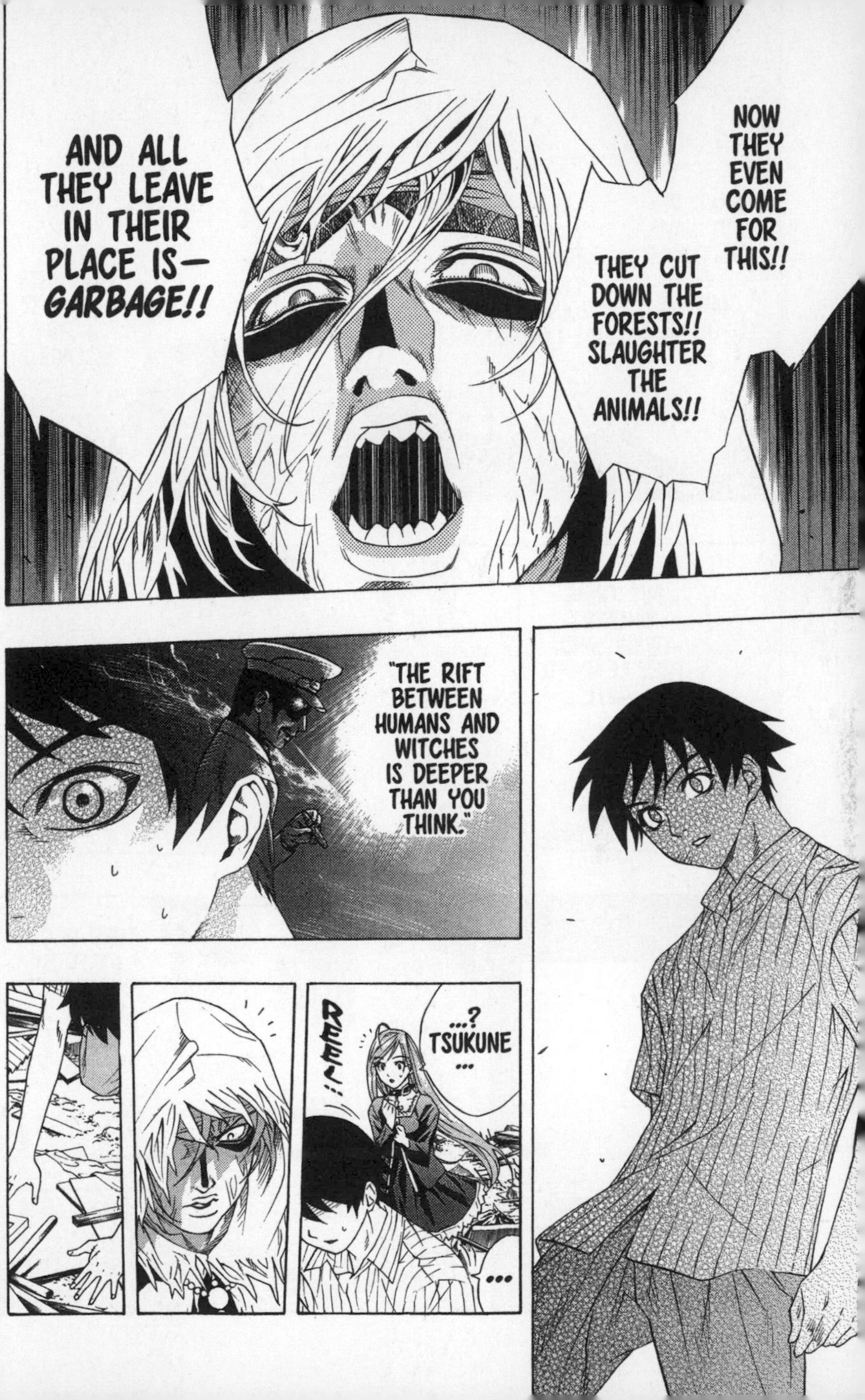
NOW THEY EVEN COME FOR THIS!!
THEY CUT DOWN THE FORESTS!! SLAUGHTER THE ANIMALS!!
AND ALL THEY LEAVE IN THEIR PLACE IS—GARBAGE!!
"THE RIFT BETWEEN HUMANS AND WITCHES IS DEEPER THAN YOU THINK."
...? TSUKUNE ...
REEL..
...

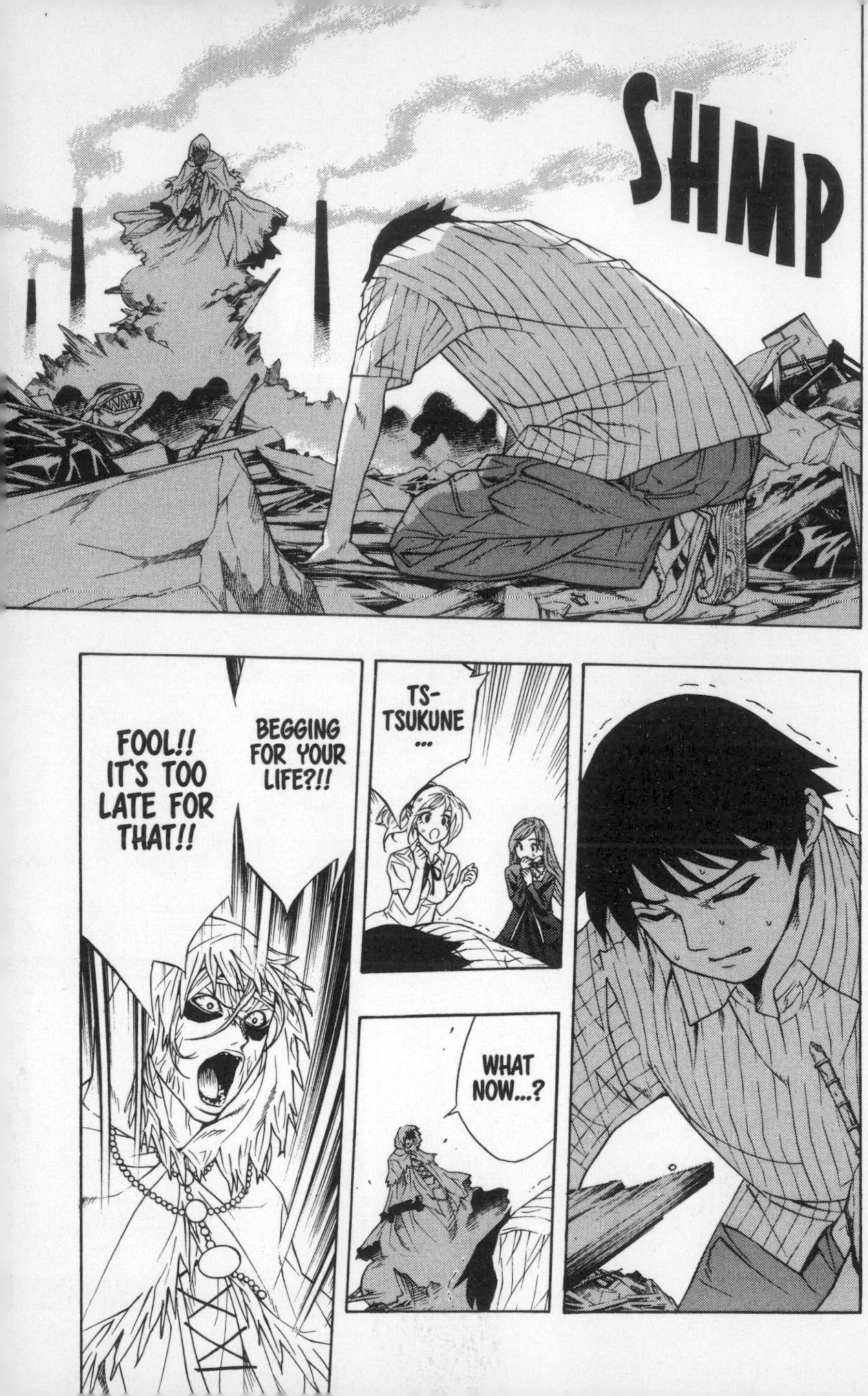
SHMP
TS-TSUKUNE...
WHAT NOW...?
BEGGING FOR YOUR LIFE?!!
FOOL!! IT'S TOO LATE FOR THAT!!

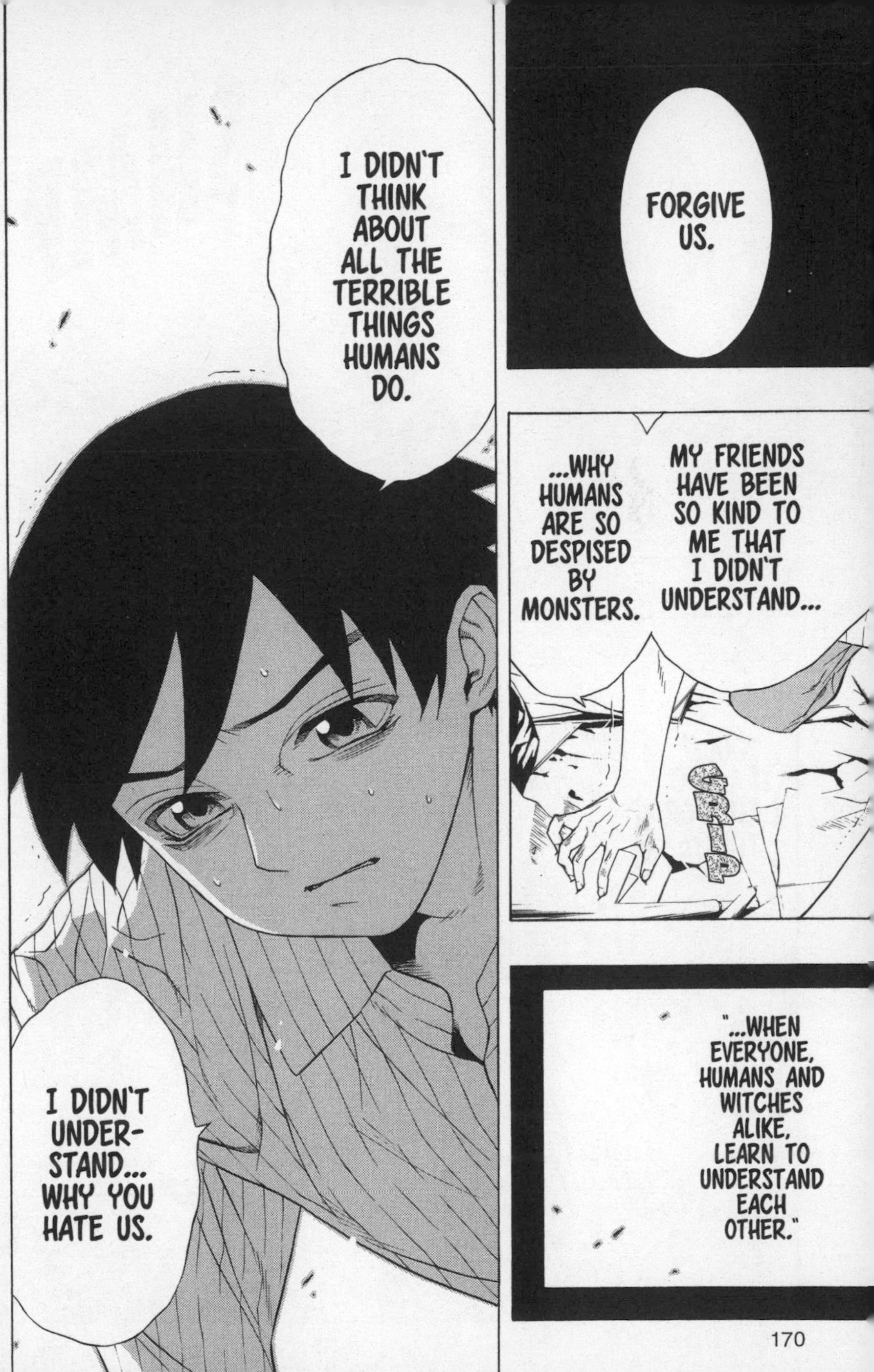
FORGIVE US.
MY FRIENDS HAVE BEEN SO KIND TO ME THAT I DIDN'T UNDERSTAND...
...WHY HUMANS ARE SO DESPISED BY MONSTERS.
GRIP
"...WHEN EVERYONE, HUMANS AND WITCHES ALIKE, LEARN TO UNDERSTAND EACH OTHER."
I DIDN'T THINK ABOUT ALL THE TERRIBLE THINGS HUMANS DO.
I DIDN'T UNDER-STAND... WHY YOU HATE US.

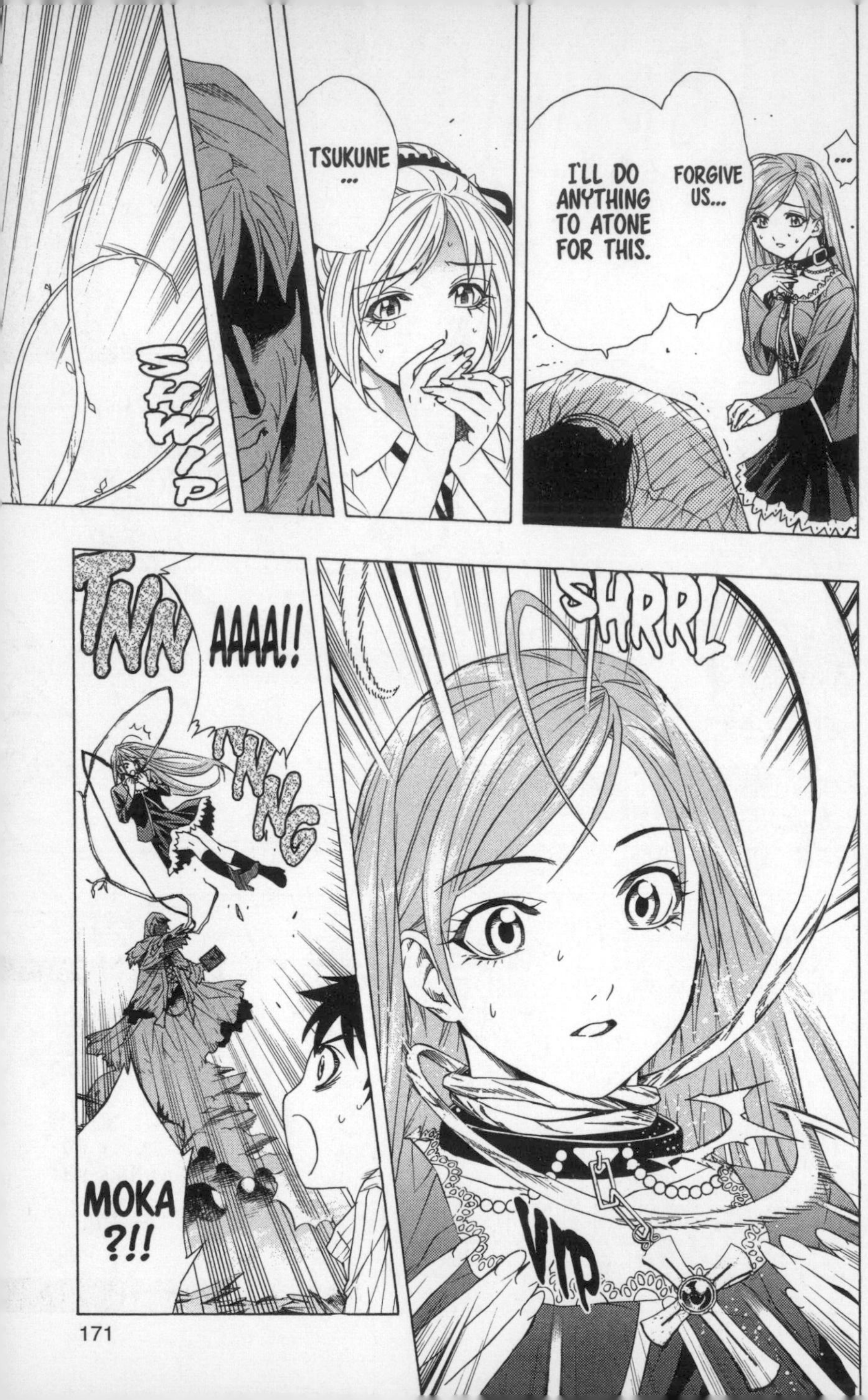
...
FORGIVE US...
I'LL DO ANYTHING TO ATONE FOR THIS.
TSUKUNE ...
SHWIP
SHRRL
VIP
TNN
AAAA!!
TWNG
MOKA ?!!

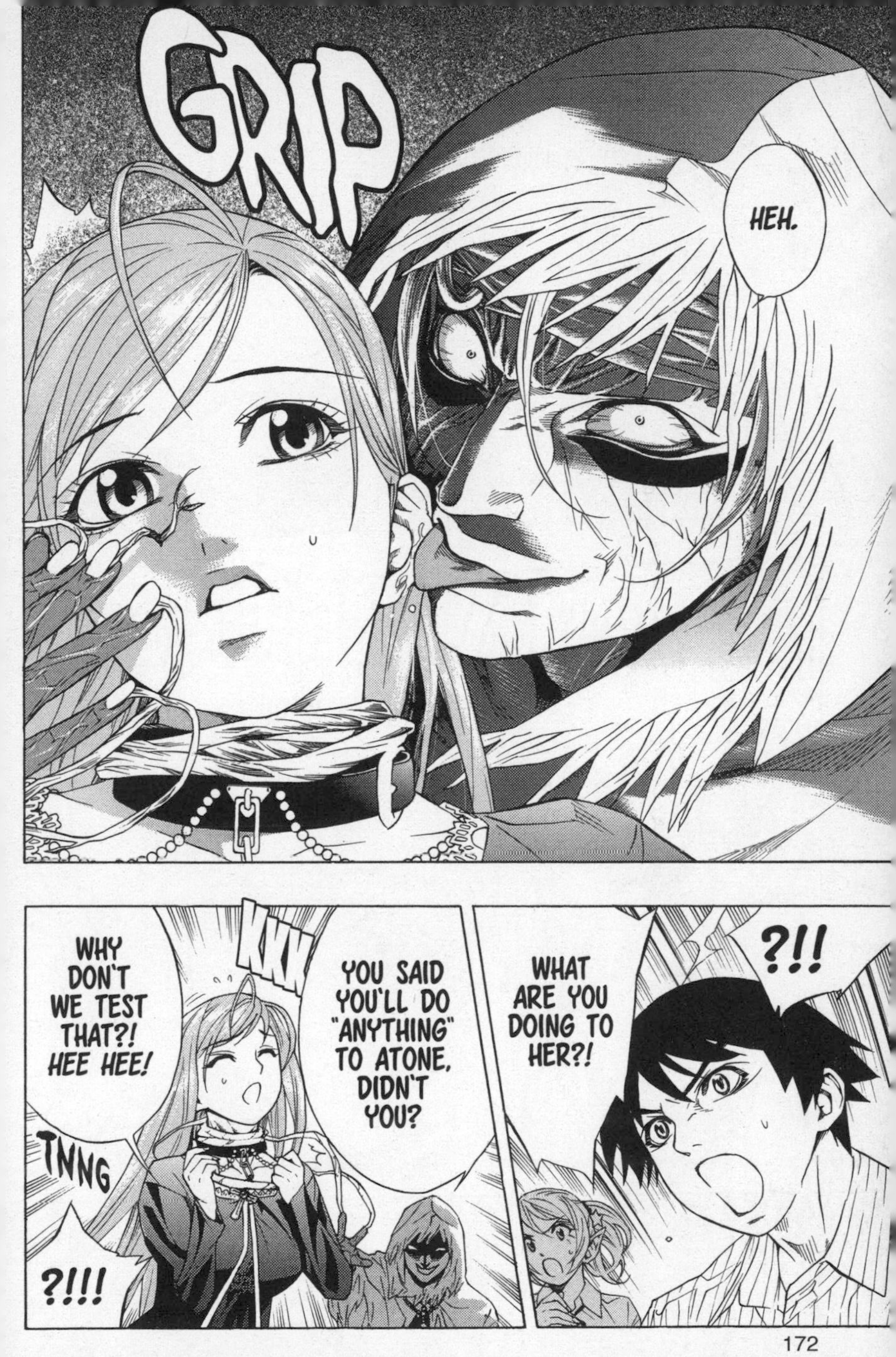
GRIP
HEH.
?!!
WHAT ARE YOU DOING TO HER?!
KNN
YOU SAID YOU'LL DO "ANYTHING" TO ATONE, DIDN'T YOU?
WHY DON'T WE TEST THAT?! HEE HEE!
TNNG
?!!!

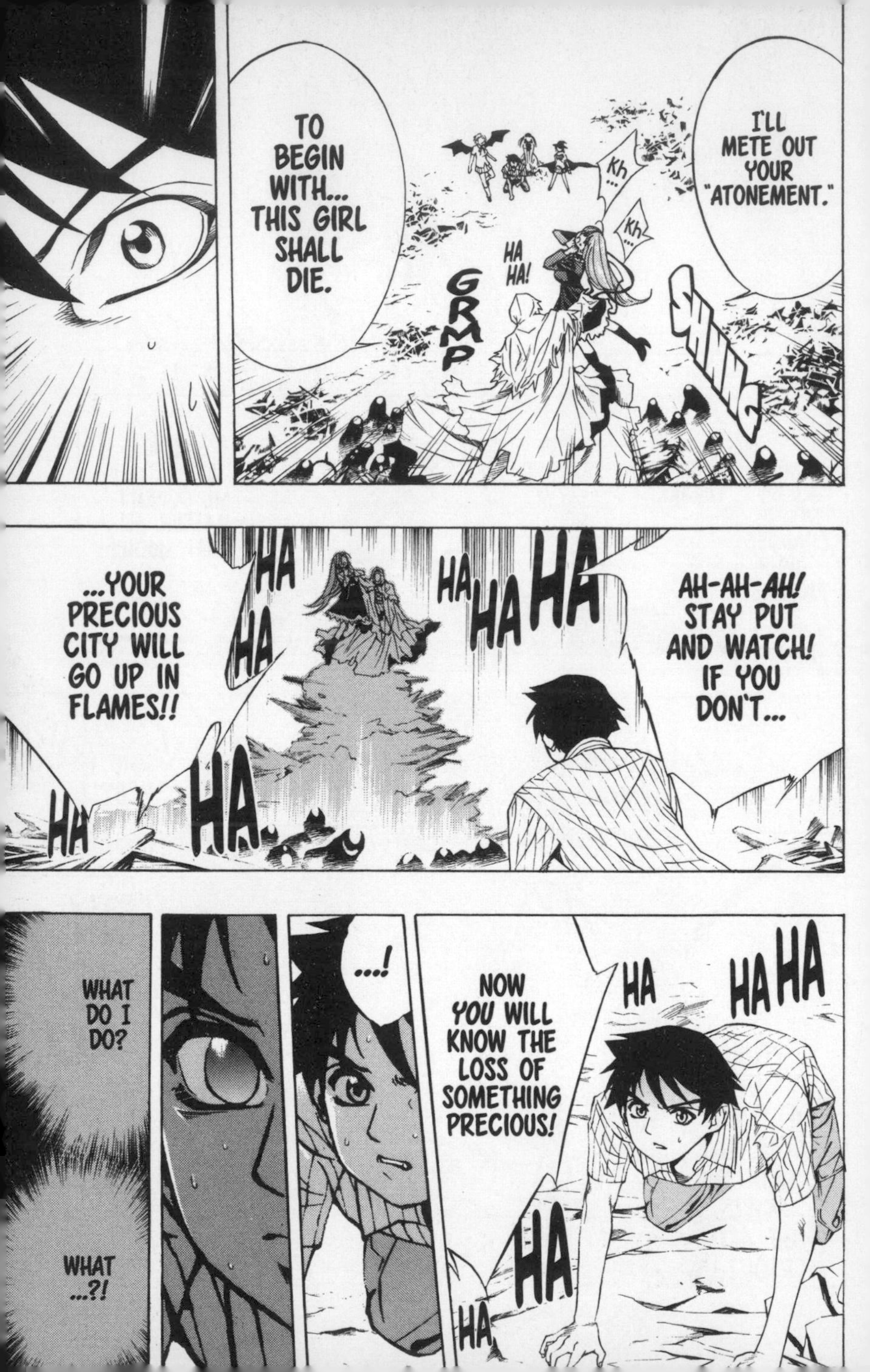
I'LL METE OUT YOUR "ATONEMENT."
Kh...
Kh...
SHING
HA HA!
GRMP
TO BEGIN WITH... THIS GIRL SHALL DIE.
AH-AH-AH! STAY PUT AND WATCH! IF YOU DON'T...
HA HA HA HA
...YOUR PRECIOUS CITY WILL GO UP IN FLAMES!!
HA HA
HA HA
HA HA HA
NOW YOU WILL KNOW THE LOSS OF SOMETHING PRECIOUS!
HA HA
...!
WHAT DO I DO?
WHAT ...?!

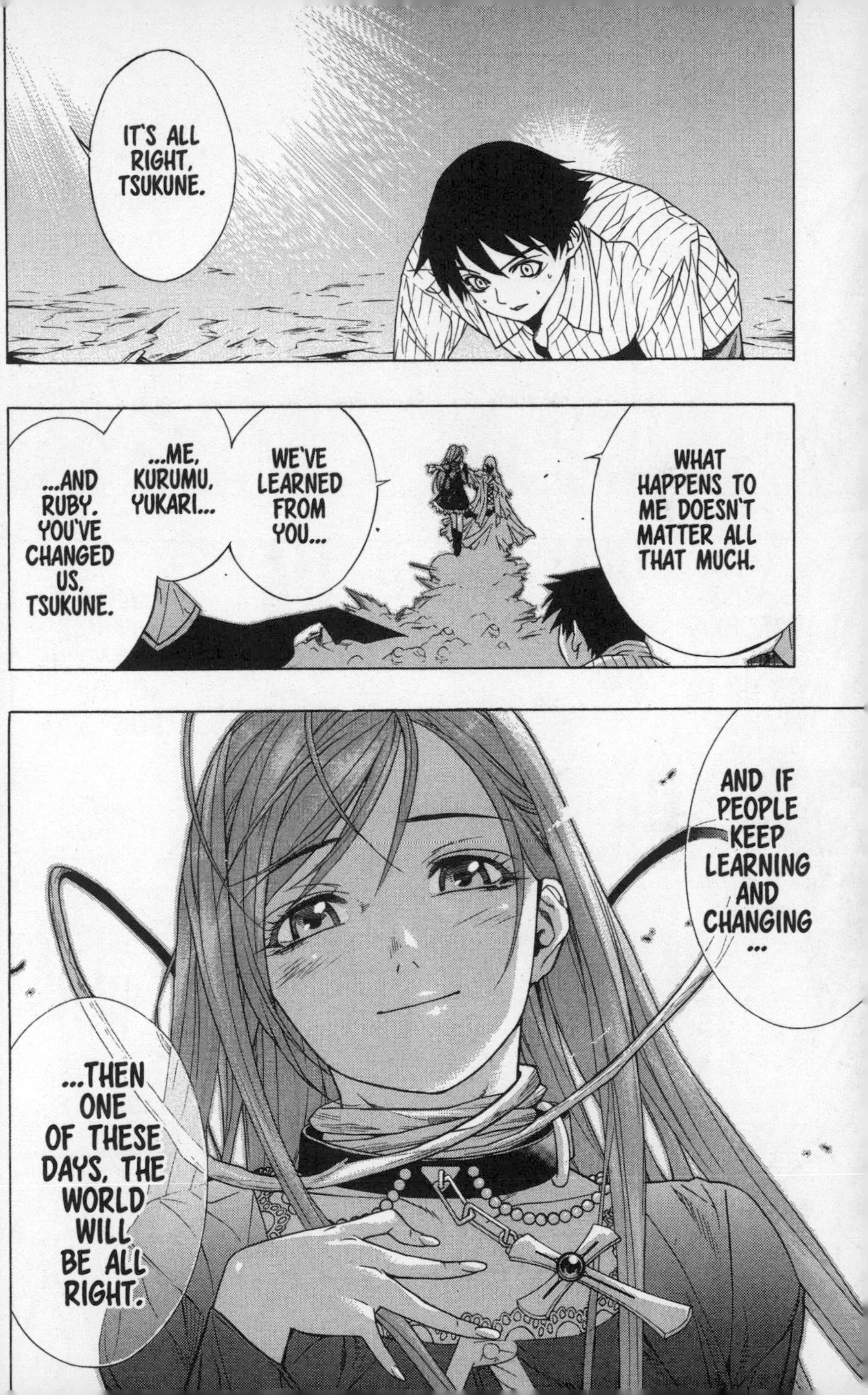
IT'S ALL RIGHT, TSUKUNE.
WHAT HAPPENS TO ME DOESN'T MATTER ALL THAT MUCH.
WE'VE LEARNED FROM YOU...
...ME, KURUMU, YUKARI...
...AND RUBY. YOU'VE CHANGED US, TSUKUNE.
AND IF PEOPLE KEEP LEARNING AND CHANGING...
...THEN ONE OF THESE DAYS, THE WORLD WILL BE ALL RIGHT.

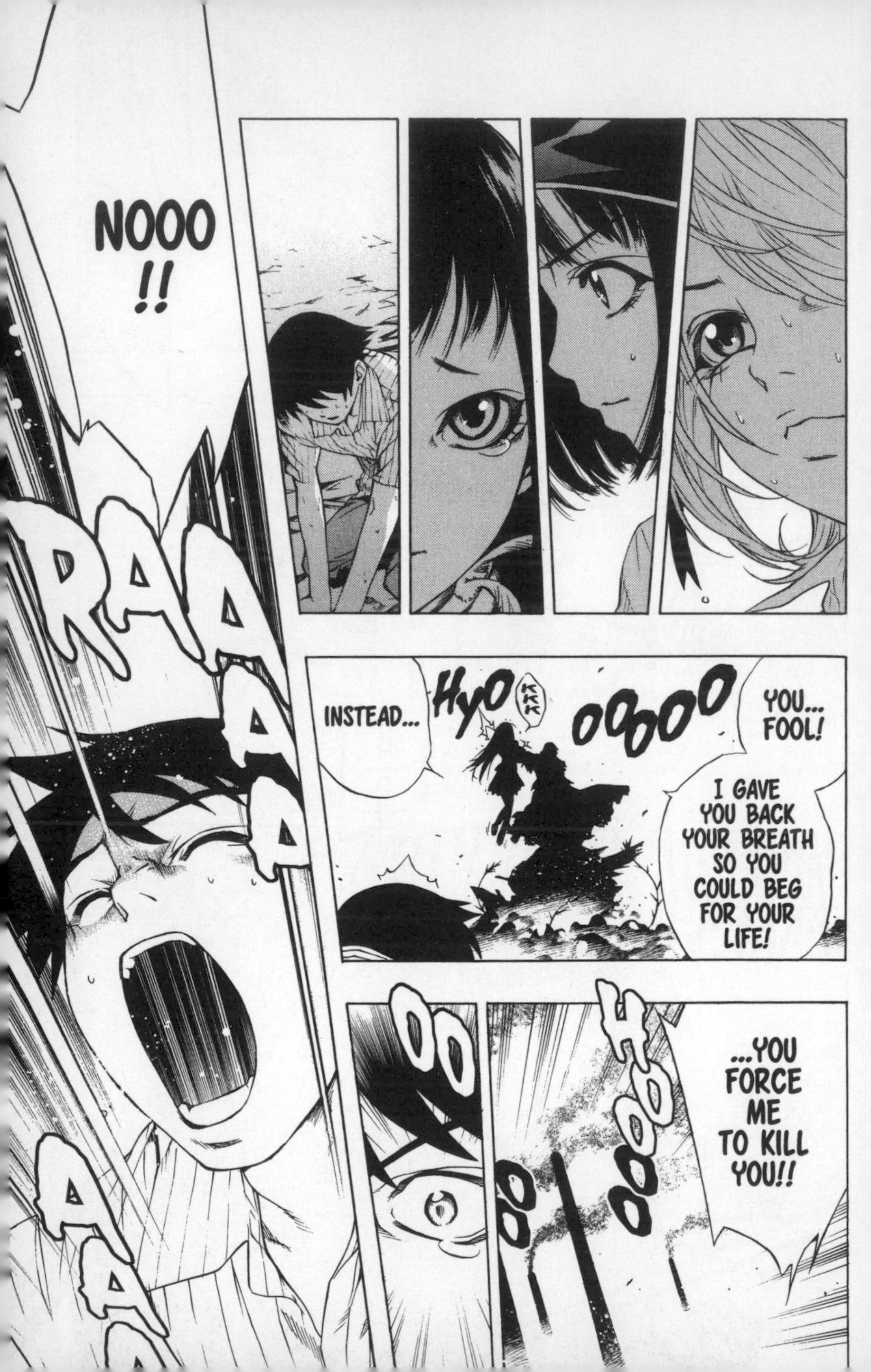
YOU... FOOL!
I GAVE YOU BACK YOUR BREATH SO YOU COULD BEG FOR YOUR LIFE!
OOOOO
KKK
HYO
INSTEAD...
...YOU FORCE ME TO KILL YOU!!
HOOOOO
OOO
NOOO !!
RAAAAAA

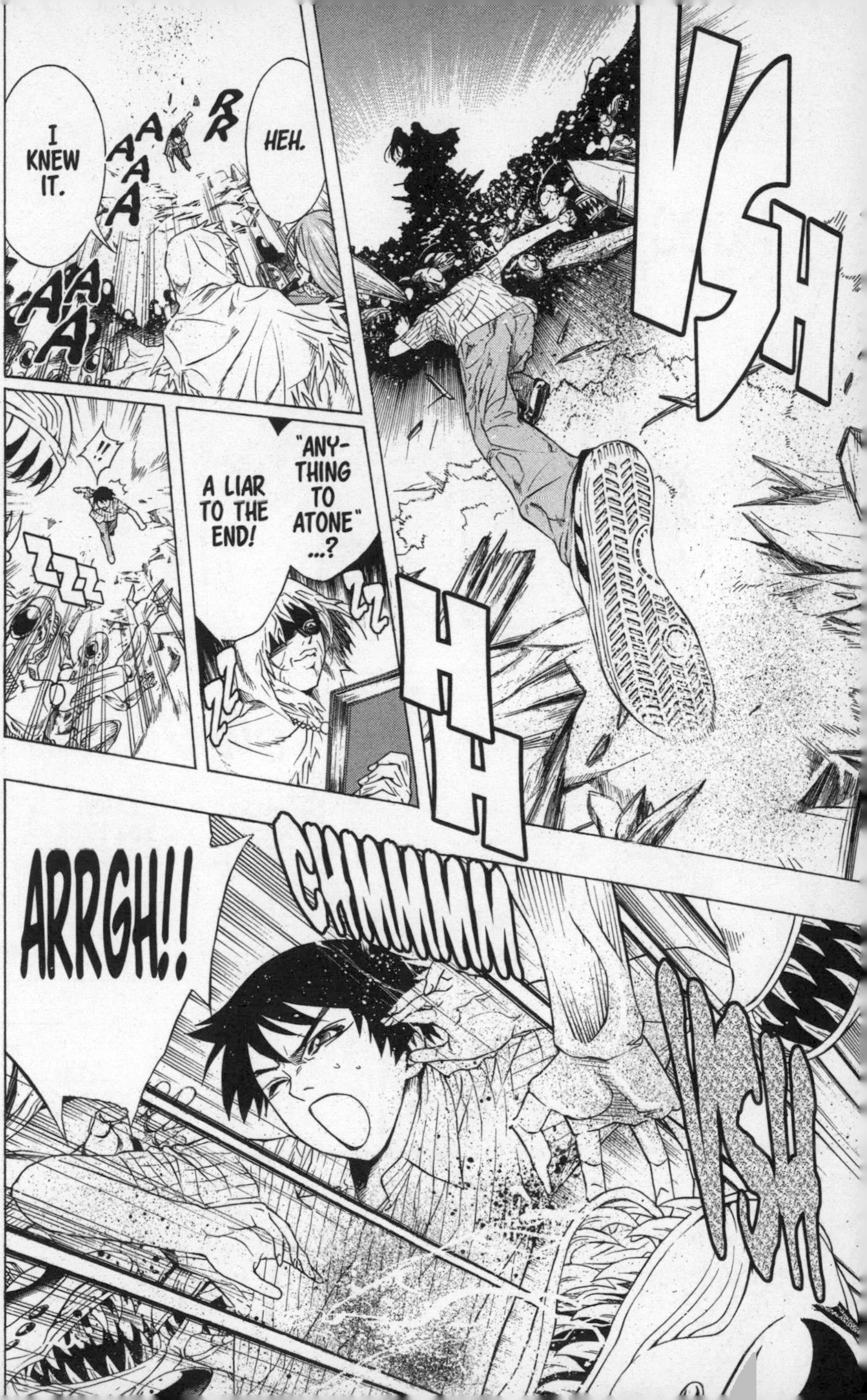
VSH
HEH.
RRAAAA
AAAA!
I KNEW IT.
"ANYTHING TO ATONE"...?
A LIAR TO THE END!
ZZ
ZZ
HHH
!!
ZZZ
CHMMMMMM
ARRGH!!

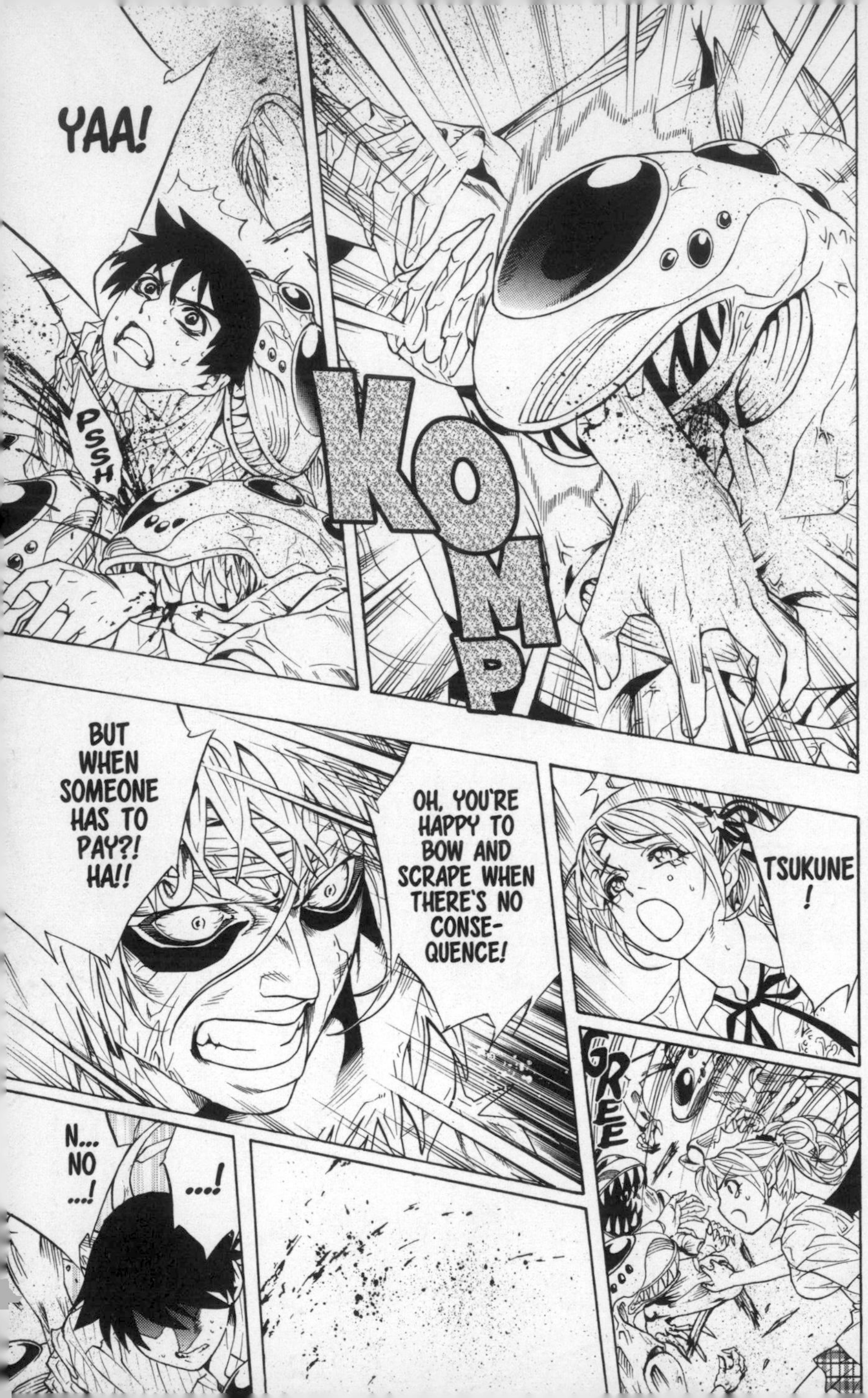
KOMP
YAA!
PSSH
TSUKUNE!
GREE
OH, YOU'RE HAPPY TO BOW AND SCRAPE WHEN THERE'S NO CONSE-QUENCE!
BUT WHEN SOMEONE HAS TO PAY?! HA!!
...!
N... NO ...!

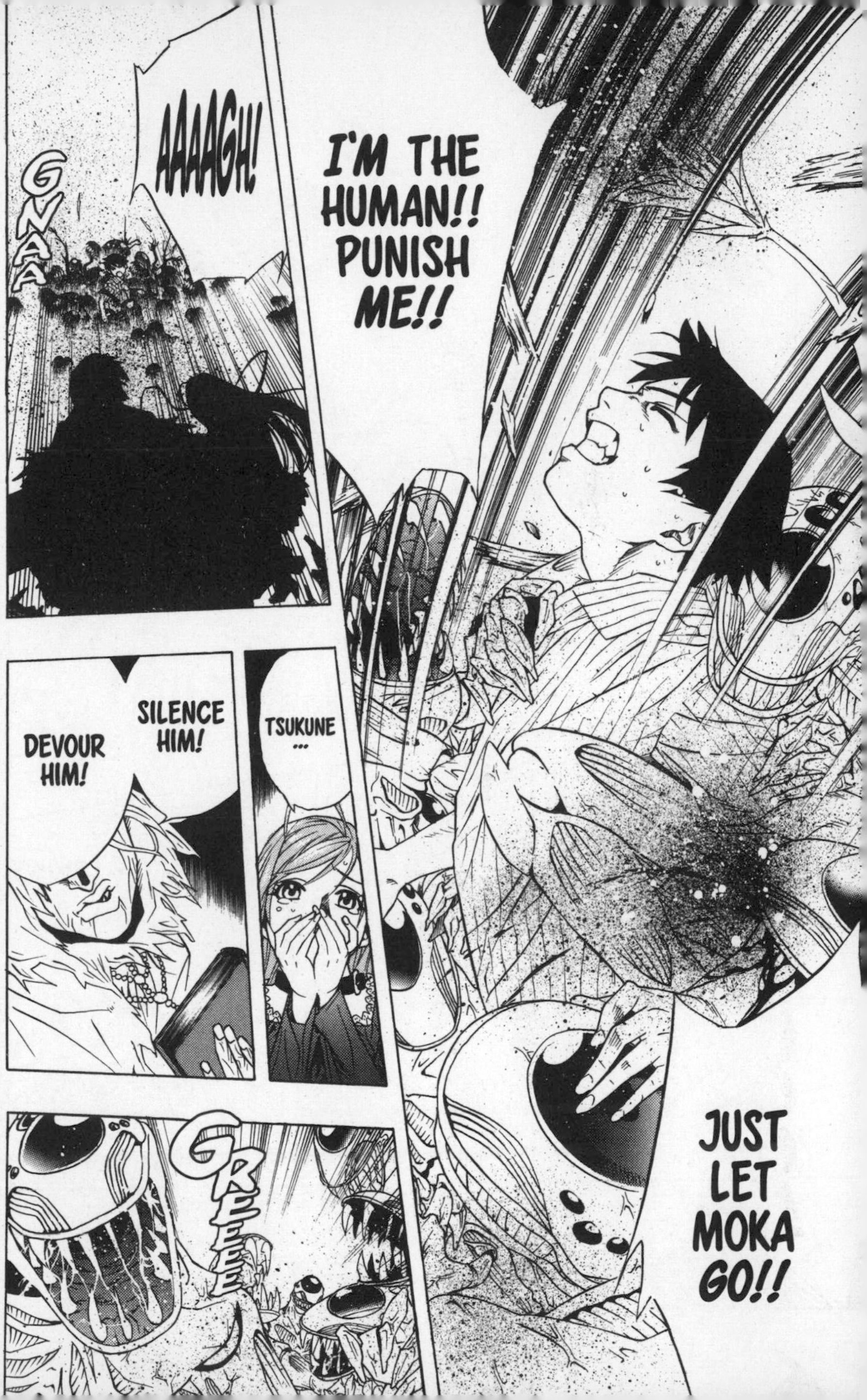
I'M THE HUMAN!! PUNISH ME!!
JUST LET MOKA GO!!
AAAAGH!
GNAA
TSUKUNE...
SILENCE HIM!
DEVOUR HIM!
GREEE

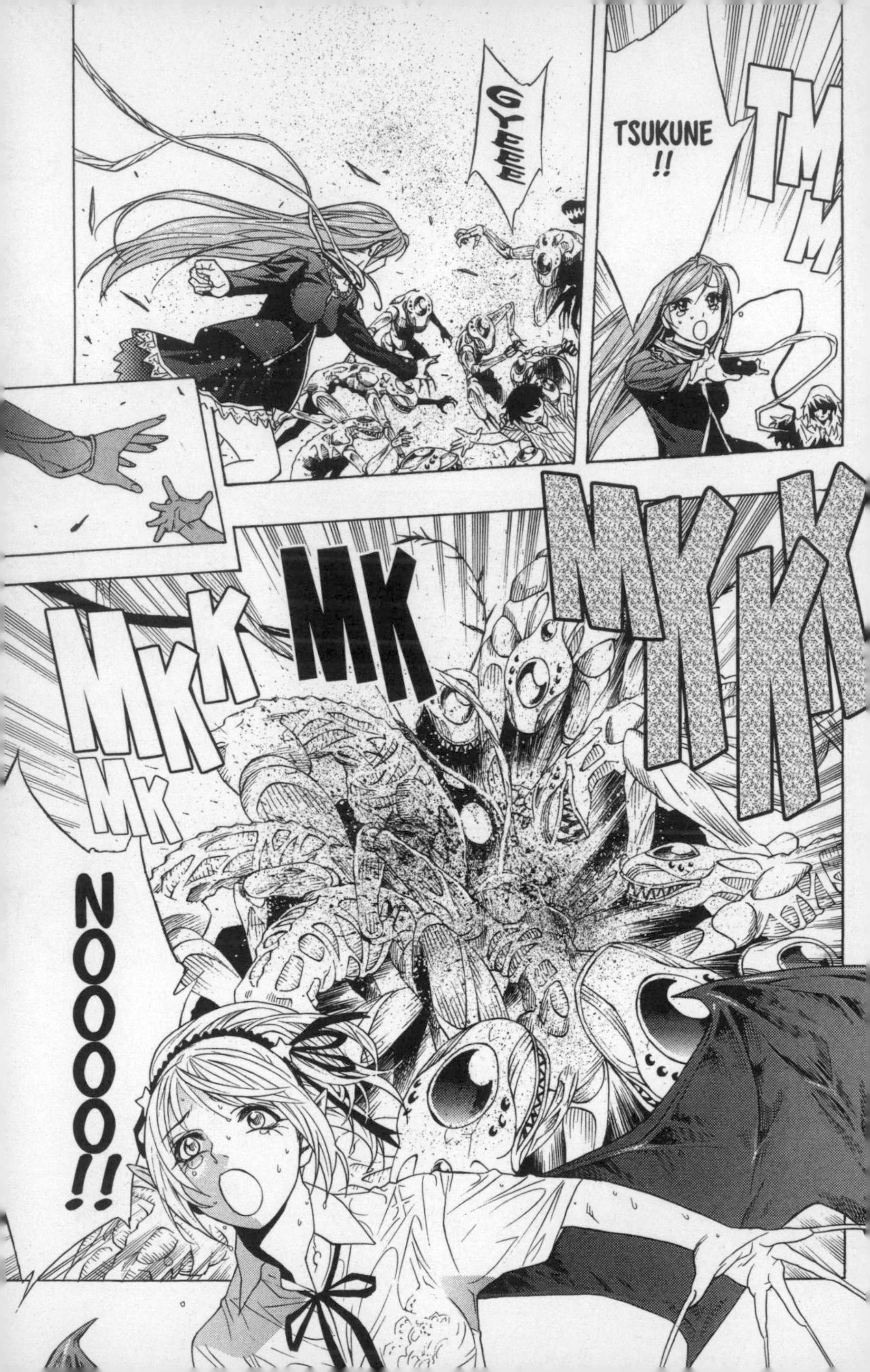
TSUKUNE !!
TMM
GYEEE
MKKK
MK
MKK
MK
NOOOO!!

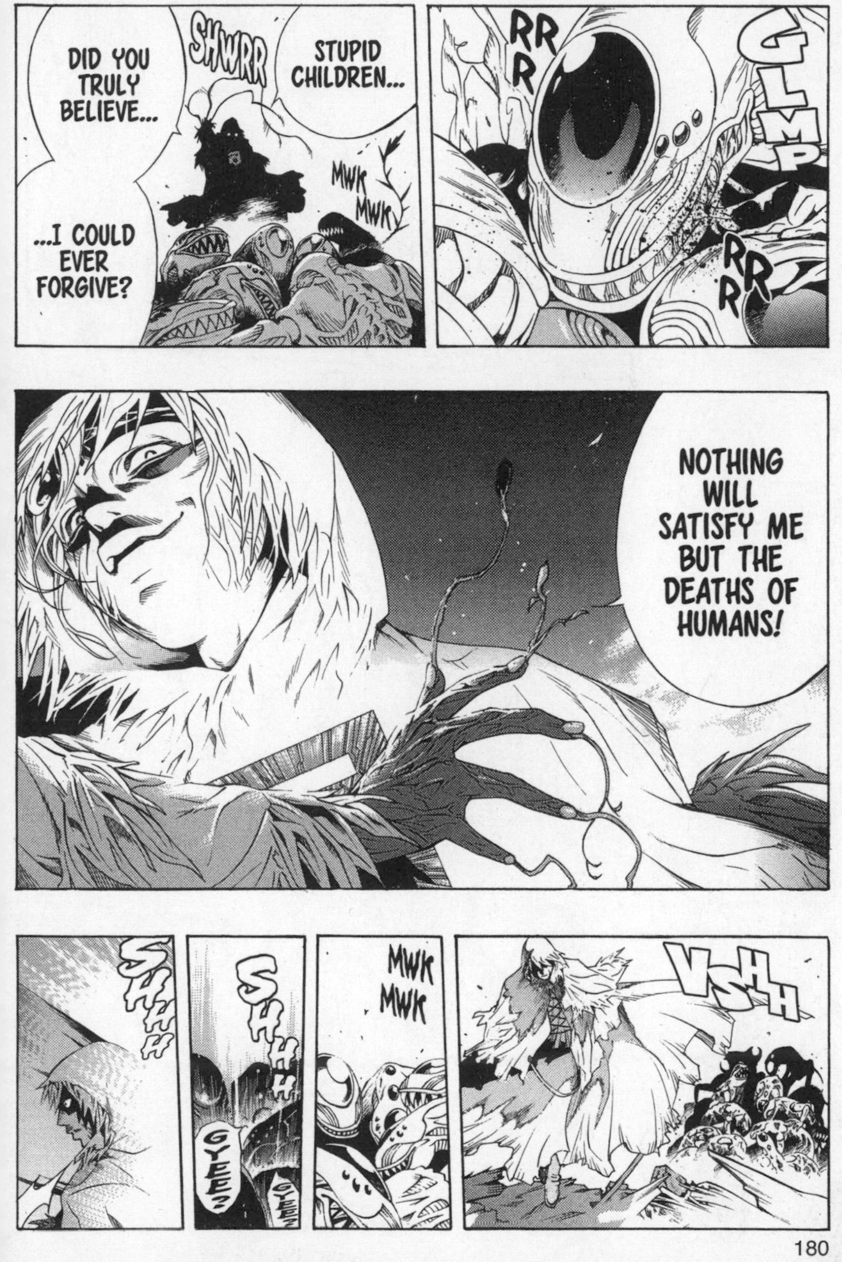
RRR
GLMP
RRR
STUPID CHILDREN...
SHWRR
DID YOU TRULY BELIEVE...
MWK MWK
...I COULD EVER FORGIVE?
NOTHING WILL SATISFY ME BUT THE DEATHS OF HUMANS!
VSHH
MWK MWK
SHHH
GYEE?
GYEE?
SHHH

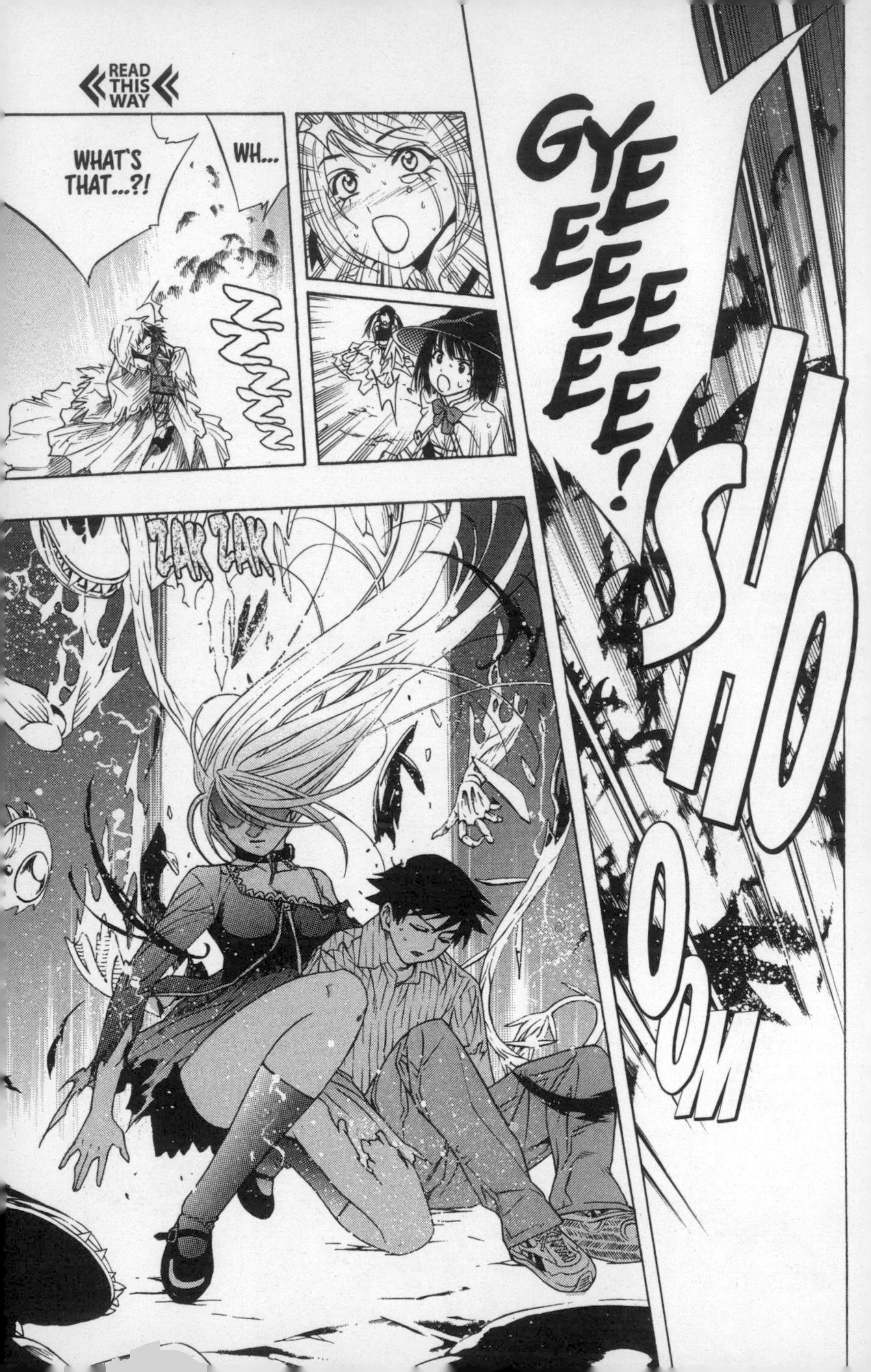
READ THIS WAY
GYEEEEEEE!
SHOOOOM
WH...
WHAT'S THAT...?!
ZZZZZ
ZAK ZAK

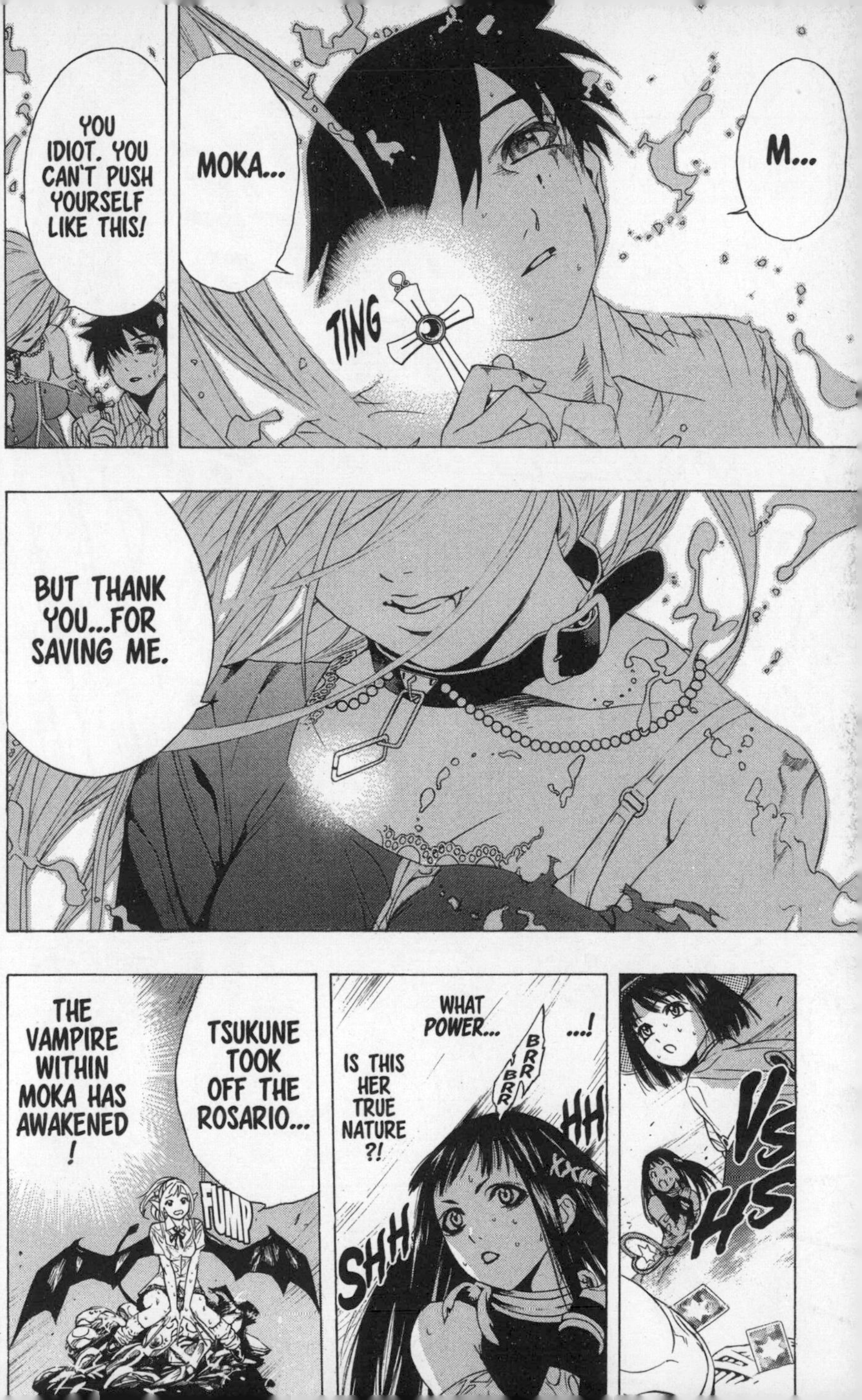
M...
MOKA...
TING
YOU IDIOT. YOU CAN'T PUSH YOURSELF LIKE THIS!
BUT THANK YOU...FOR SAVING ME.
WHAT POWER...
...!
BRR BRR BRR
IS THIS HER TRUE NATURE?!
SHH
HH
TSUKUNE TOOK OFF THE ROSARIO...
THE VAMPIRE WITHIN MOKA HAS AWAKENED!
FUMP

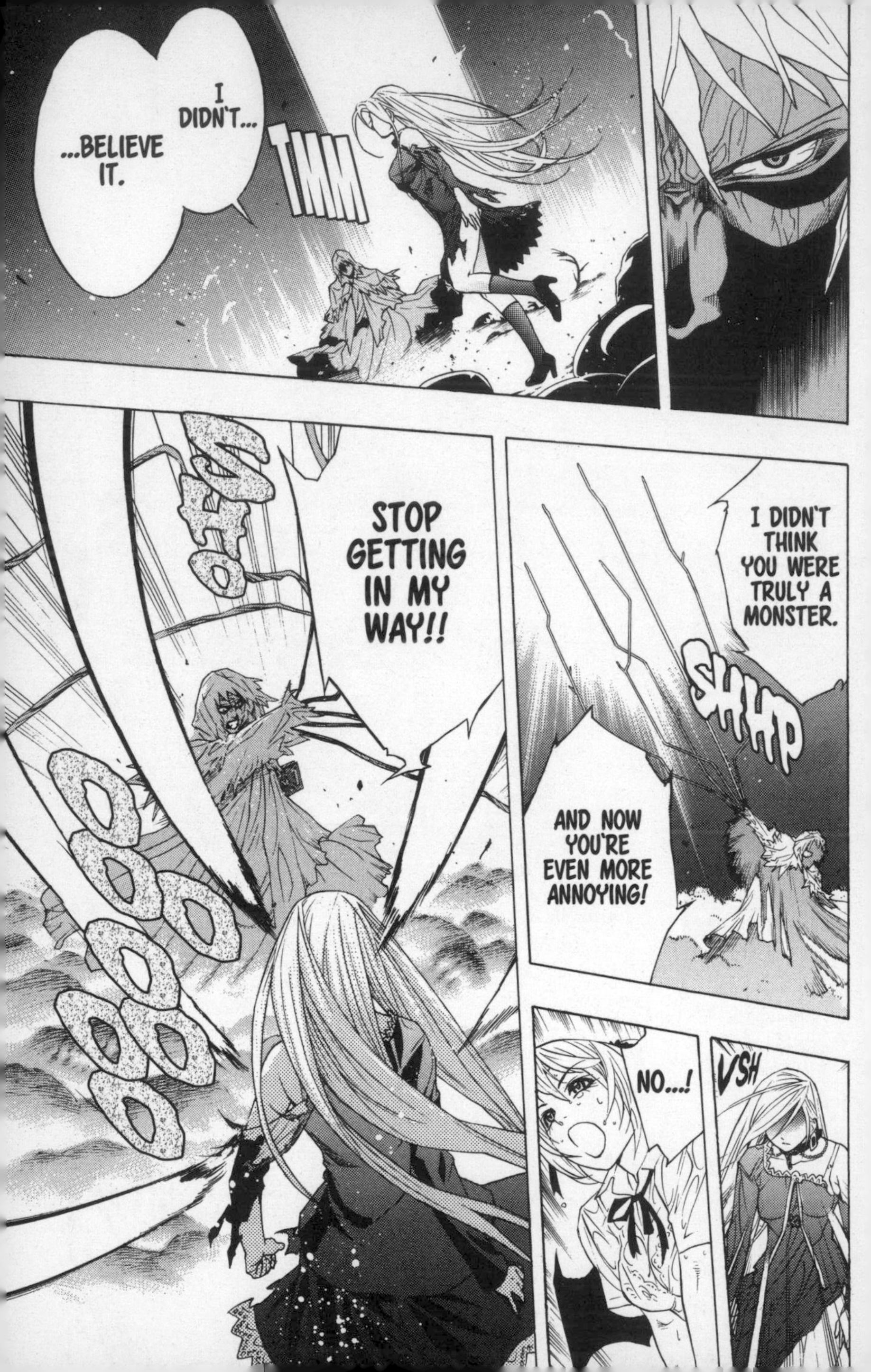
I DIDN'T...
...BELIEVE IT.
TMM
I DIDN'T THINK YOU WERE TRULY A MONSTER.
SHHP
AND NOW YOU'RE EVEN MORE ANNOYING!
VSH
NO...!
STOP GETTING IN MY WAY!!

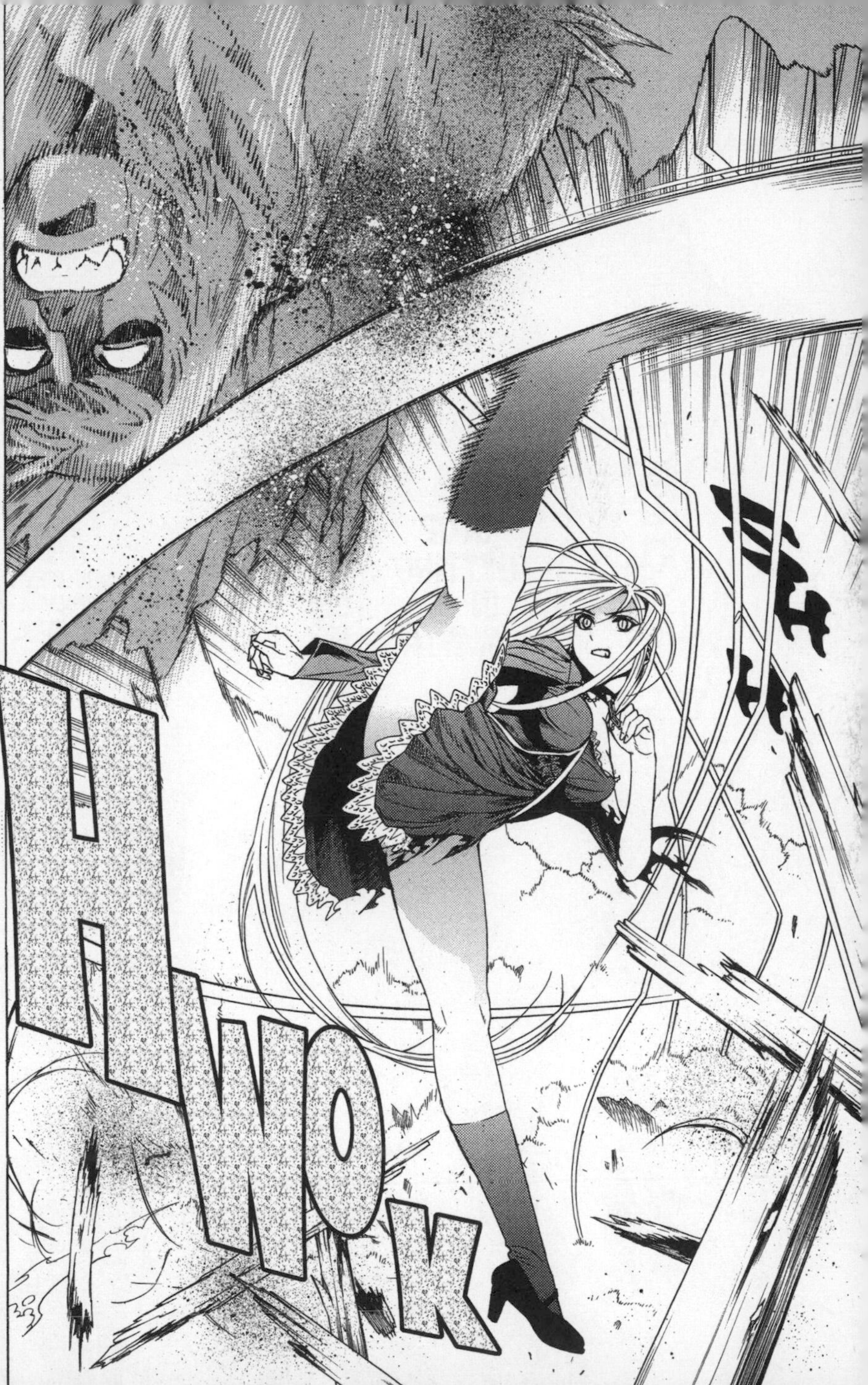
THWOK

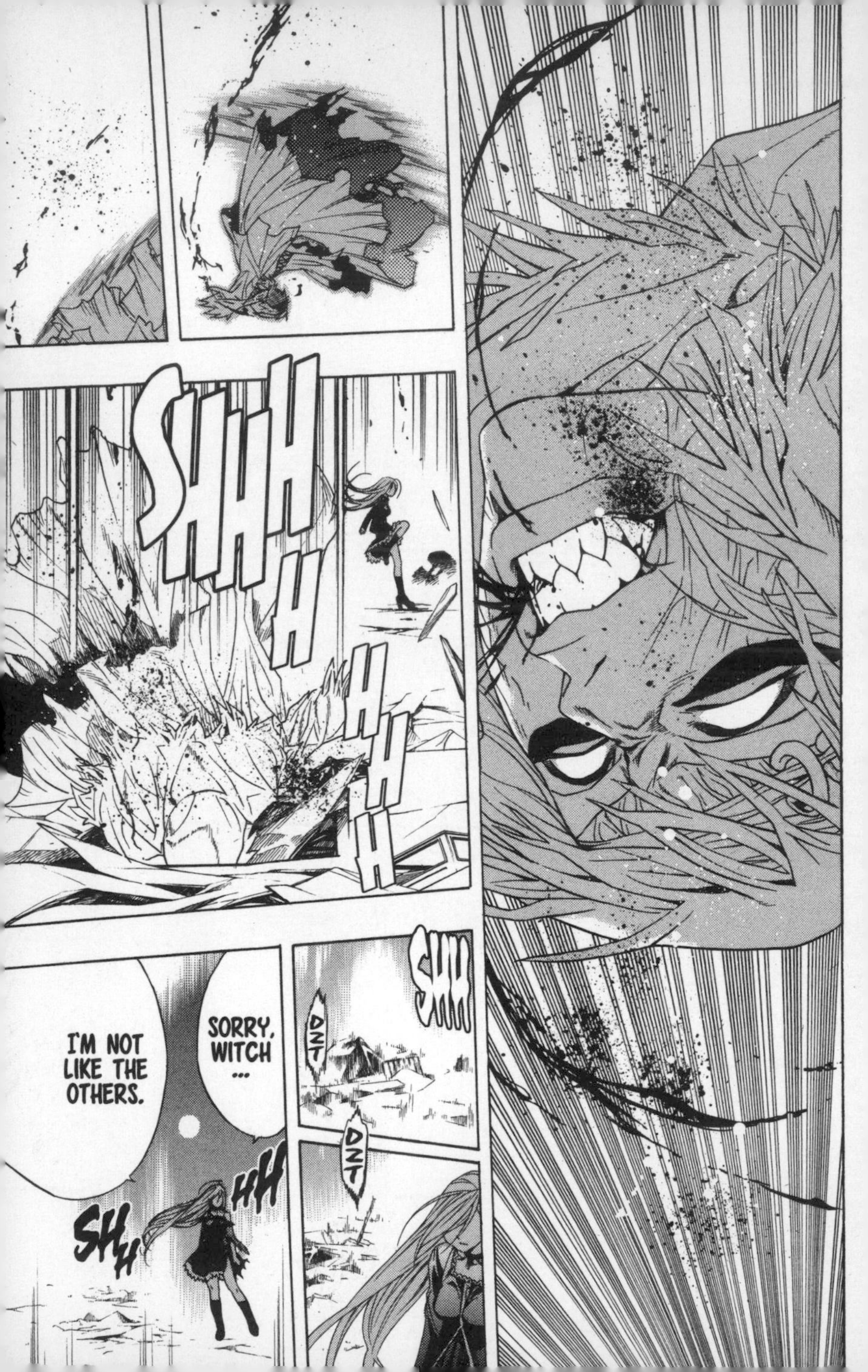
SHHHHHHHHH
SHH
DZT
DZT
SORRY, WITCH ...
I'M NOT LIKE THE OTHERS.
SHHHH

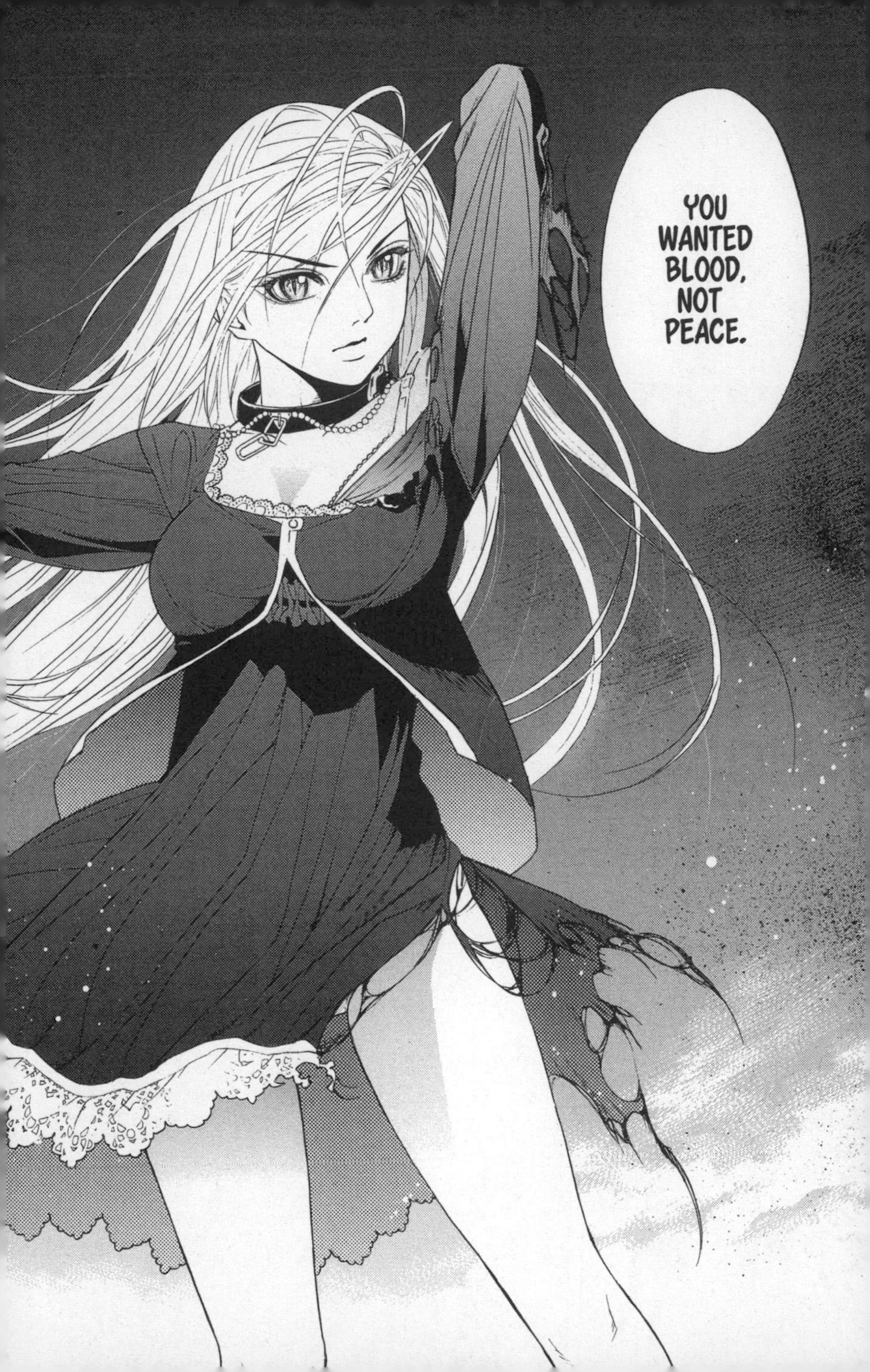
YOU WANTED BLOOD, NOT PEACE.

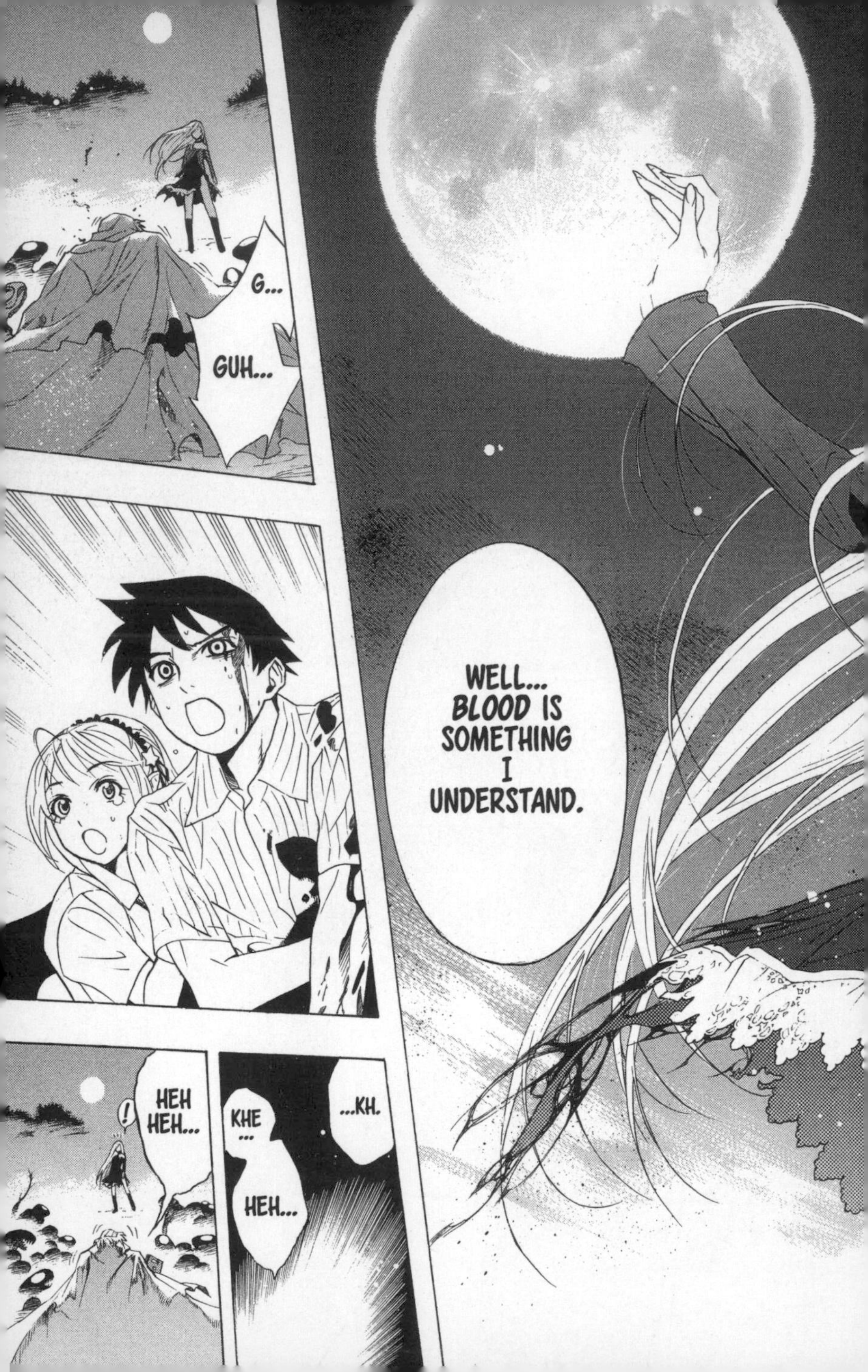
WELL... BLOOD IS SOMETHING I UNDERSTAND.
G...
GUH...
...KH.
KHE ...
HEH...
HEH HEH...
!

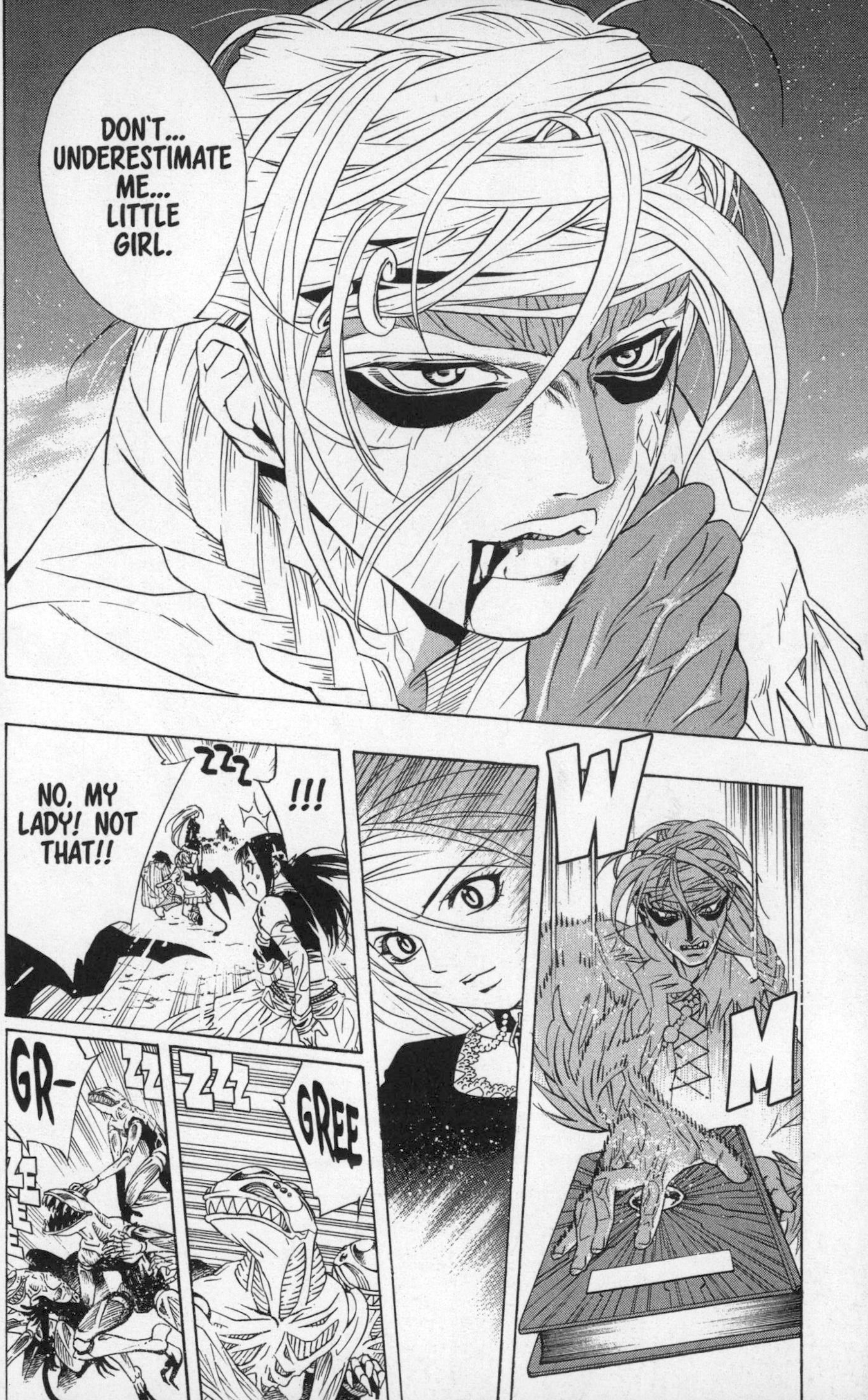
DON'T... UNDERESTIMATE ME... LITTLE GIRL.
WMM
ZZZ
!!!
NO, MY LADY! NOT THAT!!
ZZZ
GREE
GR-
ZZ

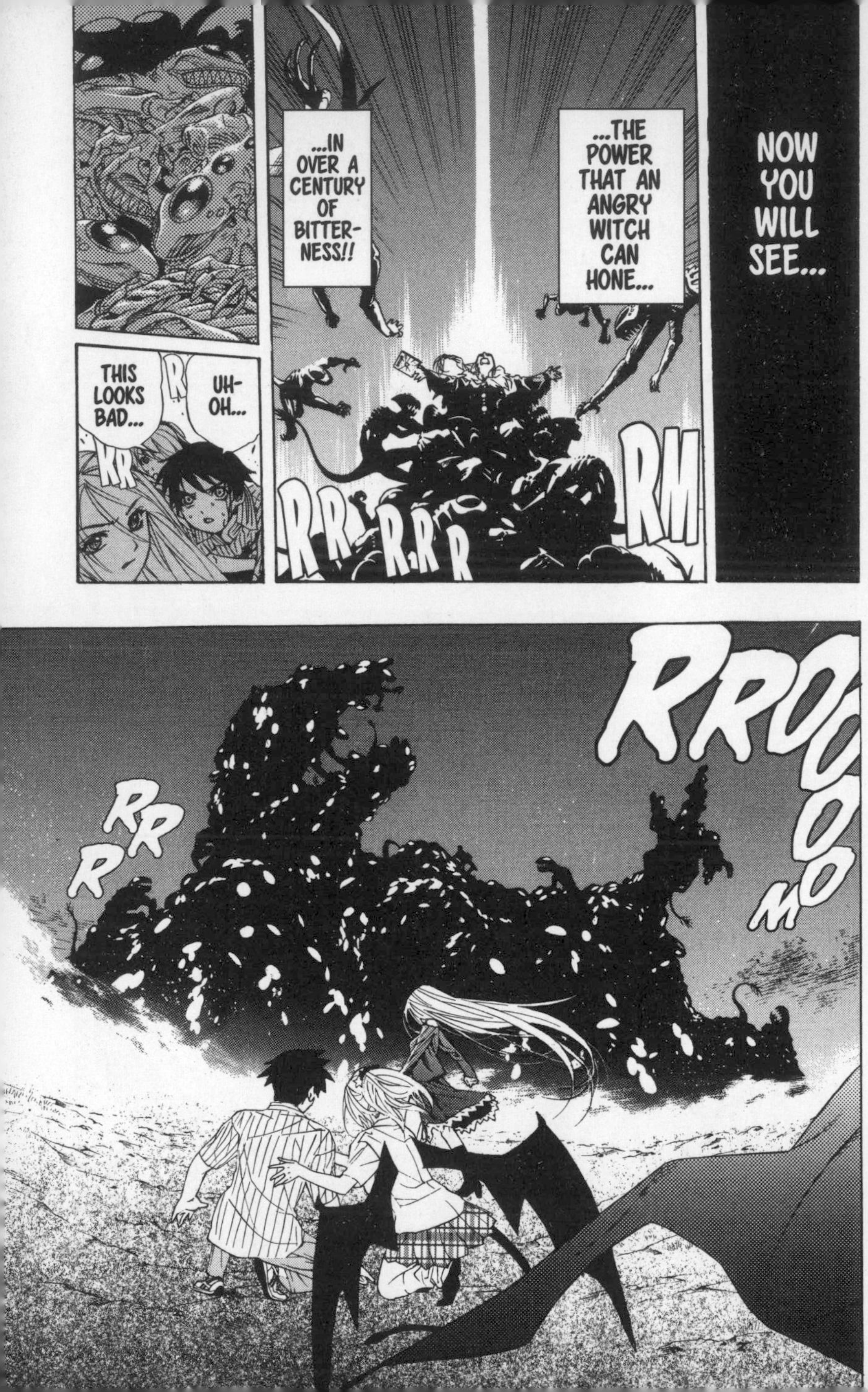
NOW YOU WILL SEE...
...THE POWER THAT AN ANGRY WITCH CAN HONE...
...IN OVER A CENTURY OF BITTER-NESS!!
RM
RRRRRR
UH-OH...
THIS LOOKS BAD...
R
KR
RROOOOOM
RRR

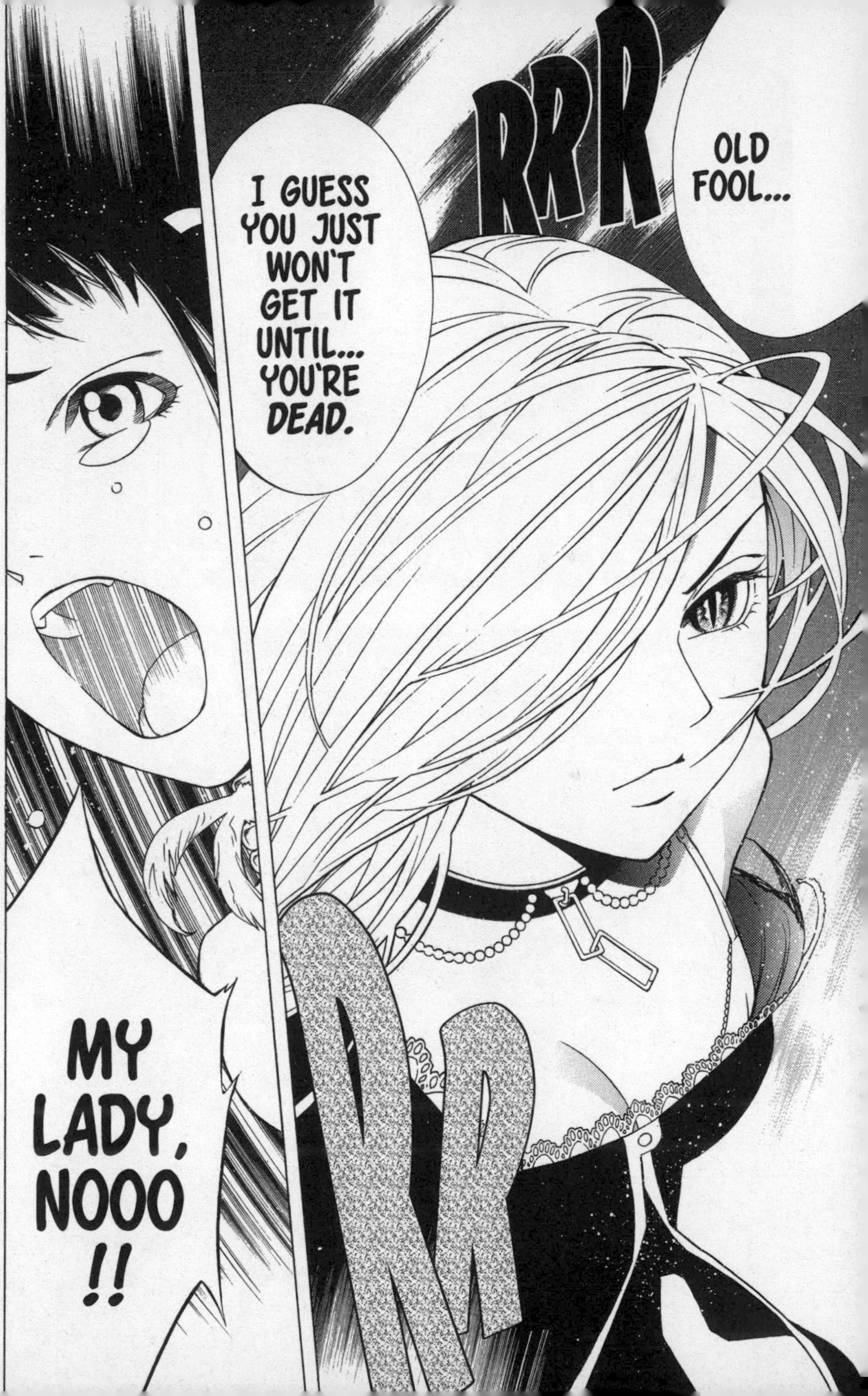
OLD FOOL...
RRR
I GUESS YOU JUST WON'T GET IT UNTIL... YOU'RE DEAD.
RRR
MY LADY, NOOO!!

READ THIS WAY

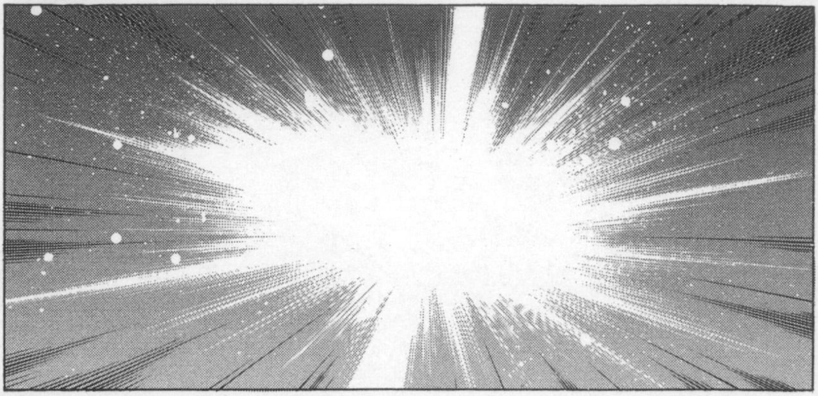

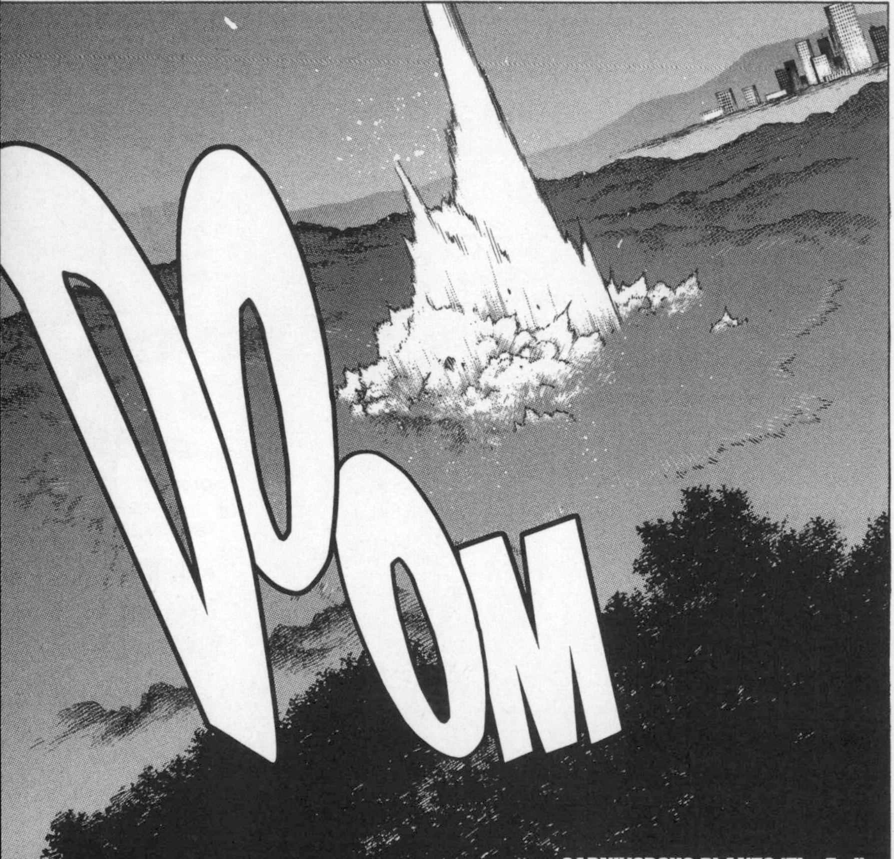
DOOM

CARNIVOROUS PLANTS [The End]

ROSARIO+VAMPIRE

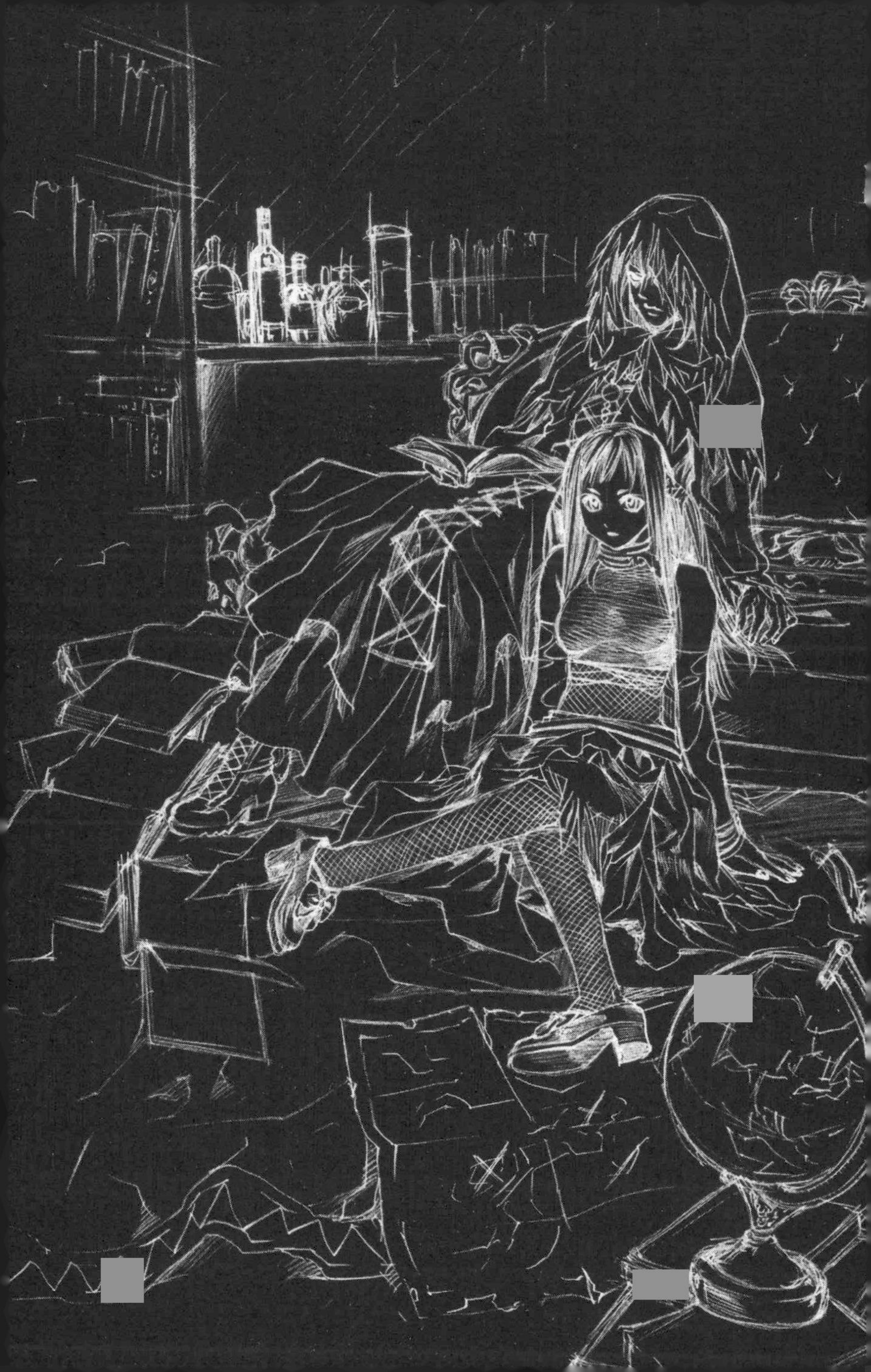

ROSARIO
+
VAMPIRE

End-of-Volume Theater

IV

• GARIGARI PLANT •

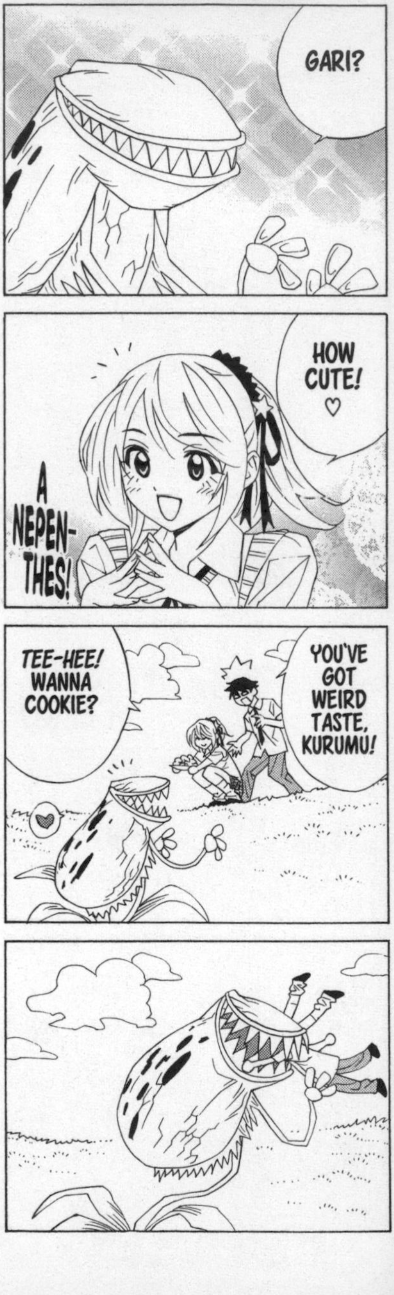
GARI?
A NEPEN-THES!
HOW CUTE! ♡
YOU'VE GOT WEIRD TASTE, KURUMU!
TEE-HEE! WANNA COOKIE?

• SUNFLOWER? •

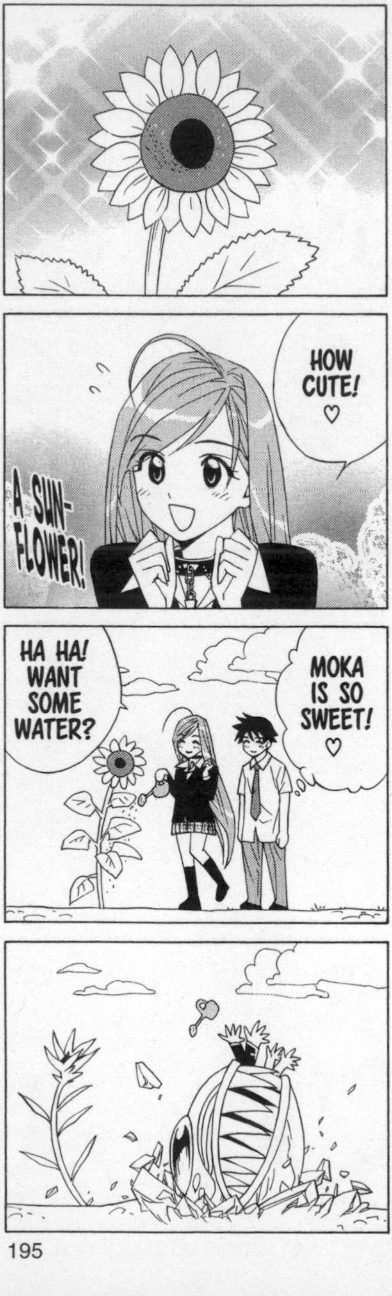
HOW CUTE! ♡
A SUN-FLOWER!
MOKA IS SO SWEET! ♡
HA HA! WANT SOME WATER?

• Sorry! •

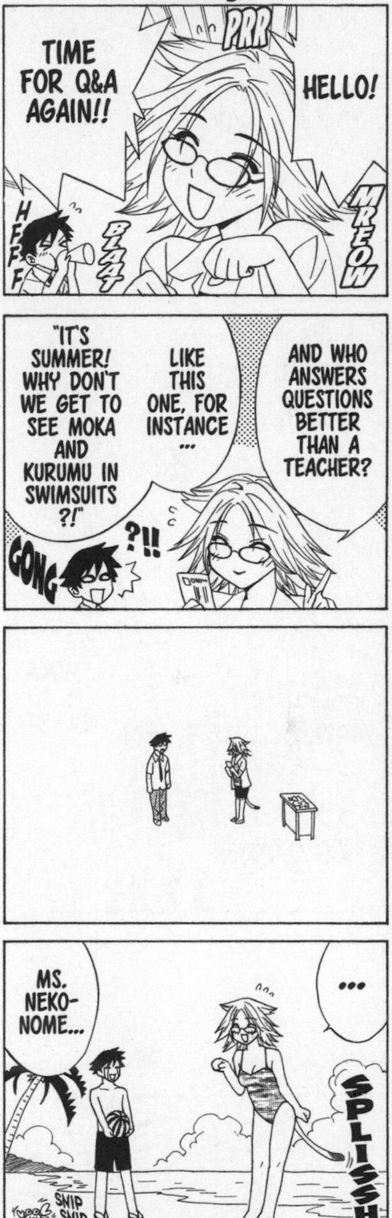
PRR
HELLO!
TIME FOR Q&A AGAIN!!
MREOW
BLAAT
HFFFF
AND WHO ANSWERS QUESTIONS BETTER THAN A TEACHER?
LIKE THIS ONE, FOR INSTANCE...
"IT'S SUMMER! WHY DON'T WE GET TO SEE MOKA AND KURUMU IN SWIMSUITS?!"
?!!
GONG
...
MS. NEKO-NOME...
SPLISSH
SNIP SNIP

SORRY I CAN'T RESPOND PERSONALLY TO LETTERS!

• Dragging Moka •

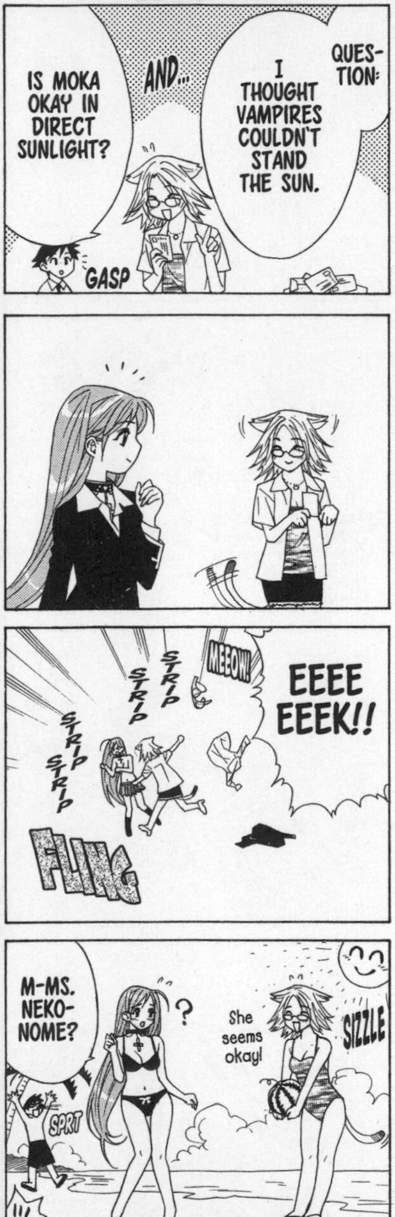
QUES-TION:
I THOUGHT VAMPIRES COULDN'T STAND THE SUN.
AND...
IS MOKA OKAY IN DIRECT SUNLIGHT?
GASP
EEEE EEEK!!
MEEOW!
STRIP STRIP
STRIP STRIP
FLING
SIZZLE
She seems okay!
?
M-MS. NEKO-NOME?
SPRT
!!!

SHE ONLY WEARS LONG SLEEVES TO AVOID GETTNG SUNBURNED! ♡

Please send your letters with any questions or words of encouragement ♡ To: Rosario+Vampire Fan Mail Viz Media P.O. Box 77064 San Francisco, CA 94107

Rosario and Vampire

Akihisa Ikeda

• Staff •
Makoto Saito
Takafumi Okubo

• Help •
Mio Isshiki
Kenji Tashiro
Ichiro Higuchi

• CG •
Takaharu Yoshizawa
Akihisa Ikeda

• Editing •
Satoshi Adachi

• Comic •
Mika Asada

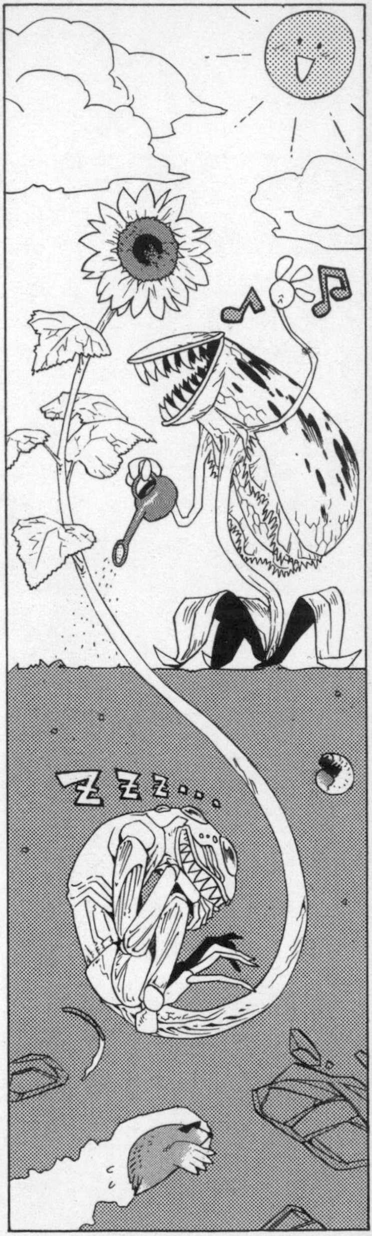
ZZZ...

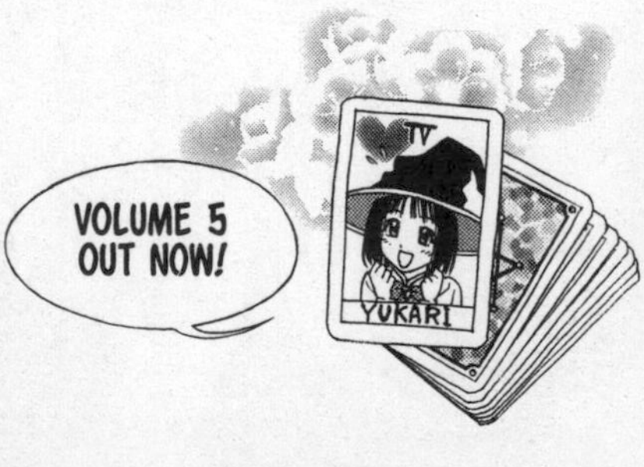
VOLUME 5
OUT NOW!
TV
YUKARI

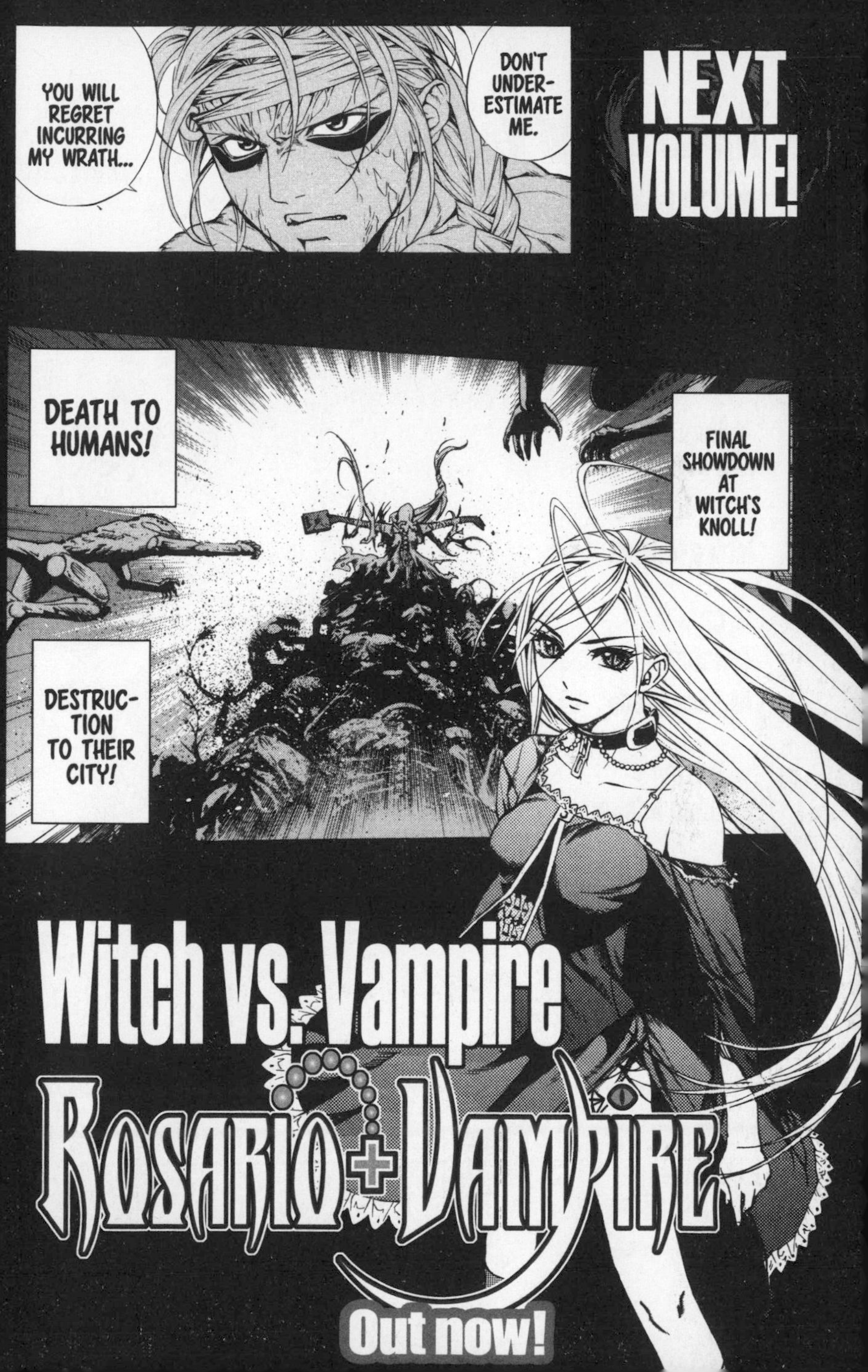
NEXT VOLUME!
DON'T UNDER-ESTIMATE ME.
YOU WILL REGRET INCURRING MY WRATH...
FINAL SHOWDOWN AT WITCH'S KNOLL!
DEATH TO HUMANS!
DESTRUC-TION TO THEIR CITY!
Witch vs. Vampire
ROSARIO+VAMPIRE
Out now!

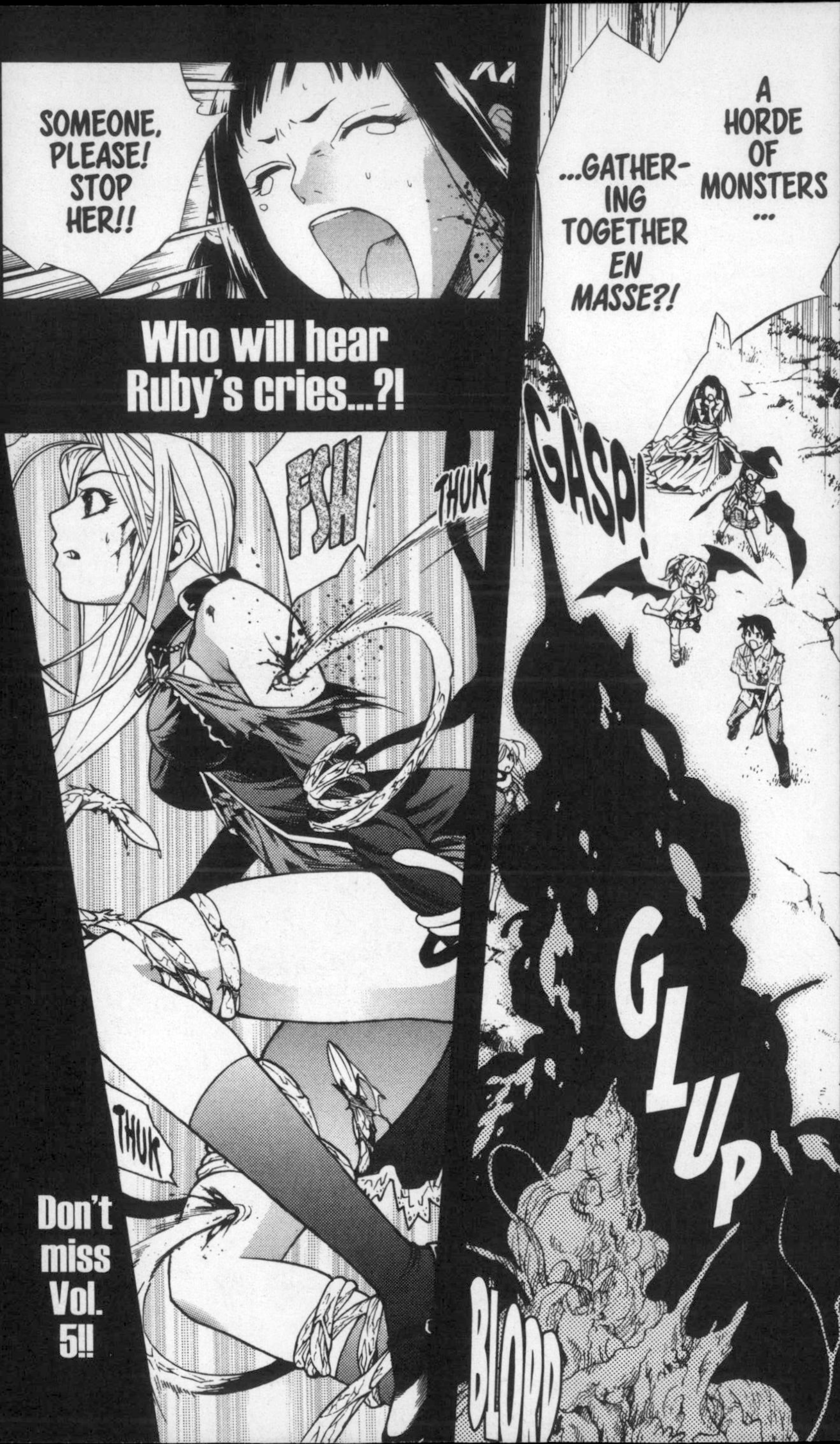
A HORDE OF MONSTERS...
...GATHERING TOGETHER EN MASSE?!
GASP!
GLUP
BLOR
SOMEONE, PLEASE! STOP HER!!
Who will hear Ruby's cries...?!
FSH
THUK
THUK
Don't miss Vol. 5!!

Crypt Sheet for Volume 5: Abominable Snowgirl

QUIZ 5

WHEN A LITERAL FROST QUEEN FALLS FOR YOU LIKE AN ICICLE OFF THE EAVES OF AN ALPINE CHALET, IT'S BEST TO TAKE…

a. a snowday

b. a chill pill

c. the heat off of her

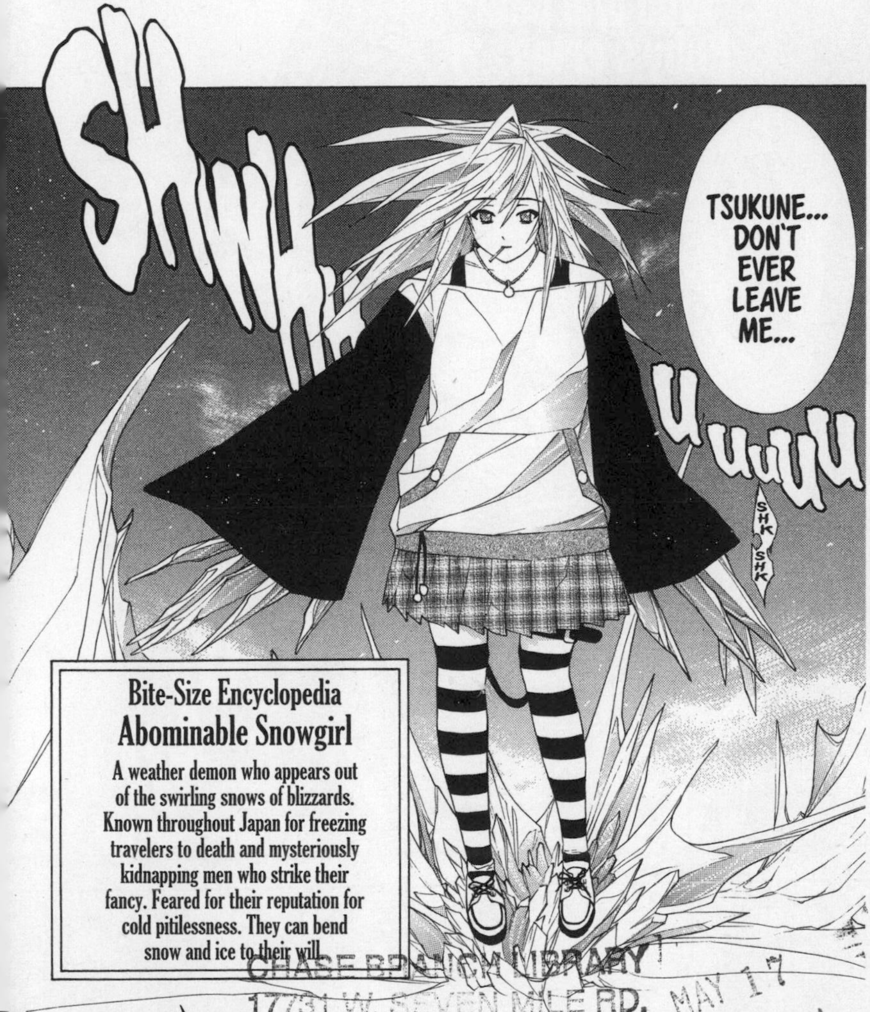
TSUKUNE... DON'T EVER LEAVE ME...
SHWH
UuuUU
SHK SHK

Bite-Size Encyclopedia
Abominable Snowgirl

A weather demon who appears out of the swirling snows of blizzards. Known throughout Japan for freezing travelers to death and mysteriously kidnapping men who strike their fancy. Feared for their reputation for cold pitilessness. They can bend snow and ice to their will.

Available Now!

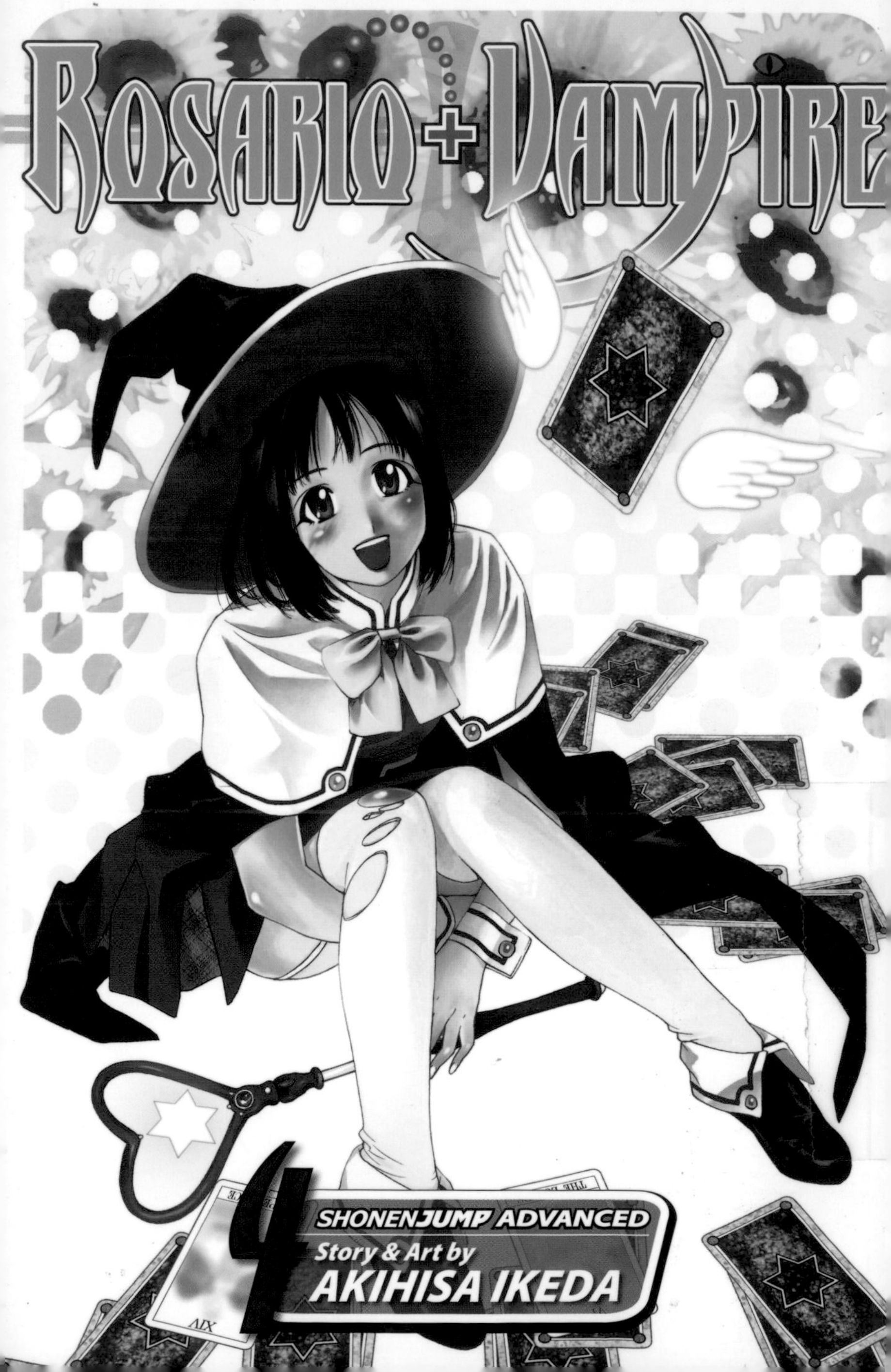
ROSARIO+VAMPIRE
4
SHONENJUMP ADVANCED
Story & Art by
AKIHISA IKEDA

35674056

P9-CDD-806